The Wisdom of the World

THE WISDOM
OF THE WORLD

*The Human Experience of the Universe
in Western Thought*

Rémi Brague

Translated by Teresa Lavender Fagan

THE UNIVERSITY OF CHICAGO PRESS   CHICAGO AND LONDON

Rémi Brague is professor of philosophy at the Université de Paris I—Sorbonne. He is the author of four previous books, including, most recently, *Eccentric Culture: A Theory of Western Civilization.* Teresa Lavender Fagan has translated more than a dozen books, including Jean-Claude Schmitt's *Ghosts in the Middle Ages* and Jean Bottéro et al., *Ancestors of the West,* both published by the University of Chicago Press.

The University of Chicago Press, Chicago 60637
The University of Chicago Press, Ltd., London
© 2003 by The University of Chicago
All rights reserved. Published 2003
Printed in the United States of America
12 11 10 09 08 07 06 05 04 03   5 4 3 2 1

ISBN (cloth): 0-226-07075-1

Originally published as *La Sagesse du monde: Histoire de l'expérience humaine de l'Univers,*
© Librairie Arthème Fayard, 1999.

The University of Chicago Press gratefully acknowledges a subvention from the government of France, through the French Ministry of Culture and Centre National du Livre, in support of the costs of translating this volume

Library of Congress Cataloging-in-Publication Data

Brague, Rémi, 1947–
    [Sagasse du monde. English]
    The wisdom of the world : the human experience of the universe in Western thought /
Rémi Brague ; translated by Teresa Lavender Fagan.
        p.   cm.
    Includes bibliographical references and index.
    ISBN 0-226-07075-1 (cloth : alk. paper)
    1. Cosmology—History.   2. Ethics—History.   I. Title.
    BD494 .B7313   2003
    113'.09—dc21

                                                    2003001353

⊗ The paper used in this publication meets the minimum requirements of the American Standard for Information Sciences—Permanence of Paper for Printed Library Materials ANSI Z39.48-1992.

Contents

Preface

In this work I propose to take a look at a historical event that has unfolded over a very long period and that consequently can only be seen from a very great distance. It concerns the changes in the way people have experienced the universe in which they have lived. I am therefore attempting something like a history of beings-in-the-world.

The phenomenon of our presence in the world does not belong to a single realm of study. It occurs everywhere: we can find traces of it in philosophical reflections, but in religion or art as well. And yet, it goes so much without saying that it is thematicized—brought into consciousness—only in very unusual circumstances.

I have therefore had to cover so broad an era that to admit as much is already a cause for amusement: this era basically corresponds to the *entire* historical progress that has occurred since the invention of writing, i.e., over five millennia. Although the time period is vast, the area however is somewhat more restricted, since I have studied only the circum-Mediterranean regions, beginning with the Egyptian Old Kingdom and continuing through Classical Antiquity, the medieval Christian, Jewish, and Muslim worlds, down to the modern West. Other civilizations have been excluded not from lack of respect for them, but simply because I do not have the linguistic abilities to study them directly and because, moreover, I am primarily interested in what has resulted in our present times.

The both omnipresent and unattainable nature of the phenomenon under study in principle invited me to look for expressions of it absolutely everywhere. However, within the realm to be covered, and even for the period on which I have focused—broadly, Classical Antiquity and the Middle Ages, from Plato to Copernicus—it goes without saying that I have only been able to proceed by casting my nets far and wide, without by definition being able to determine the comparative importance of what has been caught and what might have gotten away. When I study the modern era, from which many more texts are available, and about which I am all the more incompetent, this method becomes riskier than ever.

Readers are thus asked to rein in their skepticism and be indulgent of what is being attempted.

. . .

References have been confined to endnotes so as to interrupt the flow of the text as little as possible. However, I have quoted as many texts and secondary sources as possible. The book therefore will often appear as stiff and dry as a card file, for which I ask the reader to forgive me. But I hope the reader won't forget that I am only thinking of you: being often required to work secondhand, I have attempted as much as possible to provide direct access to primary sources. In short, I have placed in my notes what I as a reader like to have an author provide to me.

To lighten things up a bit, I have resorted to using abbreviations, the key to which may be found at the end of the book. When an author is known by only one work (Herodotus, Lucretius, Plotinus, etc.) I have omitted the name of that work.

I have cited texts in the editions I have chosen for reasons of pure convenience: because they are editions I own personally, or have easy access to—mainly in what pass for "libraries" in Paris. This is why they are not always the best editions. I prefer to refer to the originals of the works I cite, even if some have been translated since.

In most cases the translations I provide are my own. I do, though, point out references to other translations, when they exist, so that the reader may reread in their context the quotations that I make. When I must translate a translation, I point out that fact.

All non-roman alphabets have been transliterated.

. . .

I began work on the present book around 1992. Since that time I have had several opportunities to present all or part of my research. The most lengthy presentation was during my D.E.A. seminar at the Université de Paris I. I presented it a bit more rapidly to graduate students at Boston University (Spring semester of 1995), where I was able to take advantage of libraries worthy of that name. I made an even shorter presentation in three half-days to the Societat Catalana de Filosofia in Barcelona in November 1995. I presented the salient points at the University of Rennes, at the seminar *"Lebenswelt, Natur, Politik" (Graduiertenkolleg "Phänomenologie und Hermeneutik")* of the universities of Bochum and Wuppertal in Haan, at the thirteenth Taniguchi Symposium of Philosophy of Lake Biwa, at the U.F.R. of Philosophy of the Université Paris XII-Créteil, at the D.E.A. seminar of the faculty of Catholic theology of the University of Strasbourg, and finally while giving the Shlomo Pines Memorial Lecture at the Israel Academy of Sciences and Humanities in Jerusalem in January 1997, a lecture that was repeated at the University of Pennsylvania the following month.

I would like to thank all those who invited me to those occasions: Charles L. Griswold, Jr., Jordi Sales i Coderch, Frédéric Nef, Klaus Held, Tomonubu Imamichi, Monique Dixsaut, Raymond Mengus, Shaul Shaked, and Gary Hatfield. I greatly benefited from the presentations of the students in my seminars and from comments made by those who attended my lectures. I wish to thank them all, but, given their numbers, I can only do so as a whole.

However, I must mention Irène Fernandez, and my wife Françoise, who were kind enough to read my manuscript and make valuable comments on it. In addition, my wife and our children have patiently put up with a husband and father who has been both too wise and too worldly.

Translator's Note

I am privileged to have had the opportunity to work closely with Rémi Brague on this remarkable book. His gracious and encouraging help has been invaluable. *The Wisdom of the World,* which reveals the astounding breadth of the author's scholarship as he presents the ideas of the most diverse range of thinkers, as well as his own insights into the concepts introduced, has been a challenge—and an honor—to translate.

The author has reviewed the translation chapter by chapter, made important corrections and suggestions, and has provided help in locating published English-language translations of the many and varied texts he cites. When published translations could not be found, I have translated directly—unfortunately, often second-hand—from the French text.

My heartfelt thanks, once again, to the author.

Introduction

Dr. Watson, having recently moved into an apartment that he was to share with another lodger by the name of Sherlock Holmes, and having forbidden himself—like any good Englishman—to ask his flatmate any personal questions, attempts to guess Holmes's profession by making an inventory of his talents. He is surprised, among other bizarre things, at some of the facts Mr. Holmes doesn't know. For example, he hasn't a clue whether the Earth turns around the Sun, or vice versa. Once he has been told the answer, Holmes immediately declares that he will hasten to forget it, for such a fact is useless to him: "What the deuce is it to me? . . . You say that we go round the Sun. If we went round the Moon it would not make a penny-worth of difference to me or my work."[1] And what about us? Whether our work is medicine, crime, or its detection, is it truly useful to know how the world is made, where the earth upon which we walk really gravitates? Wouldn't it be better to know what we are doing on that earth?

This is the question asked by the man on the street (and who among us is not that person?) when, should the mood strike him, he finds himself in a "metaphysical" mood. By that question he is asking: What is the meaning of life? Now, the way he asks the question is not without importance. I propose taking that question seriously, and literally. The question implies that human life is defined by reference to a physical fact, that it is not only a presence in an indeterminate world, but situated at a precise location in that world, a location that is defined in relation to other elements of the same whole—in this instance, "on earth" and not "in the moon," or floating around in warm air like Avicenna's famous "flying man." At first glance this simply means that we are alive, and not six feet *under* the earth, or in some form of hell. But it is significant that human life appears physically situated from the start, and situated as such.

It is from this perspective that I wish now to examine the cosmology of a specific period in the history of thought, that of late Antiquity and its continuation into the Middle Ages within the three branches of thought that developed throughout the Mediterranean basin. During this period, knowing what the physical world truly was was supremely relevant for answering the question, "What are we doing on earth?" In reconstructing an accomplished vision of the world, I am not inspired by the simple curiosity of an antiquarian; I am attempting to situate us, us humans, in the face of a question that concerns us as much as it concerned our ancestors, a question that is nothing less, in the final analysis, than that of the nature of humankind. To know what a human being truly is, he must be examined in the arena where he most fully realizes his nature, thus where he is truly most himself.[2] Excellence *(aretē)* is the object of ethics. Anthropology is therefore inseparable from ethics.

And so it is my claim that during a long period in ancient and medieval thought (assuming we can distinguish them here), the attitude that is believed to enable man to achieve the fullness of his humanity was conceived, at least in a dominant tradition of thought, as being linked to cosmology. The wisdom through which man is or should be what he is was a "worldly wisdom." The period during which this was so had a beginning and an end. It thus forms a closed entity, one that can be distinguished from its prehistory and post-history—the one in which we now exist.

COSMOGRAPHY AND COSMOGONY

I should begin with some clarification, by specifying that I am looking at the world in the sense of an object of a cosmology, and not in one of the more common senses in which it only refers either to the inhabited earth, or to the people who inhabit it—such as in the French *"du monde"* in the sense of "people." Yet it is this very precision that will reintroduce man's concern into the heart of the question of the world. I will thus use the concept of "cosmology" in a sense that must be explained. To do this I will distinguish it from two other terms with which it is often confused. To define these concepts I will make use of words that are already present in our vocabulary but will not restrict myself to employing their commonly-held meanings.

I am therefore making a distinction between *cosmography, cosmogony,* and *cosmology.* The first two terms can be found in ancient Greek, and the first was preserved without any break in continuity in medieval Latin.[3] The third is a later term from scholarly vocabulary, one of those purely-Greek-looking words that the ancient Greeks never ventured to create.[4]

By *cosmography* I mean the drawing or description *(graphein)* of the world as it appears at a given moment, with regard to its structure, its possible division into levels, regions, and so on. This description may, indeed should, take into account the static or dynamic relationships between the various elements that make up the world: distances, proportions, etc., as well as influences, reactions, and so forth. It implies the attempt to uncover the laws that govern those relationships. It is therefore a generalized geography that, thumbing its nose at etymology, does not deal only with the earth, but with all of the visible universe.

By *cosmogony* I mean the story of the emergence of things or, perhaps, the story of cosmogenesis. It explains how things came to form *(gignesthai)* the world as we know it, in the structure in which we find it today. The way in which a given culture conceives of the world obviously influences the way in which it represents how the world came into being: a cosmogony serves to explain the world as it is imagined or conceived at a given moment by a given group of people. Consequently we know of cosmogonies with very different styles, as varied as the many cosmographies. A cosmogony can be mythical, as in the cases of the creation stories found in most of the so-called "primitive" cultures. This does not prevent those myths from being rich in thought, indeed, in reflection that may seem prephilosophical, as in Hesiod's *Theogony*. Genesis tales may also consist of the partially critical retelling of more ancient myths that have been corrected, sometimes rendered unrecognizable by being absorbed into another tale, in order to serve another doctrine. This is the case of the story of creation at the beginning of the book of Genesis. A myth can also be consciously created, in order to illustrate an earlier philosophical theory, as in Plato's *Timaeus*. A cosmogony can also be scientific. In that case it seeks to reconstruct the process by which the world as we know it today might have come into being. This occurred first with Galileo,[5] and in Descartes' *Traité du monde* (1633), and in Newtonian cosmogonies, such as for example Kant's theory of the sky (1775). Finally, this is also seen in present-day astrophysics, regardless of the role that hypothesis must play in it.

It is appropriate to note that the contents of these two concepts have drawn closer as time has gone by, to the point of being almost indistinguishable. Contemporary theories indeed conceive of the world as being in a state of flux. With this additional dimension of time, to describe the world and tell of its formation—the history and the geography of the universe, if you will—are no longer in contrast. In the past there was the contrast on the one hand between the description of a fixed and notable state, and on the other, the purely hypothetical reconstruction of its genesis, which had only heuristic value. The creation of the world by a divine craftsman (a demiurge) in *Timaeus* was, to all appearances, a way of making explicit, by listing them in the succession of operations of creation, the state of eternal things. This is how most of the ancient exegetes of Plato conceived of his cosmogonal dialogue, beginning with the ancient Academy, an interpretation that was to become rooted in tradition.[6] By contrast, modern science claims to recount a story that actually occurred: paleontology does this for living things, geology for the matter that makes up our planet, and astrophysics for the entire universe.

COSMOLOGY

Unlike the meaning I assign the two preceding concepts, what I mean here by *cosmology* is slightly different from what the word usually conveys. In fact, I use it to mean that mix of cosmography and cosmogony which as I said recent theories have rendered necessary. I prefer to reserve the term *cosmology* for a specific use. The meaning I will use, as is implied by the word *logos,* is not that of a simple discourse, but an account of the world in which a reflection on the nature of the world as a world must be expressed. We consider as cosmological a discourse, whether expressed or not (in the latter case one might speak of an "experience"), in which that which makes the world a world—what one might call "worldliness"—is not presupposed, but, on the contrary, becomes implicitly or explicitly a question to be raised. It is thus necessary that the world be explicitly posited and, already, named. The presence of a word of course does not imply the presence of a concept, but its absence indicates at the very least that the concept has not yet been thematicized. I will therefore not enter into the in-depth examination of so-called primitive "world-views" in which the word is not present; or I will mention them only in order to show the background from which human thought has had to detach itself to formulate an idea of the world, and to give it its name.

Thus a reflexive element is necessarily present in any cosmology, whereas its absence is in no way an impediment in a cosmography or a cosmogony, where it would even be out of place. A cosmology must take account of its own possibility, and of the primary condition of its existence, that is, the presence in the world of a subject capable of experiencing it as such—the human being. A cosmology must therefore necessarily imply something like an anthropology. An anthropology is not just a collection of considerations that might be made about certain dimensions of human existence—the social, economic, or anatomical dimensions, and so on. Nor is it limited to a theory that seeks to isolate the essence of the human being; it also encompasses a reflection on the way in which man can fully realize what he is—an ethics, therefore. I will not be focusing on the succession of various theories concerning the make-up of the physical universe, on the one hand because that work has already been done many times; and on the other because I do not feel I am competent to do so. On the other hand, I will attempt to reveal what might be called the *experienced cosmology* of pre-modern man.

In the sense I am using it, the word "cosmology" implies an opening onto an anthropology. Is this, then, some violence done to the language? Or worse, an attempt to reduce cosmology to a simple "vision of the world," a necessarily subjective one—whether the bearer is an individual or a society?

Let us begin by noting that the meaning of the word "world" is often anthropological. It is clear that it is increasingly used to designate human phenomena. We must examine this semantic evolution, which is itself the symptom of a revolution in mentalities. For us, therefore, "the world" designates the entire earth, considered as the resting-place of humanity, the *oikoumenē*, or society, even a part of it, the most distinguished social layer (a "man of the world"); the word can also designate a milieu ("the little world of Don Camillo"). This meaning, whether or not it is accurate, has however become the most common. For ultimately we almost never use the word "world" any more to designate a physical reality as such. For that use other words, such as "universe" or "cosmos,"[7] have more or less replaced it. Indeed, it happens that we designate cosmic realities as "the world," or as "worlds," in the plural form—precisely when we evoke the "plurality of worlds." But we only do so if those realities are considered to be inhabitable by humanity, or imagined to be peopled with hypothetical beings that would be analogous to humans ("war of the worlds"). Must we then conclude that the metaphorical use of the term has contaminated to such as extent the true meaning of the word that it has become incapable of being of use?

In fact, it is important to see that the word "world" is not itself free from all metaphor. A word does not perhaps exist to designate all of physical reality without implying a specific perspective on that reality. We can show this for the term "universe," which accentuates the way in which that whole is turned toward a unity, as if focused on it. I will be dealing here only with the word "world." We can see the appearance of its metaphorical character if we go back to its origins, and in order to do this I will now made a detour back through history.

Part One

SETTING THE STAGE

Chapter 1

Prehistory: A Pre-Cosmic Wisdom

Human thought does not begin with the Greeks. We classify them among the "Ancients," but they themselves were aware of being latecomers, or "children."[1] And it was not only within the lineage that resulted in Greek civilization that humans were thinking beings. However, the history I wish to recount here is that of a specific phylum, that of Western Civilization, that passes through Greece, experiencing a decisive turning point there. This is why I will limit myself to a few remarks about the civilizations that were in fact in contact with Greece and which might have influenced it, such as those of the ancient Near East. One must not rule out the possibility, however, that an inquiry relative to ancient China or India, for example, might yield similar results. My goal, however, is primarily to create the background of the painting upon which Greece will stand out. I will be forced to proceed at second hand, as I do not have direct access to the documents left by those civilizations. There are very few philosophers, by the way, who have reflected on the various forms of wisdom that preceded the period during which tradition places the birth of their discipline. They are paradoxically even rarer now that we possess the means to see that wisdom more directly than through the eyes of later civilizations, that is, since the deciphering of their scripts. Kant and Hegel saw Egypt from what the Greeks had reported about it. Among later authors I know of very few aside from Eric Voegelin (1901–1985) who have established an in-depth study of the civilizations of the ancient Near East based upon recent discoveries.[2]

We can group the phenomena belonging to these civilizations together under the first two headings that I have just distinguished, beginning with cosmography. They each created their own specific image of the world. There is little need to describe them here, even less to distinguish them: for example, while Egypt and Mesopotamia both represented the inhabited Earth as a flat disk floating on a primordial watery surface, those two ancient civilizations did not have the same image of the sky. For the Egyptians, it was a dais supported by four pillars; for the Mesopotamians, it was more of a cable that held a layered universe together.[3] This vision of the whole is not always presented in an explicit way; most of the time it remains in the background, which brings up an important fact: on this point the earliest civilizations are in stark contrast with the Middle Ages, when, as we shall see, summaries of cosmology were in large supply.[4]

As regards cosmogony, there are some distinctions to be made: we are unaware of any Egyptian text that might contain a tale of the entire genesis of the world in a unified version.[5] Nor did Mesopotamia exhibit very much direct interest in cosmogony; Mesopotamian storytellers speak of it primarily by way of genealogies of the gods.[6] There is in fact a tale of the emergence of the whole, the *Enuma elish*.[7] But we only have a relatively later version, in Akkadian, dating from around 1100 B.C.E. But it is not out of the question that this text gives credit to a more recent god, a parvenu, Marduk, for the creative feats that up until then had been attributed to a more ancient god, Enlil.[8] The cosmographic and the cosmogonic elements are so intertwined, consequently presenting the structure of the world in narrative form, that we often describe this view of the world as mythical.

What is of interest to me here is knowing whether such views of the world imply a cosmology, in the sense in which I use the term. Granted, even if, as in Egypt, those views do not always give special importance to the birth of man,[9] they implicitly give humans a place in the universe. Situating man is even perhaps their central function, if not their only one. Man is "on the earth," "under the sky," and above the subterranean regions. It is this that distinguishes him from the gods who are "in heaven."[10] Cosmographic facts can serve as metaphors for traits relating to anthropology; thus, one can compare the distance between heaven and earth with that which separates the limited intelligence of humans from unfathomable divine thoughts: "The plans of God [are] as [far from us] as the highest reaches of heaven."[11] Humans are disproportionate to the physical universe: "The tallest man cannot reach the heavens; the largest man cannot cover the earth."[12]

But we must make a distinction here: to situate human beings in relation to the physical universe is one thing; it is something else entirely to seek to account for the humanity of man out of considerations related to the structure of the universe. In the first case man is considered as a basic given, for which no accounting is needed. In the second case, one can raise the question of exactly what a human being is, and what he should be. So when it is necessary to explain why humans walk on two legs, why they have genders, why they must labor, why they must die, other tales take over, tales that no longer take the entire universe under consideration, but which concentrate exclusively on man. The best example of this is most certainly the simple juxtaposition of the two tales of creation at the beginning of the book of Genesis.

A MISSING WORD

The first condition required for speaking of a "cosmology," that is, a reflexive relationship with the world, is that the idea of "world" has become a theme. The sign of such "thematization" is the presence in the vocabulary of a word for "world." The word "world," or rather the series of terms that may be translated by "world," appeared at a relatively late period. If, as tradition would have it, we date the end of prehistory and the beginning of history as it is commonly known with the invention of writing, or around 3000 B.C.E., we can say that it was only at the halfway point of history that there appeared a word capable of designating all of reality in a unified way. Humanity was able to do without the idea of "world" for half of its history—not to mention the immensity of prehistory. The discovery of the idea of "world" coincides more or less then with what Karl Jaspers has called the "Axial Age" *(Achsenzeit).*[13]

The great river valley civilizations, which invented or developed writing, of course had names for the earth, not as a planet, of course, but as an inhabited domain, as *oikoumenē,* a common dwelling-place for men and animals; in this sense it contrasted with the inaccessible dwelling-place of the gods—heaven. But these civilizations do not seem to have had a word capable of designating the world in its entirety, uniting its two components. In Chinese the modern word *shì jiè* (in Japanese *se kai*) is formed from *jiè,* "circle," and *shì;* the second word also signifies "generation, duration of life," which makes it close to the Greek word *aiōn.* In India the Sanskrit *lokā,* "visible space" (as in the English *look*) can indeed be translated as "world," but in such a way that it is the expression *lokadvaya,* "the *two* worlds" (heaven and earth) that we must ultimately see as corresponding to our "*the* world."[14] In Hebrew, the medieval and modern word for "world" is *ʿōlām.* Its root is Semitic, the same as the Arabic word *ʿālam*—which itself came from Aramaic. The word is indeed found in the Bible; but there, it has only the sense of "unlimited time, eternity," and not yet that of "world," which it would only assume in the Talmudic period through the intermediary of the meaning of "era" (here, too, see the Greek word *aiōn*).[15]

For there to have been a word meaning "world," the idea that it expresses would have had to have reached human consciousness. And this assumes that people envisioned a concept in its totality, a category grasped in its two moments, that is, as a synthesis of the first two categories of quantity, plurality and unity. It is necessary, therefore, on the one hand, that the parts that make up the whole be dealt with exhaustively, without anything being excluded, and, on the other hand, that such totality be considered unified. Since we are dealing with a physical totality, its unity would consist of being ordered, well ranked, etc.

The earliest civilizations certainly did not formulate the concept of the totality of things in this way. The ancient Egyptians did not have a word for "world,"[16] any more than did the languages of Mesopotamia. But neither civilization could help but approach the concept in certain contexts, as when it was necessary to name that which resulted from the process of "creation," and they resorted to two procedures. Each resorted moreover to one of the two features of the category that have just been mentioned.

a) In the case where it was a matter of considering the whole, the solution most of the time was listing the components that it included. The list could be more or less exhaustive and drawn up following a classificatory principle that is more or less clear. They spoke of stars in this way, of plants, animals, etc. Or they would apply alternating oppositions following horizontal and vertical axes: terra firma/sea; heaven/nether world. It is possible in the long run that the multitude of the parts of the world were brought into a basic binary opposition. Thus when the Bible speaks of creation and names the result of the creative work, it names, as we all know, "the heaven and the earth."[17] This formula is very old, to the point that it is perhaps the first ever used to designate the world. It is found in Egypt in the "Instruction for Merikare," a text in a manuscript from the XVIIIth Dynasty (end of the fifteenth century B.C.E.), but whose content no doubt goes back to the end of the twentieth century.[18] The same is true of texts inscribed on sarcophagi.[19] In Mesopotamia it is found in Sumerian (AN-KI) as well as in Akkadian *(šamû u erṣetum).*[20] It exists in Sanskrit *(dyāvā-kshāmā, -prithivī* or *-bhūmi,* or the dual *rodas)* and it is also frequent among the Greeks, and after them.[21] It is conceivable that in these listings we might have a manifestation of a more general turning point in thought, which would be characteristic of civilizations earlier than the Axial Age. The Egyptologist Eva Brunner-Traut has gathered many phenomena relating to those civilizations under the concept of "aspective" (a word created to contrast with "perspective").[22] This is what she calls the mental attitude that consists of juxtaposing the various aspects of a reality without seeking to grasp them from a single point of view. But she leaves aside that aspect of cosmology.

b) These civilizations also use terms that designate the idea of totality. Thus in Egypt "creation" is in fact a self-genesis of the god Atum. What he "creates" is "everything" *(tm);* he is therefore the "master of all" *(nb tm).*[23] The word, perhaps related to Hebrew *tamam* and Arabic *tamm,* has the sense of "complete," "whole." Combined with the name Atum it creates one of those etymological plays on words of which the Egyptians were so fond. The "Onomastics of Amenemope" promises to provide an understanding of "everything that exists."[24] In Mesopotamia, it appears that the translation by "world" of certain terms is only the result of a misinterpretation.[25] But elsewhere we find words that can be translated so, even though their primary meaning is also totality. This is the case with *gimirtu,* or *kiššatu.*[26] We even find heavily pleonastic combinations, as when the gods say to Marduk: "On you alone . . . we have conferred Royalty over all of the entire Universe *(ni-id-din-ka šar-ru-tu₄ kiš-šat kal gim-re-e-ti)."*[27] The word that it was indeed necessary to render by Universe also in fact signifies totality, so that we must risk something impossible such as "the whole of all totality."

This totality, listed or substantivized into an adjective, is not yet a world. What it lacks to be one is, paradoxically, something that is too many. The world is constituted as a totality because it unfolds before a subject, before which reality is firmly established, as if independent of it. The world swells up from the absence of the subject in it. It is necessary, for the world to appear, that the organic unity that linked it to one of its inhabitants— man—be broken. Reciprocally, as we will see, it was from the moment when the world appeared in its autonomy that the presence of man in it would be able to arise as a separate issue. If this is true, what prevented the rise of the idea of world is not the incomplete nature of the listing of the elements of the world. Rather it is, on the contrary, that the concept— more or less explicit—that ancient civilizations made of that order was extended too widely, in that that order encompassed the action of the gods or men. Thus the Egyptians represented reality as a continuity in the midst of which man did not have a particularly favored place.[28] We can then see how the very division of all of reality into "heaven" and "earth," if it prepares in a way the emergence of the concept of world, is at the same time that which prevents it from coming fully into being. For that division occurs following an implicit criterion that is connected to the human: earth and heaven are contrasted as things that man can, at least in principle, grasp and that which completely escapes him. The "world" cannot appear as such until the time when that criterion is placed in parentheses. This was only to be the case in Greece. It was there, and there alone, that that "distanced" position would appear, that "Archimedes point" from which man would be able, "conscious of being a subject *(subjektbewußt)*, submit nature to objective research."[29]

So that the idea of a "physical" universe—which is specified only by factors that relate to "nature"—is in no way primitive. Just the opposite is true: the idea of "nature" *(phusis)*, even if it seeks to grasp what is original, is not originary, but derived; it is already the result of a reflection, more precisely of a separation between that which has its principle in the human activity of fabrication or estimation, i.e., the artificial *(tekhnē)* and the conventional *(nomos)*, and that which grows by itself, spontaneously, the natural.[30]

A COSMIC ORDER?

Furthermore, the concept of cosmos as a universal order scarcely arose in ancient times. The hypothesis has been made that this latency of the concept of cosmos was due to the fact that a notion of that kind was indeed the milieu in which ancient civilizations were steeped, and such a milieu, because it was a given, could not *not* remain invisible.[31] Whatever the truth may be, ancient civilizations had to conceive of man's humanity on the basis of other referents. It was not by imitating the order of the world, or by harmoniously inserting himself in it, that man fulfilled himself. The relationship of imitation, of an original where it obtains its likeness, is in a sense inverted: rather it started from social reality to go toward the cosmos. It was thus, first of all, because the cosmic order was conceived on the model of the polis.[32] In Mesopotamia, for example, the gods clearly represented elementary forces, such as the sky, the storm, the earth, the water. And the system of the world was no more than their combination, which perhaps reproduced a very ancient political situation, one that had already disappeared in the historical era, and which might have been a primitive form of democracy.[33]

Next, the cosmic order was not conceived, in Mesopotamia at any rate, simply on the basis of that of the polis. The two concepts were part of the same whole within which everything interacted. Indeed, that which occurred within the polis was supposed to exercise an influence, either positive or negative, on the cosmic order. This is an idea that would survive for a long time. One need only think of the "*waste land*" which, in Arthurian romance, punishes a human sin. Limiting ourselves to an example from ancient civilizations, it is thus that in Ugarit a disturbance in the cosmic order—a disturbance essentially located in the realm of plants, such as infertility—could only be repaired if one began by reestablishing the social order. "What this co-belonging presumed was a representation of the unity of the cosmos: if there were no order in the natural cosmos, that could be a result of a perturbation in the social cosmos. The first thing to be done to reestablish the order of the natural cosmos was to reestablish order in the social cosmos." The king, guarantor of the social order, could thus represent the god who maintained the order of the world.[34]

Was something like an order of the world, predating human activity and being proposed as a model for that activity, formulated in ancient civilizations? For some time it was believed that the Egyptians had found that formula in their concept of *ma'at,* personified as a divinity, and that it was associated with the idea of wisdom as it is presented in the Bible, as well as with the Greek idea of *themis,* or even the *logos* of Philo.[35] This concept would express the way the universe forms a harmonious whole in which man must find his rightful place—the word "rightful" implying both the idea of right, of harmony, as well as that of justice. The idea is present among the philosophers,[36] but it has also been held by philologists. This is the case of H. H. Schmid: "In Egypt one uses the term Ma'at to designate that cosmic order that was experienced as such by all the civilizations of the ancient Orient, that has been related to the creation of the world by the supreme God who is the author of it and which is guaranteed by the king who is the God's son." "He who lives rightly is in accord with the order of the world." However, one can also reverse the relationship. In that case we must say that "wisdom does not just imply an eternal, ideal, metaphysical order, to which man has only to submit. It also affirms that it is through wise behavior that the order of the world is first of all formed and becomes reality. Wise behavior shelters a completely central function, which creates the cosmos; it has a part in the establishment of the unique cosmic order." "Wherever the Ma'at is disturbed, the order in nature is carried with it and suffers. By contrast, wherever Ma'at is applied, wherever disorder is repelled, that, too, has consequences for nature and fertility."[37]

Recent work by the Egyptologist Jan Assmann has carried this interpretation even further.[38] Far from human activity having simply to insert itself into the static order of things, it is rather the just practice of man that contributes to maintaining the world in movement. Assmann retains the formula of Schmid, who entitled his book "Justice as Cosmic Order," and accepts the idea of a cosmic dimension to justice. But he does so at the cost of an inversion. He would rather speak of "the cosmic order as justice." Here we have more than just a purely verbal reversal. Indeed, all of a sudden human justice is in no way the imitation of a static cosmic order that existed before it; on the contrary, it is human justice that, assuring harmony between the realm of the gods and that of humans, contributes to keeping an essentially moving cosmic order going.

This rests on a comprehensive vision of things. For the Egyptians, the cosmos was less an order than a process.[39] They did not perceive the cosmos spatially, but temporally; not statically, but dynamically; not as a harmonious division of parts in space, but as a well-oiled course that is carried on without encountering obstacles or barriers. All order is an order of movement. In this way, good is movement, evil is the halting of that movement.[40] The Egyptians in fact knew a "negative cosmology" in which the order of the world was constantly threatened by forces that would cause it to stop and be destroyed. That order could therefore not endure all alone, but needed endlessly to be renewed. This occurred on every level: it was not just the individual who had to be justified: the State and the cosmos itself also needed justification. Far from being cosmic, Ma'at was therefore primarily social, it was justice; it was the foundation of the common life of men. But that justice essentially consisted of establishing the circularity of exchanges between men in an economy of reciprocity: that which was done or endured communicated with that which would be done or endured, action connected and obliged. On every level Ma'at ensured that the passage was free, and provided the right direction. It is the existence of that solidarity that integrated the cosmos within the sphere of linguistic communication, thereby giving it a meaning. Without the State, the cosmos could not endure.

Consequently, the order of the world—and thus that which makes the world a world—did not exist as an independent reality that hung over human activity, which was supposed to base itself on it. For anthropology, cosmology had no normative value. To repeat the system of concepts that I have proposed, we must say that the concept of "wisdom" encountered in ancient systems of thought is not a "worldly wisdom." Order did not exist prior to wisdom; it did not offer itself up, in the physical cosmos, as a model to imitate. If the world is what it is through the order that it comprises, wisdom does not result from the world, but rather produces it as such.[41]

Chapter 2

The Birth of the Cosmos in Greece

We cannot speak of a "wisdom of the world" before the idea of a world had been thematicized. In order to discover the first concrete linguistic appearance of the term, we must now look to the Greeks. The Greeks did not always have this term, one that set them apart from the civilizations of the ancient Near East. They did not possess the notion of "world" from the beginning of time; they only developed it gradually, at the end of a process that for a long time paralleled the one Egypt and Mesopotamia had undergone. We can distinguish several stages in this process.[1] In general they present the same characteristics as those that we pointed out above regarding the great river valley civilizations.

TRAJECTORY OF A WHOLE

The use of enumeration can be found in Homer (ca. tenth century B.C.E.). When Homer wishes to speak of all things, he simply juxtaposes them: sky, earth, sea, nether world, and so on. This is the case when the principal gods divide up all that exists. In Homer we also find the phrase "the heaven and the earth," a formula that would survive for many centuries after him, used with an authority that was further reinforced once the Septuagint translation of the Bible had brought the story of creation to speakers of Greek. Hesiod (ca. 730–700 B.C.E.) proceeded in the same way, but he sometimes indicated that his enumeration omitted nothing by adding the plural neuter adjective "all [things]" *(panta).*[2]

The Greek language nevertheless has a resource that not all the Semitic languages developed and which is lacking in Akkadian, as well as in

Egyptian—an article distinct from the demonstrative, which makes it possible to render just about any part of speech into a noun. Thus beginning with Heraclitus (ca. 500 B.C.E.) one often finds the same adjective, *panta*, as in Hesiod, but now turned into a noun by the article *(ta)*, "all things." It was thus no longer necessary to continue with the enumeration of its content. This appears in seven fragments of Heraclitus himself.[3] With Empedocles (ca. 485–425 B.C.E.), the adjective becomes singular and one can signify "the All" *(to pan)*. This is found in two fragments.[4]

Ancient Egypt and Mesopotamia both stopped at this stage of linguistic development. We have seen that Egypt was able to name the object of the process of the self-evolution of the world "all" *(tm)* and that Mesopotamia was able to express the realm over which the supreme god reigned by the idea of a totality that brooks no exception.[5] One might note that the Hebrew Bible does the same. This is the case, moreover, in texts that go back almost to the same period as the pre-Socratic authors that we have just mentioned. It is possible that this is the sense in which we again find the expression in Second Isaiah (chs. 40–55), which certainly dates from around 500 B.C.E. In it the God of Israel lists the sequence of his great deeds in history, up to the return of the captives from Babylon. He begins by presenting himself like this: "I am the Lord, who made all things *(anokī YHWH 'ōseh kol)*, who stretched out the heavens alone, who spread out the earth—Who was with me?" "All things" might certainly designate the world; but it is equally possible that the word *kol* also encompasses, and on the same level, historical acts of salvation. Another text clears up any ambiguity thanks to an advantage found in Hebrew; that language has an article that Akkadian does not, and can therefore turn words into nouns in a way analogous to that found in Greek. Thus, around a century before Second Isaiah, around 600 B.C.E., the prophet Jeremiah says that what the God of Israel has made is "*the* whole:" "He is the one who formed all things" *(yōṣer hak-kol hu').*[6]

In Greek all the expressions that designate the world coexist. They existed in Byzantine Hellenism, then in modern Greek up to the present time.

THE GIVEN NAME

And yet the Greeks set out on a path where other civilizations did not follow. This deviation has multiple aspects that I will not deal with here.[7] As for the topic of concern to me, the innovation was in giving the world a name of its own. The Greeks did so by choosing the word *kosmos*. Its etymology is not clear, but its meaning is, beginning with its use in the *Iliad:*

"order," always in the fixed expression *kata kosmon* "in good order," or "ornament," like the boss or stud of a horse's bit or Hera's jewels.[8] The term denotes order and beauty, even more specifically the beauty resulting from order, the beauty that is still implied today by an activity that derives its name from the word—"cosmetics." In Greek, the two meanings persisted side by side and enabled recurring plays on words.[9] Similarly, the Latin *mundus,* source of the French *monde,* or "world," is no doubt the same word as *mundus,* the French *toilette* or "woman's ornamentation," the cosmological meaning having been derived through imitation of the Greek. This is in any event what Pliny the Elder asserts: "What the Greeks call *kosmos,* we call *mundus* due to its perfect and faultless elegance *(a perfecta absolutaque elegantia).*"[10] The word *elegantia* is not simply an affectation, but a direct reference to the cosmetic usage of the term *mundus.* The usage was by no means a given and for a long time was perceived as a metaphor. Thus Tertullian recalls that, among the Greeks, the world was named from a term that actually signifies "ornament."[11] And in the ninth century Johannes Scotus Eriugena again remarked: "The Greek word *kosmos* is properly translated by ornament *(ornatus),* not by world."[12] Later, following Goethe, who spoke of *"die ewige Zier,"* in 1845 Alexander von Humboldt reintroduced the word *kosmos,* quickly explained the title of his work by recalling the Greek etymology, and paraphrased the word by "ornament of the ordered" *(Schmuck des Geordneten).*[13]

To apply such a term to the "world" assumes an implicit decision regarding the nature of the world. As to the chronological origin of such an application, it is traditionally considered an innovation attributed to Pythagoras. We consider Pythagoras to have reached his prime around 532–531 B.C.E., and we believe he died around 496–497 B.C.E. Concerning this usage we have only second-hand accounts—naturally!—that are, moreover, much later: "Pythagoras was the first to call *"kosmos"* the encompassing of all things *(hē tōn holōn periokhē),* because of the order *(taxis)* that reigns in it."[14] It is difficult to say what "encompassing of all things" means here. Is it only that which encompasses, such as the sky? Or, along with it, that which is encompassed—thus the entire "world"? A parallel in Diogenes Laertius associates this term with the affirmation of the round shape of the earth.[15] This seems to reserve the usage of the term *kosmos* to the sky *(ouranos).* In any event, it seems that we are dealing with Platonic conceptions that were retroactively projected onto Pythagoras.[16] The term is encountered in any case among various pre-Socratic authors, beginning with Heraclitus, then in Empedocles, Anaxagoras, and Diogenes of Apollonia.[17] But, as we shall see, it was above all Plato who firmly established its usage.

HERACLITUS'S DECISION

I am interested less here in the history of the word than in the conceptual decision that enabled the emergence of the idea of "world." And it is only with Heraclitus, perhaps, that we may find it formulated. The word *kosmos* is found several times in the fragments. Fragment 89, according to which wakeful people, unlike dreamers, would have one and the same *kosmos*, contains an anachronistic meaning of the word and should thus be rejected. The same is true, and with even greater reason, of fragment 75.[18] Fragment 124 remains: The most beautiful *kosmos* comes from things let loose by chance. But it says nothing of the meaning of the word, which does not necessarily designate the world.

It is the very familiar Fragment 30 that to me seems not only to contain, but in fact to create, the meaning of the word *kosmos*. I will hazard to translate it quite literally and will begin by reproducing the original text, as a sign of my hesitation: *Kosmon [tonde] ton auton hapantōn, oute tis theōn oute anthrōpōn epoiēsen, all' ēn aei kai estin kai estai: pur aeizōon, haptomenon metra kai aposbennumenon metra.* "This world, the same for all, it is neither a god nor a man who has made it, but always, it was, it is, it will be: an ever-living fire, kindling in measures, and being extinguished in measures."[19] It is not easy to see what the exact meaning of *kosmos* truly is. Is it the "world" or the "order" of things? The referent of the word is no clearer: that which "kindles and is extinguished in measures"—might it designate the adornment of the celestial vault, the stars in all their beauty? or perhaps the "fire," often interpreted as cosmic fire since the time of Theophrastus,[20] then by the Stoics? As for the idea that the *kosmos* was not made by any god or man, the second negation is obviously the more problematic. Who, indeed, has ever claimed that the world is a human work? The Ancients were already disturbed by the expression, as was Plutarch, who proposed an improbable explanation of it.[21] Most of the time modern commentators avoid the issue by seeing the expression as a "polar expression with an all-inclusive sense; its components are not to be taken separately and literally."[22] This is hardly convincing, given the extremely concise nature and significance of Heraclitus's style.

In any case we see the affirmation of the idea of an ordered totality sufficient in itself and about which it is explicitly said that it does not require the intervention of an external influence. As for the necessity of excluding an active role on the part of men, it is perhaps possible to understand this on the basis of an ancient conception, notably that of the Egyptians, as mentioned above, according to which the order of the world was maintained by the intervention of men. We need not suppose that Heraclitus was aware of Egyptian thought: Greece had analogous conceptions, for example, the idea according to which the gods were nourished by the smoke of sacrifices.[23]

THE SOCRATICS: FROM THE WORLD TO THE SKY

During the time of the Socratic revolution, the word *kosmos* was well on its way to being understood in the exclusive sense of a cosmic order. A text by Xenophon is particularly revealing in this regard.[24] He wishes to defend Socrates from the accusation of impiety that had been leveled against him. Xenophon begins by clearing his master of the suspicion that he is interested in physics, something that was viewed as the supreme impiety, a charge that had to be disproved first. Socrates, according to Xenophon, "did not discuss the nature of all things *(hē tōn pantōn phusis)* [. . .], by examining how what the specialists *(sophistai)* call "order" *(kosmos)* exists and through which necessities occurs each celestial thing *(tōn ouraniōn)*." Furthermore, not only did Socrates abstain from practicing physics, he ridiculed those who participated in the study of physics and called them fools. He criticized them on two points: (a) Before studying nature, one must already have a sufficient knowledge of human things. And that was almost impossible. One could therefore not examine "phenomena that related to the divine" *(daimonia)* except by neglecting human things; (b) The study of natural phenomena ends in nothing practical. Those who study human matters do so because they expect to be able to apply what they've learned "to themselves and to whomever they wish." By contrast, "those who seek divine things" *(theia)* do not imagine that, "once they have learned through which necessities each thing has arisen, they will make, each time they would like, winds, rains, seasons, and any other thing of this type that they might need." Perhaps just such a mastery of meteorology was envisioned by Empedocles.[25] The physicists Xenophon is thinking of do not seem to harbor such illusions; they are content with a theoretical knowledge, indeed are proud of its purity.

One can perceive a certain unease in using the word *kosmos* in the sense of world; such usage is credited to the *sophistai*. *Sophistai* did not yet designate the "sophists," with the pejorative connotation that Plato gave the term, but simply competent people, the talented, the knowledgeable. *Kosmos* was still perceived as a technical term, indeed a bit pretentious, and in any case outside the realm of good form. A "gentleman" like Xenophon took care to keep some distance from the specialists. Further, divine matters, as they are different from human matters, are above all celestial matters. They are sometimes called "divine," sometimes "demonic." The two adjectives can be distinguished elsewhere, for example in Aristotle, for whom nature was not divine, but demonic.[26] Here it indeed seems that they are used as synonyms. In other passages, it is clear that the action of the gods is carried out to ensure the "order of all things" *(hē tōn holōn taxis)*, a synonym for "the totality of the world" *(ho holos kosmos)*,[27] or, to state the same thing from the opposite direction, that this order arises out the sphere of the divine. The distinction is not made between celestial bodies, which are not mentioned in the passage, and meteorological phenomena, which are dealt with later with the "winds, waters, seasons." The accent is placed on the inaccessibility, on our inability to exercise any influence over that which we can only see, only contemplate. Whereas the knowledge of human matters provides a unified and translatable knowledge that one can use both for oneself and for others, an understanding of natural things remains closed on itself.

Finally, we can note the identification of "the nature of all things" with the *kosmos*. The distinction between the sky and the earth up to now symbolized the distinction between the realm of that which is within our reach and that which forever remains beyond us. Henceforth, it is all of nature that inherits the status of the sky. That which is natural, even if it is within our reach, even if we can point it in the direction that we choose, to the point of thwarting its effects, fundamentally escapes us, indeed because it maintains a "nature," a course that it follows without our intervention and which it will resume as soon as our action upon it ceases.

Plato's work represents a decisive point of departure in the history I wish to recount, especially his *Timaeus*, a dialogue that was doubtless created late in his literary career, and which was to have an enormous influence. As for the history of the language, it was with Plato that the word *kosmos* was installed definitively and without ambiguity in its meaning as "world." And at the same time, in this very usage, it reveals what was problematic in the underlying concept. *Timaeus* causes the concept of *kosmos* to function by providing the first description of reality as forming an ordered whole, both good and beautiful. The final words of the text sum up its meaning: ". . . this world *(hode ho kosmos)*, has thus become a visible living creature embracing all that are visible and an image of the intelligible, a perceptible god, supreme in greatness and excellence, in beauty and perfection, this Heaven *(heis ouranos hode)* single in its kind and one."[28] This pompous formula echoes the assertions made earlier: the one who created did not create two worlds or an infinity of worlds; "this Heaven has come to be and is and shall be hereafter one and unique."[29] The world is identified with the sky. That which initially designated "the sky *and* the earth" is so to speak absorbed by the sky. The all-encompassing movement is the same as in the passage from Xenophon, even though the tone is different: it is no longer a common inaccessibility that connects meteorological facts with the inaccessible celestial phenomena by tearing them together from our grasp; it is henceforth the beauty of the world that connects it to the sky.

This same movement comes to an end in Aristotle, in whom it forms the result of a passage that looks flatly lexicographical in nature. The Philosopher distinguishes three meanings of the word "sky" *(ouranos):* "(a) the substance of the last sphere of the universe or the natural body that is found in that sphere; (b) the body that is continuous with the last sphere of the universe; (c) the body enveloped by the last sphere."[30] We will have recognized respectively the sphere of the fixed stars, the heavenly bodies, indeed, all that is contained within the sphere of fixed stars, including the earth. The semantic mutation that enables that final meaning is rendered possible, indeed necessary, by an alteration in the representation of the universe. This wasn't possible so long as the sky was imagined as a flat plane above the earth. But once the sky was considered to be rounded and enveloping the earth on all sides, one could, by synecdoche, call the content by the name of the container: just as one calls "a bottle of wine" not only the glass container, but the wine it contains, so could one call "sky" all that the sky contains.

This semantic slippage is however not without consequences, for it is not a given that one can transfer all the properties of the container over to the contents. In *Timaeus*, the world is presumed to be "beautiful and good." Are these qualities compatible? The Greeks sometimes asked themselves that question.[31] Be that as it may, the outline of what appears to be a definite plan begins to emerge: an interpretation of the world taking its pattern from the sky, or, if we may say so, the *"ouranizing"* of the *kosmos*.

THE WORLD AS A CHOICE

Thus, "world" has never designated a simple description of reality: it has always translated a value judgement, the fruit of a sort of act of faith, either positive or negative. Greek scientists were aware that they not only had a knowledge of the *kosmos,* but that their use of the term had essentially constructed the *kosmos* as such, as a *kosmos*. We see the development of this awareness in a passage of Simplicius, a neo-Platonist commentator on Aristotle (beginning of the sixth century c.e.), who himself claims to reproduce a teaching of the Stoic Poseidonius (second century B.C.E.): "The task of the contemplation of nature *(theōria phusikē)* is to examine the substance of the sky and the stars, the power and the quality of generation and corruption, and, by Zeus!, it is capable of leading demonstrations on the subject of the size, the form and the order of things. As for astronomy *(astrologia)*, it does not undertake to speak of anything like that, but it demonstrates the order *(taxis)* of celestial things, having declared *(apophēnasa)* that *the sky (ouranos) is truly a world (kosmos);* it speaks of forms, sizes, distances from the Earth to the Sun and the Moon, eclipses, the conjunctions of the stars, on the quality and quantity [that are shown] in their revolutions."[32] This is a classic outline of the respective roles of astronomy, attentive to saving phenomena by proposing mathematical models, and of physics, which must explain what truly occurs. But it reveals a basic presupposition: the world is not something we can passively notice, but something that the wise man must posit as such.

We can moreover reverse the formula, in the spirit of the "philosophies [that are] suspicious" or critical of ideologies: to posit the world as a *kosmos* is the work of a wise man, who sees in it the mirror of his own wisdom. This is in any case what is suggested in an amazing aside made by Plato: "The unanimous choir of sages asserts in fact that the Intellect is for us the king of the sky and the earth, and, in doing so, *it is in reality of themselves that they make an object of veneration (heautous ontōs semnunontes)."*[33] These words are followed by a *"perhaps* they are right," which I take as ironic. Let us translate the main idea bluntly in plain language: sages give themselves a model of the world that ensures their dominion, at least symbolically. The sovereignty of the Intellect is the legitimation of "intellectuals." A much later parallel has been found in someone who however presents himself as an overt opponent of Plato—Nietzsche: "Let us distance supreme goodness from the concept of God: it is not worthy of a god. Let us also distance supreme wisdom. It is the vanity of philosophers that has become guilty of this absurdity: a God-monster of wisdom. *It was supposed to resemble them as much as possible."*[34]

These abysses, quickly opened up, were just as quickly closed, and the world was presented, in classical thought, as the ultimate case of order and rationality. We will examine the consequences of this in some depth.

Out of this Greek concept of the world as *kosmos* there arose an anthropological dimension. This might appear paradoxical if, as I have assumed, the concept of "world" only becomes possible at the moment when man has been excluded from its contents. In fact, the Greek idea of world contains an implicit appeal to the idea of subject, which it obliquely draws into it. Man is completely excluded from any active role in the construction of the world. But it is exactly because man does no "making" to the world, because his presence adds nothing to any part of the world and his absence takes nothing from it, that he is able to appear as the subject to which the world shows itself in its totality. This fact is and will remain a given, even in the most recent developments of the idea of the world, as we shall see.

Now, once the issue of the relationship of man's humanity to his presence in the physical universe has been raised, we can imagine different ways of dealing with it. Several of these models of response have been defended effectively. I now propose a summary description of them. I have chosen to group the models under four headings. Each constitutes a sort of ideal type and does not necessarily coincide in every detail with the proper name or names which I have chosen as convenient labels for them. Therefore I will examine in this order: "Timaeus," Epicurus, the revealed Scriptures, and Gnosticism. It goes without saying that they are not the only spiritual currents of Antiquity. But other currents appeared not to be as pertinent to the question I am raising here, for at least two reasons.

In fact there were spiritual currents, on the one hand, that do not appear to have envisioned the question, and therefore do not have very much to say about it. This is the case of the Sophists, the Cynics, and the Skeptics. Compared with the four models under study, they form a sort of "degree zero." Granted, this lack of interest is in itself interesting and demands an explanation, but it does not enter into the framework of my study. On the other hand, there were currents that, in relation to the four models I am highlighting, seem to propose only a variant or an intermediary approach. Stoicism, for example, at least in relation to my study, seems to boil down to the Timaean model, and this is why I will deal with it within the framework of the dominant model. I will proceed in this way for historical reasons and for other reasons that are more fundamental. Indeed, the Stoic current mixed its waters relatively early with those of middle Platonism, and it was in that form that it was able to exercise an influence on the Middle Ages, unlike ancient Stoicism, whose master works were transmitted only in very fragmented form. In addition, in the context of this syncretism, it abandoned, or indeed shaded, that by which its vision of the world was distinguished from that of *Timaeus:* above all the idea of a cosmogony interrupted by periodic conflagrations.

Part Two

Four Models

Chapter 3

Socrates' Revolution;
Plato's Restoration

The Greeks believed that the world and its human subjects were primarily connected through the existence of laws that governed them all, and that those laws were of a moral nature. This idea was not specifically Greek. It can be found, for example, in Persia; the conception of the universe as a struggle between good and evil is at the heart of the doctrine of Zoroaster. Nietzsche claimed to have named his hero Zarathustra so that the very man who was responsible for the moral interpretation of the world, for a Platonism that was more ancient than Plato himself, would be expected to compensate for his error by undoing it.[1] In Greece moral concepts also functioned as cosmology: ideas of justice, equality before the law, etc., were principles used to explain elementary cycles.[2] But it is one thing to have moral ideas intervene in an explanation of physical phenomena; it is something else again to make those ideas into the very structure of reality and that which justifies a global view of that reality as constituting a "world."

For a clear expression of this idea we have to wait for a well-known text by Plato, which has remained a favorite in anthologies since Antiquity: "Wise men tell us . . . that heaven and earth and gods and men are held together by communion *(koinōnia)* and friendship, by orderliness *(kosmiotēs)*, temperance, and justice; and that is the reason . . . why they call the whole of this world *(to holon touto)* by the name of order *(kosmos)*, not of disorder *(akosmia)* or dissoluteness."[3] The *kosmos* formed by the universe, however gigantic it may be, is ultimately only a specific case: that which is said about it is the application of a rule that holds for all reality: it is the sort of order *(kosmos)* found in each being that renders a being good.[4] The "wise men," or competent people, are not pointed out by name.

Socrates lists five virtues that make the world a world. The final two were to take their place among the four cardinal virtues. The central virtue bears a name that is formed from the same root as the word *kosmos.* Might one use this idea as the principle for an explanation of things? Is justice cosmic as the *kosmos* is just?

THE SOCRATIC REVOLUTION

Such a way of viewing things could not make headway until an obstacle had been overcome: this is what has been called the "Socratic revolution."[5] It is important to examine this phenomenon but I will do so only from the point of view that concerns us here. The formula, which has become traditional, assumes a particular interpretation of the facts as related by the Ancients, and that interpretation assumes an excessive simplification of a very complex process.[6] Aristotle was content to distinguish what Socrates was talking about, that is, things that related to the moral qualities of people *(ta ēthika),* from what he did not mention, that is, nature in its totality *(phusis).*[7] Elsewhere, he even seems to regret Socrates' lack of interest in physics: "In Socrates' time, [the preoccupation with verbal definitions] increased, while one ceased to seek that which concerned nature *(ta peri phuseōs),* so that those who philosophized *deviated (apeklinan)* toward useful virtue, that is, politics."[8] Earlier, Xenophon had portrayed, at least as an initial approach, a Socrates who disapproved the study of nature, or, in any event, the in-depth study of it.[9] The difference between the two concerns is not always presented as a diachronic passage from one to the other. But Aristophanes in his own way shows that this turn of events was not simply a pure reconstruction: the *Clouds* shows indirectly that the young Socrates was indeed interested in physics; otherwise the play would be incomprehensible. It is even possible that the play was not only the reflection of a historical fact, but the cause of it: Socrates may have been warned of the dangers of physics while seeing the play, and might then have turned his attention elsewhere.[10]

We have the henceforth canonical formula for this revolution in a familiar passage by Cicero. I will cite it here in order to emphasize an aspect of it that seems of prime importance: "Socrates was the first to recall the philosophy of the sky, to place it in the cities, even to introduce it into homes and forced it to seek out in regard to life, customs, and things both good and evil *(de vita et moribus rebusque bonis et malis).*"[11] The implications of this are remarkable: turning away from the study of nature in order to turn toward a study of good and evil things obviously implies that it is not in the sky (natural reality *par excellence*) that one will find good and evil things. The difference between good and evil does not apply to natural realities. These implications are made explicit elsewhere: the knowledge of natural realities, assuming such knowledge is possible, "has nothing to do with a good life" *(nihil . . . ad bene vivendum)*.[12] For us, viewing physical realities as being axiologically neutral has been a given for a very long time. We therefore no longer see that such a conclusion is a result, that it had to be taken by force. It is precisely just such a conquest that can be read in the tales of the Socratic revolution.

The most complete account is the stylized reconstruction Plato gives of the intellectual biography of Socrates in the confession of the *Phaedo*. Yet Plato's work does not exactly include the description of a passage that begins with a study of objective nature free of any consideration of values, and that results in moral questioning. Rather the work shows a limiting of the search for good and evil to the realm of human relationships. For Socrates himself this resignation was only a second choice, a *deuteros plous*. Socrates' dream was not only to discover a rigorous physics; it was above all to uncover a unified system of concepts, unequivocally valid for both physics and ethics. If Socrates based such hopes on the *nous* of Anaxagoras, it is because that concept could explain both moral actions and physical events: "[It seemed to me that] starting with this principle *(logos)* [the principle of the best], it was appropriate for man to seek nothing other, *on the subject of oneself or on the subject of other* [*things*] *(peri hautou ekeinou kai peri tōn allōn)*, than that which is better and most excellent."[13] The important element here is the establishment of a correspondence between the self and things. The chasm that separates the mode of being of the self and that of things present in the world is thus bridged—as was the case, it seems, in Greek thought in general.[14]

Thus Socrates renounced that unification of experience in favor of considering solely phenomena relating to the polis, that is, the being-together of men. In this way he disconnected anthropology from cosmology and introduced his plan to found an anthropology based solely on itself.

AWAKING FROM THE DREAM: THE *TIMAEUS*

In the history of ancient philosophy the "Socratic revolution" did not represent an irrevocable break. It only appears as such after the fact, in a schematic reconstruction of the history of thought. In fact, the situation was quite different since the revolution was followed, within Plato's work itself, by a sort of restoration. This was seen very clearly beginning in

Antiquity, and it was explained as needed through more or less artificial biographical data.[15] Plato rebuilt a bridge over the abyss Socrates had opened, by positing Good as the supreme principle. Good exercises its sovereignty over physical reality; but it equally rules the conduct through which the human individual turns his soul into a coherent whole (ethics) and gives the polis where his humanity must come to its fulfilment the unity without which the polis must fall (politics). Socrates thus once again evokes the figure of Anaxagoras and the advantage that Pericles derived from his association with him. Here we have an example of the way in which right knowledge of that which dominates us *(meteōrologia)* and of the nature of intelligence *(nous)* and of its absence opens up onto political rhetoric.[16] In the *Laws*, which in the chronological order of Plato's works is no doubt the very last dialogue, the Stranger of Athens shows that reason does not just intervene in a derived fashion, like man's attempt to adapt as best he can, through his technical abilities, to an initial situation of unreason, but on the contrary that it is there from the beginning, at the very birth *(phusis)* of that which exists. Consequently no piety is possible without the awareness that the Intellect *(nous)* guides all that is.[17]

The dialogue that most clearly asserts the interdependent link between a particular cosmology and the task that falls to man is the *Timaeus*. It is all the more important to give this work a place of honor here within the history of ideas because its influence on ancient, medieval, and emerging modern philosophy can hardly be overestimated. It is as if the *Timaeus* were attempting to reestablish, doubtless on another level, that which the Socrates of the *Phaedo* had renounced—perhaps unwillingly. We obviously cannot undertake an in-depth analysis of this complex dialogue here. I will limit myself to a few general remarks before examining that which, though probably not the most original in the *Timaeus*, was the most influential.

The *Timaeus* is commonly viewed as a cosmology. One of the most authoritative commentaries is even entitled "Plato's Cosmology."[18] I do, however, have some reservations before this so-called evidence and am tempted to consider the dialogue as being thoroughly ironic, as the best vision of the cosmos but not necessarily the truest, as the best possible exposé of a fundamentally impossible knowledge, just as unattainable as the ideal city of the *Republic*.[19] Whatever the case may be, the work deals with anthropology at least as much as, or perhaps even more than, with cosmology. More specifically, Timaeus, who gives the dialogue its name, describes the cosmology required by a particular anthropology. This is in any event what he begins by saying most explicitly: the text will reveal the formation of the world up to that of man.[20] And, in a more discrete fashion, it seems to me that the very structure of the text parallels the structure and functions of the human body, as the dialogue itself describes them—the first part corresponds to the head, the second to the torso, with its major connection at the diaphragm.[21]

The plan for human life can be summed up as an imitation of the *kosmos*. According to the *Timaeus* the *kosmos* was created by a divine craftsman who strove to render his work as similar as possible to the perfect model. He made the sky and the secondary gods who inhabit it, and to whom he delegated the creation of man. The sky was placed in motion by a soul that ensures the regularity of its movement. Similarly, man possesses a soul that derives from the same mixture as the soul of the world, but with a lesser degree of purity. At birth that soul is plunged into the flow of bodily humors which carry it along in their disordered current. The soul only gradually reestablishes internal order, at the price of an education. The individual soul must imitate the regularity of the movements of the soul of the world. This task is preset by an already established similarity in the very structure of things: the head in which the individual soul turns in circles has the same rounded shape as the perfect sphere formed by the entire universe.[22] In order to imitate the cosmos, one must have knowledge of it. The first part of the dialogue, which considers reality only from a teleological perspective, thus explains from that perspective the presence of the sense of sight: "The god invented and gave us vision in order that we might observe the circuits of intelligence in the heaven and profit by them for the revolutions of our own thought, which are akin to them, though ours be troubled and they are unperturbed; and that, by learning to know them and acquiring the power to compute them rightly according to nature, we might reproduce the perfectly unerring revolutions of the god and reduce to settled order the wandering motions in ourselves."[23] This passage expresses through images the connection between the theoretical dimension of philosophy and its practical dimension.[24] The theory is at first simple vision, but the text quickly goes on to a consideration of invisible mathematical regularities that underlie the visible texture of the heavens. Astronomy, not a naive gaze, is beatifying. It is therefore necessary that the citizens of the just polis study it, the elite in-depth, and the masses minimally.[25]

The second part adds a consideration of necessity to that of what is best. A passage located at the end of the first subdivision of this new consideration recalls the ethical importance of the division of causes: "We must accordingly distinguish two kinds of cause, the necessary and the divine. The divine we should search out *(zētein)* in all things for the sake of a life of such happiness as our nature admits; the necessary for the sake of the divine, reflecting that apart from the necessary those other objects of our serious study cannot by themselves be perceived *(katanoein)* or [understood *(labein)*] or communicated, nor can we in any other way have part or lot in them."[26] How are we to understand this "searching out" of the divine cause? Is it a study whose method Timaeus will indicate to us? Or is it a more practical knowledge to be obtained? Near the end of the second part the theme is taken up again, with in addition the reminder of the cause of the disturbance of the circles of the soul, whose presence the first passage had simply evoked without explaining why it occurred: "The motions akin to the divine part in us are the thoughts and revolutions of the universe; these, therefore, every man should follow, and correcting those circuits in the head that were deranged at birth, by learning to know the harmonies and revolutions of the world, he should bring the intelligent part, according to its pristine nature, into the likeness of that which intelligence discerns, and thereby win the fulfillment of the best life set by the gods before mankind both for this present time and for the time to come."[27]

The link between the cosmological and the anthropological is thereby restored. But it is henceforth inverted: contrary to what occurred in the ancient visions of the world, it is no longer man who assures the order of the world; it is the imitation of the preexisting order of non-human, physical realities that helps man to achieve the plenitude of his humanity. As we shall see, wisdom will be an imitation of the world.

And yet we see that to the theme of the imitation of celestial regularities there was an ironic counterpoint in the idea that gymnastics must also be ruled by cosmic movements. But whereas the passage cited above seemed to discourage an imitation of the errant cause in favor of the "divine" cause, now the model is the irregular, Brownian movement, of the primal qualities in the container. The movement must be reproduced by assuring the body a maximum amount of motion, either through gymnastic exercise, or at least—by rocking the cradle of newborns: "But if he will imitate what we have called the foster-mother and nurse of the universe and never, if possible, allow the body to rest in torpor; if he will keep it in motion and, by perpetually giving it a shake, constantly hold in check the internal and external motions in a natural balance; if by thus shaking it in moderation, he will bring into orderly arrangement, one with another, such as we described in speaking of the universe, those affections and particles that wander according to their affinities about the body."[28]

The *Timaeus* is thus not only the first work in which the idea of the world as *kosmos* was thematicized in a central way, but it was also the first to define human excellence as a "wisdom of the world."[29] The same theme is dealt with in the dialogues Plato wrote in his old age, as well as in the *Epinomis*.[30] The model that emerges from it remained preeminent until the modern era. It did so in the developed form that it assumed during a secular journey, which began immediately following Plato. I have presented it here in its germinal state; I will describe it later enriched with accretions that ultimately revealed all that it implied.[31]

Chapter 4

The Other Greece:
The Atomists

The Platonic, or rather "Timaean," model was not the first, nor did it remain the only one. It became dominant only after a long history. Before Plato, reference to the cosmos was in fact what some Sophists brushed aside. Not all those who were classified as Sophists were uninterested in cosmological issues.[1] Hippias is one such example. But Protagoras's statement, which portrays man as the measure of all things, whatever that might mean, rejects out of hand any claim to apply a cosmic model to man or to human phenomena (and above all to the *logos*).[2] There were non-cosmic wisdoms. We have seen this in the ancient Near East. And it remained true in pre-Platonic Greece as well as afterward. Some wisdoms were born of the Socratic revolution and might be more faithful to it than Plato was in the *Timaeus*. The Cynics were not concerned with nature;[3] the same is true of the Cyrenaics who claimed that nature was unattainable.[4] They reasoned following a notion that came out of the *Treatise on Non-Being* by Gorgias: nature escapes our grasp and even when we understand it, such knowledge is useless to us. Indeed, even if, high above in the sky, we could take a global view of nature, we would not be more virtuous for all that.[5] The Pyrrhonian Skeptics, just like the Epicureans, dealt with physics *(phusiologia)* only with a view to tranquility *(ataraxia);* but for them, that tranquility was obtained in an even more indirect fashion: the study of physics did not lead to possible explanations of phenomena; rather it enabled one to refute the explanations of others with equally strong evidence.[6]

I will spend more time looking at another school, the one which is called, no doubt inadequately, "atomistic," and which is notably associated with the names of Democritus, Epicurus, and Lucretius. This school appears to respond directly to the central theme of this study, and to quite consciously construct a well-thought-out model that enables a consideration of nature and of the status of a knowledge of the physical universe, a knowledge it begins by declaring possible, while arguing against the Skeptics.[7] This school is of even greater interest to the present study since beginning with Epicurus it appears quite explicitly to challenge the Platonic model. It can be interpreted as a dismissal of the anthropological importance of the notion of the world. In this tradition, the structure of the universe is in the final analysis indifferent to human existence and to its unbridled development. Happiness is in no sense favored by an examination of celestial phenomena. In fact, examining such phenomena too closely could even threaten human happiness. A model for human excellence must be sought elsewhere.

DEMOCRITUS

What we know of Democritus does not tell us how he envisioned the role of nature and/or of a knowledge of nature in the formation of an ethics. Some scholars even believe that his thinking is quite simply incoherent and that his physics does not lead to the establishment of an ethical system, indeed, that it precludes the very possibility of one—in particular due to his necessitarianism, which seems to exclude freedom and thus responsibility.[8] Cicero states that Democritus "had placed beatitude in the knowledge of things, as if he wanted happiness to result from research carried out on nature."[9] But as the thesis being upheld in this context is that happiness resides in knowledge, the statement was probably "adapted," and Democritus was added to Epicurus to further strengthen the argument. In addition, the doxographer Aetius presents the doctrine of Leucippus, Democritus, and Epicurus, saying that the world has no soul and no providential government.[10] But how can the authentic doctrine be distinguished from the reconstruction carried out following ideas borrowed from the *Timaeus?* Does this mean that the Democritean universe was not aware of the Platonic doctrine of the "soul of the world"? The notion that man is a "miniature world" is indeed found in Democritus, but it does not seem to imply an invitation for the "miniature world" to imitate the larger one. On the contrary, it seems to imply that the same laws apply to both—laws that impose certain properties upon them—and which, since those laws are followed in any case, could not be imitated. For Democritus, the internal harmony of the soul and of the human body is more important than that of the world.[11]

EPICUREANISM
A. The Interest of Physics

With Epicurus and his disciples, an original conception of nature and its study was born. As was the case with Plato, and in the tradition pioneered by him, the study of physics had a moral goal. As almost everywhere in ancient philosophy, the emphasis was placed on not doing violence to nature and on letting oneself be guided by nature.[12] The Epicureans did not believe that morality could become perfect without physics;[13] and they argued against a purely theoretical use of physics, which in their opinion was a complete waste of time.[14]

But unlike what occurred within the Platonic model, the moral goal was reached indirectly. It was not from being inspired by the known world, but by the *knowledge* of the world, that such a moral reform could be obtained. This is what the Epicurean Torquatus explains in Cicero: "Thus one derives from [the study of] physics *(e physicis)* the courage to face the fear of death, the strength to fight the fear [that comes] from superstition, a calming of the mind, once the ignorance of all hidden things has been expelled, and temperance, once the nature of desires and their like have been explained."[15] The effect of physics is not objective, but purely subjective. The physical universe in itself is not truly interesting in the strict sense: we do not have to go through it *(inter-est)* to become that which we ought to be. The goal of the exercise is not specifically knowledge, but the absence of disturbance *(ataraxia)*, life without upsets *(athorubos)*.

Certainly, knowledge might provide great joy, as intense as if it were an end in itself, and concomitant joys in exercising that knowledge: "In philosophy enjoyment keeps pace with knowledge. It is not learning followed by entertainment, but learning and entertainment at the same time."[16] But it remains true that the effect of knowledge is not the same. It is no longer a question, as in Plato, of an imitation, but of a distancing. The goal of knowledge is not assimilation, rather it is objectification, as a means of dissimilation. The object of knowledge, like death, must be "nothing for us."

This goal is recalled at the end of discussions of certain specific topics, such as the face of the moon or the regularity of celestial revolutions, a passage the conclusion of which, according to the text of the manuscripts, suggests that "we rejoice with the god."[17] Epicurus begins by stating the goal of his physics: "First of all, therefore, not to believe that there is any other goal of knowledge in the realm of celestial phenomena *(meteōra)* . . . than tranquility *(ataraxia)* and strong certainty, just as for everything else. . . . If fears *(hupopsiai)* of the phenomena of the sky did not disturb us *(ēnōkhloun)*, nor those that we experience regarding death, that it may be something that relates to us, and the fact of not knowing the reasons for pain and desires, we would not have an additional need *(prosdeisthai)* for a knowledge of substances *(phusiologia)*."[18] The second fragment is composed using a structure that is found elsewhere in the Epicurean school and is perhaps typical of its method or, at least, of the Epicurean attitude: the reconstruction of a virtual state in which what is now a need was not; the necessity of adding what should not have been useful to make up for something that is henceforth truly lacking. Porphyry has handed down a long fragment of political philosophy by an otherwise little known Epicurean, Hermarchus. In it we read: "If everyone were equally able to observe that which is useful and to respect it, we would not have the additional need *(prosdeisthai)* for laws."[19]

B. An Anti-Timaeus

This attitude was itself developed to respond to a model that rendered it necessary. That model, it seems to me, is the one I previously derived from Plato's *Timaeus*. We have already noted the presence in Epicurus of passages in which Plato, and more precisely the *Timaeus*, is taken to task. Thus the doctrine of the elements is criticized in the treatise *On Nature*.[20]

In a passage that comes closest to the one—essential for our purposes—on the imitation of celestial movements, Plato discusses the complex movements of the planets. Astronomical speculations provide reason to fear the future "to those who are incapable of calculating *(tois ou* [*si vera lectio*] *dunamenois logizesthai)*." It is possible that Epicurus meant to parody that phrase. Indeed he speaks of those who are capable of experiencing the supreme and stable joy that comes out of a very balanced condition of the flesh and a credible anticipation of it, a joy reserved for "those who are capable of calculating *(tois epilogizesthai dunamenois)*."[21] The context is the same: a relationship with the future. The addition of the prefix *epi* to the verb indicates the surpassing of the present through calculation. But the most external support, the heavenly bodies, is replaced by the most intimate one, the flesh.

Similarly, regarding the connection between physics and ethics, we have the impression that Epicurus is responding to Plato point by point. For Plato assigned the same goal to astronomy as Epicurus did, and in the same words: to do away with *disturbance (tarakhē)*, to put the disordered periods of the soul into order through the imitation of the ordered periods of celestial bodies *(ataraktois tetaragmenas)*.[22] However, if Epicurus adopts Platonic vocabulary, it is to subvert it. Celestial phenomena cannot favor the absence of disturbances *(ataraxia)* that they in fact bring about. The fact that the movements of the celestial spheres themselves know a sort of ataraxia does not imply that they are likely to communicate it. They are not peaceful and peace-bringing objects of contemplation. On the contrary, they cause disturbance and anguish.[23] It even appears as if the sky is the paradigm of the place where all our trouble comes from, including tectonic phenomena. The Epicurean poet of the *Etna* suggests that, faced with a volcanic eruption, knowledge enables us not to be misled, not to remain mute, pale with anguish, imagining that "threats from the sky have traveled toward the subterranean world."[24] There is no question of escaping the terrors of this earthly world by taking refuge in the sky: it is the sky that is the primary source of terror. It is knowledge that must remove the sting from all sources of disturbance, both celestial and terrestrial.

This primordial goal of physics explains the "endless nonchalance"[25] with which Epicurus proceeds with regard to an explanation of natural phenomena. His method does not involve indifference toward truth. There is a need for truth: only true knowledge of nature *(phusiologia)* is able to deliver us from disturbance.[26] But the true is not transposed into the one. What is important is that there be at least one explanation, lest we remain faced with a disturbing mystery. Thus nothing prevents the possibility of a choice of several concurrent explanations. Epicurus thus proposes, especially in meteorology, several solutions without seeking to reduce them to a single principle believed to account for everything.[27] And Lucretius goes so far as to say that, out of several explanations, since there are several worlds, one of the explanations applies at the very least to one of those worlds.[28]

C. An Inimitable World

To this attitude toward the world and the knowledge that we obtain of it there corresponds, as if it were the foundation, a new concept of the *kosmos*. It contrasts on every point with that proposed by Plato and Aristotle and can even be conceived as destined to render the idea of an imitation of the world unthinkable. This Epicurean concept is moreover a return to the original meaning of the Greek word, "ordering." Atoms are distinguished from their arrangement. The arrangement in which we live is one of many possible arrangements, even one of the arrangements that actually coexist. Furthermore, unlike eternal atoms, this arrangement is perishable. Granted, the laws that govern the formation of worlds are the same, regardless of the determined organization of one or another of the worlds. But the resulting forms vary.[29] The spherical form, in particular, so dear to Plato and Aristotle, is by no means the only one. Thus in Cicero, the Epicurean Velleius claims not to understand why that form would be more beautiful and more worthy of the world than any other.[30]

The plurality of worlds is not simply a physical theory.[31] It bears on the very idea of *kosmos,* which becomes relativized through its passage into the plural form. The final reality is not order, such and such a particular arrangement, but atoms and the void. The relationship between the world in which we live and the final reality is not a relationship of a copy to an original. Knowledge of the world does not enable us to go back to an organizing wisdom upon which we might govern ourselves, for this world is no more than that which it happens to be. The fact that our world is only one *exemplar* prevents it from being an *example.*

Classical cosmologies are crowned by theologies, both implicitly, in the identification of deities with the stars, the most elevated and most beautiful bodies among all that is, according to Plato and Aristotle, and very explicitly so in Stoicism, for which theology (or rather theiology, the science of an impersonal divine) is a part of physics. Thus imitation of the world and assimilation to a god or gods are intricately connected. Now, it is as if the Epicurean conception of the gods aimed directly at rendering both of these attitudes impossible. Several indirect accounts (but not a text proceeding directly from Epicurus) place the gods in "inter-worlds," in Greek *metakosmia,* in Latin *intermundia.* Epicurus was familiar with the first word[32] but does not apply it to his doctrine of the gods in any of the texts available to us. However, we do have witnesses that clearly point in that direction.[33] For it is of the greatest importance that the gods be placed in the "inter-worlds."[34] The gods exist, their existence is never doubted. But it is essential that they be extremely non-cosmic, that they belong neither to this world or to another—whether it be this "low" world or a supracelestial world. They must not hang over the things of the world: one reaches them without climbing or descending, without leaving the world in any way: if they are between worlds, one can leave one world only by heading toward another. There are so-to-speak horizontal inter-worlds. Epicurus does not speak of the supra-worldly existence of his gods. Their interworldly existence does not so much serve to establish their position as, negatively, to attempt to present them as a counterexample; it serves to prevent them from sliding into the position of the supra-worldly. Imitating the gods remains an ideal to propose,[35] but it is no longer an imitation of the world; it is an imitation of their non-cosmic beatitude.

LUCRETIUS

The Latin poet places his writing in the wake of Epicurus, but he does more than simply give a versified translation of him. We find elements in Lucretius that are missing in his mentor, although we are unable to say with complete certainty whether they are original. Among them one finds a critique of that Stoic providentialism according to which the world was made to serve as a dwelling-place for man. Lucretius argues that the earth includes vast expanses that are uninhabitable and unfit for cultivation, not to mention that the largest portion of the globe is covered by water.[36]

The second point, the temporary nature of the groupings that form worlds, does not seem to have been made explicit by Epicurus, who perhaps saw in it only a thought-experiment. In Lucretius, on the other hand, the notion is presented emphatically, and in an existential manner. The world is not a stable *kosmos*. It is experienced as essentially fragile. Its ruin is possible: "A single day . . . and the mass that has stood firm for many years will crumble, and with it the structure of the world."[37] It is even possible that such ruin might be announced by the signs of a decline leading to a relative infertility in nature.[38] Nothing prevents us from thinking that the end of the world is imminent: "The thing itself will confirm my words, perhaps, and, after the lands have been strongly shaken, you will soon see everything break apart."[39] The idea was expressed by other Latin authors, such as Ovid or the anonymous author of *Octavia*,[40] but especially the poet of the *Etna* who, after talking about earthquakes, wrote that they represent "the most authentic omen that the world must eventually return to its primitive appearance."[41]

This essential fragility of the world prevents us from seeing it as a source of support or a place of refuge. Thus Epicurean consciousness contains an element that might be called eschatological. But it includes a specific nuance with respect to the Stoic idea of *ekpurōsis* or with respect to the awareness of the end of the world found in Judaism and Christianity. Indeed, on the one hand, the Stoic conflagration is replaced by the cyclic temporality of the "great year";[42] it is thus foreseen for a date that can be calculated. The destruction of the world, according to Lucretius, remains unforeseeable. One cannot count on the dissolution of the world any more than one can count on its survival. Moreover, unlike what is supposed by apocalypses, the soul is also led to perish—not to be judged. Anguish is caused by the idea that the soul might survive the world, which atomism renders impossible.

In the Epicurean tradition, the world is something upon which one must not rely. Human wisdom is not a wisdom of the world. An essentially non-cosmic wisdom is required. For Epicurus the accent placed on friendship *(philia)* is not simply a call for harmony; it implies that a connection between men is more important than a correspondence with cosmic realities. But there can no longer be any question of ignoring the physical realm. The path to pre-philosophical wisdoms was henceforth cut off. Wisdom could no longer be *acosmic;* since it came after the Platonic attempt to edify a wisdom of the world, it was henceforth to be *metacosmic.*

Chapter 5

Other than Greece:
The Scriptures

The vision of the world I am attempting to reconstruct is not only the development of ideas born in Greece—a name that designates both a country and an all-encompassing attitude. That vision has roots in "Jerusalem" as well as in "Athens," and as regards Islam, in Mecca and Medina. A determined attitude toward the world can be found in this second, non-Greek source, an attitude that became a component of the synthesis that was formed at the end of Antiquity, and which I will describe; but that attitude also served as a counterpoint to it.

As we know, the Bible does not constitute a single text, but is an entire library made up of books whose literary genres, authors, and the eras in which they wrote all differ. Thus it would be useless to attempt to hypostasize something like a "Biblical vision of the world." The unity of the Bible does not reside in the text itself, but in the experience of the people of Israel. That experience constitutes the common background upon which and in the light of which the texts have been continuously read and reread. Furthermore, the intention of the Biblical authors was only rarely to form an explicit vision of the world. Such a vision in most cases appears only as scenery. The Bible doesn't contain any unified cosmological doctrine; rather it provides various insights, which we will examine in succession. I will limit myself here to a few texts, chosen because they seem to best represent the points on which the Bible provides elements responding to the question at hand.[1]

THE OLD TESTAMENT

On the whole the Old Testament provides the same vision of the structure of the physical universe as is found in the civilizations of the ancient Near East.[2] Most of the time this cosmography remains subordinate to the tales for which it provides only an implicit framework; a cosmography is only rarely presented for itself, as in the vast panorama in Psalm 104, which comes close, as we know, to the Egyptian hymn to Aton.[3] The object of the Old Testament authors was not to indulge in physics, but to dispense religious teachings.[4] Even an evocation of the wonders of the world opens up onto praise of the God of Israel. Thus Psalm 19 continues the assertion that "the heavens are telling the glory of God *(El),*" by praising the law of the God of Israel *(YHWH).* And this is indeed the central and primary goal of the texts of the Old Testament: to establish and recall the exclusive covenant between the people of Israel and their God, who gave them the land upon which they settled.

Such teaching however, affects the way the world is represented, and precisely because it does not have direct bearing on it. The exclusivity of the cult of the God of Israel indeed demanded the condemnation of the other cults in the land of Canaan. Those cults for the most part worshipped agrarian and pastoral deities, lords of rain and fertility. Later a new adversary appeared, the cult of celestial deities imported from Assyrian religion.[5] Now the prophets' protests were directed toward the cult of the stars, specifically that of the sun (Jeremiah 8:2; Ezekiel 8:16). To direct a kiss to the Sun or the Moon was a sin (Job 31:26–28). Later the emphasis was redirected from criticism of the cult of the stars to that of the foolishness of those who, admiring the beauty of creation, were unable to recognize the craftsman who created it (Wisdom of Solomon 13:1–5).

The polemics against other gods, both earthly and celestial, implies that they were seen as comprising a unit, if only in order to be rejected in one fell swoop. Consequently, the common realm that underlies both earthly and heavenly things, in spite of the immense difference between them (what resemblance is there between animals and stars?), had necessarily to come to the fore as such. That common realm was something like "nature." Thus the idea of nature was not unique to Greece; but Greece did have the distinction of having made nature into a theme and thus to have named it, by contrasting nature to artifice and the conventional.[6] But Israel, too, situated nature opposite another entity which was at first indeterminate and was nothing other than the empty place kept vacant for its jealous God.

A. The Moral Order of the World

We have seen that the notion of a correspondence between the physical and the moral was present in Greece, but that it came from elsewhere. It should not be surprising to note that that idea was also found in ancient Israel. It came out of the pre-Biblical idea that human action exercises an influence over natural rhythms: to human justice toward the God of Israel—in this case abiding by the rules of worship—there responded a "justice" of rain and harvest.[7]

It seems that this correspondence was the object of a reflection that generalized it. In this regard there is a passage from Second Isaiah, written after the exile to Babylon. God is emphasizing at the same time the stability of his creation and the rectitude of his words: "For thus says the LORD, who created the heavens (he is God!), who formed the earth and made it (he established it; he did not create it a chaos *(tohu)*, he formed it to be inhabited!): 'I am the LORD, and there is no other. I did not speak in secret, in a land of darkness; I did not say to the offspring of Jacob, 'Seek me in chaos *(tohu).*' I the LORD speak the truth *(dōber ṣédeq)*, I declare what is right *(maggid meyšarim).*'" (45:18–19). The text begins by asserting, without belaboring the point, the identity of the creator: the God who created the heavens is the same one who created the earth. The God of Israel does not create the world without giving it maximal consistency. To create is to establish firmly, to install forever. Creation is the result of an irrevocable decision, a promise from God. The God of creation is as faithful and worthy of faith as the God of the Covenant. His word therefore has the same stability as his creation. What he says and what he does are mutually confirmed. God does not speak in secret (see 48:16), and yet he is hidden (see 45:15). It is not in the chaos preceding creation that he must be sought, precisely because that chaos was overcome by the order of creation. One must seek him in the order of the created world, in what is intelligible in that world. The stability that the God of Israel introduces into creation is a preparation that enables one to understand his historical word. His "word" perhaps designates the gift of the Law on Mount Sinai. This is what medieval commentators readily assumed.[8] But regardless of the content of God's communication, it is remarkable that the communication takes place in the form of words. God manifests himself by speaking, not by infusing some unspeakable experience—drunkenness, desire, a state of heightened consciousness. Unlike the ecstatic cults of "idols," God did not speak to troubled feelings, but to the clarity of the intelligence and of the heart. He thus agreed to place himself on the same level as that upon which man might respond, and to encourage freedom. Ultimately his words possess a rectitude that is not only of a speculative nature, but is also practical. What he says is "correct," like the result of an exact calculation, but also reflect a decent attitude. His words are "right," in the double sense of righteousness and exactness.

Here we witness the appearance of what might be called a triangle of rationalities: there is a *logos* present in creation, in the history of God with his people (the words of the prophets), and in moral consciousness. And these three dimensions are mutually confirmed. (a) The unshakable permanence of what the Greeks called *phusis* is akin to the historical and evolving word of the Covenant, since Creation is the first stage of the economy of salvation: the world is saved from chaos as Israel is saved from the Red Sea. (b) The order (in the sense of "regularity") that the sky and the earth obviously follow reflects the order (in the sense of "commandment") that the conscience gives in the secret depths of the heart: the universe is not permanent as that which rests on itself, but as that which is established, settled. It is the image of the constancy of love, of the faithfulness of the creator. (c) The Law given in history reflects the aspirations of our conscience. It does not invite ecstatic disturbances, but encourages a reflective choice of life.

The idea of creation was formulated along the lines of these notions: when the wise men of Israel reflected on the universe that surrounded them or, in any case, on what they knew about it, they imagined a creation that was not the result of the work of God, let alone the result of a combat between God and some primitive monster, but of speech. That which is to be created does not resist divine speech, but allows itself be brought into existence by it. The psalmist comes to this conclusion: "By the word of the Lord the heavens were made" (Psalm 33:6). Later Philo uncovered the principle of creation and gave it a Greek name that evokes a thousand resonances: *logos.*

Creation conceived in this way is above all a production. The position in being of that which is is illustrated by an entire gamut of craftsmanlike images: modeling of clay, foundation of a house, the unfolding of fabric, etc, are mentioned in turn. And yet creation is also the instilling of a meaning through a word and the attachment of a value: the creative word is the word of justice. In this way it unites the two principles, artifice and convention, which contrasted with the Greek *phusis.* And in Israel, as well, a concept developed that was also in contrast to their union—"nature." The "world," in the Greek sense of *kosmos,* is what it is thanks to the order it manifests. The world of the Old Testament was produced with wisdom *(ḥōkhmah)*,[9] but that wisdom did not belong to man. There was indeed a wisdom of the world, but its subject was God, not man.

B. Devaluing the World in Favor of "History"

The first ordered description of what we call "nature" can be found at the beginning of the Bible, in the first of the two creation stories that open Genesis. This story is far from being the oldest text in the Bible; on the contrary, it was most probably written after the Exile. It deserves a meticulous analysis, for despite its apparent simplicity, the text is extremely complex.[10]

I will comment here only on the account of what occurred on the fourth day: "And God said, 'Let there be lights *(ma'or)* in the firmament of the heavens to separate the day from the night; and let them be for signs and for seasons and for days and years, and let them be lights in the firmament of the heavens to give light upon the earth.' And it was so. And God made the two great lights, the greater light to rule the day, and the lesser light to rule the night; he made the stars also. And God set them in the firmament of the heavens to give light upon the earth, to rule over the day and over the night, and to separate the light from the darkness. And God saw that it was good. And there was evening and there was morning, a fourth day" (Genesis 1:14–19). This text is situated within a general movement in which the Creator delegates more and more of his power to what he has created. This creative power is a power of separation: after having separated the light and darkness on the first day, on the second he creates the firmament whose function is to separate the waters above and the waters below. Here we see that the primary task of God—the separation on the very first day between light and darkness—is conferred upon the entities that were created on the fourth day (see 1:18). Those entities are not called by their names, they have no personality. The firmament is a lamppost, the stars are simple lamps that God places after lighting them, or (this is the literal meaning, contained in the verbal schema of the names of instruments applied here to the root 'WR) "instruments to illuminate," "luminaria."[11] They are, quite obviously, the Sun and the Moon. The prophets readily call them by their names: "The LORD, who gives the sun for light by day and the fixed order of the moon and the stars for light by night" (Jeremiah 31:35). Here, the absence of a name suggests a devaluing of the heavenly bodies. They are called "big" only from the point of view of the light that they provide. Ibn Ezra notes this fact and explains it: the Sun and the Moon are viewed solely from the point of view of their light, not of their size, for, if they are not in themselves the largest of stars, they are the ones that shed most light upon the earth.[12] From our perspective it is clearly a matter of a discrete dismissal of the "pagan" gods. But it is interesting to wonder why the Bible proceeds in this way. It might have employed other, more polemical means, as is the case in other passages. Here, the stars cannot be served, because they themselves serve. They have a function: to distinguish times *(zemanim)* and festivals *(mo'adim).*[13] Space is put at the service of time. Among the dates thus fixed, festivals are named first (1:14), although they are much less apparent than the alternation of day and night, and even the phases of the moon, which require a bit more observation. It is indeed that which renders them pertinent—and more than elsewhere—in Israel. Indeed, those festivals do not celebrate the return of natural cycles (seasons, harvests, etc.), but commemorate a single event, one that occurred once and for all. Thus Passover, which was no doubt originally a pastoral festival, is associated with the Exodus. "Nature" is not envisioned for itself, in its cyclical affirmation of itself, but to be the framework for events situated in time. There is nothing surprising, then, in the fact that nature appears to have been established through a single event, creation.

A second detail follows in the same direction. Throughout the entire creation story, the curtain rises on a scene that is to be one of a history. We see this at the beginning, in a detail that at first appears pointless: the Spirit of God that initially hovers over *(merahhéphet)* the face of the waters (1:2). He does not intervene throughout the entire pageant of creatures, but remains like an unfulfilled threat or promise. This is because he is destined to land upon a predetermined people, Israel. Only one other passage uses the same root, RHP, in the same intensive form, precisely the one that describes the way in which the god of Israel leads his people: "Like an eagle . . . that flutters over *(yerahheph)* its young . . . the LORD alone did lead [us, Israel], and there was no foreign god with him" (Deuteronomy 32:11).[14]

The devaluing of celestial bodies was intended to extirpate the worship of the stars. The cult of the stars is forbidden in a very explicit commandment in Deuteronomy: "And beware lest you lift up your eyes to heaven, and when you see the sun and the moon and the stars, all the host of heaven, you be drawn away *(niddahta)* and worship them and serve them, things which *the LORD* your God has allotted to all the peoples under the whole heaven. But the LORD has taken you, and brought you forth out of the iron furnace, out of Egypt, to be a people of his own possession, as at this day."[15] The expression to describe misguidance and the cult of foreign gods, "to be drawn away" *(niddaḥ),* is common (see Deuteronomy 30:17). The prohibition is accompanied by a sentence: whoever bows down before the sun, the moon, or any other of the host of heaven will be stoned (Deuteronomy 17:3). As for the *Sitz im Leben,* one must no doubt think of the reign of King Josiah—during which Deuteronomy was allegedly "rediscovered." King Josiah, a pious Yahwist, eliminated those who made sacrifices in high places, "those also who burned incense to Baal, to the sun, and the moon, and the constellations, and all the host of the heavens" (2 Kings 23:5), and destroyed their places of worship. The quoted text is one justification for that policy. The most interesting point is clearly the reason provided, which is, however, not clear in itself: one can understand that the stars were given to all people throughout the world, all the stars spreading their influence indiscriminately over all of humanity.[16] But one can also understand that they were spread out among all people in such a way that each people would be under the protection of a specific constellation or planet, and of the angels placed in charge of them—with the exception of Israel, whom YHWH personally watched over. This idea is found elsewhere in Deuteronomy 32:8ff. ("sons of angels," Septuagint reading). The idea was eagerly adopted later, among the rabbis of the Talmud *(eyn mazzal le-Israel)* as well as among the Church Fathers.[17] In the Middle Ages that is the way Ibn Ezra, for example, interpreted the passage.[18] Furthermore, if the stars had been given to all peoples, what was the reason for that? Simply to illuminate them? Or so that they would be their gods, to tempt them in that way? Rashi favored the first interpretation, but discusses the second in some detail: "He did not prevent them from wandering, from following them, but he made them slide due to their vain words, to chase them from the world."[19] According to rabbinical tradition, there was an addition to the Greek of the Septuagint to dispel any ambiguity in favor of the first interpretation.[20]

Whatever the case may have been, the heavenly bodies belong to all peoples, whereas the Law was given only to Israel. Consequently, the Law was not to be found in the sky (Deuteronomy 30:12), which covers the entire *oikoumenē* without favoring any particular historical unit. Thus the passage perhaps constitutes the first appearance—not literally, of course—of the ideas of *nature* and *history.* It deals with that which exists everywhere in the same way, with what is characteristic of that which is by nature: "That which is by nature is unchanging and everywhere has the same strength *(dunamis).*"[21] It was long known that celestial phenomena belong to that realm, and there are texts in which that fact is reflected: the sun, the moon, the sky, the earth, and the sea are common to all but receive different names.[22] One would therefore expect that constant phenomena, those that exist everywhere and forever, and thus for all peoples, would be more important than an event, datable and localized, that concerns only one group of human beings. Yet the exact opposite is true here. The relationship to the Absolute does not pass through "nature," but through "history." It is the intervention of the God of Israel, a datable and localized intervention, that singles out the Jewish people. This idea would persist in Judaism, for example in the writings of Judah Halevi.[23]

C. Apocalyptic

The facts of nature were introduced into history in such a radical way that, later in the history of Israel, thinkers came to believe that those facts, or in any case, their present state, would exist only for a time. The sky and the earth would perish, would wear out, would change. Prophets announced the destruction of the heavens and the earth, indeed the creation of new heavens and a new earth.[24]

The intertestamental literature, outside the Jewish and Christian canons, further emphasizes this aspect of things. Although medieval thinkers were only slightly aware of it, having received from the Bible only the selection of writings that make up the Old and New Testaments, this literature nonetheless is interesting in itself. It assumes a composite cosmology, one that had already entered into the orbit of Hellenism but that was marked by Babylonian and Persian representations.[25] One can find several new themes in it, such as a certain superiority of earth over heaven: men are worth more than angels—note, it is on earth that the story of God and his people is played out.[26] And again, a theme that would be taken up throughout the Middle Ages with much fanfare: the idea that Abraham discovered the uniqueness of God through astronomical considerations, an idea found for the first time in the second century B.C.E. in the book of Jubilees.[27]

Apocalyptic literature contains a teaching about the world: "the age is hastening swiftly to its end" *(festinans festinat saeculum pertransire).*[28] This literature presents the devaluing of the stars by representing those paragons of regularity as subjected to disorder,[29] and by envisioning something like a dismissal of the spirits responsible for governing them. Moreover, it also had an influence on the New Testament. The message of Jesus, who announced the coming of the reign of God, was formulated, by himself or by the early Christian community, using the vocabulary of apocalyptic, which was itself not exempt from Greek influence. Thus the description of the end of the world in 2 Peter (3:10–13) is expressed in the Stoic vocabulary of the final conflagration.

THE NEW TESTAMENT
A. The Words of Jesus

In the teachings of Jesus one finds very little concerning "nature." In the apocalyptic addresses attributed to him, the devaluing of the stars already extant in the Old Testament is translated along the lines of an event, like an announcement of their temporary nature. Physical phenomena are included among eschatological signs, the sun darkens, the moon no longer sheds its light, the stars fall from the sky, the powers of the sky are shaken (Matthew 24:29). The vocabulary and the arsenal of images are those traditionally associated with apocalyptic. But that which was only a more or less long-term forecast became the announcement of an imminent event which required an urgent decision.

At the same time a physical image is used to express that urgency, in two parallel passages on the signs of the times: Matthew 16:2–3, and Luke 12:54–56—the latter interestingly juxtaposing "the sky and the earth," both in contrast to the *kairos.* Jesus is asked for a sign from heaven. Which means, according to the euphemism that avoids naming the God of Israel directly: from God. He replies by harshly rejecting the pious metaphor and uses the word "sky" in the literal sense. There is then a list of examples of inferences from meterological occurrences (the sky is red, thus the weather will be fair; the clouds are gathering, thus it will rain). But the meaning is reversed: the regularity of meteorological phenomena is no longer an example of the stability of the cosmos. It functions as an image of the sureness of the eschatological coming of God. The reasoning no longer leads from the present to the future within a cyclical nature; it opens up onto an absolute future.

The relationship with nature takes a paradoxical turn. One passage invites the consideration of natural phenomena, in this case living things, birds in the sky that should be watched *(emblepein),* the lilies of the field that should be studied *(katamanthanein).*[30] We are close here to an exhortation to imitate the moral qualities attributed to certain animals, found in the Bible and elsewhere.[31] But the recommended behavior—not to be concerned with one's food or clothing—is certainly not an imitation of the makeup of natural beings or even their activity, but solely their relationship of absolute dependency upon the goodness of God.

Another passage offers the same teaching, but from the opposite point of view. Here we are told to love our enemies and thereby to imitate God, who makes his sun shine and his rain fall indiscriminately upon the just as well as the unjust (Matthew 5:45). One must not imitate the sun, the traditional image of good before and after the New Testament, but God. One must be perfect like the Father, not like his creatures. Unlike in the *Timaeus*, the creature enables the Creator to be known (Romans 1:20), whereas Plato never suggests this. But the creature itself is not an object of imitation.

There is something more stable than the world, something that will not only survive its upheaval, but against which the world measures up, indeed, that created it: "Heaven and earth will pass away, but my words will not pass away."[32] This sentence seems to be echoed in a commandment addressed to the disciples. I will indulge myself with an explication: "But I say to you, Do not swear at all, either by heaven, for it is the throne of God, or by the earth, for it is his footstool."[33] The phrase is situated within the context of a rabbinical discussion: "the sky and the earth" being able to designate either the sky and the earth themselves, or their Creator, the path is ambiguous and therefore is not binding.[34] Philo emphasized that rather than explicitly invoking the primary Cause, it was better to name the entire world.[35] Human speech cannot lean on anything of this world, for the things of the world belong to God who created them. To claim that one can stick to one's word as long as the earth and the sky exist, is to call upon God to conserve that which he is perhaps about to revoke. Such a possibility is brought to the fore in the eschatological atmosphere of the New Testament. One can derive an essential, anthropological consequence from it: the word must be risked alone. In theology one would say that the Word cannot come from the world, but is incarnated as it comes from elsewhere. Speech is what makes man a "logical" animal. This is above all the case when it manifests the freedom expressed by the "yes" or the "no," the commitment whose definitive character is marked by the irrevocable nature of the given word. One might interpret as follows: man must not attribute that which makes him a man to anything of this world. The humanity of man transcends his worldliness. The Synoptic Gospels therefore have a strange kinship with Epicurus.

B. *The Johannine Writings*

With the Fourth Gospel[36] and the Epistles of John, there appears a new meaning of the term "world." The word no longer designates the object of a cosmography, physical realities in their ordered totality; this is why that meaning does not directly concern us. We should however take a quick look at the meaning, for two reasons: first, because in the history of West-ern thought it has never ceased to interfere with the sense upon which I am basing the present study; and second, because it presents a philosoph-ical pertinence itself, wherefore I will need to return to it later.[37]

In the writings of John the use of the Greek word for "world," *kosmos,* is in the same vein as the meaning that the Hebrew *'olam* was beginning to have at the time. "World" first designates human life. The expression "to enter into the world" is found in the familiar Prologue to the Fourth Gospel, where it is a question, according to interpretations, of "every man," or of the divine Word that "was coming into the world" (John 1:9, and see 3:19). The writings of John are moreover among the first texts in which the syntagm "in the world" appears in Greek.[38]

The world is the creation of God (John 1:3). But men are separated from Him. The world is darkness that revels in itself and shuts itself off from light (3:19), a lie that denies the truth (18:37), death that refuses life. It is sub-jected to Evil, "father of lies" (8:43f.), "murderer from the beginning" (8:44), and therefore "ruler of this world" (12:31, etc.). The Son, who is the Word, is a light that comes into the world (8:12, 12:46), truth, life. He reveals him-self in the world in order to save it (3:17). But he does not come from the world (18:36). Those who have welcomed him are the objects of the hatred of the world (1 John 3:13). They must therefore adopt something like an ethics of beings-in-the-world, as Christ defined it just before the "High-Priestly Prayer": "In the world you have tribulation *(thlipsis);* but be of good cheer, I have overcome the world." (John 16:33). This state of affairs is, however, temporary: "And the world passes away, and the lust of it; but he who does the will of God abides forever" (1 John 2:17). Henceforth faith, which puts the believer in contact with God, "overcomes the world" (5:4).

The world here designates the men that inhabit it and the situation in which they exist. The writings of John contain nothing that reveals an in-ventory of the contents of the created world, no form of cosmography.

C. The Pauline Writings

I am looking at the writings of Paul[39] here, after discussing those of John, despite their likely chronology given the majority view that the writings of John are the latest texts in the New Testament. I am doing this for reasons of substance. Indeed, in Paul's writings one already finds within the con-cept of world *(kosmos)* a movement from the anthropological to the cos-mographic.

The word "world" sometimes designates the creation (Romans 1:20), or the inhabited earth (1:8). But it above all designates human life. To live, for man, is to "deal with the world" *(khrēsthai ton kosmon)* (1 Corinthians 7:31). The world, constituted by the concerns of fallen man (the "flesh"), turns against him and enslaves him (vv. 32–34). To govern himself according to the order of the world is to define a rule of action, the "wisdom of the world" (1:20, 27–28; 2:6, 8; 3:18–19). And like John, Paul is familiar with the apocalyptic idea according to which the world "passes away." If the world is only temporary, to rely upon it is foolishness: God has "made foolish the wisdom of the world" (1:20). In addition to the world, everything that structures it is accused of foolishness, the Jewish Law as well as Greek philosophy.[40] It is thus recommended to Christians: "Do not be conformed *(suskhēmatizesthe)* to this world *(aiōn)* but be transformed by the renewal of your mind" (Romans 12:2). That which "passes away," and that to which one must not conform, is the *skhēma* of the world: "The form *(skhēma)* of the world is passing away" (1 Corinthians 7:31). The *skhēma* is not the image as a simple representation, as a "vision of the world"; the word designates the image that enables a practice, the one that enables one to "have a hold on life" insofar as it makes the world hold *(ekhein)*. The idea of something like a structure of the world thus appears, accompanied by a cosmography.

It is implicit in the Christology of the Captivity Letters: the death of Christ establishes contact with God, an access to Him (Ephesians 2:18), which no longer goes through the elements of the world. The world has in fact entered under the control of "worldly" powers that consider themselves independent from God and therefore are evil. This is the case with what Paul calls the "power of the air" (2:2). But those powers are unaware of God's plan. In particular, the coming of Christ is unknown to them (1:21, 3:10, 6:12). They are consequently stripped of their sovereignty by Christ (1 Corinthians 15:24).

The cosmic dimension of salvation appears clearly in a passage in which the overall context is a simultaneous critique of astrology and of the attachment to the Jewish festivals whose dates are determined by the movement of the moon and the sun. Those are two ways of being under the influence of the celestial bodies which are, in the world, what is most cosmic. But they are also what is most rudimentary in the world: "When we were children we were slaves to the elemental spirits *(stoikheia)* of the universe" (Galatians 4:3).[41] They were our tutors whose care we have now left—perhaps this is the first appearance of the idea of an adult age of humanity, an emancipation. "Now that you have come to know God, or rather to be known by God, how can you turn back again to the weak and beggarly elemental spirits *(stoikheia)*, whose slaves you want to be once more?" (v. 9). Placed back through baptism into Christ himself, we are dead with him to the elemental spirits of the world: "If with Christ you died to the elemental spirits *(stoikheia)* of the universe, why do you live as if you still belonged to the world?" (Colossians 2:20–21).

The writings of Paul thus contain a cosmography. But it remains implicit, and it hardly needs to be made explicit: on the one hand, because Paul adopts the image of the world of his time, and, on the other, because it only serves as a backdrop. That which makes up the physical universe is significant only because it is led into the drama of salvation. And the story is in fact that of it being put out of circulation.

. . .

Thus, with the New Testament the "wisdom of the world" is named explicitly for the first time. But this is for the purpose of being immediately rejected and deemed foolish. The wise man is indeed he who knows how to read the signs of the world. But those signs are "signs of the times" (Matthew 16:3); they are read in relation to a world that passes away, and they designate, beyond that world, the historical intervention of its creator.

THE KORAN

The sacred Book of Islam[42] is different from those of Judaism and Christianity in more than one way. In particular, the two Testaments are composites and were written over a long period of time—several centuries for the Old Testament, and several decades for the New Testament. The Koran, however, has a unity that dates from its origins: a single author—Allah,[43] for the Muslims, and Muhammad for others—and it was composed over a period of around twenty years, although the posthumous assembly of its elements occurred over a longer period. It is therefore not surprising that we find a rather unified doctrine in it. On the other hand, as we have known for some time, the Koran develops many of the elements found in the earlier sacred Books and the Apocrypha that reached Muhammad through different sources, both oral and written.[44] The principal elements of his vision of the world thus adopt certain givens from the Old and New Testaments but place the emphasis elsewhere, which has given rise, in later Muslim tradition, to somewhat original developments.

A. The World as Creation

The idea of the world is not clearly present in the Koran. The borrowed word (from Aramaic), *ʿālam*, which renders it in Classical Arabic, is found in the Koran only in the plural, and not in the usual form, *ʿawālim*, but as *ʿalamūn*, which designates the inhabitants of the world and men in particular. The recurring form, *rabb ʾul-ʾalamīn*, traditionally rendered as "Lord of the worlds" or "of the universe," probably means "Lord of men."[45]

The unnamed "world" is all of the objects created by Allah, which is tautological, as Allah alone can create; the deities of the idolaters are not capable of creating, not even a fly. Allah creates tirelessly. Indeed, to create he need only say "So be it!" to something, and it is.[46] As in Genesis, Creation takes place in six days. According to one passage, the earth was created in two days.[47] Several others show Allah creating, then sitting on his throne.[48] Allah can add anything he likes to his creation. The idea of a creation continuing through providence is perhaps present where it is said that Allah "ordains all things [in the sense of commandment]" *(yudabbiru ʾl-ʾamr).*[49] It even seems that the Koran, which does not contain the Biblical ideal of a sabbatical rest for God after his work of creation, does not distinguish initial creation and the maintenance of the created through providence. Thus Allah "keeps the heavens and the earth from falling."[50]

The object of the creative act is not subsumed under a single term. As in the Bible, it is often designated as "heaven and earth," to which is often added "that which is between them" or "the stars." Lists can be summed up by "all things," this last expression also appearing alone.[51] The exclamation "[He] who excelled in the creation of all things" recalls the Priestly tale of creation.[52] But there is an essential, though subtle, difference: the totality in the Bible is additive, and here it is distributive; according to the Bible the object of admiration is the entirety of creatures, in the connection that gives them their consistency; according to the Koran it is every creature viewed individually, without any connection to the rest of creation, indeed, without any link other than that with Allah.

The structure of the world is portrayed marginally alongside a few specifications concerning its production by Allah. Thus the heavens do not rest on any visible pillar. One passage reiterates the idea of an initial separation of the sky and the earth. Another suggests a sketch of a spherical cosmography[53] that distinguishes seven heavens to which seven earths correspond.[54] It seems that the stars are a barrier against the demons that are enclosed by it.[55]

B. The Signs

The first suras, dictated in Mecca, begin by using the phenomena of creation as testimony in an oath. They then turn to the apocalypse and announce a cosmic catastrophe, an earthquake, an opening of the sky or a series of extraordinary phenomena.[56]

The Koran adopts the apocalyptic transposition of the "signs of the times," which already appeared in the Gospels,[57] turning natural regularities into signs of a definitive irruption of Judgment Day: Allah, who created man from a drop of semen, will of course be able to resuscitate him; Allah, through the rain, makes vegetation appear, and that is how he will make the resuscitated come out of the earth. He who had no difficulty creating the sky will have none resuscitating man.[58] In a general way, natural phenomena are proof of divine goodness.[59]

The theme of "signs" *(āyāt)*, no doubt announced during the first Meccan period, became pervasive during the second.[60] Let us cite a few examples: "Surely in this there are signs for men of judgement;" "Surely in the heavens and the earth there are signs for the faithful; in your own creation, and in the beasts He scatters far and near, signs for true believers; in the alternation of night and day, in the sustenance God sends down from heaven with which He resurrects the earth after its death, and in the marshalling of the winds, signs for men of understanding." The idea is summed up in a sentence: Allah "created the heavens and the earth to establish the truth. Surely in this there is a sign for true believers."[61]

We can describe the theme by looking at a few points: *(a)* Concrete reality is a language through which Allah speaks to man. It is called, most of the time, a sign, but also a reminder, a memory-jogger *(dikrā)*. *(b)* Man can decipher it and deduce the existence and the generosity of Allah from it. *(c)* Still he must exhibit intelligence *(nuhan)* and "heart" *(lubb)*. *(d)* Thus he must make use of those faculties and listen *(sama‘a)*, reflect *(tafakkara)*, understand *(‘aqala, tadakkara, or iddakara)* or believe *(’āmana)*.[62] We are invited to "consider" *(nazara)* the kingdom of heaven and earth, as Abraham did, he who deduced the oneness of the Creator from it—a theme that came from Judaism.[63] Thus the sura "the Bee" presents a vast tableau of creation: heaven and earth, man, the animals, rain and the vegetation it causes to grow, the stars, the earth with its varied colors, the sea with its fish and pearls, the mountains; it continues the theme farther on when it repeats the phrase: "for men of understanding" three times.[64]

In this respect it does not appear that Muhammad distinguished the "natural" from the "cultural." Indeed, the signs invoked could belong to the most varied realms and be the objects of lists that juxtapose phenomena whose ontological statuses were completely different. This is the case with what is "natural," "historical," and "artificial."[65] Natural regularities are on the same level as the *gesta Dei* of history. Thus the sura "*Yā Sīn*" mentions as signs the fertility of the earth, the night, and the sun, then the story of Noah's Ark. The idea of "sign" encompasses historical reminders, in particular those of the Bible: the hospitality (philoxeny) of Abraham or Noah's Ark. It forms the refrain for the sura "The Poets."[66] The historical is constantly juxtaposed to examples taken from nature.[67] And the same expressions, for example "reminder" (*ḏikrā*), designate the roles of both natural signs and historical tales.[68]

Moreover, artifacts are just as much "signs" as are meteorological phenomena or those relating to vegetation. This is quite specifically the case of boats *(fulk),* which are cited no fewer than sixteen times.[69] It is true that the emphasis is placed less on the vessel as manufactured object than on the way in which the water was made capable of floating such a massive object. If this is so, the idea is found in Saint Ephraem, who perhaps indirectly influenced Muhammad.[70] Allah put the sea at man's disposal so that boats could sail on it; he causes the wind that moves them to blow; he brings the lull and ensures them a peaceful journey.[71]

C. Man

Man, the reader of those signs, is a favored creature: Allah gave him a harmonious form. That which has been created is subject to man's use, including the sun and the moon.[72] But what is unique to man is only rarely compared with what relates to the cosmological. Nor does it appear that the world and the "self" are clearly distinguished, as is suggested by the juxtaposition, in a single series, of natural phenomena and the soul. This is very clear in: "On earth, and in yourselves (*fī anfusikim,* literally "in your souls") there are signs for firm believers *(li-'l-mūqinīna).*"[73] It seems that this distinction is practiced elsewhere, as in the famous verse in which Allah is supposed to say: "We offered Our trust *('amāna)* to the heavens, to the earth and to the mountains, but they refused the burden and were afraid to receive it. Man undertook to bear it." But the rest of the verse, which emphasizes man's injustice and ignorance, seems to qualify the privileged status first recognized in man.[74] Every created thing, and not only man, adores Allah—even the mountains.[75]

Does the Koran contain a doctrine on the duty of man who conceives that duty on the basis of his relationship to the physical universe? In several places the Koran insists on the idea that creation was not accomplished in jest: "It was not in jest *(lā 'ibīna)* that We created the heavens and the earth and all that lies between them. We created them to reveal the truth *(bi-'l-ḥaqqi)*." "It was not in sport that We created the heaven and the earth and all that lies between them. Had it been Our will to find a diversion *(lahw)*, We could have found one near at hand." "It was not in vain *(bāṭilan)* that We created the heavens and the earth and all that lies between them. That is what the unbelievers *(ẓann)* think."[76] It is possible that the recurring formula according to which Allah created, *bi-'l-ḥaqqi*, should also be translated in the other passages as "seriously," and not by "in truth," as one might also do.[77] It is not impossible that the Koran's insistence on the seriousness of human life and its rejection of a hedonistic interpretation of that life goes hand in hand with the very seriousness of creation. However, it is unlikely that we are dealing here with a metaphysical affirmation of the final goal of creation, which would contrast with theories on the playful nature of the being.[78] It is affirmed alongside the idea of a fixed amount of time *('ajal musammā)*.[79] This is why I wonder whether the text should be considered in a judicial context[80] and it should be understood that Allah did not make the world without collateral, but as an investment that would show returns.

In a single passage, and one often commented on, Allah announces that in man he will create a *xalīfa* on earth. We have fairly recently come to believe that this should be interpreted as saying that man received the dignity of "Vicar of Allah" ("Caliph") on earth. But the Arabic word thus rendered signifies "successor," more specifically someone who succeeds the owner of land that has escheated—which cannot be the case for Allah. It is therefore not impossible that the underlying idea is that man succeeds as occupier of the earth—the angels.[81] It is out of the question that Allah delegate anything to man. We can see this when we compare the Koranic and the biblical versions of the same scene: according to the Koran, Allah teaches Adam the names of all things; but the biblical God names only five things (day/night, sky/earth/sea) and leaves it to Man to name the animals, thus agreeing to learn something from his creature.[82]

. . .

I would now like to highlight the elements common to the Scriptures considered to be revealed, and sketch something like an "Abrahamic" model. The world is created by a good God, who affirms at every stage of creation that what he has just freely brought into being is "good," indeed in his ordered edifice "very good" (Genesis 1). But the phenomena that seem most sublime within the physical world are not those of the highest level. They are in fact of lesser value compared with man, whom they serve. Man therefore is not meant to govern himself according to the phenomena of the world but must seek elsewhere for a model of behavior. In the final analysis, that model is God himself. God manifests himself less through his creation than through a more direct intervention: He can either give the world his law, as in Judaism and Islam, or he can indeed enter into that world through incarnation, as in Christianity.

Chapter 6

The Other Other: Gnosticism

THE LAST MODEL

The fourth and last model I will now describe is Gnosticism or, more exactly, an aspect of Gnosticism: anticosmism.[1] The word "Gnosticism" designates a complex group of movements that do not in fact share a common doctrinal corpus. Their unity is perhaps only artificial, but in them one can identify something like a common "sensibility," and this is what is of interest to us here. Furthermore, this *Stimmung* goes beyond the boundaries of Gnosticism, coloring the entire Mediterranean world around the second century C.E., a period that has been characterized as an "age of anxiety," owing perhaps to a "failure of nerve."[2]

I have chosen to place Gnosticism at the end of this gallery of cosmological models, first of all for simple reasons of chronology. Indeed, it does not appear that the Gnostic movement predated the Christian era, nor even the destruction of the Temple of Jerusalem in 70 C.E. Gnosticism occurred after the birth of Christianity or, at least, is situated after the apocalyptic movements of the end of Old Testament Judaism. It is possible that Gnosticism was one of the responses to those movements. I will not deal with the contested issue of its origins. They are perhaps Judaic, and are in any case post-Judaic. Gnosticism is also post-biblical for fundamental reasons: it is a response to certain theses in biblical theology; its mythology is an inversion of the Jewish exegesis of the beginning of Genesis.[3] A somewhat negative valuation of the world is present in certain Jewish sects and perhaps even in Qumran.[4]

Gnosticism also postdates the philosophers. It is possible to find various aspects of Greek thought echoed in Gnosticism. And the accent Gnosticism places on knowledge is Greek.[5] Certain Gnostic traits are even present in Platonism, first in Plato himself—out of whom, according to Plotinus, comes all that is good in Gnosticism.[6] And this is corroborated by the presence of a passage by Plato, translated into Coptic, in the Gnostic library of Nag Hammadi.[7] The Platonic themes that enable a Gnostic reinterpretation include the demiurge and the idea that he might not be good.[8]

The reality of the presence of the soul in the world inevitably leads to a problem. The presence of a soul in it is the consequence of a fall, the reason for which is unclear in middle Platonism, including in Plotinus, and it is still hotly debated among various interpreters.[9] But beginning with Plato, a problem appears: the presence of the soul in the world is good for the world, but bad for the soul. In *Timaeus* the fall of the soul is the price to be paid for the perfection of the world: the gods must achieve a perfect world that thus includes the four types of living beings. But in the beginning only primitive Man is created, a sort of *Adam qadmon*, who, in principle, should be exempt from a fall.[10] And the animals can only emerge from it once man has fallen. Thus Gnosticism remythologized what philosophy had rationalized. In this way it did not only undergo the influence of philosophy; it was situated explicitly in relation to philosophy, to provide a response to—and a distance from—it.[11]

ANTICOSMISM

If I feel compelled to speak of Gnosticism here, it is because it also proposed a model of a relationship with the world. What is more, that relationship seems to be one of the keys to Gnostic thinking, a point that was made by Hans Jonas, then by Henri-Charles Puech.[12] The way in which Gnosticism views the world indeed explains an entire range of other features of the Gnostic mentality. This is the case, for example, of the Gnostic attitude toward the body, following a logic Tertullian observed: if the body is that through which we are in the world, and if the world is bad, the body must not be able to be resurrected.[13]

On this point Gnosticism contrasts both with the "Greek" vision of the world and with biblical Revelation in its orthodox interpretation, in that it rejects the postulate common to these two models. These models might disagree as to the origin of the world, which for the Greeks was eternal (whether that eternity concerned only matter or also extended to the arrangement of its parts) but for the followers of biblical religions was created. But they are in agreement as to the value of that which exists, that is, its fundamental "goodness." That goodness can in turn be due to several factors. According to the Bible and, with some slight differences, according to *Timaeus,* it is a consequence of its origins in a perfectly good Creator; for Aristotle the goodness of the world was connected to its perfect permanence; for the Stoics, perfection expressed the world's identity with God Himself. But the principle was secure. And it was precisely to that principle that Gnosticism was diametrically opposed.

It has been argued, against Hans Jonas, that in Gnosticism and the religions that grew out of it, anticosmism is not present everywhere with the same intensity. In this view Manicheism seems to have expressed less harsh attitudes, as can be seen in this text: "The wise men and the ones by whom the right is chosen are capable of recognizing the boundless and timeless and unmixed goodness of the Paradise in the limited and temporal and mixed goodness of the world. And in the same way from the numbered and limited evil, which one sees in the world, the numberless and boundless evil of the hell is recognized, that it (i.e. the numberless evil) exists. And when one does not see in the world the limited and passing goodness and evil, and the mixture of the one with the other (viz. the mixture of goodness and evil), (then) the commandment to keep far from evil and to go to the goodness cannot come (in)to the thought of someone."[14]

Furthermore, in Manichaeism the world is a machine for salvation, a mechanism intended to liberate, to gather up, and to purify the Light that is held captive in it: "The meaning of the world is the redemption that men [more precisely: the elect] must operate. And insofar as that redemption . . . is interpreted as a purely physical process, the cosmos in its totality appears henceforth as the bearer and the instrument of that very process: from the three "wheels" [the sublunary spheres: water, wind, and fire] to the two "luminous vessels," the moon and the sun, to the wheel with twelve buckets of the zodiac, and to the paradise of light, it forms a gigantic machine, artistically arranged and manipulated, whose goal is the "renewal" *(ahramisn)* of the liberated Light. It is thus, in the physicomechanical myth, that is presented the submission of the cosmic apparatus to the goal which is the redemption of the Light: the earthly world is no longer, as in the doctrine of Zoroaster, only the *scene* of the battle against the world; it is a device to be used to that effect."[15]

In Gnosticism itself anticosmism isn't as uniformly clear, either. It is clear above all in Marcion; Valentinus, however, represents a cosmogonic Gnosticism, in which the world is already present in the pleroma and is thus not entirely evil. Others are more nuanced, such as Hermogenes. In his Platonistic cosmology, the *kosmos* indeed deserves its name but preserves a disordered portion of wild matter: the Demiurge "took a part of the Whole and tamed it *(hēmerōse),* and left the other carried away in disorder. He said that which is tamed is the *kosmos,* and that the rest will remain wild *(agrios)* and is called matter without order *(hulē akosmos)."*[16] In the best of all cases the role of the world is pedagogical. This is the case in Ptolemy: "The spiritual elements, which Wisdom [Achamoth] sows from the beginning to the present in righteous souls, *educated on earth and raised,* and, from the fact that they had been sent as children, having later reached perfection, will be given as intended to the angels of the Savior."[17]

A DEVALUED WORLD

These nuances aside, the fundamental tenor remains a devaluation of the physical universe. Not even Ioan Couliano can cite a single text in which it is affirmed that the world is good; at the most he deduces a relative innocuousness about the world.[18] He is forced, moreover, to admit that for the Gnostics the world is an error, useless, and that its final disappearance will be a liberation.[19] A text from Nag Hammadi asserts this explicitly: "The world *(kosmos)* came about through a mistake *(paraptōma)."*[20] It is an illusion *(phantasia).*[21] The world was made by a demiurge who was not the supreme God, but a being subordinate to him. Different Gnostics can place the accent on different negative characteristics. For some the demiurge is ignorant. Thus for Basilides, the Demiurge does not know that something more perfect exists above him.[22] For others, such as Ptolemy, he is simply evil.[23]

In classical Hellenism there was an almost unbreakable association between the beautiful and the good. In *Timaeus* they constitute two characteristics of the world that were believed to be inseparable and mutually involved—even if that connection appears more problematic when examined closely.[24] In Gnosticism, however, the world could be beautiful, but it is not good. Indeed, it is material, easily corrupting, incomplete, moving. It is good *(agathos)* in that it produces all things, but it is not good as regards its other aspects, since it is corruptible, moving, and the producer of corruptible beings. The world is even the epitome of evil *(plērōma tēs kakias),* whereas God is the epitome of good.[25] The world is the full measure *(to sumpan horos)* of evil.[26]

The bad quality of the world can be related to the fact that it is botched and thus simply badly made. This is the case in certain texts of the *Corpus hermeticum,* in which the fact that the world is bad—the "badness" of the world, if we like—is not an evil act, an evil deed. But true Gnosticism goes one step further. In Gnosticism the world is essentially evil. There is an evil power that reigns in the firmament—that is, exactly where, according to "classical" Greek thought, Good should be at its highest point.[27] One text speaks of the "firmament where the prince of this world lives," and in a parallel text we read: "I see Satan seated in the firmament of the sky."[28] This is why it is essential that the world disappear entirely: "The All is being dissolved, both the earthly (things) and the heavenly."[29]

The world does indeed display a rigorous and incontestable order, even a fascinating beauty. But its beauty is devilish, it is a trap intended to seduce the soul. And its order serves in fact to make it impossible to escape it. For the prisoner, to inhabit a well-constructed prison is in fact a cause for despair rather than one of encouragement. Gnosticism further emphasizes the regularity and the power of the *kosmos* of classical Hellenism, but while changing its influence from positive to negative.[30]

COSMIC TERROR

In Manichaeism the world is a place of torture for the Light: the world is its cross, in a generalized crucifixion.[31] For Gnosticism, such is, in any event, the case for the soul. Plotinus speaks of the huge "drama" *(tragōdia)* created by the Gnostics about the dangers that the soul risks in the spheres of the world.[32] And a text from Nag Hammadi indeed says: "We possess nothing in this world, out of fear that the Domination that has occurred in the world might retain us in the celestial spheres, those in which universal death surrounded by individual [deaths] resides."[33] The powers in the world appear as a source of terror. This is the case in a Greek magical papyrus which contains an invocation to Ursa Major.[34] Or further in another magical text according to which the seven planets are launched in pursuit of man, who cannot escape their influence.[35]

A Mandaean text, which in its current form no doubt goes back to the eighth century, but which brings together more ancient representations, expresses this sentiment vis-à-vis the physical world.[36] The person speaking is described contemplating the entire world above him: not only the stars, but "the angels who are placed above the sky, who are also placed above the earth, the twelve signs of the zodiac." The evocation of the celestial and terrestrial world, from the angels who preside over the four elements to the trees and the fruit, lead to a questioning concerning origins: "Who can tell me where they came from, upon what they rely, and upon what they stand?" The static structure is animated by an ordered movement: the angels who day and night attract the stars turn them into a succession comparable to a system of recurrences. This regularly alternating return of celestial phenomena does not provoke the same reactions in men. On the contrary: "There are many people who rejoice in that, and many [others] who are troubled by it and say: 'Why has the day dawned and why has the morning arrived?' And that other, nocturnal, recurrence: there are many people who rejoice in it, and many [others] who are troubled by it, cry, and say: 'Why has the night come and why has the moon risen?'" Our dissatisfaction is comparable to that of Job longing for the night when it is day, only to then await impatiently for the day to return. We are thus constantly out of phase: no time is favorable. Instability exists in things themselves: the stars "change by day and by night, turn and turn again in the sky, and have no permanence in a place." Their only consistent trait is negative: "They produce nothing good for the children of men: they impoverish some, and enrich others; they cause damage to all; they turn a slave into a free man, and a free man into a slave." In addition, stars don't simply upset and ruin material situations. Their evil action is deeper, since it extends to souls, which they plunge into error: "They circumvent the souls of the children of men and seduce them, so that they err. They trick them and keep a good number of their souls for themselves until the final day." He who becomes the spectator of a world thus construed trembles and shakes; his body contracts in a painful spasm, sighs rise in his heart, his legs collapse beneath him. Considering the situation, he understands his dereliction in an evil world and concludes: "My older brothers have abandoned me in *this world of evil*, they do not come and they do not rescue me from here."

It is of little importance that this very dark scene is merely the prologue to a deliverance and that it is a prelude, here as throughout Gnosticism, to the coming of a Savior. What interests me is the way in which the world is perceived. It is a place of anguish for the soul: "Pain *(ponos)* and anguish *(phobos)* cover things like rust covers iron."[37] According to a text from Nag Hammadi, anguish can become as thick as fog.[38] Anguish is in fact the raw material of the world: the world is not only *in* anguish, it is so to speak *"of"* anguish the way a plank is made *of* wood. According to the Valentinians, the Demiurge created evil spirits out of sadness *(lupē)*, animals out of fear *(phobos)*, "and that which is created out of fright *([ek]plēxis)* and out of the impossibility of escaping it *(aporia)*, those are the elements of the world." The same doctrine is voiced by Irenaeus.[39]

THE SOUL IN THE WORLD

For the "classical" Greeks, our presence in the world did not develop into a theme, for it went without saying. For the Gnostics, it ceased to be obvious and became a pressing issue that was divided up into a series of questions: "How are we detained in this dwelling place? How did we come to this place? In what manner shall we depart? How do we have [the] authority of boldness? Why do the powers fight against us?"[40]

Our presence in the world is conceived through several negative images, such as nightmare,[41] or abandonment: the soul is abandoned in the world like an aborted fetus in the formless void.[42] We were brought into the world through a violent movement. Our presence in the world is the consequence of a *propulsion.*[43] The image constantly recurs, as in the well-known catechism, close to the text that has just been cited: "Who were we? What have we become? Where were we? Where have we been tossed *(pou eneblēthēmen)?* Toward what goal do we hasten? Whence have we been rescued? What is generation? And regeneration?"[44] The image recurs in the *Pistis Sophia;*[45] among the Naassenes the soul, "thrown *(errimenē)* toward unhappiness *(eleos),* laments."[46] Elsewhere the soul pleads: "Rescue us from the darkness of this world, into which we have been thrown."[47] Granted, the image of a propulsion is not unique to Gnosticism. It can be associated with the famous Epicurean comparison according to which man, at birth, is like a castaway washed up *(proiectus)* onto the shore.[48] The image of the world as something shaken by a storm where thousands are shipwrecked is also found in Mani.[49] However, behind the similarity of the metaphors, two diametrically opposed representations confront one another. Indeed, in Lucretius the image serves to show that the world is not made for man: the world has its own laws that are not regulated upon the needs of man, who is as if superfluous in it. In Gnosticism it is rather a question of showing, conversely, that man is not made for the world: man is too good for the world. The cosmological pessimism of the Gnostics is balanced by a "dizzying anthropological optimism."[50] The association, which has become accepted since Hans Jonas, with the concept of "being thrown" *(Geworfenheit)* as forged by Heidegger is not truly convincing.[51]

The world is not our natural habitat. That is why "the good will not enter into the world."[52] Or, if they are in it, they are lost in it. According to Heracleion, "that which is unique *(oikeion)* to the Father—that is, the spirit—is lost *(apolōlenai)* in the profound matter *(hulē)* of wandering *(planē).*"[53] To enter into it is in fact to enter into death, it is less to be born than to die: "The one who is born of the Mother is led toward death, that is, toward the world *(eis thanaton . . . kai eis kosmon).*"[54] The world is ultimately not our dwelling place, but either a prison,[55] or in any case that which is not appropriate or familiar to us, uninhabitable, one might say, at the cost of the over-translation of the technical term *anoikeion.*[56] The play on words implicit in that which is "unique" *(oikeios)* and that which is a "dwelling place" *(oikia)*—one might think of terms such as "inhabit/habitual," "familiar"—

is present in Heracleion: that which has fallen into matter is "unique" to the Father;[57] Capernaum (John 2:12) designates "those extremities of the world, those material things toward which he descended. And it is because that place was uninhabitable *(anoikeion)*, it is said, that one says he neither said nor did anything. When Jesus announced to the centurion: 'your son lives,' he means that 'he is as he should be *(oikeiōos)* and appropriately, without any longer doing what is not appropriate to do *(anoikeia).'*"[58]

For the Stoics, it is the evil one who is a stranger in the world, where the wise man is the good citizen;[59] for the Gnostics, in comparison with the world we are too good not to be strangers in it. This is true first for Christ, who left the world for that reason. Mani also felt, in relation to other religious groups, foreign and alone *(othneios kai monērēs)* in the world,[60] and his isolation indeed corresponded to his ontological situation: the soul is like a stranger in the world.[61] The Gnostic revelation is often attributed to a Stranger: thus the assumed author of an apocalypse, Seth the Allogene, and perhaps Elisha ben Abuya, the "Aḥer" ("The Other") of the Talmud.[62] Gnostic awareness is essentially "foreign awareness" *(xenē gnōsis)*. Election and its subject are also strangers, for they are supra-cosmic: "'I [the soul of the wise man and of the Gnostic] am a stranger *(parepidēmos)* and a sojourner *(paroikos)* among you' (Genesis 23:4, Psalm 38:13). Basilides began there to say that the elite of the world are strangers *(xenēn tēn eklogēn tou kosmou)*, in that they are by nature supra-cosmic *(huperkosmion)*."[63]

Feeling a stranger in the world, the soul seeks an exit which will enable it to leave and return to its true world. According to the Naassenes, Jesus asked the Father to send him to help the soul. That soul "seeks to flee the bitter chaos, and does not know where to go." Elsewhere God is praised, "He who has thus given man a door in a foreign world."[64] The soul must perceive the beckoning that comes from elsewhere and that reveals its true nature to it. The liberation provided by the Savior (who can be Christ) liberates from the powers of the world, in particular the influence of the stars, suddenly enabling one to rise up to the transcendent Father. Thus: "This is why the Lord descended to create peace, the peace that comes from heaven to earth. . . . This is why a foreign *(xenos)* and new *(kainos)* star has risen, destroying the former order of the stars *(astrothesia)*, shining with a new and non-cosmic light *(kainōi phōti, ou kosmikōi)*, and tracing new and salutary paths."[65] One can note the implicit equivalence between "new" and "extra-cosmic."

In such a model there can be no question of a "wisdom of the world" in the sense in which I understand it. Using the expression only surpasses its pejorative sense as it appears in the writings of Saint Paul.[66] It is perhaps in this sense that it appears in a text from Nag Hammadi: "The wisdom of the world overcame them from the day when it created the sun and the moon and when it placed its seal on its sky for all eternity."[67] The wisdom of the world could only be, in the subjective sense of the genitive, the diabolical ease with which this world captivates us. The authentic wisdom of "he who knows," that of the Gnostic, is the knowledge of ways of evading, a wisdom of the negation of the world.

. . .

The four models I have just sketched form a system and might be rather loosely arranged into a tableau with two means of access, by way of the intrinsic ontological value of the world and of the interest a knowledge of it has for man.

In the *Timaeus* Plato responds in a very positive way to the two questions about the value and the interest of the world: the world is what is best, and knowledge of it is supremely interesting, since such knowledge, and it alone, enables us to reach the fullness of our own humanity. For Epicurus, the world such as it is is not bad, but it has no more value than any other arrangement of atoms; a knowledge of it, in theory, is not indispensable, but it is useful in fact, since it enables one to be reassured. For those who claim to be of Abraham, the world is good, and even "very good," because it is the work of a good God; a knowledge of it is also useful, since it leads to a knowledge of the Creator. For Gnostics the world, the work of a clumsy or perverted demiurge, is bad.

The *value* of the world in Platonism, at least in that of the *Timaeus*, is greater than that found in "Abraham." For Plato that which transcends the world remains vague; for Abraham the Creator is "the only (truly) good." Conversely, the Epicurean world is better than that which Gnosticism imagines; it is in fact not truly bad, but morally indifferent. The world according to the Gnostics is on the contrary the epitome of evil, a trap and a prison.

The *interest* of the world, in Platonism, again looking only at the *Timaeus*, is considerable, since knowledge of it constitutes the only path to excellence in human conduct. It exists for those who follow Abraham: the world is a completely legitimate and practical path to God; it is therefore not without interest, but a detour through it is not indispensable, as revelation can more immediately provide the believer with a more precise knowledge and clearer prescriptions for action. Epicureanism considers "physiology" as having only a negative, indirect value; it is nevertheless indispensable, for without it wisdom would remain beyond our reach. For Gnostics a knowledge of the world is useless, as the only liberating knowledge is indeed rather that which enables one to escape it.

Part Three

THE MEDIEVAL MODEL

Chapter 7

Marginal Models

As we have just seen, Antiquity produced four models that dealt with the issue of the link between cosmology and anthropology. But among the schools of thought whose responses we have briefly looked at, not all were able to survive intact. Some disappeared, or were buried below the surface. Others made compromises with models that were able to emerge triumphant. I will now examine a succession of different cases. But it must first be noted that the fundamental theory underlying the triumphant model was not unanimously accepted.

IMPERTINENCE
A. Negation of the very notion of Kosmos

There are a few examples of complete rejection of the major premise of the dominant model, that is, the idea of the ordered nature of the world as *kosmos*. This rejection was sometimes expressed through parody, a genre that refused to take the model of the world seriously, and that, moreover, expressed the same attitude toward anything that claimed to be serious. This is the case of the master of that style, Lucian (120–180 C.E.?). Inspired perhaps by a text by the real Menippus, Lucian parodies the literary theme that had become classic of the ascension and the voyage into the celestial regions, a theme illustrated by Cicero, Lucan, and others.[1] He begins with a phrase that parodies the philosophical tales of conversion, the tone of which is found as late as Spinoza, in the famous beginning of the *Tractatus de Intellectus Emendatione:* "As for me, as soon as I had examined things in life and had found all human things ridiculous, base and inconstant, I mean fortunes, dominations, reigns, since I scorned them and considered that to be concerned with them *(spoudē)* was to neglect truly serious things *(spoudaia)*, I forced myself to raise my head and to look at the Whole." The inflated tone of the moralist might make such a declaration appear serious, if it were not followed by a development that aims to show that the disorder of the sky is equal to that of the earth: "But then, what plunged me into great confusion, was first the very thing that wise people *(sophis-tai)* call the "world" *(kosmos)*." Lucian examines the structure of the phys-ical universe beginning with the last sphere and descending to the earth, the opposite of the movement of ascension that had carried his hero off to the sky. He mentions one after the other the stars (no doubt the sphere of the fixed stars), the Sun, the Moon, then atmospheric phenomena. This is all summed up by an expression which, curiously, Helm leaves without commentary and by which Menippus indirectly designates the physical universe: "what the wise men call *kosmos*."

This seems very clearly to allude to the passage by Xenophon that has already been cited in which the word *kosmos* in the sense of "universe" ap-pears for the first time, at least in the Greek literature that has survived.[2] In Lucian's time, or even earlier, if we acknowledge that the text for the most part goes back to the time of Menippus, the word had long been un-derstood to mean "universe." Lucian, by emphasizing the word's forgotten etymology, invites us to question the legitimacy of the decision that is im-plicitly made about the nature of the universe: that the decoration must also represent an order. And if it is already troubling that questions about the universe such as "how it was born, or who the artisan of it was, or the principle of it, or what is its goal" could not be answered, the problem be-comes critical with regard to the celestial bodies, that part of the world that is more than just a part of it, since not only do they enclose the whole, but they guarantee its coherence and legitimize the name of "order" that is given to it: "When I then examined the world in detail, I was forced to ex-perience a much greater confusion, for I found the stars thrown around everywhere in the sky *(hōs etukhe tou ouranou dierrimenous)*." The stars are not carefully positioned on the celestial vault; far from forming an intelli-gible design or even a simply regular one, they are "thrown around" hap-hazardly. This notion continued to torment thinkers up to the modern era, to the extent that Descartes dreamed of finding the law hidden behind the phenomenon.[3] The metaphor of "propulsion," or of "being thrown into," as we have seen, is often used to describe the way in which man appears as an intruder and, at worst, as trouble-maker, in a splendidly ordered world. Here it is turned around and applied to the world itself. Its nature as *kos-*

mos is placed in doubt. It is possible that the world, to repeat the common interpretation of a fragment of Heraclitus, is made only "of things poured out haphazardly."[4]

B. A Cosmology without Anthropological Relevance

One might also, without formally refusing to see the world as a *kosmos*, reject the notion of an anthropological orientation of cosmology, such as is developed in the *Timaeus*. This was the case, again in Lucian's time, of Galen (121–199).[5] Plato, as we shall see, explained man's unique upright posture as orienting him toward contemplation of the sky.[6] But Galen was content with a purely immanentist explanation of man's posture and argued against those who associated anatomical facts with a final causality. He places standing erect or sitting, another position unique to man, within the overall context of a physical anthropology in which the characteristics unique to man form a system. These two positions are necessary since they are the most convenient for an animal with hands: "All the actions which the hands perform in the exercise of the arts require these two positions; for some we perform standing and some sitting, but nobody does anything lying supine or prone. It was right for Nature not to give any other animal a structure enabling it to stand erect or to sit, since the other animals were not meant to make use of hands." Galen then ridicules those who see the erect posture as an orientation toward the sublime dimension of height. Man, in this regard, is rather less well suited than certain flat fishes whose two eyes are on the same side of its head, or even the donkey, an animal that hardly symbolizes intelligence: "To think that man has an erect posture for the sake of looking readily up to heaven and being able to say, 'I reflect Olympian light from my undaunted countenance,' is to be expected of men who have never seen the fish called *uranoscopus* (heaven-gazer), which looks perpetually up to heaven whether it wants to or not, whereas man would never see the heavens if he did not bend his neck back. Moreover, this ability to bend the neck is not, of course, characteristic of the human animal alone, but is found to an equal degree in the ass as well, not to mention long-necked birds that can look up easily when they wish and can also readily turn their eyes in every direction." In conclusion, Galen even indulges in playing Plato against himself, the *Republic* against the *Timaeus*— a dialogue which, according to him, as we shall see, does not express Plato's most authentic thinking. Socrates ridiculed a too-literal interpretation of the way in which knowledge is supposed to turn the soul's gaze on high. What is seen above is not material, as if all it took to be a philosopher were to float on one's back: "It is a mark of gross carelessness if a person fails to listen to Plato when he says, 'Looking up does not mean lying on one's back and yawning, but . . . means using one's reason to meditate on the nature of things.'"

Moreover, still looking at the Middle Ages, the notion that man is the goal of creation was demolished by the strict followers of Aristotelian philosophy. Avicenna is perhaps the first medieval author to rise up explicitly against the idea that the movements of the stars would have as their ultimate purpose the well-being of the sublunar region and its inhabitants. Yet he doesn't indicate who had argued in favor of the theory he is attacking. He speaks of "certain people" who had taken literally a phrase of Alexander of Aphrodisias that might have been interpreted in that way.[7] The formula is found in the commentator's writings—if indeed the treatise in which it is found is in fact his.[8] But Avicenna does not name those whom he reproaches for that mistaken interpretation.

Elsewhere he does name, in a similar context, Abū 'l-Ḥasan al-ʿĀmirī.[9] We find the same attitude in the scholarly itinerant Bible commentator Abraham Ibn Ezra (d. 1167), a rationalist thinker who was, moreover, under Avicenna's influence. In a long digression in the second version of his commentary on the first verse of Genesis, he launches into a stock attack on any sort of anthropomorphism, more specifically against the idea of man's superiority over the angels, a recurring criticism in his writings.[10]

C. A Cosmology without Moral Relevance

The model could be protested less for its premises than for its consequences, to wit, for its ethical relevance. Lucian is commonly contrasted with the emperor Marcus Aurelius, his exact contemporary (121–180): for Lucian, nature does not lead to anything, a description of it is meaningless; for Marcus Aurelius, it does have a meaning.[11] It is all the more remarkable that they are in agreement on at least one point: that which Lucian proclaims to be irrelevant in the comic register, Marcus Aurelius declares to be indifferent using a tragic tone—as if to illustrate Marx's famous quip. The philosopher emperor asserts that, even if one assumes the world is in disorder, that would not be a reason to imitate it. He then provides an alternative, but only to reject it: "[it is] either an ordered universe *(kosmos)* or a medley heaped together *(kukeōn)*, but still an order; or can order subsist in you and disorder *(akosmia)* in the Whole *(to pan)!* And that, too, when all things are so distinguished and yet intermingled and sympathetic *(sumpathōn)*. . . . And whether the Whole *(to holon)* be God, all is well—or whether it be Chance *(to eikēi)*, somehow molecules or atoms, be not yourself there ruled by Chance."[12] Are we in the presence here of a seriously imagined alternative, or simply of an extreme case, an *a fortiori* reasoning ("even if, considering the impossible, the world were in disorder, that would not be a reason to let oneself go"), or even a "nightmare," similar to what has been called "Plato's nightmare?"[13] As for the two terms that Marcus Aurelius contrasts, they form the fundamental alternative of ancient cosmology,[14] and their formulation does not in itself present any specific interest. However, their relativization as regards the ethical domain is interesting, in that it presents the program of a de-solidifying in relation to the world, a program destined to be adopted later in a completely different atmosphere.

The passage by Galen that we looked at above is only a detailed illustration of the thinker's general attitude, and it is found notably in a passage from the voluminous work in which he compares Hippocrates and Plato.[15] In that passage he declares that physical facts in general are irrelevant to how one conducts one's life: "To inquire also into matters that are not useful for ethics and political action is appropriate *(akolouthon)* only for those philosophers who have chosen speculative philosophy." Galen draws up a very classic list of questions in advanced physics (indeed, "meta-physics") asking "whether there is anything after this universe *(kosmos)*, and if there is, what its character is, and whether this universe is self-contained, whether there is more than one universe, whether the number of universes is very large, and similarly whether this universe is generated or ungenerated, and if it had a beginning, whether some god was the artisan of it, or whether it was no god but some irrational and artless cause that by chance made it as beautiful as if a god supreme in wisdom *(sophōtatos)* and power had supervised its construction." Such questioning is useless for the domestic economy, politics, or justice in general: they "contribute nothing to managing one's own household well or caring properly for the public interest or acting with justice and friendliness toward kinsmen, citizens, and foreigners." However, Galen has just introduced an essential theme here: the beauty of the world might just as easily be the result either of what a god effectively achieved, or of factors devoid of reason, art, or necessity, but which rendered it the same as what a god might have achieved. In any case, everything occurs *as if* the world were the work of a wise demiurge; the question of knowing whether that is in fact the case therefore loses its urgency.

The same approach is applied to the idea of providence: "While it is useless to ask whether the universe had a beginning or not, this is not the case with an inquiry about divine providence. It is better for all of us to examine the statement that there is something in the universe superior to men in power and wisdom; but it is not necessary to consider the question what sort of substance the gods have, whether they are entirely bodiless or whether they too have bodies, as we do. These matters and many others are completely useless for those virtues and actions that we call ethical and political, and no less for the cure of the soul's ills." Whereas one can dismiss research into advanced physics without further ado, one can be content here with "acting as if," with a philosophy of the *als ob* . . . It is meaningless to practical life whether the world was made by a god or by a blind cause, as long as that cause acted *as if* it had followed a plan.

Galen expressly asserts the Socratic genealogy of his attitude with an implicit citation from the passage of the *Memorabilia* that we looked at above: "Xenophon's statement about them is best; not only did he condemn them as useless himself, but he said that Socrates also held this view. The other companions of Socrates agree, among them Plato himself; for when he adds to his philosophy a theory of nature he gives the exposition of it to Timaeus, not to Socrates." Plato is thus put back into the lineage of Socrates, and the considerations of physics in the *Timaeus* are attributed only to the eponymous character, an attitude found not only in Galen, but also, two centuries later, in the writings of the emperor Julian.[16] Galen places physics and logic alongside each other in order to reject what is excessively technical about those two disciplines: "just as he gives the more extended dialectic to Parmenides and his pupil Zeno." However, with a view to healthy politics, Galen maintains the necessity of carrying out some studies in physics and logic: "For in a theoretical study of ethics and politics it is impossible not to touch at all on the theory of nature and of reasoning," even if, when they are considered by themselves, "you will find that these [theoretical inquiries] too are among the useless things." It is a pity that Galen does not say precisely which physical and logical knowledge has a moral and/or political usefulness. In any case, physics thus appears as a simple appendage to philosophy in the strict sense. It has nothing to teach us in the realm of behavior. There is nothing surprising, therefore, in the fact that in his summary of the *Timaeus,* a summary we have only in Arabic, Galen omits passages that concern the imitation of the stars.[17]

AN "ABRAHAMIC" SOCRATISM

All these thinkers follow the Socratic tradition, sometimes by very explicitly invoking Socrates' name. In the medieval choir that voice is not truly discordant but sings a counterpoint. It abstains from any judgment on the world itself, even less any depreciative judgment. It sees the world in the same way the Platonic model does, but, simply put, it does not consider the world relevant in the final analysis. In fact it proposes a different anthropological model. It asserts a certain primacy of a knowledge of self over that of the world, thereby radicalizing the "Socratic revolution" or undermining the restoration carried out by Plato in the *Timaeus*. It is better that man examine himself rather than study the physical world. Several themes are intertwined here: the vanity of knowing nature, for those who do not know themselves; the impossibility that knowing nature might provide us with peace of mind.

The earliest author in whom this tendency clearly appears is no doubt Philo of Alexandria (ca. 15 B.C.E.?).[18] He represents a synthesis (whose elements are difficult to isolate) of Platonism (rather, of Socratism) and biblical thought. He presents his concept of a knowledge of nature within the general framework of his work, the exegesis of the book of Genesis. More specifically, he reflects on the allegorical meaning of the migration of Abraham. Abraham, born in Ur, first settled in Harran before going on to Palestine. Each of these towns corresponds to a fundamental dimension of human activity. Abraham begins first with an involvement in astronomy.[19] He is thus associated with one particular type of man. Philo distinguishes three types: by nature, some belong to the earth, others to the sky; still others belong to God.[20] Those who pursue the pleasures of the body are of the earth; artists, scholars, and lovers of knowledge *(philomathēs)* are of the sky. Indeed, among our faculties the celestial faculty is the intellect. This association of the intellect with the sky has a cosmological foundation, since each of the celestial bodies is itself an intellect. The men of God are the priests and the prophets. Such men refuse to mix with the republic of the universe or to become citizens of the world. They thus transcend everything relating to the senses to attain the intelligible world, where they relocate after becoming naturalized citizens of the republic of Ideas. Before becoming a man of God, while he still lived among the Chaldeans, Abraham was thus a man of the sky. He sought to know the higher reality, which is the ether, and philosophized on events and their causes.

Philo also uses the traditional tripartite division of types of life into a life of pleasure, an active life in search of honor (politics), and a contemplative life. But he combines the two upper levels differently: the contemplative life is divided in two, depending on whether it bears on the world or on God. The first kind is thus related to political life, through the intermediary of the Stoic idea that man is a citizen of the world. One can thus radically transcend the realm of the political only by also leaving the walls of the cosmic City.

This is exactly what Abraham did. God allowed him to go beyond astronomical knowledge.[21] That knowledge was essentially idolatrous: it "taught the creed that the world was not God's work, but itself God." It led to fatalism, "that the vicissitudes of better and worse are reckoned by the courses and ordered revolutions of the stars, and that on these depends the birth of good and ill." God gives Abraham a new advantage. He makes him the heir to a "wisdom which cannot be received by sense, but is apprehended by a wholly pure and clear mind." Philo reiterates the Platonic theme of knowledge capable of disregarding the multi-colored spectacle of worldly phenomena and of raising oneself to an understanding that is possible only for the intellect. "Through this wisdom the best of all migrations becomes an established fact, the migration of the soul which passes from astrology to real nature," not, of course, toward the physics of the sublunary, but toward the knowledge of the primary principles of nature. Philo, going beyond Plato, thus connects to the Bible: this migration leads "from the created to the uncreated, *from the world to the Maker and Father of the world,*" toward Him whom the *Timaeus* declared to be essentially unknowable. He is accessible through faith: "Those whose views are of the Chaldean type have put their trust in heaven, while he who has migrated from this home has given his trust to . . . God."

This migration, however, is not, as we might expect, centrifugal. Quite to the contrary, it leads us toward the center, toward the subject of knowledge, a subject that is constantly tempted to forget itself, favoring the object of its desired knowledge.[22] Philo heaps sarcasm on the so-called sages who speak of every thing and claim to grasp the essence of it, as if they had been present at the creation of the world, as if they had been the advisors of the Creator when he created all things. He invites them to set aside prying questions and choose a much closer object: themselves. Once a knowledge of oneself has been acquired, every other knowledge becomes credible: "Do not . . . spin your airy fables about moon or sun or the other objects in the sky and the universe so far removed from us and so varied in their natures, until you have scrutinized and come to know yourselves. After that, we may perhaps believe you when you hold forth on other subjects."

Our inability to place ourselves before the creation of the world and thus, all the more so, before our own creation, is found in the Bible. There we already see the ironic questions that Philo asks of the self-important physicists.[23] But he effects an interesting connection, which justifies the expression "Abrahamic Socratism" that I have hazarded. Indeed he places biblical facts alongside Socrates' experience, which is explicitly invoked.[24] The Holy Scriptures reproach those who scrutinize the physical universe with being indiscreetly involved in what does not concern them, things on high. They are invited to be concerned with that which is close to them, with that which cannot be closer: themselves. The tendency toward a knowledge of external things should be directed rather toward knowing the instruments of knowledge themselves, the organs of the senses. In fact, the name of the town where Abraham resided for a time—Harran-the-Hollow (this epithet is Philo's pseudo-etymological elucidation)—allegorically alludes to those windows of the body. This critical examination of knowledge is "the most necessary and most appropriate philosophy for man." In this way, the Bible not only voices the exhortation to know things that are close, as formulated in Pindar and illustrated by the famous story of Thales who fell in a well;[25] it also carries out the order that Socrates had borrowed from the Delphic Apollo: "Bring the explorer down from heaven and away from these researches draw the 'Know thyself.' . . . This character Hebrews call 'Terah,' Greeks 'Socrates.' For they say that 'Know thyself' was likewise the theme of life-long pondering to Socrates, and that his philosophy was concerned exclusively with his own self."

The fulfillment of this sort of Socratic revolution does not only end up in an ethics or politics; it opens up onto a gnoseology. The subject toward which it invites one to descend is also the perceiving subject who should examine himself and measure his power for knowledge. The "Know yourself" is vaguely founded on biblical passages that recommend to "take heed (to yourself)," in which this imperative is a translation of *hiššāmer (lekha)*.[26] This is not the final stage. The goal is and remains knowledge of God. But going through what is represented by the town of Harran enables a shortcut to knowledge of God, which no longer need be obtained via a detour through physics.[27] To descend from the sky is nothing, if one only applies the same research methods to the earth. The danger is not in one object of study or another, the sky, for example, but in the curiosity with which one studies it. Philo can therefore exhort us to change our land, to "quit, then, your meddling with heavenly concerns, and take up your abode . . . in yourselves." The field of inquiry we require is ourselves. It is from that point that one can know God: "For by observing the conditions prevailing in your own individual household, the element that is master in it, and that which is in subjection, the living and the lifeless element, the rational and the irrational, the immortal and the mortal, the better and the worse, you will gain *forthwith (euthus)* a sure knowledge of God and of his works." The method for doing this corresponds to a widespread idea in Antiquity:

one can conclude from the presence of a spirit in oneself to the presence of that same spirit in the universe.[28] Just as our spirit directs what is in us, so it conducts the universe. I want to stress the revolution in the method carried out by Philo: there is no longer any need, for those who can examine themselves, for a detour through a consideration of nature; the spirit passes in a straight line from the self to God.

THE TWO DEFEATED MODELS AND THEIR RETURN

The two rejected models reacted in many ways. In certain contexts their rejection itself conferred a greater impact upon them. In others, their presence only imbued the model that remained dominant with a specific tone.

A. Revolts and Repressions

The Epicurean model is among those that became virtually invisible. It was not alone: Seneca pointed out that there was no longer anyone who defended the ideas of Pyrrho.[29] But later, the emperor Julian, among the authors whose books have been lost, adds the writings of Epicurus to those of Pyrrho.[30] In the Middle Ages Alain de Lille was able to write that he was living in an age when Epicurus and Manichaeism had disappeared.[31] Epicureanism was in fact no longer anything but a subterranean trickle, and the image of Epicurus was reduced to that of a pleasure-seeker.[32] For Talmudic Judaism, his name even became a proper name *(apiqoros)* to designate the unbeliever, specifically the negator of providence.[33] Those who proposed an atomistic physics, such as William of Conches, were eager to keep their distance from Epicurus.[34]

The same is true of Gnosticism. Christianity was the most radical in rejecting it. Christianity was in fact founded on the affirmation not only of the goodness of the Creator (which it shares with Judaism and Islam), but also, and perhaps above all, of the Incarnation, which is prolonged in the sacramental economy of the Church. The Christian God is so to speak involved in the world. An attack against the world must therefore be a full-strength attack against God as well, and a more direct one, in any case, than it would be in Judaism and Islam, where the connection between God and the world is only one of creation.

Thus on Christian land Gnosticism underwent several revivals, catalogued by the doxographers of the official Church under the heading of "heresies." This was the case in the Byzantine Balkans, among the Bogomils. It was again the case, later, and perhaps in the wake of the former, among the Cathars of Languedoc. According to the Bogomils, darkness, matter, and the visible world are the work of the demon. The Cathars have similar doctrines.[35] The question of the soul's entering into the world, or of the origin of the union of the soul and the body, did not receive a clear response from them. That union nevertheless remained abnormal. We are not part of the world. According to a Cathar prayer: "We are not of the world and the world is not of us *(Car nos no em del mon nil mon no es de nos)*."[36]

In Islamic lands we find Gnostic elements among certain unorthodox thinkers. Thus the exaggerated Platonism of the doctor and free-thinker Abu Zakariyya ar-Râzî expresses a similar idea: "As long as the soul exists in this material world, it will not escape from its evils"; the commentary by Kazwanî in this regard adds that the soul then knows that it is "a stranger *(jarība)* in this world."[37] The myth is presented in more detail elsewhere, in Nasir-i Khusraw, with the image of sleep and awakening, of a return to a superior world, etc., and in the discussion between the two Razis, our own and the Isma'ili propagandist Abû Hatim.[38] It is true that Razi seems to have derived a more positive opinion of the world, akin to Manicheism, since, according to his central myth, the creation of the world is the work of God helping the soul. Certain extremist Shi'ites go so far as to distinguish Allah from the Intellect, the first thing created, with the typically Gnostic role of the demiurge who, forgetting his origins, believes he is alone.[39]

B. Domestication: Abrahamic Gnosticism

A reserved sensibility in relation to the world, even a sensation of foreignness with regard to it, are frequent occurrences in more orthodox religious expressions. But they are held at bay by the fundamental assertion of the basic goodness of creation. Thus one very frequently finds assertions that the world is nothing but a dream. The theme is already old; in Gnosticism it takes on a sinister form: the dream turns into a nightmare.[40] The simple, neutralized, image of a dream in the three religions remained active in the Middle Ages and ended up in the assertion that gives its name to the most famous play by Calderón.[41]

This is the case in Christianity and in its founding documents, which contain, as we have seen, a certain number of negative formulas concerning the *kosmos*, understood in the sense of everything that turns away from God.[42] Later tradition sometimes voiced a "scorn for the world *(contemptus mundi)*" or "for the century *(saeculi)*," to the point of conceiving man as an a-cosmic being. It sometimes went so far as to preach escape from the world.[43] Monasticism even knew exercises intended to develop a feeling of foreignness, such as that aimed at a desired alienation *(xeniteia),* which habituated one to not feeling at home anywhere, except beyond the world. In Syrian monasticism, inner alienation led to a true life of wandering; in Egypt, one could practice alienation in one place, as what was essential was to make oneself foreign to the world itself, not to a specific place.[44] Even contemporary Christianity experiences a sensibility of this kind, as is sometimes seen in Chesterton—especially before his conversion to Catholicism, to be sure—or in the Catholic novelist from the Southern United States, Walker Percy.[45] But in all cases the world from which one must escape is not physical nature, which is the work of a good God.[46] The "world" or the "century" is a particular attitude toward God, indeed it simply designates, in monastic literature, all other conditions of life. Evil comes only from an unruled attachment to the *goods* of this world—which still remain only goods. We can see what separates the most ascetic monk from Gnosticism: the Gnostic is essentially foreign to the world and becomes so radically once he has become aware of it; the monk is part of the world and must separate himself from it at the price of an effort at asceticism.[47]

The case of Islam is a bit different. A positive concept of "Gnosticism" *('irfān)* endured there more durably than on Christian land. One can find a gnosticizing sensibility in several locations. Thus, for example, among the "Brethren of Purity," but also in the Sufism of 'Aṭṭār.[48] This sensibility seeks legitimacy by leaning, of course, on words attributed to Muhammad. It is therefore said that "this world below *(dunyā)* is a prison for believers and a paradise for the impious," as well as the recommendation: "Be in this world below as if you were a foreigner *(ġarīb)*."[49] The image of the world as a bridge that must be crossed over, but on which one must not settle, is found almost everywhere, as a *logion* attributed to Jesus.[50] It is a question, however, of "the here below," of the inferior world, and certainly not of all creation.

Finally, in Judaism we find traces of the same sensibility: here, too, man, or the intellect that makes him human, is a foreigner.[51] Judaism also has the formula of the uninhabitable bridge.[52] And one could spot Gnostic elements in the Kabbala and perhaps even points of contact with Catharism on the issue of evil.[53]

Chapter 8

The Standard Vision of the World

The models we have just looked at remained marginal, and for the most part only the first and the third—the Timaean and Abrahamic models—remained in the forefront as rivals. The Timaean model had in its favor the philosophical syncretism that dominated late Antiquity: a Neo(?)platonism that had received an Aristotelian foundation in logic, physics, and ethics, which also readily borrowed ethics from Stoicism. The Abrahamic model came to the forefront when the revealed religions triumphed together on the social and spiritual levels. All the same, at the moment we cannot claim that the two models were foreign to each other. The dominant philosophy and religion did in fact exchange many elements. The medieval model for the most part was the fruit of a compromise between "Timaeus" and "Abraham." In the medieval worlds of "Abrahamic" religion, Plato's dialogue was accepted both directly and indirectly almost without interruption. Plato was "the greatest among those who have philosophized on the world."[1] The guiding question regarding the relationship between cosmology and ethics thus received a specific model of response. This model dominated the period extending from classical Greek philosophy to the end of the Middle Ages. It is that model we will now examine.

COMMON GROUND

The four models were able to confront each other, and two come out winners, because they did so on one and the same terrain. Indeed, during a long period in the history of thought—a period that corresponds to what we call Classical Antiquity and the Middle Ages—the way the world was represented remained roughly the same. This representation was, in short, the spheres imagined by Eudoxus, then adopted by Aristotle and Ptolemy. These thinkers conferred an authority upon them that for a long time remained uncontested.

As for those who pondered this cosmographic science, I am including here only educated people, those who had access to written culture and who therefore left traces—they were in a very small minority. The common man might have imagined the world as fantastically as he wanted, but his way of viewing things would have been written down only in the most unusual of circumstances—and with the help of others. This was the case of the people of Montaillou, who were visited by an Inquisitor in the twelfth century. Or of the miller in sixteenth-century Italy whose opinions were also preserved by the Inquisitors there, and for whom the world was a huge cheese.[2] Such ways of seeing belong to a succession of immemorial representations. Sometimes educated people also defended deviant cosmographies, such as the egg-shaped world of Hildegarde von Bingen, or Robert Grosseteste's cosmogony founded on light, not to mention the archaising image, supposedly faithful to the Bible, provided by the merchant who became a monk, Cosmas Indicopleustes, who in late sixth-century Byzantium argued against the roundness of the earth.[3]

I will recall here that such knowledge prevailed for a period that had a definite beginning and end. Before that period there was not one cosmography on which everyone could agree. Each thinker could present his or her personal vision of the universe, a vision that also inevitably included a cosmogony, and could defend its plausibility as best he could. In ancient Greece we do not find a unified vision of the physical universe farther back than the fourth century B.C.E.[4] The subsequent triumph of a single cosmography eliminated or stripped of relevance any previous attempt at a cosmogony, for example, by relegating it to the realm of myth (as in Plato's *Timaeus*).

It was thus within the same framework that what I am calling "cosmologies" were able to confront each other or, rather, that the cosmological issue was henceforth able to be addressed. One knew against what, or in what, one had to place oneself in order to resolve the problem of man's place in the world. Based on an interpretation of the facts, one could go from a positive to a negative view, or vice versa: some Gnostics saw the world as a prison, whereas the dominant tendency (Plato, Aristotle, the Stoics, the Neoplatonists) saw themselves as living in a splendid palace. The world's affective value could consequently change its sign, from positive to negative: the artistic arrangement of the spheres inspired joy in some when they were faced with the harmony, and despair in others about ever escaping from it. But everyone had the same description of the world.[5] We can fathom the breakthrough represented by Classical Greece: before then the "wisdom of the world," wherever it existed, conceived the world, in relation to which it was a matter of man's situating himself, in a mythical fashion; after ancient Greece, man's insertion into the cosmic order was based on a *known* world—no longer one experienced in myth—on a vision of the world that was of course rudimentary, but nevertheless established through means that were derived from scientific knowledge. A single unified cosmography, broadly sketched, provided a basis for all cosmologies. It even favored those with which it had more affinity. The scientific representation of the world was prolonged therefore without interruption into a response to the existential question of being-in-the-world. "Knowledge" and "sensibility" were in phase.

From this point of view it is interesting to note that the period I am envisioning here produced, alongside highly technical treatises, such as those of Ptolemy, several cosmological summaries for the general public. Many examples of such writings may be cited. In the ancient, "pagan," world, Ocellus Lucanus (second century B.C.E.) comes to mind.[6] In Islam, a popular encyclopedia such as that of the Brethren of Purity in several places, not to say ad nauseam, presents the overall schema of the universe in onion-like layers. A work such as the "Secret of Creation" *(Sirr al-Xalīqa)* is completely devoted to presenting accepted cosmology.[7] In the Christian world, we possess accounts in Latin, such as the *Hortus Deliciarum* by Herrad of Landsberg. But it is remarkable that texts are also found in the vernacular, in French or Middle High German, such as the *Lucidarius*.[8] Finally, so that the illiterate might also know how the world was made, there were abundant graphic representations, both pictorial and sculptural.[9]

As for the philosophers, they presented sketches of the structure of the physical universe in various contexts that provided a sort of lowest common denominator of the ancient and medieval vision of the world in nontechnical terms. Averroes is one such example.[10] Maimonides undertook this exercise twice, once in a work addressed to an elite, the *Guide of the Perplexed*, but also, more surprisingly, at the beginning of a juridical work in which he presents a picture of the whole of the created universe as an integral part of knowledge that nevertheless has God as its object.[11]

This cosmography was not simply the object of speculation. In principle it could be experienced. Such experience is illustrated poetically in the tales of the ascent of the soul into the upper spheres, which we find among various Latin authors and their medieval imitators.[12] These tales could be pure literary fictions. But they might also describe an experience that a magical ritual was supposed to cause to occur.[13] Tales of the soul's ascent into the upper world are quite ancient, since they go back to Sumer: Etana, on the wings of an eagle, sees the world below become smaller and smaller.[14] But it was only later that they were associated with a description of the world like that provided by science. One of these tales even has the prophet of Islam as its hero, which conferred an uncommon authority upon it. This is the famous hadith of the "nocturnal voyage" of Muhammad. It fed the Muslim imagination, but it also passed into the Latin West in the form of *Mohammed's Ladder*, whose influence extended as late as Dante.[15] The same cosmology could be presented in the form of a dream, as in that described by Savonarola in 1495, in his sermon on the Annunciation.[16] It could also serve as farce, as in Cervantes' *Don Quixote*, specifically in the second part of that work (1615). The hero, blindfolded, mounted on a wooden horse, is supposed to have traveled quick as lightning over a fabulous distance, at the cost of a detour through the celestial regions. And he recognizes perfectly the places where he is led to believe he has traveled: the three regions of the air (the second is the province of hail and snow, the third that of thunder and lightning), and the place of fire, located between the sky of the moon and the last region of the air.[17]

The success of this type of literature is not simply a fact to be noted. It is evidence that the questions it dealt with appeared relevant to the educated man. Such a man owed it to himself to have an exact representation of the world. For ancient and medieval man, the structure of the physical universe was important, it was *interesting*. Neither of the two questions, "who am I?" and "where am I?"—or, if we wish, "what is man?" and "what is the world?"—could be answered without an answer to the other.[18]

A MULTI-LEVEL WORLD

I will now describe that structure. I will do so only in very broad outline, relying on the work of historians.[19] Further, I will not mention a great many details that to me appear less relevant to the subject at hand.

According to the cosmography in question, celestial realities and things of this world below are not on the same level. The sublunary is separated from the supralunary. It is so, as the word suggests, by the barrier created by the sphere of the Moon. In addition, the different levels in space are endowed with different values, favor being given to the sky. The sky, explains Plato in the *Timaeus*, was made directly by the Demiurge, whereas the creation of the earth and its inhabitants was relegated to secondary divinities.[20] Consequently the respective works are unequally perfect.

In Aristotle, the two realms are formed of two different types of matter: whereas the sublunary is formed of four elements, whose natural movement is rectilinear, the supralunary is made of a fifth element *(quinta essentia)* whose nature is to move around in a circle.[21] The first Stoics knew only a single matter and therefore refused the idea of a fifth substance. Nevertheless fire admitted different degrees of purity. Their physics were therefore different, before a certain syncretism came to erase the borders with Middle Platonism and peripateticism.[22] In any case, the practical result is the same: a cosmological scale is doubled by an axiological layering.

There is no medieval text to suggest that the sky must be made of elements completely identical to those found on earth. But the question of knowing whether the difference is of degree or kind remained in dispute.[23] Not all medievals admitted a celestial matter, and some preferred a vision along Stoic lines, such as, among the Christians, Johannes Scotus Eriugena or William of Conches.[24] The same is true of certain Jewish authors.[25]

But those who believed so were in the majority. Among them one finds Christians such as Bonaventure.[26] The same belief is found among the Jews, and above all when they were highly observant Aristotelians, such as Ibn Ezra or the radical Averroist Isaac Albalag.[27] Maimonides attributed traditional authority to the doctrine by claiming to have discovered it in a passage from the *Pirqê d-Rabbi Eliezer.*[28] Those who had Neoplatonic tendencies, such as Ibn Gabirol (Avicebron), for example, introduced some modifications: the substance of the sky and of the sublunary elements is the same as for quantity; but the substance of the sky does not have the same qualities as the sublunary elements and is not subjected to generation and corruption.[29] Still, the doctrine of two matters is found among Platonist Kabbalists such as Bahya ben Asher or Nachmanides.[30] Gersonides conceived of a single substance, the differentiation of which produced supra- and sublunary matter. It was not having recognized this primary substance that led the Ancients to dualism.[31]

According to Averroes, it was necessary to distinguish two types of matter and two types of presence of form in that matter. For supralunary substances, the form does not subsist in the matter, and the matter is only substrate, not potential matter; for sublunary substances, the form subsists in the matter, which is potential. We will not dwell on this here. But it is interesting to note Averroes' emphasis that knowledge of that difference is so important that a lack of such knowledge prevents the attainment of human perfection.[32] We can see that cosmography was of supreme interest; to be concerned with it was certainly not idle curiosity.

Here below, one finds the theater of the generation and corruption of things that emerge from the four elements and which return to them. Above, the stars are eternal as individuals. Below, things cannot be repeated identically. Not being able to experience the infinite revolution of the celestial bodies, at the very least earthly things imitate that revolution through cyclical occurrences, such as those involving water, which evaporates, then falls back down as rain; or the seasons that recur; or animal species, among whom reproduction imitates eternity, although no one individual survives eternally; or the great land and water masses: they change places following a very slow rhythm, as seen by the presence of fossil shells in mountains, which were discovered in most distant Antiquity, and which medieval observers continuously noted.[33]

The earth is only an imperceptible point, invisible to whoever observes things as a whole.[34] Whoever carries out this experiment practically by going up in the sky can see the earth only as an object of scorn, and laugh at the smallness of reasons for men to go to war—so say the Pompey of Lucan, and Dante himself, or the Troilus of Chaucer.[35] In addition, the earth is formed of a vile, heavy, opaque matter. The authors who play with the idea of a cosmogony see earth as the concretization of the debris from higher spheres, and sometimes use powerful images to describe it, such as a sewer.[36] This did not, however, prevent a more positive vision of the earth, where it is represented as the dwelling place of man, from his point of view, and on his scale. Need we recall that ancient and medieval poets were as aware as was the *sapeur* Camember that "the spa-ring [is] a period of ru-newal"? It is more useful, however, to note that certain thinkers, going from feeling to reflection, remarked that a study of the earth is not only more useful and appropriate to us than a study of the heavens, but such a study gives us an affinity with the sky. The period that concerns us is therefore marked by an oscillation between "faithfulness to the earth" and "forgetting the earth," favoring either the stars, or the ultimate destiny of man, which is celestial.[37]

MAN

The question "What is man?" which Kant elevated to the rank of the central question of all thought,[38] was not often raised in Antiquity and during the Middle Ages. And when the question was explicitly formulated,[39] it rarely received an answer. It was only in very unusual circumstances that man's humanity appeared as an issue, as in Augustine's *factus eram ipse mihi magna quaestio,* or in the famous formula of Abū Ḥayyān al-Tawḥīd ī (d. 1023): "Man has become an issue for man *(inna al-insāna qad aškala ʿalayhi 'l-insān)."*[40] Man, in the period that concerns us here, was characterized in a whole series of ways that would be too tedious to list and which, in any case, have already been the object of scholarly monographs. Thus, for example, man is a double, amphibious animal.[41] He is the limit or the horizon between the material and the spiritual.[42] Or yet, he is a resourceless animal, neglected by his wicked stepmother, Nature, etc.[43]

In the Middle Ages the question of who—man or the angels—was the best of all creatures remained in dispute. And the responses usually given to that question were not the same in different religious traditions. Among Jewish thinkers, a majority decided in favor of the angels.[44] In the Muslim world the Koran clearly pronounces in favor of man.[45] And in the Christian world one detects a discordant, although discrete, note. The accent is placed in a more decisive way on man's historicity, which is a consequence of his carnal nature. Human love must reach its maturity in charity, which implies time. The angel makes his decision outside time and remains eternally what he has chosen once. Man can fall and be redeemed. From this point of view man is worth more than the angels. The angels can learn something from man, for what occurs in human history is inaccessible to angelic spirits.[46] This is one of the arguments that encouraged certain medieval authors to speak of man's relative superiority over the angels.[47]

Among man's characteristics, I will look only at the traits that involve his relationship to the physical universe. First, as for quantity, man is something very small compared to the world. He is not what is greatest in the world. He is in fact only an insignificant part of it.[48] And as for quality, man is not the best of what the world contains, either. The "best" are the celestial bodies, as Aristotle suggests rather clearly, an idea that would later be adopted by an entire tradition.[49] However, man is the best of the sublunary beings, the most perfect animal. Psalm 8, which contains one of the rare occurrences of the question "what is man?"—which here is an exclamation more than an interrogation—very clearly sums up man's intermediary place in the universe: he is insignificant compared to the heavens; in the immediate surroundings of the angels; and superior to the animals.

The position of "neighbor of what is above" for ancient and medieval man was not necessarily occupied by a living being in the sense in which we understand it—even if our experience with angels has become more difficult in modern times. It could involve physical bodies, celestial bodies, which possess a life all their own, more intense than our own. An example of this point of view can be found in Hierocles, a fifth-century Platonist: "Nature . . . has attributed perpetual movement to the sky, and permanence to the earth, so that each of them bears the trace of divine resemblance. It distributed to the celestial body the perimeter of the Whole, and the center to that which surrounds the earth. . . . Things on high are decorated with multicolored stars, and animals endowed with intellect; the earth is decorated with plants and animals who use only sensations. Man appears as the middle ground *(mesotēs)* of these beings, who are separated by such a distance. He is amphibious, the last thing from on high, the first of those below. This is why sometimes he is carried along with the immortals, and, through his conversion to Intellect, receives his unique fate; sometimes he is incorporated into mortal species and, by the fact that he escapes divine laws, is deprived of the dignity *(axia)* appropriate to him."[50] Hierocles adopts the idea of man as an amphibious animal. He also adopts another, equally widespread idea, that man's place among all beings is not assigned to him at the outset, but is the result of his freedom to assimilate either into what exists above him, or into that which he ought to overcome—a commonplace that, last but, as a matter of fact, perhaps least, Pico della Mirandola voices in the exordium of a discourse that many modern commentators believe to be original.[51] However, what is interesting for my purposes is how physical realities (stars/earth) are placed alongside living things that are seen as various modes of life or forms of soul ("angels"/plants and animals).

The ambitions of ancient and medieval man are therefore aimed at the cosmos. They are inspired, and at the same time limited, by the place assigned to man in the hierarchy of completely physical realities that make up the cosmos. Man's craziest dream (literally speaking) is expressed in a phrase by Maimonides, in which I detect an avowal. In a medical treatise Maimonides devotes a chapter to mental health. There he explains that it is useless to regret the past, that it is impossible to change it, "and there is no difference between a man's being grieved because of the loss of his money or similar things and his being grieved because he is a man and not an angel *or a star (kawkab),* or similar thinking about impossible things."[52] Maimonides also alludes to the legend of Nimrod and his metamorphosis into a star. What is astonishing to Maimonides about it is that the transformation is an ontological promotion, which shockingly seems to reward a rebellion against God and injustice toward men.[53] In the passage cited, the choice of examples is revealing. Perhaps the childish dream of being all-powerful can be expressed, for us, as well, through the fantasy of having wings and being invisible. But the example is surprising: a modern writer would never dream of coveting the characteristics of a celestial body. And it is just that dream that is found behind the representations of astral immortality. Marsilio Ficino echoes this when he bases his invitation to contemplate the sky on the kinship between man and the stars: "Why do you watch so long, divine beings? Raise your eyes to the sky, citizens of a celestial fatherland, residing on the earth! Yes, man is a terrestrial star *(terrena stella)* surrounded by a cloud, and the star, for its part, is a celestial man *(celestis homo)*."[54]

Thus to live on earth does not correspond to our most profound aspiration. The final sphere would suit us much better. It is this yearning that is expressed in a few verses which a biographer and doxographer attributes to al-Farabi. They can be rendered as follows: "Brother, pierce the realm of what is vain / and be in the realm of truths. Our abode is not one in which we linger / and man's being on earth is no marvel. What are we, if not lines we enter / on a globe, an entering that awaits us. This one vies with this one for / the smallest and most concise of words. What encompasses the heavens is what we most deserve / now, how many are crowded together in the center! *(muḥīt as-samāwāti awlā binā / fa-kam ḏā 'l-tazāḥum fī 'l-markaz).*"[55] Ibn Bājja attributes a verse that is almost identical to the one we have just cited to a poet by the name of Ibn al-Jallāb, who is perhaps the person of the same name who is known as an astronomer:[56] "That which surrounds the skies is what we deserve. Why, then, do we linger in the center? *(fa-maḏā al-xulūd ilā 'l-markaz).*"[57]

PHYSICAL PREFIGURATION OF ANTHROPOLOGY

Furthermore, in this line of thought the presence of an anthropological dimension does not just arise from the fact that a certain image of man and his behavior is proposed as a moral model by the structure of the physical universe. It is also just as rooted in the belief that man's condition is as if prepared by the physical world, which thus calls man to a fuller realization, through his will, of what his presence in the world already suggests to him.

A. Microcosm

On the one hand, man is himself conceived as a small world (microcosm), as containing in himself, in miniature, all the components of the physical universe. This idea has previously been studied at length.[58] It is of timeless antiquity and is found beyond the realm we are looking at here, for example in India with the legend of Prajapati, or in ancient Iran.[59] In Greece it is at least as old as the pseudo-Hippocratic treatise of the *Weeks:* it finds its most ancient and explicit formulation in Democritus.[60] The theme remains one of the most common, indeed, one of the most recurrent in medieval thought. It is found in the three (or four) medieval monotheisms: Latin and Greek Christianity, Judaism, and Islam. Its presence in Arabic is ancient. In particular, the *falāsifa* were aware of it since al-Kindī. In Islamic lands the Brethren of Purity made the image the title of two of their epistles, only the second of which deals with the notion in a more central way.[61] The idea flourished in the twelfth century: among the Jews, Joseph Ibn Ṣaddīq (d. 1149), who was greatly inspired by the "Brethren," made it the title of a complete book, in which, moreover, the theme is not dominant; among the Christians, Bernard of Tours (Bernardus Silvestris) divided his *De universitate mundi* (ca. 1150) into a "Megacosmos" and a "Microcosmos," and Godfrey of Saint-Victor (d. 1194) wrote a *Microcosmus.* It was more or less popular depending on the philosophical schools. Thus the Aristotelians had a tendency to see the image of microcosm only as a metaphor.[62]

The idea was rendered in sculpted, imagined, or concretely drawn representations, for example, in Hildegarde von Bingen, who described man inscribed within a circle.[63] Thus in miniatures in which a man is shown nude, his arms extended to form a cross, inscribed in a square, his head surrounded by a circle, or simply inscribed within a circle—two images that a familiar drawing by Leonardo di Vinci ingeniously attempts to combine. The human form, presented as a *chi* (X), imitates not only the Cross of Christ, but the intersection of the circles of the soul which, according to the *Timaeus,* defines the world.[64]

I will not examine this theme in greater detail, either its complete historical journey or all of its aspects. In particular I will leave aside that which nevertheless constitutes the best-known developments to which it leads, that is, the careful listing of more or less arbitrary parallels between the parts of the human body and those of the physical universe (the so-called "melothesy"). This is found in Antiquity,[65] then in the Middle Ages, among the Jews[66] as well as among the Christians[67] and Muslims.[68]

There is, however, an idea that concerns this study more directly: that the correspondence between the two worlds—the large and the small—is a sign of the presence in both of one and the same wisdom. The idea is found in Galen.[69] Later, some thinkers insisted on the fact that the true principle of resemblance between the world and man is the presence in man of an intelligence that communicates with that of The One who created the world. This idea is found in Judah Halevi and Maimonides.[70]

There is an occasionally recurring idea that seems even more interesting to me, which accentuates the theoretical aspect of a use of the microcosm: man contains within himself what he needs to know the entire universe. He constitutes a summary, a "magic mirror" in which every reality can be known. As the astrologer Manilius expressed at the beginning of our era: "What is surprising in the fact that men can know the world, they for whom there is a world in themselves *(quibus est et mundus in ipsis)*, and each is a copy of God on a reduced scale."[71] Worldliness is so to speak inside of man. Thus a knowledge of oneself logically leads to knowledge of all things. After Porphyry, this idea is found in Kindī, the Brethren of Purity, and Joseph Ibn Ṣaddīq, who interprets the famous verse Job 19:26—"from my flesh I shall see God"—in that sense.[72]

It remains to be explained why all things are found in man. One might assume that the soul knew all things before it was incarnated into a particular body. This idea is Platonic—even if Plato himself had his sources. It goes back to the *Meno*, of course, but also to the *Timaeus*. The latter work gives a mythical representation of the notion by explaining that souls, before being incarnated into the body of man, tour the universe on the back of a star.[73] Man knows everything because his soul, before it is born, has traveled, or seen, the great world in its entirety.

One can also find an answer by assuming that everything was contained in primitive Adam, and that God drew it out of him and made him see it. Let us recall, for example, the famous passage from *Midrash Rabbah* on Genesis in which Adam sees all generations and their scholars *(dōr dōr we-dorŝaw)*.[74] It is in this spirit that the Brethren of Purity proposed an unusual interpretation of a famous Koranic passage, the one on the pre-eternal Pact *(mītāq)* between God and the descendants of Adam.[75] In the Koran, God "brought forth descendants from the loins of Adam's children." For the Brethren, God showed Adam all of creation. According to perhaps the clearest passage on the subject: "The Creator . . . created man 'in the most beautiful stature,' formed him in the most perfect shape, and made his shape a mirror for his soul, so that he might see the shape of the whole world in it. Indeed, since the Creator . . . wanted to inform the human soul about the treasures of its worlds and show it the world in its totality, and since He knew that the world is vast and great, and that man does not have the ability to go around the world and see it all, because of the brevity of his life and the vastness of the inhabited world, He decided in His wisdom to create for him a little world to reflect the great world. He thus included in the little world all there is in the big world, showed it to him and made it known to him. He . . . then said: 'He made them testify against themselves *(ašhadahum 'alāâ anfusihim):* Am I not your Lord?' They all responded: 'Yes.'"[76] The Brethren daringly reinterpreted a scene that is fundamental in Islam. It explains the primitive faith in the single God (Allah) of humanity, which was drawn from the loins of its father, the first man. Successive prophets, up to their "seal," Muhammad, scarcely made anything of that faith other than to recall it to the forgetful sons of Adam: the primordial alliance, transhistorical, in pre-eternity. The Brethren interpreted the "testify against *('alā)* oneself" as a testifying based on a consideration of oneself. The root šHD is called upon: "to cause to testify" becomes "to cause to see," whereas the Koran does not say that the men drawn in an instant from the loins of Adam had *seen* anything of creation. The passage is commented on again and again in the *Risāâla Jāmi'a,* which is supposed to clarify all of the epistles, and in which I have counted as many as six such occurrences.[77]

The lists with which the Ancients and the Medievals illustrate the idea of microcosm can be forced and tedious. However, they do reveal an important mindset: man is so far from being a stranger in the world because he is woven from the same material as the world. In a sense, the imitation of the world thus only solidifies an already assured kinship. It will then be a matter only of directing the innate resemblance that connects man to the world toward that which makes the world worthy to be called a cosmos, that is, the celestial world.

B. Influences

And yet this celestial world is not confined to the role of waiting passively to be imitated, either. It is equally active, in that it exercises influences over the world below.

The first influence is massive and invokes one-time occurrences. It is the object of the theory of cataclysms, tidal waves, floods of celestial fire encountered beginning with Plato, which was subsequently developed by later thinkers. In Plato the theory aims above all to account for the progress of the sciences and philosophy.[78] Next, it serves to refute an objection against the idea of the eternity of the world. Its adversaries assert that if the world were eternal, progress in the sciences and technology should have attained an extraordinary level, and the maximum knowledge possible would have already been attained.[79] The response invokes setbacks consecutive to cataclysms, which have allowed only a few unpolished beings to survive, shepherds whose lives in the mountains shelter them from floods.[80] These catastrophes can also be seen as means to prevent excessive population growth. Such is the case in the writings of several medieval authors, who were more or less clear forerunners of Malthus.[81]

Let us consider the example of al-Biruni. He begins by stating the principle that every living being has a tendency to grow and multiply, then mentions the images of the farmer who pulls up weeds and of the arborist who prunes dead branches. In addition, the same process, applied in those examples through human effort, is found in nature. Bees kill unproductive consumers. "Nature does the same; except that it makes no distinction, because its action is unique." In trees nature eliminates superfluous leaves and fruits and prevents them from doing that which they were intended to do. Biruni continues: "Similarly, this world below, when it is corrupted due to a large population, or is on the verge of being so, possesses a rector *(mudabbir),* and the providence [that it exercises] over the whole is present in all parts of it [the world below], so that it sends toward it someone who diminishes the great numbers and stops the matter of evil."[82] This text is not without its difficulties. Does providence act like nature, which does not distinguish between the good and the evil? The biblical flood was selective. The cataclysms to which the passage alludes destroy what Biruni calls "the matter of evil"; not evil itself, but the power of the opposites—which is also, therefore, the matter of good. What is this rector of the world, which also exercises something like providence *(mudabbir/tadbīr)?* Biruni doesn't call it God. Elsewhere, on the basis of the existence of exceptions, he suggests the possibility of the existence of a demiurge and governor other than nature, which he designates using expressions that apply only to God.[83] In any event, the issue has been raised: the issue of an influence of a celestial power (regardless of how one imagines its content) over the sublunary, an influence that is believed to possess a moral value, acting as it does to promote good or, at the very least, to curb evil.

There is a second way that the celestial acts upon the terrestrial. Its influence is no longer effected through a one-time intervention, but it permanently weighs upon the earth. The sky exercises an influence over the earth, in the strict sense.[84] This is the foundation of astrological theory, which, although it was not followed unanimously by pre-modern thinkers, was accepted by a comfortable majority of those thinkers as a legitimate field of knowledge. This was the case, as we know, of the founding fathers of modern astronomy, such as Kepler, although many had reservations concerning the lack of freedom implied by astral determinism. But the notion of influence is broader than its astrological application, and ancient and medieval man were quick to admit the reality of a certain parallelism between the sky and the earth, and of an influence of the former over the latter. This idea is broader than the word that expresses it, *influentia,* which, perhaps in too concrete a fashion, evokes a flowing. It is also translated by the words that designate "power" *(dunamis, virtus).*

Early on, one finds a passage by Aristotle in which the Philosopher presents his cosmology as if in miniature.[85] The Sky's effect on the Earth is limited here, however, to a very elementary, and empirically obvious, awareness that the annual cycle of the Sun—usually the seasons—is accompanied by a renewal or a numbing of the life of sublunary beings. Elsewhere, Aristotle remarks in passing that the world that surrounds the earth is "of a single piece with the revolutions on high, so that all that it has the power to do, is steered from on high." Subsequently, even if the material cause of sublunary phenomena, and above all, of the meteors being discussed here, is the four elements, the efficient cause is "the power *(dunamis)* of the [phenomena] that are always moving."[86] With this shift to the plural there is the possibility of a more nuanced causality. If all the celestial bodies play a role, the variety of their movements, which is almost infinite, enables one to account for the diversity of earthly facts with less obvious arbitrariness. In addition, Stoic cosmology enables the introduction of the idea of a unity of the whole universe, an organism linked by the same spirit *(pneuma)* in which all that affects the part must affect the whole, through com-passion *(sumpatheia).*

Through influences, the world calls on man, as if magnetically, to allow himself to be infused by it. One must still proceed to making a prudent distinction between good influences from on high and supposedly evil influences. In any case, it is the superior that influences the inferior. Man can in no way modify the order of celestial phenomena. Again in the fifteenth century, for an Aristotelian (and even an Averroist) such as Elijah del Medigo, the claims of the Kabbalists to "repair *(tiqqûn)*" divine realities through practices analogous to magic was scandalous, to the point that he had to reassert that the influence could only be exercised in a single direction: "The superior [beings] act upon us but are not subjected to any action from us; it is they who direct the inferior world through the power of God, and they are not directed by inferior beings."[87]

The idea of a celestial influence does not have just a spatial dimension, in that the superior flows onto the inferior. It is doubled by a chronological dimension: the circular temporality that rules the celestial bodies is believed to govern the linear temporality of human history.[88] In this way it suggests a cyclical interpretation of the historical future and thus relativizes the aspect of adventure without return that human history might assume.[89] The result is something like a cosmologization of history. Conversely, the Christian polemics against astrology, as we shall see, accompanied a historization of cosmology.[90]

C. Erect Posture

Finally, the necessity of imitating supralunary reality provides our being with the very final cause that accounts for its structure: the very structure of our bodies, detached from the humility of the earth and aimed toward the sky, enables us to contemplate the stars. Nature has thus drawn us upright so that we might be inspired by the example of what it has produced that is most "cosmic." The idea of contemplation of the sky thus intersects, though it is not confused with, a very ancient theme, that man's erect posture is one of his advantages over the rest of the animals.[91] Indeed, erect posture is a necessary but not sufficient condition for contemplating the physical sky.[92]

The theme of the advantage of erect posture can be traced to the most ancient of times. When a scientific explanation has been sought, the fact was first considered to be an element of a physiological system. Aristotle developed the theme lavishly, placing it within a highly nuanced context that combines the physical properties of the elements and the reciprocal implications of the various organs, in particular the hand and the vocal tract, which form a system.[93] On this last point, Aristotle's ideas are echoed by Gregory of Nyssa, who probably borrowed them from Poseidonius. They are found in a modern anthropologist like André Leroi-Gourhan, who, curiously, does not mention Aristotle, but cites Gregory.[94]

In the Arab world, the physical explanations emphasize the balance of the four humours in the human body, as in the work of Pseudo-Apollonius of Tyana or the famous treatise on magic, *Picatrix*.[95] One might be content with an immanentist explanation, like Galen's.[96] But his criticism misfired and did not prevent the introduction of a final cause. Aristotle had not clearly drawn a conclusion from his treatment of the orientation of the human gaze toward the sky. Medieval authors connected the Aristotelian deduction of human morphology to its assumed final cause, which was lacking in Aristotle's work. They defined man *(anthrōpos)* using a fantastic etymology, as the one who looks up *(anō-athrein)*. Plato gave this explanation in a way that was undoubtedly not entirely serious.[97] But it is reiterated with no apparent irony by an entire series of authors, such as Isidore of Seville or, inspired by him, Abelard.[98] The same idea is expressed in another image from the *Timaeus*, of man as a celestial plant having roots toward the sky. It is present in Philo. In the Middle Ages it is found in the Christian twelfth century, in Islamic lands, and in Kabbalistic Judaism.[99]

If the name of man constitutes something like a program for his action, that program is preformed in his very structure. The erect posture is an invitation to stand up toward the sky. The idea is present starting with the *Timaeus,* and it was passed on to the most diverse authors through the centuries. It is present in the work of the Greek-educated Jew Philo, who indicates very clearly the final cause, contemplation of the sky.[100]

The theme is ubiquitous in Latin literature. It is found in Cicero,[101] but above all in two verses by Ovid, which are very often cited: "Whereas the other animals, crouching on the earth, look at the earth, He gave man a sublime face, ordered him to look at the sky and to direct his raised face to the stars."[102] It is adopted, sometimes along with the quotation from Ovid, by several later authors.[103] Finally, Macrobius adds the notion, which is also Platonic, of the resemblance between the celestial sphere and the human head.[104]

These themes went from paganism to patristic literature, in which they are frequently found, in Greek beginning with the *Letter to Diognetus,* and in Latin beginning with Minucius Felix.[105] Their common ground is in commenting on the biblical passage asserting that man was created in God's image (Genesis 1:26). We do not know clearly how the sacred writer himself conceived man's resemblance to God. Modern exegetes are not in agreement on this point. Nor does the question receive a unanimous response from the Church Fathers or medieval writers: is it a matter, for example, of reason? or of freedom? In any case, the theme of standing upright according to the *Timaeus* is sometimes reproduced with very little modification. This is the case in Lactantius, in a passage that is in effect a summary of the *Timaeus:* the erect posture that allows man to contemplate the sky is for him a reminder of his origin; his mind is lodged in the citadel of his head, which is of a perfectly round shape to imitate the universe. Proof of the nobility of the origin of man are "right reason, his sublime condition, and his face which he has in common with God the father and which is very close to His."[106] However, the celestial origin of man does not assume the preexistence of souls, but creation by God, who is in the heavens. A certain murkiness persists as to the *sublimis status:* is it a matter of the rectitude of the stature, or simply a vague "dignity"?

Most often, however, the theme of standing upright is placed within the context of a general anthropology,[107] into which a new organizing principle, the tale of creation according to Genesis, was introduced. One then sees several inflections. On the one hand, the theme only appears in second place, after it has been declared that resemblance to God is not through the body, but through intelligence, and only as a supplementary argument. This is very clear in Augustine: man is not the image of God through his body, but indeed through his intelligence; erect posture is at most a sign of that superiority, but does not confer it.[108] On the other hand, the rectitude of the human body is passed over toward that of which it claims only to be the image, that is, of the intellect. The direction upward becomes that of the "sky" in general, without further specifics. The "superior things" are not the celestial bodies, but are phenomena that only the intellect is capable of grasping ("ideas"), or spiritual phenomena (Christ after the Ascension, next to the Father).[109] Their order is no longer the astral *kosmos*, but the logical system of intelligible things. Thus, according to Cassiodorus, man is upright so that he can contemplate superior things, that is, intelligible things *(ad res* supernas et rationabiles *intuendas)*, whose harmonious disposition reveals profound mysteries to us.[110]

Augustine takes up the Platonic theme that the contemplation of the material sky does not raise the soul, but on the contrary, fixes it on the ground. He has a very revealing formula: man is upright so that he can see not the visible ground, but the sky, which is "the principle of invisible things *(principium invisibilium).*"[111] One can note a subtle reversal, but one heavy with meaning: the sky was previously all that was visible, according to the constantly reiterated etymology that connected its name, *ouranos*, with the adjective signifying "visible" *(horatos).*[112] It is henceforth, on the contrary, the paradigm of all that is invisible.

Finally, two other inflections appear in patristic literature: superiority over the animals becomes the reason for a moral imperative. This is the case in Basil of Caesarea.[113] That superiority is explicitly drawn toward the legitimization of man's dominion over the animals, in Gregory of Nyssa and others.[114]

Conversely, man's abandonment of his dignity forces him to lose both his moral rectitude and the upright posture that is the sign of it. Hence the theme of the curved soul, which is the opposite of that of the rectitude of the soul. The term came from Persius: "Oh souls curved toward the ground and incapable of celestial things *(o curvae in terris animae et caelestium inanes).*"[115] The idea also comes from the anthropology of Plato's *Timaeus*. It remained present among pagans beginning with Sallust.[116] It then went on to the Church Fathers, and is finally found among medieval authors.[117]

COSMOLOGY AND HUMAN DIGNITY

The predominant current of ancient and medieval thought only rarely saw human dignity as resting on cosmological factors. One author who did, however, was the Jewish apologist Saadia Gaon (d. 962), who saw man's place at the center of the created world as an indication. He points out that nature has the custom of placing what is most precious at the center: the seed in the middle of the leaves, the pit at the center of the fruit, the yolk in the egg, the heart in man, the visual spirit in the eye. And the earth is at the center of the celestial spheres. The last object of creation thus must be on the earth. One can eliminate the elements, which are inanimate, and the animals, which are irrational. Only man remains.[118]

Saadia establishes a certain anthropocentrism on a geocentric cosmology. All the same, he is not defending a naive teleology: his discussion of botany does not envision nature from the point of view of its usefulness to man. And yet, the rigor of his reasoning is mitigated by a shift in the criterion. Saadia begins with the thesis, arrived at by induction, of the natural centrality of the most important. But once he reaches the earth, he abandons the criterion of centrality for that of life, and disregards the inert. He then takes as a criterion reason, which enables him to disregard animals.

We find a similar idea in the Ismaili propagandist Nāsir-i Khusraw (d. 1088): "The stars and the sky are, due to divine imperative, like the servants of natures [the elements], for they lavish advantages on them; they revolve around the natures like servants and slaves that surround their master. In another way, the natures are like the slaves of the sky and the stars, since they derive their power from them in order to become rich."[119] The text takes away with one hand what it has just given with the other: the superior is at the service of the inferior only from a certain point of view, quickly counterbalanced by another, less metaphorical one. The same idea is found in Hildegarde von Bingen (d. 1179) and in Ibn Arabi (d. 1240).[120]

Some authors explain the structure of the world by God's intent to install man on it and thus to render it inhabitable by him. This is especially the case in the physics of the sublunary world, it being primarily the dwelling place of man. Thus the existence of emerged land caused a problem, as soon as one conceived of the elements as forming concentric spheres. Water, lighter than earth, should submerge the earth everywhere if the earth had a regular form. It is the irregularity of the earth's surface that enables some of its parts to be dry, and thus habitable. The problem continued to torment certain medieval thinkers, such as Avicenna, and remained active until the eighteenth century.[121] The translator of Maimonides, Samuel Ibn Tibbon, used the problem as a pretext for an entire book, written between 1220 and 1230, in which digressions occupy more space than the solution that's actually proposed.[122] Some authors attributed the fact to a cause other than nature, that is, divine Providence.[123] Others, such as Miskawayh, for example, invoke the influence of celestial bodies.[124] Averroes attributes the emergence of the earth to the action of the stars, and above all of the sun. The stars, which are themselves eternal as individuals (their individuality not being distinguished, moreover, from their being as species), only maintain the perpetuity of sublunary species. They thus see to it that the animal species are preserved, whereas individuals disappear. Similarly, they assure permanence as to the fact of emerging earth: even if their distribution might change, there will always be a balance between dry and wet surfaces. Averroes does not precisely explain here the way the celestial bodies play their role. He does so elsewhere, attributing the emergence of the land to the Sun, but with the cooperation of the fixed stars. Their greater numbers in the north would explain the unequal distribution of the emerged land, more vast in the arctic hemisphere.[125]

Once the influence of celestial bodies over a phenomenon that makes human life possible had been established, only one step remained to be taken to make that life a final cause, and to put the stars in the service of man. That step was taken more than a century before Averroes by al-Biruni.[126] After summing up the argument over the respective natures of water and earth, he maintains that the emergence of the earth was due to divine will. It was because God intended to create man that he began by giving the earth a shape that was different from that which its nature would have conferred upon it. He then cites a lost passage by Ṭābit Ibn Qurra in which the author is seen as resolving in his own way the old problem of the salinity of the oceans, which never ceased to preoccupy ancient and medieval thinkers.[127] Here, too, he brings in a teleology: the salinity enabled an avoidance of decay which would have been dangerous to man. Since man needed fresh water for himself and his domestic animals, God put the sun and moon in his service, assigning them the task of putting the water in motion, by making it evaporate. The goal of the movements of the celestial bodies and their variety was to spread heat all the way to the center of the world. It therefore seemed that the ultimate goal of the celestial was the terrestrial.

In the Christian world, this relationship was asserted more or less clearly. We find the idea that the central placement of man is not completely humiliating, since being entirely below enables him to receive all the influences that come from the upper spheres. In this way, the pure passivity of the receiver is turned around to take on a more positive meaning. We find this idea in William of Conches and in Bonaventure.[128] We owe a particularly interesting text to Robert Grosseteste. He writes: "All things are for man, that is, so that human generation is carried out up until the completeness of the body of Christ which is the Church is accomplished. The movement of the skies is thus only for the generation of man. . . . And the movement by which the heavens produce generation in these inferior regions consists only in making the star or the stars situated in the sky itself [the sphere] turn around. Indeed, the revolution of the stars around the earth is by itself the efficient cause of generation. Now, the sky, apart from the star, is everywhere similar to itself, and it could not influence *(immutare)* inferior things in a certain situation rather than in another one if there were not a star in it. This is why every movement of the sky through which no star would move would contribute nothing to generation, and by this token its movement would be useless."[129] Cosmology is very explicitly placed in the service of the history of salvation: the world only endures to ensure that the greatest number of elect be reached. But Grosseteste deduces from that old patristic idea what is necessary to gradually clarify a very precise astronomical problem. The static structure of the world must be able to encourage generation, which is not cyclical, but directed toward an end.

Among Jewish authors, Gershonides (d. 1344) devotes an entire chapter to the influence of the spheres on the inferior world. He uses an argument that is very close to that of Grosseteste. The chapter is constructed as a *disputatio* following the Scholastic method. The objection—*videtur quod non*—to circumvent is the impossibility for the superior in the universe to be in the service of the inferior. Aristotle's authority—*sed contra*—sets forth that the stars are the cause of things below. Gershonides presents a subtle argument while following a guiding question: Why do the celestial spheres contain stars? The fifth substance is simple. Here below, the diversity of the organs in a living being is explained by the complexity of the elements that make it up, as well as by the necessity with which it lives to conclude its existence in perfection. But the celestial body, simple and perfect, does not need to be organized. Then why is it spread out in spheres? Why do they contain stars? Why is there the diversity of colors in the light they emit? The response: "In so far as the spheres apprehend something of the law, order and rightness of the sub-lunar world and as a result of this very apprehension they desire to do something to perfect this order, it is necessary that they have an organ [or instrument], to accomplish this activity, and this organ is the planet or star. This suggestion, however, implies that the stars or planets are not in the sphere for their own sake but [are there in order] to bring about what the apprehension of the spheres necessitates with respect to the perfection of sub-lunar phenomena."[130] The objection is resolved by a distinction: the clarity of the stars is owed to the things on earth, but their substance is owed to itself. The idea that the influences to be exercised over man are the final cause of the universe continued for quite some time.[131]

. . .

According to this line of thought, man and the world are connected by a reciprocal involvement. The being-in-the-world possesses a relevance before a level of existential experience; it is significant in cosmography before it is so in a cosmology. What is more, cosmology is guided, prefigured by cosmography.

To say what man is is to rank him in an order that is spatial, dynamic and axiological. As for simple localization, it is not without meaning for man, and for his very humanity, that he be located on the earth and under the sky: his very place is enough to assign him a specific value, a value that is rather weak, moreover, compared to the rest of the world, and which becomes almost nothing when it is compared to that of celestial phenomena. And, when other factors come to increase that value, as is the case for medieval man, they no longer relate to cosmography. As for the dynamic relationship between man and that which surrounds him, man is not simply in the world; the world is also in man. It gives rhythm to his history, even prevents that history from gaining independence by forcing the development of human achievements to periodically return to zero. It defines the aspirations of man. It directs his physical structure.

In all of this there is scarcely anything that modern man might condescendingly call a naive anthropomorphism. Man is just as much cosmomorphous, so to speak, as the cosmos is anthropomorphous, The cosmos exists in function of man, granted. But it would be too much to say that it is *for* him. First, because man is not alone, but is preceded by more noble beings, stars or angels. Then, more dramatically, because man is so intensely cosmic that one might wonder whether the distinction that first places man opposite the world only to then relate them to each other can be maintained to the end; it is rather the cosmos that affirms itself in man.

Thus we have seen that for thinkers of late Antiquity and the Middle Ages, man's being was cosmic from the outset; we will now see that what man ought to be, man's task, was decidedly just as much so.

Chapter 9

An Ethical Cosmos

This presentation of the way the world was imagined in Late Antiquity and the Middle Ages is not merely a description of things as they were. It also has an inseparable ethical significance. I am therefore well aware of the arbitrary nature of the separation I have made here between the physical and the ethical aspects of things.

During the period in question, some thinkers were aware of the relevance of the image of the physical world to matters of practical philosophy. This elevation to the reflective realm is present from the beginning in the works of Plato. In the *Sophist,* he shows that the way one conceives of the world depends on the type of person one is.[1] In the *Laws,* book 10 develops Plato's theology in terms of moral and political considerations. This awareness continued for a long time. Thus in Abd al-Latif al-Baghdadi (d. 1231): "The view of Plato and Zeno is the opposite of the previous view [Democritus]. For they assume that nothing in this world is outside Providence and that everything is filled with God and that He penetrates all things. This is excellent and very true. It is the view to be followed by the great mass and one which one must believe. *It leads to orderly political life and social harmony.* The prophets have proposed it and the divine books expressed it. In my opinion one must believe in it."[2]

A HAPPY WORLD

Ethical determinations can be applied to the physical. The world is content with its fate; one can say that nothing affects the good condition of the world, even if not everything is perfect in the sublunary. Thus, it is reasonable to say that the world—the entire world—experiences happiness *(eudaimonia)*.[3]

But this world is not specifically the one in which we live, surrounded by plants and animals, the world where the living are born and die, the world where, far from willingly accommodating one another, animals and cities seek to overcome each other or, at least, are in competition to appropriate important resources. For the Ancients, that was only one aspect of the whole. What occurs around us is less the rule than the exception. Where the world truly is what it is, this battle does not occur. The place where the world appears in its true light is the celestial realm. The most perfect harmony reigns there. It does so is a figurative sense, but the same is true in a literal sense as well. The Pythagorean idea of the "harmony of the spheres," even if it was not shared by Aristotle and his philosopher disciples, is an integral part of a poetic vision of the world, and it was perhaps accompanied by musical illustrations.[4] Nietzsche rightly sees an image of the "moral significance of existence."[5]

Regardless of the details, one fact is obvious: order is the characteristic of the supralunary incomparably more than of the sublunary. Aristotle says this clearly: "There is much clearer evidence of definite ordering in the heavenly bodies than there is in us; for what is mortal bears the marks of change and chance."[6] A later philosopher expresses the separation of the two realms with an image: "The course of the moon is the isthmus *(isthmos)* of immortality and generation. All that is above it and upon it, the race of the gods occupies, that which is below the moon [is occupied by the race] of discord *(neikos)* and nature."[7]

Augustine uses this image as well. He emphasizes the difference between the human bodies that hide the movements of the soul, thus enabling lies, and the celestial bodies. Human bodies are carnal. In fact: "[After they sinned] God changed [Adam and Eve's] bodies into this mortal flesh in which deceitful hearts are hidden. For we should not believe that thoughts could be hidden in those heavenly bodies, as they lie hidden in these bodies. Rather as some states of soul are apparent on the countenance, and especially in the eyes, so I think that in the clarity and simplicity of those heavenly bodies absolutely no states of the soul are hidden."[8] The underlying image is interesting: the sky is that which, in nature, cannot lie. It is the unveiled face of nature.

Thus, cosmography has direct axiological relevance: good and evil are divided up just like the "above" and the "below," like the earth and the sky. We find an extremely clear formulation of this point of view, one leading toward Gnosticism, in the *Corpus Hermeticum:* "There is nothing good on the earth; there is nothing evil in the sky."[9] To assume that something evil can be located in the sky appears as more than a mistake; it is blasphemous.[10] Alexander of Lycopolis in his polemics against the Manichaeans, who asserted that the celestial bodies contained evil even if that evil were moderate, points out that: "In their view evil is conceived as disorder and random motion. But the heavenly things are always the same and in the same condition, and one cannot find fault with any of the planets for wanting to remain longer than its allotted time in some sign of the zodiac, nor with any of the fixed stars for not staying in the self-same position and for moving one degree to the right in the course of a century, and for not continuing its circling around with the revolution of the universe."[11]

EVIL AS THE EXCEPTION

In the intellectual universe of Late Antiquity and the Middle Ages, or, in any case, in its dominant current, one can find traces of a certain fundamental attitude voiced from all directions. It constitutes a recurrent theme in the ethical attitude of this period: the evil that reigns here on earth is basically only an exception. The rule that it confirms is manifest in the regularity and the majestic order of celestial movements. It is owing to that order that the world deserves its Greek name of *kosmos,* which rightly means "order," good arrangement, arranged and harmoniously articulated totality, etc. Here below it is possible that everything is falling apart; above, "all is order there, and beauty."

Now, the place where everything functions well is incomparably larger than the tiny spot where we pine away, at the center of the world, that is, for the Ancients, at the lowest place, below everything else.[12] Evil can very easily be unleashed where we exist, to the point of giving the impression that the gods are neglecting men.[13] But it remains an almost invisible exception, if one compares it to the overwhelming majority of Good. So says Aristotle already when he expresses the idea in the language of the law: "For only that region of the sensible world which immediately surrounds us is always in process of destruction and generation; but this is—so to speak—not even a fraction of the whole, so that it would have been juster to acquit this part of the world because of the other part, than to condemn the other because of this."[14]

Immediately following Aristotle, Theophrastus reiterates the same idea: "But to say that *in general* the good is something rare and found only in a few things, while the evil is a great multitude, and does not consist solely in indefiniteness and exist by way of matter, as is the case with the things of nature, is the act of a most ignorant person. For quite random is the talk of those who speak of the whole of reality as Speusippus does when he makes the valuable element *(timion)* to be something scanty, namely, what is found in the region of the centre of the universe, the rest forming the extremes and being to each side of the centre. Rather, reality in fact is and always has been good *(kalōs)*."[15] This cosmological passage concludes with a declaration of ontological import, that is, the explicit identification of that which would later be called two transcendentals, the being and the good.

The idea is also found in the writings of Alexander of Aphrodisias. In his treatise on the soul, he attempts an explanation of the presence of evil in the world. He presents his solution in a central formula that uncannily recalls a fundamental image from the ontology of Jean-Paul Sartre: nothingness is spread out *(paresparmenon)* in the being. This explains the relaxed softness *(atonia)* and weakness *(astheneia)* that are the reality of all that is not eternal. Except that, according to Alexander, this does not occur everywhere, but, on the contrary, only in exceptional circumstances: "The non-being is not mixed into most beings, and, wherever it is, it isn't very important, either. It is a small part of things that are themselves a small part of the whole. Among the beings, it is there where there is the non-eternal. That is what surrounds the earth, and that place is very small *(elakhistos)* compared to the entire world. Indeed, if the earth, according to the astronomers, is like a point compared to all of the sky, and if the non-being is found around it and in it, it is indeed something very small."[16]

The idea is found again in the doxography on Aristotle, as for example in the one most probably used by the Church Father Hippolytus to write the chapter in which he associates Aristotle, as the source, with the heresy of the Gnostic Basilides: "He [Aristotle] says that evil things are under the auspices of the moon, and above the moon there are none."[17]

Themistius is situated at a turning point. In religion, he remains a pagan in the service of emperors who were already Christian; in philosophy, his work, which paraphrases Aristotle, is located midway between pure peripateticism and Neoplatonism. In one of his ceremonial speeches he writes: "Order *(taxis)* is a sign not of weakness, but of a nature exempt from change and disturbance. And that in the universe which is closest to it enjoys the highest point of order. As for disturbance *(tarakhē)*, tumult, and agitation, they are found in a small part of the being, and relate to things that, by a defective character *(elleipsis)* corresponding to their weakness, are deprived of the name of being."[18]

The idea, with nuances that we will see below, passed into the revealed religions. Thus Augustine suggests that sin only occurs under the sky: "Men sin under the sky, all the evil they do, men do under the sky."[19]

The Brethren of Purity (tenth century, perhaps shortly after 960) criticize a form of dualism that they attribute to "certain Greek wise men" (no doubt the Stoics) for whom the two principles are one, active, and the other, passive: "The order of the world is clear for them, and they know the harmony of the creation of the skies, in spite of their vastness, the grandeur of their parts and the great number of the creatures that are found there; they know that there is nothing above that is corruption and evil, and that everything there is in the most beautiful order, the best hierarchical ordering and arrangement; they know that *evil is found only in the world of generation and corruption which is below the sphere of the moon,* and even, evil, in the world of generation and corruption, is found only in the plants and animals, unlike the other [things] that exist, and not even at every moment, but at one moment and not another; and through causes that do not derive from an agent following a primary intention, but following a defect in the matter and an inability in it to receive good at every moment and in every situation."[20]

The idea is also in Avicenna, who alludes to it in his doctrine on evil.[21] It is the thinking of a good Aristotelian, showing some Neoplatonism, since he attributes evil to matter, which is incapable of receiving perfect order.[22] This ontological inferiority of evil transfers into the register of quantity: "Evil things are very rare compared to existence since existence is entirely or mostly Good. . . . Harmful effects and evil are only exceptions."[23] And this rarity of evil itself is translated in cosmological terms: "The totality of the cause of evil is found only in that which is below the sphere of the moon, and all that is below the sphere of the moon is insignificant compared with the rest of being."[24]

Finally, the idea is powerfully proclaimed by Maimonides in his polemics against the doctor and free-thinker Râzî: "If man considered and represented to himself that which exists and knew the smallness of his part in it, the truth would become clear and manifest to him. For this extensive raving entertained by men with regard to the multitude of evils in the world is not said by them to hold good with regard to the angels, or with regard to the spheres and the stars, or with regard to the elements and the minerals and the plants composed of them, or with regard to the various species of animals, but their whole thought only goes out to some individuals belonging to the human species. . . . The true way of considering *(i'tibār)* this is that all the existent individuals of the human species and, all the more, those of the other species of animals are things of no value *(qadar)* at all in comparison with the whole that exists and endures. . . . [Man] should not make the mistake of thinking that what exists is in existence only for the sake of him as an individual. According to us, on the other hand, . . . the species of man is the least in comparison to the superior existents—I refer to the spheres and the stars."[25] Râzî, the doctor, saw reality as a huge hospital in which, by definition, the patients were in the majority: in the world, too, evil dominated good. Maimonides reestablished the correct proportions by placing man within the whole of things. At worst, evil affects only a tiny part of the whole. Good triumphs in the superior world, which constitutes the rule; from the point of view of that world, man is only a negligible exception.

Finally, the argument passed on to medieval and modern Christian thinkers. St. Thomas Aquinas cites our passage from Avicenna. And in the seventeenth century Leibniz quotes approvingly the text by Maimonides that I have just reproduced above.[26]

THE HERE BELOW

Once it was established that good was safely tucked away above the sphere of the moon, nothing prevented ancient and medieval man from recognizing that evil affected the restricted realm in which he was confined with full force and that it even formed an essential motivation in it. Thus the balance among animal species rested on the way animals conducted themselves toward each other, engaging in relationships of pure strength. Herodotus, for example, knew that the overall survival of the animals was assured by the ratio between their greater or lesser fertility and their predatory abilities. The foresight *(pronoiē)* of the divine is thus seen to be quite capable *(sophē):* the rabbit, fearful and without defenses, is fertile; the lioness, on the other hand, gives birth only once, since the cub is only able to be born, it was believed, by tearing the womb with its claws.[27] Lucretius knew that each living being had some weapon or defense, without which it could not survive.[28]

The Ancients did not see man as an exception and had no illusions about his natural goodness: Thucydides knew that man wanted all the power he could obtain, and the dialogue he recounts between the Athenians and the Melians provides us a vision alongside which Machiavelli appears to be almost naive.[29] Ancient and medieval thinkers were not unaware that large fish ate smaller fish.[30] This example was even proverbial for them: it is seen in the formula through which Indian thought expresses what we would call the "law of the jungle": the "logic of the fish" *(mātsyanyāya).*[31] But observation of animal behavior acted as a negative example for human ethics.

Thus for Hesiod the example of the fishes is the model of what man should *not* do.[32] He is followed by Theophilus of Antioch and Basil of Caesarea.[33] Nemesius of Emesa, in a passage for which the editors do not mention sources, qualifies by recalling that the food chain has an end: certain fish, the smallest ones, which he calls *fukia,* eat what might be called the grass of the sea.[34] The Talmudic rabbis evoke the risk of falling back onto the law of the jungle to justify the necessity of government. Without law, "men would eat each other alive."[35] In doing this they would not be content with simply transgressing against the commandment that forbids murder, but would even disregard the most basic of the Noachic laws forbidding "tearing someone's limb off,"[36] a command that distinguishes man from the animal which throws itself on its prey to devour it raw.

It seems, however, that authors were sometimes tempted to propose the balance of nature as a model for human behavior. We have at least one example of this, in one of the principal treatises on political philosophy by al-Farabi (d. 950).[37] It deals with opinions held by the inhabitants of ignorant or perplexed cities, rivals of the virtuous city he describes. Farabi speaks of it as relating to ancient opinions—no doubt those of the Greeks— but he names no authors. The opinions are prefaced by a factual statement: things that exist are in opposition, and each one tries to annihilate the other. Each being possesses means to preserve itself, to repel that which is the opposite of it, to annihilate it and to assimilate it, and finally, to overcome other things to make them serve its own purposes. Each being is equipped with weapons that enable it to conquer its enemies. One is therefore tempted to imagine that the individual's search for well-being was nature's intention; the existence in the individual of an instinct for survival, of defensive and nutritive organs, finally, of technical abilities enabling him to transform his environment, seems to indicate this. But there is more: Farabi states that some animals, which he does not, however, name, sometimes attack other animals and kill them, without deriving any obvious advantage from that. Everything occurs, thus, not only as if every living being saw itself as the supreme goal of nature, but even as if it believed that only its own existence were legitimate, and that the raw existence of anything else was harmful to it.

In addition, every being attempts to dominate others. This is a spontaneous instinct independent of will. This situation of rivalry exists between one animal species and another, but also, within most species, between one individual and another: mutual attacks and aggression do not cease, each being seeking either to destroy the other if it is harmful, or to use it for its own ends if it can be of use. Observation backs this up: everything happens without order, hierarchies are shaken, what happens to people does not depend on their merits. We can leave the responsibility for this gloomy diagnosis to Farabi's adversaries. We can argue against some details of it, such as the existence in the animal of a purposeless aggressiveness, or of a struggle to the death between individuals of the same species of animal. The main point is the dual conclusion that, according to Farabi, his adversaries draw from it. It is first of all a generalization attributing that state of reality to nature: "Some say, following that, that this situation is natural for beings and is their innate character." It is then, and above all, "that [things] that natural bodies do out of their nature are those that it is appropriate *(yanbaġī)* for animals capable of choice to do through their choices and their [actions of] will, and for those that are capable of reflecting to do through their reflection."

This Hobbesian description of a war of all against all may have ancient sources. Plato comes to mind immediately, as do the theories defended by the characters of Thrasymachus and, above all, of Callicles, the latter mentioning, fleetingly, moreover, the example of the animals.[38] On the other hand, I know of no precedent for the very movement of Farabi's reasoning. And what is above all unique and perhaps new is the succinct way in which the equation between "is" and "should" is proposed: what irrational animals do without wishing to is what reasonable animals should do, with full awareness and deliberate intent. Farabi does not approve of this equation; or, in any case, he does not approve of the terms of the comparison. For him, as we shall see, there is indeed an exemplary reality whose effective behavior should serve as a rule for us. But the good model to follow is not the animal, nor any other sublunary thing; it is the order of the sky.[39]

AN APPEAL

One essential fact remains: one can *appeal against* evil to a higher jurisdiction. In this cosmology, human activity occurs only in a lost corner of the world. It is only in this tiny hole in the cosmic order that one can and must distinguish between good and evil and, let us hope, choose the good. Everywhere else the choice in favor of the good has been made since the very beginning. And that "being" is identified with the good. Well before Scholasticism raised the formula to the rank of axiom, the Being and the Good were interchangeable *(ens et bonum convertuntur)*.[40]

It is possible that acknowledging this fact might help us to understand why the Ancients hardly ever formulated a distinction between "is" and "ought." Granted, all morality practices this implicitly, and the Stoics have a concept of the *deon* that corresponds more or less to the "ought." But its formulation as a contrast between two principles underwent a long period of incubation from which it emerged only in the modern era.[41] To my knowledge it budded for the first time implicitly in Machiavelli, in the famous text in which he speaks of the great distancing *(discosto)* between "what is done" and "what should be done."[42] In Hume it is proposed as a principle.[43] But according to the ancient and medieval vision of the world, every "ought" *(Sollen)* is surrounded by a gigantic "is" *(Sein)* which renders it relative, indeed negligible.

Furthermore, that which does not yet coincide perfectly with the good is en route toward it. From this point of view, what would correspond to our "ought" is only temporary and tends toward its reabsorption into the "is." The "ought" is the expectantly suffering "is" which would indeed suffer from not yet truly being itself if its potential being were not a way of forcing itself to reach its potential. The world is animated on every level by a movement of ascent: at the bottom, as already seen in Aristotle, matter desires a form.[44] Medieval thinkers continued what was scarcely more than an image: every form tends toward a more perfect form.[45] Meister Eckhart puts it very well: "The nature of every seed aims to become wheat, the nature of all metal aims to become gold, every birth *(geberunge)* aims to become a man."[46] Man's imitation of higher realities is thus placed into a more extensive movement of which it is in the end only one particular case. It is how an intelligent and free being accomplishes what all located below him on the scale of being does without knowing or choosing it.

Thus, up until a specific period in the history of the human mind, nature was one of the sources of morality. By this I do not mean the attempts to base morality on "human nature." For in that case "nature" above all means "essence," as it is grasped and elucidated by an ontology of the human, in other words, by a philosophical anthropology. The nature of man is then that which man is deep down, that which constitutes his most complete form. And it is a matter of concretely realizing the perfection of man's humanity through a *praxis* that makes the unfolding of that essence possible—indeed, that demands it.[47]

Quite the opposite is true in the world view I am attempting to reconstruct here. The nature that determines ethics is indeed that which is usually understood by "nature," that is, all the things that man neither makes (through his *poiēsis*), nor does (through his *praxis*), but which are there in themselves. This nature is subsequently the object of a purely passive relationship, one that occurs when an object is given for observation. But for us, today, nature understood in this way has no relationship to ethics. Or if it has one, it is at best in the capacity of one realm of application among others. It even comes after the primary realm of moral actions, which is, of course, interhuman relationships. For our ancestors, however, man could—in fact should—borrow the criterion of his action from nature. Nature was then a source of morality.

As a consequence one could turn physics into a propaedeutic to ethics. The Stoics, the first to clearly formulate the division of philosophy into various realms, were also the first to connect them to each other. In this case, as regards the objective order (as distinguished from the order of learning), ethics is always to physics what the fruit is to the tree.[48] Chrysippus even stresses that "there is no other means, or more appropriate means, to reach a definition of good and bad things, of virtue and happiness, than by starting from common nature and from the government *(dioikēsis)* of the world."[49]

It is indeed nature, and not physical science alone, that determines man's humanity; nature as an object of study, not the study of nature as the activity of a subject. The ethical value of physics does not come from the human process of learning, but from nature itself. It is not a matter of recalling what is obvious: a study of nature can lead us to the practice of certain virtues, because it awakens them or because it implies them. Thus the effort to bring to light the mysteries of nature can train us to be courageous; the reflection on the marvelous order of things can lead us to admiration and gratitude toward the Creator—whether that creator be a personal god or the unconscious soul of the world; to consider the small amount of space that we occupy in the world can teach us humility, etc. All these elements have been illustrated throughout the history of thought by the most diverse authors: by Pascal, but also by Spinoza, Goethe, and others. And physicists today often repeat this hymn to the educative value of physics.

We find these ideas in ancient texts. But we also find passages in which it is clearly a question of nature as an object of study, not of its study as an activity. Thus, for Cicero: "The study of the heavenly phenomena bestows a power of self-control that arises from the perception of the consummate restraint and order that obtain even among the gods; also loftiness of mind is inspired by contemplating the creations and actions of the gods, and justice by realizing the will, design and purpose of the Supreme Lord and Ruler to whose nature we are told by philosophers that the True Reason and Supreme Law are conformed."[50]

ETHICS IN THE COSMOLOGICAL

A text by Simplicius seems especially relevant here. It appears in the prologue to his famous commentary on Aristotle's *Physics.* It was written at the beginning of the sixth century, but it is highly likely that it borrows from a much earlier commentary, that of Alexander of Aphrodisias (second–third century). Simplicius cites him very often elsewhere and probably takes material from his commentary, without naming him. As for the passage we are going to look at, it has a parallel in the "great commentary" *(tafsīr)* of Averroes on the same work, a parallel that is presented as a quotation by Alexander. What I will say about Simplicius's text will therefore apply also, at least in part, to Alexander.

Following a procedure that was commonly practiced by ancient commentators, Simplicius precedes his explanation of the words of Aristotle with an introduction in which he responds to several previous, canonical questions: What is the work's intent? What is the name of its author? Where should the work be placed in the body of the writings of the author? etc. Now, one of these questions concerns the usefulness of the work and, thus, that of the knowledge it claims to impart. It is within this framework that Simplicius wonders about the extent to which a study of nature is useful. To do this he distinguishes five successive points, which he places in order of increasing importance.[51] Physics *(phusiologia)* is useful: in the affairs of daily life, because it provides the principles of technologies such as medicine and mechanics (understood above all as the art of manufacturing machines of war); because it contributes to leading the superior part of the soul, which is the intellect, toward its perfection—for which a study of theology is particularly valuable; it is an auxiliary for moral virtues; a ladder that leads toward knowledge of God and ideas; and finally, it incites us to piety and to acts of thanksgiving toward God. The advantages of the study of nature are thus classed in ascending order. The more important they are, the later they are mentioned. From this perspective it is interesting that physics' contribution to technical matters is placed in first place and is dealt with only very concisely. What we other moderns would insist on the most, that is, the conquests of medicine and mechanics, is of course mentioned clearly. But the relevant passage is extremely brief. In it there is only a taste of what is essential, which is yet to come. Simplicius stresses explicitly that the fourth advantage, ascension to God, is the most decisive, which reduces the fifth (religious feeling) to the status of an appendix. On the other hand, a qualification is necessary if one pays attention to the more or less important place reserved for the various arguments. The passage devoted to the third of these includes no fewer than twenty-five lines, that is, more than the other four put together, which add up to only seventeen lines (respectively, four, three, seven, and five). In addition, this part is divided carefully: one paragraph for each cardinal virtue. This is why I will take a closer look at it.

Consideration of nature teaches temperance, for two reasons: it exposes the nature of pleasure and shows that it is only a consequence, a sort of epiphenomenon *(parakolouthēma),* and never an end in itself; what is violent about it comes from what is against nature. One would therefore not be tempted to place pleasure at the highest level of one's choices *(proēgoumenon);* next, to be concerned with physics *(phusikē theōria)* deflects from the enjoyments of the body and consequently from passion for external things. This second argument also holds for justice, moderation, and generosity in negotiations and contracts. In addition, physics teaches courage, by showing how tiny our body appears compared to the whole of things that exist, how short our lives are, and how necessary is the dissolution of our being. Knowledge of the superiority of the soul over the body helps to approach death with serenity: "Who would be more courageous than the one who has recognized, thanks to physics *(phusiologia),* that the living being that we are is not a perceptible part of the universe, any more than the measure of our life in the totality of time, that it is necessary that all that is born be followed by corruption *(phthora),* which is decomposition into simple [components], restoration of the parts into the totalities to which they belong *(oikeiai holotētes),* rejuvenation of [phenomena] that had grown old, and return in strength of tired *(kekmēkos)* [phenomena]? To be corrupted now or after a few years would be negligible for him who recognizes the infinitude of time. And if, understanding *(ennoein)* the distinctive superiority *(khōristē huperokhē)* of the soul, he compares it to the troubles *(askholia)* that come to him from the body, then he will easily accept death. And he who has such as attitude toward death, what else among what passes as terrible could frighten him?" Physics also teaches wisdom *(phronēsis),* because the conscious part of the soul, out of which comes knowledge of nature, is related to it. We can note a shift here: in good Aristotelianism, wisdom *(phronēsis)* is a dianoetic virtue, not an ethical one. It is wisdom that provides ethical virtues with the *logos* that enables them to attain a happy medium. Simplicius, using the more or less clear image of kinship or affinity *(suggenes),* conceals the difference between *sophia* and *phronēsis,* which Aristotle, for whom that difference holds a central place, asserted strongly. Physics "renders [those who study it] magnanimous and proud *(megalophrōn),* by convincing them not to consider any human [concerns] great. It sees to it that they are content with little and, as a consequence, they are ready to put in common what they have and need nothing from others, [and thus] it renders them generous *(eleutherios)*." The argument is interesting, because one might expect that it would invite us less toward magnanimity and more to humility. It seems that the wise man no longer considers himself as belonging to humanity. He feels from the start above everything that is human.

The virtue of justice is placed in fifth place. Simplicius risks a bold formula with regard to that virtue, which seems to me to be of the greatest importance here. The study of nature contributes "to justice, insofar as it shows that the elements and the parts of the Whole *(to pan)* make way for each other, are content with *(agapān)* their place *(taxis)*, respect geometrical equality and, by that fact, stand apart from greed *(pleonexia)*."[52] Contemplation of nature inspires justice because nature conducts itself with justice. The text does not point out completely clearly the realm in which this justice is most specifically manifest. It might in fact be a matter of the four elements that change within each other, in the spirit of the fragment of Anaximander;[53] or of the concentric arrangement of the parts of the *kosmos,* none of which encroaches upon its neighbor; or of the order of astronomical phenomena, etc. Similarly, Farabi sees a perfect cycle among the elements: since matter cannot achieve the same forms at the same time, each renders its place to the other, taking turns.[54] However this justice may be concretely achieved, the "geometric equality," a phrase borrowed from a well-known passage by Plato, cited above,[55] is *in things themselves.* Nature itself practices virtues.

Averroes presents the same list of virtues, successively naming courage, temperance, justice, generosity, and magnanimity.[56] He adds, as regards what concerns us here, an essential element that he formulates quite clearly and again might be derived from the lost commentary of Alexander of Aphrodisias: *the moral model is found in things themselves.* Concerning the virtue of justice, he thus writes that wise men seek it: "For they know that the nature of justice resides in the substance of things (Latin: *naturam justitiae existentem in substantia rerum;* Hebrew: *tebha' ḥay-yōšer ḥan-nimṣa' be-'eṣem ḥan-nimṣā'ōt*), this is why they wish to imitate that nature and acquire that form."[57]

The idea is not rare. Well before Averroes, and on Christian land, Bernard of Chartres (d. 1126) said that the subject of Plato's *Timaeus* was natural justice *(naturalis justitia):* "Since Plato wanted to deal in depth with natural justice, he began with the generation of the perceptible world. In its creation and the just ordering of its parts, in the distinction between celestial and non-celestial things, he taught the strength of natural justice which the Creator used toward the created, he who, through pure charity, granted each thing that which naturally related to it."[58] Bernard adopts the classical definition of distributive justice. But whereas it normally occurs between creatures, he places it in the relationships between the Creator and his creatures. Justice is indeed present in things themselves, but it is the result of the agreement of each with its own nature, as it is instilled by God. The Platonists linked to the Chartres school adopted this idea. But they were not the exception: all medieval scholars—both the common man who received the idea through tradition and philosophers—were in agreement that "by [means of] right *(yōšer)* the Heavens and the Earth endure."[59] And the idea did not disappear in the modern era, since it is explicitly encountered in Schiller and Herder.[60]

Within this context can be placed an entire complex of ideas that constitute a fundamental feature of the medieval vision of the world, that is, what is called symbolism. Much has already been written on the subject, and in various styles, both by drawing up lists of correspondences and by studying the mindset that underlies it.[61] The basic idea is that the world is linked to man through the presence in both of the same system of signification. The world is full of meaning, and of a meaning that man is capable of deciphering and applying to himself. Wisdom would be a wisdom of the world in that it would consist of correctly interpreting the messages contained in things. For Christians, such messages bear above all on God, who left his mark on the created and filters through creation. But through the world, God also presents us with models of how we should behave. We have just recalled that moral virtues are present in things. One can thus see them in those things, with more or less clarity depending on their level of being. Thus the celestial world clearly shows us the four cardinal virtues.[62]

. . .

According to this view there are not, on the one hand, a physical world devoid of "values" and, on the other, "values" without roots in perceptible reality. The very trite notion of "values" is perhaps itself the result of a separation that ancient and medieval cosmology renders impossible. To speak of "values" indeed causes good and evil to depend on subjectivity: what "matters," what is "valuable," is what one esteems, what "has a price," is what one prizes, what one appreciates. The principle that sets forth values must therefore be worth more than the values it sets down, which are by that fact always revocable: "Among all the things we value, it is the evaluation *(Schätzen)* itself that is the valuable *(Schatz)* and the jewel."[63] "Values" are therefore stricken with an intrinsic weakness, since posing them as such is to recognize at the same time that they cannot subsist by themselves. There is nothing surprising, therefore, in our speaking so much of "defending values": they are too weak to do so themselves, much less to defend us, we who set them forth.

This difficulty could not present itself in ancient and medieval thinking. For that thinking, the being is good at the outset and therefore has no need to receive that quality elsewhere than from itself. The interconvertibility of the Being and the Good not only governs metaphysics, in the doctrine of transcendentals; it has a cosmological version. It allows itself to be seen in the very structure of the world. This situation has ethical consequences: it asks for nothing less than a specific way to define human moral action. Good is not something that must be injected from outside into a neutral receptacle; it is already there, indeed, it imposes itself with brio into reality. This does not lead to any form of quietism. Ethics remain a task. But "to do" good consists less of *producing* than of *reproducing,* than of transporting from one domain to another that which is already there.

Chapter 10

A Cosmological Ethics

Numquid nosti ordinem caeli
Et pones rationem eius in terra?
Job 38:33 Vulg.

The world, and above all that which is most cosmic in the world—the sky—provided ancient and medieval man with brilliant evidence that good is not only a possibility, but a triumphant reality. Cosmology has an ethical dimension. In turn, the task of transporting such good into the here below where we live enriches ethics with a cosmological dimension. It is through the mediation of the world that man becomes what he must be, and consequently, what he is. Wisdom thus defined is indeed a "wisdom of the world."

The mediation exercised by the world and the wisdom that it enables are however theoretical before they are practical, or first theoretical in order to become practical—assuming that this separation of the theoretical and the practical allows us to adequately grasp what is at issue here.

THE WORLD AS OBJECT OF CONTEMPLATION

Contemplation is the form taken, in certain cases, by the universal aspiration to attain the good located above us. Contemplation is therefore a reality more immense than man, and in a sense all things, even the inanimate, wish to contemplate.[1] Nevertheless, man is the only creature in whom contemplation becomes a precursor to ethical action. In the *Protrepticus* Aristotle resolved the already classic dispute regarding the three types of life in favor of the contemplative life. He also gave classic form to the idea of contemplation *(theōria),* but not without leaving his doctrine on this issue strangely incomplete. Indeed he does not immediately answer the question of whether the object of contemplation is the world *(kosmos)* or something else.[2] We learn at the end of his principal treatise on ethics that contemplation constitutes the most elevated and most worthy mode of life. But he never really tells us what we are to contemplate, what is the *object* of contemplation. Other passages in his work indicate a nuanced response. The highest being, the god, contemplates nothing but himself. But he cannot serve as an example in this regard. Examining humble beings such as the animals compensates through the ease of the research for the dignity they lack as compared to the celestial bodies, so that the charm of biology is equal to that of astronomy.[3] One passage suggests that philosophy is service to and contemplation of the god. But is it the god of the *Metaphysics?* Mightn't Aristotle rather be thinking of the inner god, human intellect?[4]

Later thinkers, in particular those of the Stoic tradition, have a ready response: the supreme object of contemplation is the world as indistinguishable from God. The dignity of contemplation and the dignity of the world are mutually reinforced: it is because contemplation is the loftiest activity that it has bearing on the world; reciprocally, it is the supreme dignity of the world that endows contemplation with all its worth.[5] The goal of human existence is to be a *kosmotheōros* (the word is not ancient, and was no doubt coined by Huygens).[6] This response was anticipated, moreover, even before Aristotle by thinkers like Anaxagoras, to whom are ascribed suggestions that the goal of human life is the contemplation of the sky.[7] The model he presents is cited throughout the Middle Ages: it is found in Chalcidius,[8] from whom it passed on to the thinkers of the Chartres school and elsewhere. Thus, Bernard of Tours attributes it to Empedocles and adds a striking formula: "Take away the firmament, I will be nothing *(celum subtrahe, nullus ero)."[9] The idea is found, moreover, not only among the Christians, but is also present in Jewish tradition beginning with the Talmud.[10]

To believe that the world is an object of contemplation is all the easier in that the world is endowed with divine traits. Aristotle already considered the celestial bodies to be divine.[11] The Stoics rendered the entire world divine, by identifying it with Jupiter. Pliny the Elder writes: "[The world] is sacred, eternal, huge, all of it, or rather it is itself everything, outside, inside, containing all things in it, it is at the same time the work of the nature of things and the very nature of things."[12] There is the pseudo-Aristotelian, somewhat Stoic, treatise, *De mundo* [On the world], which, perhaps for the first time, assigns contemplation its own object: knowledge of the world and knowledge of what is most excellent in it—that is the supreme business of philosophy.[13]

The comic author Menander (342–293) corrects a traditional pessimistic declaration. According to that declaration the greatest good, after that of never having been born, is to die as quickly as possible: "The man who I declare has had the best fortune is he who has quickly gone back to where he came from, but not without having contemplated without difficulty *(alupōs)* those venerable beings: the sun, common [to all], the stars, water, clouds, fire. These beings, even if he lives for a hundred years, are always visible; and if he lives only for a few years, he will never see anything more venerable."[14] Contemplation of the world is the greatest thing life can offer. It justifies life, but also neutralizes any consideration of duration. However short life may be, it will at least allow one to grasp the immutable order of the sky, the eternity of which is seen as easily in the short as in the long term.

In Cicero's *Lucullus,* the eponymous character gives an oration inspired by Antiochus of Ascalon against the skepticism of the New Academy. Cicero replies. He stresses that the Stoics themselves are in disagreement on certain points in physics, in particular on the relative importance of the sun and the ether. He adds: "I do not think, however, that one must discard these questions . . . that come from physicists. Indeed, the consideration and contemplation of nature are like a sort of fodder for minds and intelligences; we stand up, we seem to become taller, we look from above upon human things and, by dint of reflecting on superior and celestial [things], we scorn those things that are of us, as being narrow and tiny. The very fact of hunting down things that are both the greatest and the best hidden already includes charm, and if, moreover, something appears that has the appearance of truth, the mind is filled with a typically human pleasure *(humanissima voluptas)*."[15]

The dignity of contemplation is a principle admitted by all philosophers, transcending different schools of thought. It persists even if the expected degree of certainty varies, from Stoic confidence to skeptical reservations that are content with likelihood. The approach of the investigation takes precedence over the results obtained, as if Cicero were anticipating specifically modern attitudes here.[16] Contemplation is not distinguished from consideration, if one can apply the distinction, which was transmitted through later sources, between the possession of truth and the seeking of it.[17] Both nourish the soul, not only, as was the case with Plato, their object: divine truth.[18]

With more restraint, Alexander of Aphrodisias confirms the choice in favor of the world as object of philosophical contemplation.[19] He distinguishes two types of knowledge worthy of interest *(spoudēē):* one which is so only indirectly, because it relates to other knowledge that is worthy of being chosen for itself; and the other which is so directly because it includes in itself that which is worthy of interest. Philosophy does not consist of knowing just anything, and there are even things it is better not to know: "Knowledge of these things being completely superfluous, it no doubt does not belong to philosophy, since it is a way of giving oneself trouble in vain." Just as the philosopher does not act haphazardly, nor does he consider just anything, and "contemplation must have a limit, just as action has one." Philosophy therefore desires to know only divine and honorable things. And those things are the ones of which nature is the craftsman, nature which is divine art. Alexander repeats a play on words that was already hoary in his own time on the verb "to contemplate" *(theōrein)*. It is supposed to show that the objects of contemplation are divine things, that contemplation "sees divine things" *(horân ta theia)*. Consequently, theoretical philosophy is the science of divine things and of things that are naturally born and constituted. It is knowing those things that is in itself worthy of interest. Alexander expresses himself vaguely, but it seems that he is taking astronomy to be the paradigmatic science. He says in fact that it is the only part of geometry that envisions divine and natural substances. Astronomy has the advantage of best concretizing the theoretical model of man's relationship to that which exists.

A TEXT BY SENECA

But it is without doubt Seneca who voices the idea most clearly. He did so around 63 C.E., in the treatise *De otio,* whose title is best translated as "On Availability."[20] Seneca begins by repeating the ancient question, disputed at least since the time of Euripides, regarding the preeminence of the active life or the contemplative life. He neutralizes the issue by connecting both options to different versions of the same basic attitude: to be concerned with the objects of contemplation is to be actively involved in the highest form of politics. The response he thus proposes is not found in his writings alone. It is also shared by Plotinus: contemplation is the highest form of action.[21] And for an Ancient, "action" *(praxis)* designates above all political life, the affairs of the polis. The assimilation of contemplation with action is therefore rendered possible by assimilating the universe to a polis, "cosmopolitanism" in the strict sense, as it is supported by the Stoics. "Idleness," the effort to free oneself for contemplation, is in this way also a way of serving the polis.

Seneca lists an entire program of ethical and physical investigation. To contemplate is thus not simply to passively amass observations of the spectacle of things, but to open up an inquiry into a reality that is not immediately apparent. The final goal, then, is for the work of God not to remain without a witness. To live according to nature was the old Stoic ideal and remains so here in a new form: the formula henceforth designates the fulfillment of a mission assigned by nature. This is a dual mission: to act and to contemplate: "I live according to nature if I give myself to it entirely, if I devote my life to admiring and adoring it. And nature wants me to do two things: to act and to devote myself to contemplation; I do both these things, since even contemplation cannot be conceived without action."

The desire to know hidden things proves that we are naturally drawn toward contemplation. The desire to know in the realms of geography, theater, history, ethnography—and even voyeurism—shows this. The natural desire to know, upon which Aristotle already based his thinking, but which he left at the theoretical level, is connected here to its concrete source. Aristotle also took into evidence our taste for traveling.[22] This impulse was finally given a name, which remained classic:[23] curiosity: "Curiosity in us is a gift of nature." Except that the word "curiosity" did not yet mean for Seneca what it means today. It suggests a very important concept, *cura*, the restless attention given to a thing, the concern that one has for it. The totality of things, considered to be beautiful, well organized, thus of *kosmos*, must have a spectator: "Being aware of its genius and its beauty, [nature] created us to be the spectators of such a marvelous spectacle; it would have wasted its effort, if these so great works, so pure, so finely conforming, so brilliant, rich with so much varied beauty, were offered only to the void."

The spectator nature requires is man. Man's physical characteristics—erect posture, a flexible neck—and foremost his central location are connected to his role as spectator. Seneca mentions a theme that became commonplace:[24] "What proves that nature wants us to contemplate it, and not simply to glance at it, is the place where it has put us: nature has established us in its center, arranging around us the panorama of the world; and nature did not stop at placing man upright, but, since it wanted to make contemplation easy for him, so he could follow the movement of the stars from their rising to their setting and turn his face to follow the movement of the Universe, nature placed man's head toward the sky and placed it on a flexible neck." Man's central location is therefore not an advantage that he can attribute to himself. He fulfills here, in the theater of nature, not the function of the hero, but that, less glorious, of the claque.[25] Similarly, diurnal movement is assumed to enable nature to successively present the totality of its riches for human observation: "Then, by making the signs of the zodiac progress, [nature] has successively deployed to his eyes all the parts of itself." Seneca derives a curious consequence from this: nature manifests itself to man "so that what it shows him of it inspires him to want to know the rest." The fact that nature shows itself entirely serves only to heighten the desire to know hidden things. The formula is awkward, however: one might wonder what the "other things" are if what is shown is already "all things."

We do not see everything; nor do we see all things according to their exact dimensions. Sight only functions as a scout, it only opens the path that leads beyond the world: "There are in fact objects that our sight does not reach and those that we see appear shortened to us: it is indeed our eye, however, that opens the path of investigation to us and which poses the first givens of our knowledge of the true. We can then, through induction, pass from the perceptible to the obscure and conceive a reality more ancient than the firmament itself." Once again, Seneca lists questions relating to physics. The questions are ranked from high to low, from the stars to men, in such a way that the final questions reproduce as in a mirror, on a smaller scale, the progress of the entire passage. All the questions concern the genesis of the world rather than its structure, its cosmogony rather than its cosmography. The yon . . . is rather the hither. . . ! By thus transcending the perceptible, "our thought goes through the ramparts of the sky and is not content to know what falls under the senses: 'I delve,' it says, 'into the expanse that opens beyond the firmament.'" The image is ancient and not specifically Stoic. On the contrary, it has a classic form in the Epicurean Lucretius.[26] What is original, however, is the idea of knowledge that appears here: knowledge is not conquered by human effort over a nature that would only offer itself passively as an object; it is part of a strategy of nature itself that desires to accede, through man, to something resembling self-awareness.

THE PRIMACY OF THE SKY

The study of nature is thus above all the study of the celestial world.[27] This settles an old quarrel. Aristotle had hesitated between two possible objects for philosophical contemplation, each compensating for what is lacking in the other: divine realities are, in themselves, more valuable, but they most often escape us; but things of this world, however mundane they may be, are easily accessible.[28] While Aristotle, enthralled with biology and less interested in astronomy, makes it clear that he leaned toward the former, the balance is subsequently upset in favor of astronomy. This is, for example, the case in Gersonides, himself an astronomer by profession: "Because of the high rank of this investigation, the small degree of understanding that we reached in it is more precious and more noble to us than the entire investigation of matters less noble and of lesser rank, and this is quite clear from the nature of human desires."[29]

But already Proclus, for purely theoretical reasons, gave precedence to astronomy, knowledge of divine bodies, over alchemy, the study of the transmutations of earthly elements: "On the subject of the stars, an investigation of them has a justification *(prophasis)*, their discovery has a legitimacy *(katorthōsis)* which is not small, [that is:] so that they demonstrate that the bodies that are transported in a circle move in a uniform way. They say in fact that it is what is appropriate for divine bodies."[30] It is particularly interesting here that in order to claim the dignity that it has by nature, astronomy requires a comparison with alchemy that to our knowledge never appears before Proclus. Alchemy is not just a knowledge of the terrestrial. In that case it would have been enough to contrast astronomy to geography or to zoology. Alchemy is also a claim to intervene in the course of nature, to lead nature to a perfection of which it would be incapable by itself. Alchemy is the first instance of a technological approach to the modification of nature[31]—an approach that, as is known, often appeared in the modern era, above all in Francis Bacon, under the guise of magic. Alchemy is thus the ultimate non-contemplative science, and doubly so, through its object of study and also through its methods. It therefore contrasts with astronomy, the nature of whose object prevents one from acting upon it, so that it is purely contemplative.

Astronomy also legitimizes its existence by arguing its moral usefulness. First, by asserting that contemplation brings happiness: without the contemplation of the ocean of beings made possible by geometry, there is no happiness, recalls Maximus of Tyre.[32] But on the other hand, the idea of an imitation of the sky, which came from the *Timaeus,* is again found here. Thus the idea that we encountered above among the philosophers— Simplicius and, no doubt, as his source, Alexander of Aphrodisias before him—is applied to the only rigorously mathematical discipline of the pre-Galilean period.[33] It is interesting that it is practitioners of science who thus endorse the idea of the commentators. Would this be a transgression of the Platonic distinction between empirical astronomy and rational astronomy?[34] Not really, since, on the one hand, the contemplation in question is intellectual, not tangible; and on the other, astronomy is purely hypothetical, it does not "dirty its hands" with physics.

Ptolemy writes in the preface to the *Almagest:* "In addition, as to the excellence *(kalokagathia)* that concerns actions and character, it is [astronomy] among all [the sciences] that can render one clear-sighted to the highest degree: from the regularity *(homoiotēs)*, the good order *(eutaxia)*, the harmony *(summetria)*, the absence of pompousness *(atuphia)* that one contemplates on the subject of divine things, it renders those who are aware of it lovers of that divine beauty, and it accustoms and, so to speak, naturizes *(phusiō)* to a state similar to one's soul."[35]

The famous epigram attributed to the same astronomer is cited by the Brethren of Purity: "It is said that Ptolemy desired a knowledge of the stars *(nujūm)* and he made the science of geometry into a ladder to climb to the spheres, following which he measured the spheres and their distances, the stars and their dimensions, then noted them in the *Almagest,* and that ascension was made by the soul, not by the body."[36] It is interesting that this passage was placed within a context concerning the liberation of the soul with regard to matter, in a file of quotations including the famous passage on ecstasy from the *Theology of Aristotle* as well as a saying attributed to Christ. An "epistemological" reflection is turned into a "mystical" one.

Aratus, in his poem on celestial phenomena, expresses this notion in the form of a myth.[37] The digression on the virgin Dikē, who lived among men during the golden age and who had henceforth disappeared only to return in an eschatological age, like the one Virgil describes,[38] has as its framework the notion of the departure of the gods. In the past, communication with the gods was immediate. Today, although the gods have gone away, there remains a path toward them, and that is celestial phenomena. The movement is the reverse of that of the "Socratic revolution": it is no longer a question of descending from the sky into the polities, but to go up from the polities, whence justice has disappeared, to the sky. In this way Aratus's passage is the poetic version of the moral justification for astronomy.

Finally, studying the sky is not something purely external for the soul. By studying astronomy, the soul fundamentally studies itself. This is expressed in a text by Seneca.[39] As an introduction to the investigation of nature through general considerations, he compares ethics with physics. The physics under consideration is that of the Stoics, which also includes theology, since it studies a nature that is not radically distinct from God: "There is no more difference between philosophy and the other sciences than there is, in my opinion, within philosophy itself, between the part that has man *(ad homines)* as an object and the part that considers the divine *(ad deos)*. . . . From one to the other there is the distance that separates God from man." The analogy is simple: physics is to philosophy-in-general as philosophy is to knowledge-in-general. The comparison turns to the advantage of physics, which is not surprising, since, before dealing with physics, it is appropriate to increase its value. But the criterion that assures its superiority is very interesting: "The science of the human teaches what must be done *(quid . . . agendum sit)* on earth; that of the divine what is done *(quid agatur)* in the sky." Physics, the science of what is, triumphs over ethics, the science of what ought to be.

This passage is thus one of the very rare early formulations of the distinction that would be at the foundation of moral philosophy in the modern era, between *is* and *ought (Sein* and *Sollen).* We Moderns would spontaneously place what ought to be higher than what is, and Kant justified this ranking by the primacy of practical reason.[40] For Seneca, primacy incontestably belongs to theoretical reason: the "is" is worth more than the "ought." Moral practice is purely preparatory, a *via purgativa* that finishes higher than itself: "The first [morals] dissipates our errors and places within our reach the flame that enables us to see clearly in the perplexities of life." Physics alone achieves what morality only promises: "The other [physics] rises considerably above the darkness in which we struggle, and those that it has pulled out of the darkness are led by it toward the source of the light. . . . The virtue to which we aspire is splendid *(magnifica),* not that it is sufficient, to be happy, to have been able to keep oneself from vice, but because it liberates the soul, prepares it for a knowledge of things of the sky and renders it worthy to participate in divine existence. The soul has, in its perfection and its plenitude, the happiness that the human condition can attain, when, full of scorn for all that is evil, it reaches the heights of the sky and penetrates as far as the intimate recesses of nature. . . . This globe is only a point. . . . In the sky the space is immense, and the soul *(animus)* is admitted to take possession of it. . . . Having arrived above, it feeds on it and grows. It seems that, freed from its bonds, it returns to its source." These are all expressions that should be taken literally, according to Stoic physics. Or rather, one must constantly transpose physics and what one might call spirituality onto each other: physics explains the very being of the soul, which is assumed to be a spark of the divine fire. Study of the sky makes the soul aware of its kinship.

This is why "in the charm that divine things have for it, it finds a proof of its own divinity *(hoc habet argumentum divinitatis suae quod illum divina delectant).* It therefore takes the interest in it that one has, not for that which is foreign, but for that which is one's own *(nec ut alienis, sed ut suis interest).* . . . It knows well that all of that concerns it directly *(scit illa ad se pertinere).* . . . It is there that the soul finally learns what it has sought for a long time, there that it begins to know God. . . . To be interested in these questions, to study them, to be absorbed in them, is this not to free oneself from one's mortal condition and pass into a superior category of beings?" We can note Seneca's play on the idea of interest, present as regards the thing itself, and going as far as the verb chosen by Seneca. The soul has a natural interest in the study of nature. One might think on the contrary that nature would be of less concern than morality, which indicates how to behave, and therefore, that interest in nature would be purely theoretical, indeed the pursuit of a curiosity in the pejorative sense of the term. But here, the interest quite literally lies in the fact that the soul is involved. The Socratic revolution is overthrown: if the soul is a part of the world, self-knowledge and knowledge of the world are no longer in opposition.[41] One must then pass through physics to reach oneself. In the strict sense of the term, the study of nature is *interesting*.

AN IMITATION OF THE WORLD

The view of the world I am examining is not simply a static description of reality in its hierarchical structure. It also contains a model for moral practice. The appeal to the good order of celestial phenomena is not solely theoretical. It is at the same time an instance of what is asked of man, the most noble of beings relegated within the contingency of the sublunary. The order of the superior world is a model for men of correct behavior in life. It is through imitation of the perfect regularity of the celestial figures that man can successfully put his own sublunary life in order. He can thus transpose the "Socratic revolution" onto the practical register and "make the sky descend to the cities."

A. The Imitation of Order

Plato introduced the idea of an order to be imitated, but the idea had already been prepared in earlier Hellenism. We have just seen this: the object of contemplation was not mentioned at the outset and remained vague. The same is true of the exact nature of the order to be imitated. This is the case in Euripides, who sketches the portrait of the "contemplative man": "Happy is he who possesses the knowledge brought by investigation *(tēs historias . . . mathēsin)*, without rushing toward the harm of his co-citizens nor toward unjust actions, but who contemplates the ageless order of immortal nature *(athanatou kathorōn physeōs kosmon agērōn)*, whence he is constituted, whence and how. Such [men], never does the concern of shameful actions appear before them."[42] The text is not without its problems. What is the referent of the pronoun I have translated here as "such [men]"? Does it relate to "he who," passing from the singular to the plural, drawing from the idea of the "type of man"? Does it relate to "the order" which, here too, implies an organized plurality? That seems more likely, for the moral qualities of the "contemplative one" are already mentioned in lines 3 and following. The justice of that person would thus be the consequence of his familiarity with the order *(kosmos)* formed by nature *(phusis)*.

Plato himself does not immediately present the world as the object of an effort of imitation. In the *Republic,* Socrates explains to Adeimantus: "For, presumably, Adeimantus, a man who has his understanding truly turned toward the things that *are* has no leisure to look down toward the affairs of human beings and to be filled with envy and ill will as a result of fighting with them. But, rather, because he sees and contemplates things that are set in a regular arrangement and are always in the same condition—things that neither do injustice to one another nor suffer it at one another's hands, but remain all in order according to reason—he imitates them and, as much as possible, makes himself like them. Or do you suppose there is any way of keeping someone from imitating that which he admires and therefore keeps company with?"[43] The passage remains open: we do not know whether it concerns stars or ideas, the latter more likely because of a parallel passage, a bit earlier; and in the same dialogue, the "sky" in which is found the paradigm of the just city *(en ouranōi)* is not necessarily a physical reality.[44] What is important, however, is that the basic structure is set: looking above, turning away from the below, the order *(kosmos)* as the object of love, the impossibility of *not* imitating what one loves. This last assertion, presented in the form of a rhetorical question, assumes the intellectualist conviction: one cannot know good without wanting to, and therefore, "no one is evil by choice." If it is a matter here, as everything leads to believe, of ideas, it is remarkable that this structure is found again elsewhere, transposed onto other objects.

B. The Whole as Example

The basic structure we have just exposed, the imitation of an order, can be realized in several ways, depending on whether the order to be imitated is assumed to be manifest in the Whole itself or in a privileged part of it. In the first case, imitation and adaptation tend to coincide. Stoicism emphasized this aspect, especially in its early days. Primitive Stoicism, in fact, does not assume that the world is stable, but sees it destined to reintegrate the primitive fire out of which it emerged. Subsequently, the world does not offer a permanent model. Its present structure is destined to disappear, and the question of whether eternal recurrence will bring exactly the same situation remains obscure: it seems that, beginning with the assertion that there is strict repetition (Socrates once again accused by Anytos, once again drinking hemlock, etc.), Stoicism evolved toward a less rigid theory. The same is true, moreover, of the idea of the final conflagration, which, in middle Stoicism, gives way to the notion of the world's eternity. Consequently, the object of imitation must above all be the world in its totality, more than the structure of the world at any given moment.

It is thus that Poseidonius defines man's final goal: "To live while contemplating *(theōrein)* the truth *(alōtheia)* and the order *(taxis)* of all things and by contributing to the establishment of them *(sunkataskeuazonta)* insofar as possible."[45] We can contribute to seeing that order reigns in all things to the extent that we are ourselves a part of that order. But we must still become aware of that order by having an exact vision of it, by interpreting it correctly.[46] This is why, according to Cicero, "man is born to contemplate and to imitate the world; he is in no way perfect, but he is a part of what is perfect."[47]

Seneca also considers that the aspect of the world that we should imitate resides in the very "worldliness" of it, in what makes it a totality: "Do not shine out toward the external. What you have that is good is turned inside. Thus it is that the world scorns that which is external, for it is content with its own spectacle. . . . Reason, excited by the senses, goes in search and, borrowing principles from them (in fact it has nothing else upon which it might lean in its quest for the true), returns to itself. Indeed, the world, the one that surrounds all things, and the god who directs the universe lean toward the external, but nonetheless return from everywhere toward their inner self. Let our mind do the same when, following the senses, it tends through their mediation toward exterior things, let it be master of them and of its self."[48]

Seneca assumes a theory of occasionalist knowledge: knowledge begins with sensation, but that is only its point of departure. Elsewhere the same Seneca establishes man's humanity on his very worldliness: "Nature has endowed us with a large soul *(magnanimos)* and, just as it has given some animals a ferocious spirit, to others a clever spirit, and to others a fearful spirit, so has it given us a spirit avid for glory and haughty, which does not seek the place where it will live most securely, but where it will live most honorably. *It is completely similar to the world it is following, as much as mor-*

tals are allowed to be, and that it imitates (simillimum mundo, quem, quantum mortalium passibus licet, sequitur aemulaturque); it places itself in front, it wants to be praised and looked at."[49] Man's magnanimity is such—literally, the human soul is so great—that it is equal to the entire world. The comparison with the souls of animals is only mentioned to be passed over: in the end our soul is not comparable to that of this or that animal, thus of this or that part of the world; its model must be the world itself.

To be wise, then, would be to be perfectly "worldly." The play on words is constant, beginning with the hermetic writings, in which it is a matter of *munde mundum servare.*[50] In a fourth-century text, which constitutes something like a catechism of the popular Neoplatonism that the emperor Julian wanted to establish or reestablish, one reads: "We who imitate the world *(ton kosmon mimoumenoi),* how could we be better put in order *(kosmētheiēmen)?*"[51]

A century later, the Neoplatonic commentator Elias established the parallel between the order of the world and the order of the conduct of the one who studies it.[52] The world is divided into that which only commands, that which only obeys, and that which both commands and obeys: the divine commands everything, the sublunary obeys, angels and celestial powers obey God and command the inferior world. Similarly, we can reinterpret the Platonic tripartition in ourselves in that sense: reason only commands, desire obeys, the heart *(thumos)* receives orders from reason and passes them on to desire. Elias concludes from this: "Thus then, let the student in his life be ordered *(tetagmenos)* and [form] a *mikros kosmos,* so that through the intermediary of the order that is in him he knows the unique principle of the Whole (in fact the order is directed toward the One, the disorder toward plurality), and that, through the intermediary of the *mikros kosmos* that is in him, he recognizes the *kosmos.* And he will be a *mikros kosmos* if, as in the universe *(kosmos),* better things win out over the less good." One of the traditional definitions of so-called "civic" *(politikē)* philosophy includes an imitation of God insofar as that is possible for man. Subsequently: "If the philosopher imitates God, he puts his conduct in order *(kosmein)* in all ways and he makes himself a little world *(mikros kosmos).*"

The theme is a common one: during the same period, another commentator, David, also mentions Democritus and the idea of microcosm, but without connecting it to a definition of philosophy. On the other hand, on several occasions he plays with the verb *kosmein* as the goal of philosophy.[53] Written earlier, a text by Proclus is interesting in that it connects the theme to an exegesis of the *Timaeus.*[54] In fact it questions the reasons for the presence of an anthropology in a dialogue that is above all on physics. It cites several reasons: first, the consideration of man is appropriate to us since we propose to live together as men; then, we are a microcosm, and "the motions akin to the divine part in us are the thoughts and revolutions of the universe." But the decisive reason is the practice, attributed to the Pythagoreans, "of connecting to the contemplated object a discourse on the contemplating subject: when in fact we know what the World is, it is necessary . . . to add to it the knowledge of what can indeed be the subject that examines it and grasps it through reason. Now, . . . Plato . . . has said expressly at the end that, if one wishes to attain a happy life, "one must assimilate that which contemplates to that which is contemplated." For the Whole is eternally happy, and we will also be happy when we will be assimilated to the Whole, for in that way, we will have climbed to our Cause. Since, in fact, man below has the same relationship with the Universe as the Ideal Man has with the Living in Self . . . when the man below will be assimilated to the Universe, he will also imitate its model in the mode that is appropriate to him, for he will have become "ordered" *(kosmios)* by the fact of his resemblance with the Order of the World *(kosmos),* and happy since he will be rendered like the Blessed God."

These texts, like those attributed to the Stoics, propose the world in its entirety as an object of imitation. However, they place the accent on the ordered, hierarchized nature of the world. It is less a matter of imitating the totality as such than the ordering and layering that turn it, right through, into a *kosmos.*

CELESTIAL MOTIONS AS CENTRAL OBJECTS

In addition, most of the time what we are supposed to imitate is not so much "nature" in general as it is the celestial world. The difference between the sublunary and the supralunary becomes the basis for a morality, in a process that began in the first century B.C.E. and culminated in the third century C.E.[55] Seneca returns to this theme on several occasions. He begins with a comparison which aims at exhorting whoever wields authority to wonder "whether the state of the world is more pleasant and more beautiful for the eyes on a serene and pure day or when all things are shaken up by claps [of thunder] and fires blaze here and there. The face of a tranquil and measured reign is none other than that of a serene and luminous sky."[56] Then the analogy is completed by receiving its cosmological dimension: "The superior and best ordered *(ordinatior)* part of the universe, that which is close to the stars, does not bunch together in clouds, is not pushed into a storm, does not whirl around in a cyclone; it is exempt from all upsets; the thunder claps lower down. Similarly a sublime spirit, always calm and placed in a tranquil sphere *(statio)*, stifling in it all the seeds of anger, is moderate, venerable, harmonious."[57] It is no longer a question of regulating oneself on meteorological phenomena, but on those at a higher level; Seneca derives a rule from this, which designates the model by its name: "The soul of the wise man is similar to the supralunary world, where the weather is always fine *(Talis est sapientis animus, qualis mundus* [*mundi status,* varia lectio] *super lunam: semper illic serenum est).*"[58] This always serene world (in the strict sense) is the *kosmos,* the world that, due to its perfect order, truly deserves its name.

Ancient and medieval ethics therefore contains a dimension in which moral practice must take the regularity of the world as its model. Such imitation is not prescribed for the individual alone. The cosmic order is a norm for the polis, as well. This is because the universe, according to an ancient metaphor that continued to be upheld, is itself conceived as a polis. Thus, according to Philo, "for anyone who contemplates the order in nature and the constitution *(politeia)* enjoyed by the world-city whose excellence no words *(logos)* can describe, needs no speaker to teach him to practise a law-abiding and peaceful life and to aim at assimilating himself to its beauties."[59]

In addition, to repeat a classic Aristotelian distinction, imitation is not only practical, it is also poetic. We do not have to seek conformity with the world only through the rectitude of our ethical actions. We can also produce works that reproduce its structure, for example, cathedrals.[60] Here, too, the idea is ancient. Architects have sought to construct cities whose structure imitates that of the *kosmos.*[61]

I will now follow the theme of the imitation of celestial motions in the ancient world, then in each of the three medieval religious worlds we have been examining.

A. Antiquity

One might assume that the idea of imitating celestial bodies was present, at least in inchoate form, as early as Hesiod: the structure of the *Works and Days* and the ethical significance of the entire work suggest that astronomy has an influence on the good order of human life.[62] Euripides presents the lunar and solar cycles as examples of equality *(isotēs)* and of an absence of envy *(phtonos).*[63] But as we have seen,[64] it is only the *Timaeus* that unequivocally says that the object to be imitated is the regulated movement of the celestial bodies. This dialogue is therefore the direct or indirect source of the idea of the imitation of the sky and the object of an immense series of quotations or allusions.

Cicero repeats the idea without referring to its source: "I believe that the immortal gods planted souls *(animos)* in human bodies so that there would be people to take care of things on earth and who, while contemplating the order of celestial things, imitate it through the measure and the constancy of their lives *(caelestium ordinem contemplantes imitarentur eum vitae modo atque constantia)*."[65]

On the other hand, Plutarch expresses the idea without going much farther than paraphrasing the *Timaeus:* "For Plato, God placed himself in the center of everything as a model for all perfection and he grants human virtue, which is in some way an assimilation *(exomoiōsis)* to himself, to beings capable of 'following God.' Indeed, the Universe which was by nature anarchic found the principle of its metamorphosis into an organized world *(kosmos)* in a resemblance, a participation in the ideal virtue that belongs to the divinity. This same philosopher also asserts that nature has granted us sight so that our soul, through the marveled contemplation of the stars that travel in the sky, becomes accustomed to tasting and seeking order and harmony *(to euskhēmon kai tetagmenon),* to be horrified by the unbalance and the wandering of the passions *(anarmosta kai planeta pathe),* to avoid the approximate and pleasure, the source of all evil and all discord."[66]

The idea that the order of the world is a model by which man must be inspired becomes common, not to say commonplace. Thus the Neoplatonist Iamblichus sings the praises of friendship: Pythagoras had it reign between all things, gods and men, soul and body, men among themselves. He brought it to the body through "the pacification and the reinforcement of faculties hidden within it, by means of health, of the diet that leads to it, and of temperance *(sōphrosunē)* by imitating the prosperity *(euetēria)* that reigns in the elements of the world."[67]

Other authors develop the idea more fully. We have the example of a representative of the "second sophistics," Dio Chrysostomus (ca. 40–after 110).[68] The orator recommends that his co-citizens of Prusa reconcile with their neighbors from Apamea. He presents them with the example of the good order that reigns among the celestial bodies, in which he sees the results of moral virtues: "Do you not see the eternal order, the agreement, the temperance of all the sky and the divine and blessed beings who are there?" On the earth, elements maintain a harmony among them that comes out of the virtue of justice: "Do you not see . . . with what justice in reasoning and what moderation they naturally exist, conserving themselves and the totality of the world?" Dio then goes on to systematically develop the idea of a cosmic order of a moral nature and to propose it as a model for human behavior.

It is remarkable that he appears quite aware of the difficulty presented by this type of parallel, since he begins with a concession: "Even if the argument will appear to some to go too high and not to be at all adaptable to us." Unfortunately Dio does not specifically name these fearful minds, but their hesitation is plausible: do we not transgress the limits assigned to the human by such a comparison? He himself does not hesitate to suggest: "These beings, incorruptible by nature, divine, and guided by the thought of the first god, the greatest one, are preserved by reciprocal friendship and concord, both those who are stronger and bigger and those who seem smaller." Such an agreement is indispensable for them to continue to exist: "If this community were dissolved and if discord arrived, their nature would not be to such a degree sheltered from perdition and corruption that they would not be disturbed and they would not undergo the corruption . . . that leads from being to nothingness. . . . But the greed and dissention of the other [elements], which occur in spite of the law, contain an extreme danger of perdition." Fortunately, this is only a speculative hypothesis: this perdition would never affect the entire universe "due to the fact that there exists between those elements full peace and full justice, and that everywhere all things serve and follow a reasonable law, obeying it and giving in to it." Thus the Sun makes way for the stars and the Moon, allows itself to be eclipsed by the Moon, indeed to be hidden by thin clouds; the Earth accepts last place and endures everything there. The text continues with a passage on the harmony between the animal species, which seek not to trouble each other, rather, to collaborate with each other.

The cosmology underlying this exhortation is essentially Stoic. It is certainly not a goal in itself: the world is evoked only as a background on which stands out, for the shame of man, his inability to get along with his neighbors. This view of the world is interesting, however, in that it puts a cyclical rather than a static view of the world at the service of a moral exhortation. When it is a matter of presenting the cosmos as a model, it is most often seen as an eternal order. Here, however, the order unfolds in time. Furthermore, as a good Stoic, Dio does not establish a clear-cut border between the supralunary and the meteorological: the eclipse of the Sun and the fog are placed on the same level. He even assumes a certain continuity between the air and the terrestrial world, which enables him to continue with a consideration of the animals. In any case, the good order of the universe is expressed in a constant way through the moral virtues of justice, temperance, and calm. However, although the overall context of the passage clearly indicates that nature is valuable as an example, the idea of the imitation of nature is not explicitly mentioned.

B. Christians

The idea expressed in the text of the *Timaeus* survived for a long time in Antiquity and the Middle Ages, whether its source was explicitly mentioned or not. Its fundamental message is found among the pagans that have just been cited, but also later among Christian thinkers. These thinkers had access to the *Timaeus,* either directly, like the Byzantines, or through the intermediary of a Latin translation. Cicero's stopped—the coincidence is curious—at 47b2, just before the passage that contains the idea of an imitation of celestial bodies.[69] However, Chalcidius continues as far as 53c4 and comments on our passage and was followed by medieval writers such as William of Conches.[70]

First among the witnesses of the indirect tradition is Boethius (d. 524), who develops the theme powerfully in the *Consolation of Philosophy.* The book had an enormous influence on thinkers of the Middle Ages: it was translated into many languages, including Catalan and Castilian. It was done into English by translators as distinguished as King Alfred, Chaucer, and also Queen Elizabeth I. The French version was made by Jean de Meung. Finally, it was no doubt the only Latin text to have been simultaneously translated into Greek by the Byzantines and adapted into Hebrew.[71] Its Latin commentators insisted on the idea of imitation of the sky.[72] Boethius sees the world as the *Timaeus* sees it. And one of the poems that appears in the *Consolation* constitutes a sort of compendium of Plato's dialogue. Nothing can exist without a minimum of order that preserves its nature. The skies are an example of that law. They are admirable less through their vastness than through the reason that governs them.[73] It is in them that the will of God is most clearly visible and readable: "If you would see, with pure discerning mind, / The lofty Thunderer's laws, / Look up to the heights of the topmost heaven; / There the stars keep their ancient peace / In the just compact of the universe."[74] Philosophy helped Boethius to point out the paths of the stars so that we might "shape our character and the whole manner of our life according to celestial models."[75] It is God who assures the regularity of the celestial movements. Only the actions of men are free, and disorder reigns on the earth. Let God apply the same law there by which he dominates the skies: "Steady with that stability of law / By which you rule the vastness of the heavens."[76] The eighth poem of the second part concludes: "O happy race of men, / If the love that rules the stars / May also rule your hearts!"[77] The earth is only a point in the universe. But the man who inhabits it is worth more than precious stones. Standing erect, he can look at the sky. Let him raise his eyes to the sky then instead of lowering them to the mud.[78] Thus, going beyond the earth, he will be made worthy of the sky: "Earth overcome / Grants you the stars."[79]

The idea seems to have undergone a particular blossoming in the twelfth century. Bernard of Tours, in his *Cosmographia* (ca. 1150), which is also inspired by Plato's *Timaeus*, reformulates its teaching within the framework of the idea of the correspondence between macrocosm and microcosm. Man was made on the model of the world: "A compound formed of the two, body and soul, on the model of the celestial order."[80] The microcosm thus needs the macrocosm: "The second world, man, needs the knowledge and the care of the first and best."[81] This concern would be addressed by an imitation of the large world by the small one: "In the small world, which is man, Physis understands that she is not mistaken, if she takes the resemblance of the large world as an example for her."[82] This is why man must be led by the muse Urania through the sky, so that he may know it: "The human soul must be guided by me [Urania] through all the spaces of the ether, in order to increase its wisdom."[83] It becomes aware of the sky in order to strive to resemble it: "Only man, whose configuration bears witness to the nobility of his mind, will elevate to the stars his noble chief, so that he can have a model in the inalterable laws and paths of the sky to lead his life."[84]

In his *Anticlaudianus,* Alain of Lille gives the idea an original spin. The goal of perfect Man created by Nature with the help of Phronesis and Theologia is to "*vivere lege poli.*"[85] Let us understand by this that human action must be regulated according to equity more than the strict letter of the law, which kills. The letter is the forensic law, which is debated in the forum, which is thus named *ius fori.* One can appeal this law to a superior jurisdiction. It is interesting that this jurisdiction is designated by the term, obviously called by assonance, but perhaps not only for that reason, "law of the pole" *(ius poli).*[86] The formula refers to that which is in force in the sky, which is conceived, not only as the dwelling place of the divinity, but, in the most concrete way, as a sphere launched into the motion of rotation on itself and having as an axis the straight line that passes through the poles. The formula comes from St. Augustine, who had used it of a man who had donated his goods to the Church and then changed his mind. Did he have to deprive his children of that of which the bishop had become the owner? "The bishop had the power not to make restitution, but only according to the law of the forum, not according to the law of the sky *(jure fori, non jure poli)*."[87] Augustine's context does not emphasize the cosmic aspect of the idea, and the expression scarcely suggests more than "the Heaven," as a euphemism substituted for the divine name. This is again the case in Gratian, who cites the passage by Augustine, thus conferring upon it the dignity of a principle of law.[88] But the image was subsequently taken more literally, to refer to the order of the spheres.

Gerhoh of Reichersberg (d. 1169) closely follows a text by Rupert of Deutz (d. ca. 1130) while subjecting it to interesting changes. Rupert places the seven gifts of the Holy Spirit and the seven days of creation side by side. The work of the fourth day, the creation of the stars, corresponds to the spirit of strength or courage *(fortitudo),* since philosophers, pagans and Christians alike, have forever admired the strength and the power of the stars, "which maintain their course with such a determined and stable regularity," established on the order of God, (Rupert continues with a purely doxographic outpouring) "that people thought they were alive and controlled the destiny of men."[89] However, Gerhoh, who up until then had been copying word for word, draws a different conclusion from this: "so that their strength is justifiably an object of admiration and at the same time of emulation for rational man, convincing man of disobedience if he happens to leave the orbit of the commandment that is proposed to him *(a proposito sibi exorbitat praecepto)*."[90] The "strength" or rather the constancy of the stars should not only awaken our admiration, but should also inspire us to imitate it, indeed, to make us ashamed of our disobedience, which then appears, as Gerhoh suggests, to be as serious as a star leaving its orbit.

Dante uses the idea of imitation of the sky to develop an argument in favor of monarchical government: "Every son is in a good (indeed, ideal) state when he follows in the footsteps of a perfect father, insofar as his own nature allows. Mankind is the son of heaven, which is quite perfect in all its workings; for man and the sun generate man, as we read in the second book of the *Physics.* Therefore mankind is in its ideal state when it follows the footsteps of [the skies], insofar as its nature allows. And, since the whole sphere of [the skies] is guided by a single movement . . . and by a single source of motion . . . , then . . . mankind is in its ideal state when it is guided by a single ruler (as by a single source of motion) and in accordance with a single law (as by a single movement)."[91] Dante bases his argument explicitly on a text by Aristotle. In the second book of the *Physics,* Aristotle gives an interesting variant of his common formula "man engenders man" by completing it with "and the sun" (that is: with the help of the sun). It was thus a matter of placing animal generation in the larger context of cosmology.[92] From it Dante derives the terse formula that we are "sons of heaven/the sky." To the sun are added the other celestial bodies and their influences, in the spirit of the astrology of the period. The kinship between the sky and man is not just a metaphor, since the celestial influences form the human embryo when the condition of the sky and the mixture of matter in it allow.[93]

The same idea is found among post-Copernican writers, such as Petrus Ramus (d. 1572). Ramus takes the Platonic praise of astronomy literally but substitutes music as its object: "Music (as Plato thought of it), sister of astronomy and completely similar to it, not only produces for the mind an honorable relaxation and agreeably causes the troubles that concern it to cease, but through the imitation of celestial revolutions *(conversiones)* calms the floating and wandering revolutions of the human mind, which are related to them."[94]

The idea of imitating the sky contains something like an internal dialectic. Such an imitation cannot in fact be fully accomplished without having to neutralize the distinction on which it is based and to equate the earth with the sky. This would be all the more true when that moral neutralizing coincided with the assertion of a physical homogeneity between celestial and terrestrial matter. An idea of this sort is already present in Epicureanism. This is the case in the famous passage by Lucretius asserting that victory over the gods of Olympus makes us equal to the skies. It is even clearer when the anonymous author of the *Poem of the Etna* asserts that seeking to know the earth is a concern that connects us to the stars of the sky.[95] In the Christian realm, the distinction between the sky and the earth is only temporary. At the Resurrection, "sky and earth will be joined, and there will only be the sky remaining."[96] Alain of Lille develops the idea. His point of departure is a conception of nature that already relativizes the clear distinction between the sky and the earth. The garden of Nature, which is described according to the rules of the topos of the *locus amoenus,* although located on the earth, goes up to the sky. It also includes the stars: "Adorned with its own stars . . . the earth risks painting a new sky."[97] Once perfect man has won a victory over the vices, the earth no longer has anything to envy the sky: "Virtues govern the world. Henceforth, the stars and the dwelling of the axis [of the world] do not have more charm than the terrestrial globe; henceforth the land rivals the sky, henceforth the earth is wrapped in the shine of the ether, henceforth Olympus covers the earth."[98]

Meister Eckhart also unfolds a complex dialectic of the reversal of opposites. He indulges in etymological games on *homo, humus*—identified with *terra*—and *humilis,* and on several occasions recalls the paradox of geocentrism: for the earth, to want to distance itself from the sky would be to get closer to it. One text formulates his conclusion in a way similar to Alain of Lille's: "Humility and patience make a sky from the earth. . . . Among the humble, the earth is a sky, the lowest is the highest. What is deep and what is high *(altum)* are the same thing. Humility and the earth are of the deep, the sky is of the high."[99]

C. Muslims

At the beginning of philosophical reflection in Islamic lands, Muslim thinkers adopted the Platonic theme with great enthusiasm. It is difficult to know through which channels the influence of the *Timaeus* was able to reach the Muslim world. But due to that influence we have a summary of this dialogue by Galen, lost in Greek but preserved in Arabic translation. However, as we have seen, the passages containing the idea of the imitation of the sky are not included.[100] On the other hand, one of the most famous books of magic in the Middle Ages, known in Latin by the title *Picatrix,* relates a warning given by Aristotle to Alexander. The Wise Man is supposed to have recommended to the Emperor to make no movement that does not imitate the movement of the sky and does not correspond to it.[101]

Al-Farabi gives a clearly collective, political version of the idea.[102] He puts into place a three-sided correspondence between the structure of the organism, the hierarchy of the cosmic spheres, and the order of the virtuous city, which should imitate those two orders. The parts of the city are arranged in an order of mutual dependency. In this way, artificial reality, produced out of political art, "will become similar to natural beings, and its ranks will be similar to those beings who begin with the First and finish at the raw matter and at the elements; their connection and their attachment will be similar to those of the various beings with each other. . . . It is clear . . . that the political assembling and the whole that comes out of it in the cities resembles the assembling of the bodies in the entire world. It is also clear . . . that there is in the whole of what the city and the nation contain equivalents of what the whole world contains." Farabi develops the idea by more or less accentuating this or that aspect, depending on the subtly varied contexts of his different works in political philosophy. The most constantly stressed aspect is that of the hierarchical construction of reality: "In the world there is first of all a principle, then other principles according to their ranks, beings that come from those principles, other beings that follow those beings according to their ranks, until one reaches the last of the beings through its rank in the being. Similarly, in the whole of what the nation or the city contains, there is a primary principle, then other principles follow it, other citizens who follow those principles, and others who follow them, until one reaches the last citizens through the ranking in the city and humanity. There are therefore in what the city contains the equivalents of what the whole world contains."

Avicenna is perhaps the author in whose writing the idea is best situated within an overall view of the soul's destiny. The idea is dealt with in the context of a cosmology, which, far from functioning as a metaphor for a human order, is taken in the physical sense of the word. Avicenna sets forth the idea in a short treatise which is probably his last work: "The celestial bodies are not constituted from a mixture of these four elements but . . . are totally lacking in these opposites. Furthermore, it is only the involvement with these opposites that hinders the reception of the divine effluence. . . . The closer, therefore, a temperament is to a balanced state, the more is a person predisposed to receive this effluence. Since the celestial bodies are totally devoid of the opposites, they are receptive to the divine effluence; human beings, on the other hand, no matter how balanced their temperaments may be, are not free from flaws [due to the involvement with] the opposites. As long as the rational soul is associated with the human body, no corporeal entity [*jirm*] can be completely ready to receive the divine effluence or to have perfectly revealed to it all the intelligibles. But when a person expends all his efforts to purify [his rational soul] through knowledge, acquires the propensity for contact with the divine effluence. . . , has a balanced temperament, and lacks these opposites which hinder his reception of the divine effluence, *then there comes about in him a certain similarity to the celestial bodies and he resembles in his purity the seven mighty ones, i.e., the seven celestial spheres.*"[103] The resemblance to celestial bodies and, in particular, to the seven mobile stars, here called the seven mighty ones, is not, as in most of the texts we have seen, the result of a direct effort of imitation. It is the consequence, not targeted for itself, of an effort of purification of the self. Man is handicapped by the presence of his rational soul in a body, a sublunary body. Such a body is composed of the four elements. As those elements come from a combination of two of the primordial qualities, which are contrasted in pairs (hot/cold; dry/moist), they do not have the absolute stability of the celestial bodies which are made of a fifth element, of a perfect purity and free of all opposites. It is this stability that the wise man imitates from his place on earth. The philosophical practice ends up, if we may say so, in quintessentializing man.

In other texts, perhaps more representative of his most mature thought,

Avicenna presents an original concept of the imitation of the world that pulls imitation out of the commonplace realm of a simple physical mimicking: "The perfection belonging to the rational soul is to become an intellectual world *('ālam 'aqlī)*, in which is imprinted the form of the Whole, intelligent ordering *(niẓām ma'qūl)* of the Whole and the good that spreads over the Whole, beginning with the principle of the Whole, advancing as far as the noble substances, then the absolute spiritual realities, then the spiritual realities that are suspended in a certain way from the bodies, then to the superior bodies through their dispositions and their strengths, then [the soul] continues in this way until achieving fully in itself the disposition of the entire Being, and changes into an intelligent world *('ālam ma'qūl)*, parallel to the entire existing world, contemplating what is absolute truth, absolute good, true beauty, united to it, painted in its image and in its disposition, affiliated to its company and having become part of its substance."[104] The idea that the soul is transformed into the intelligible world is originally from Plotinus.[105] It is encountered in the *Theology of Aristotle*,[106] whereas that work—the fact is interesting as regards the transmission of the Neoplatonic legacy to the Arab world—does not paraphrase the passages of Plotinus where the idea is found. The idea is again found in Miskawayh,[107] and elsewhere in Avicenna's early writings.[108] But the passage I have just quoted is important because it clearly shows that this transformation is parallel to Avicenna's view of the entire universe, including the physical universe. The order of the soul consists of reproducing the order of the universe. It thus also encompasses knowledge of the physical universe or, at the very least, of the superior, celestial bodies. To imitate the whole is also to enact the intelligible reverse side of the sensible world—an idea that would leave traces in Gersonides' conception of beatitude. On the other hand, Avicenna leaves the moral dimension of the imitation of the world in the shadows.

Finally, there is another dimension of Avicenna's thought in which the celestial bodies play a more direct role in the destiny of the human soul, since it seems that they help make up for the disappearance of the vital breath after the soul's separation from the body. Indeed they provide the soul with a minimum of materiality that enables it to continue to exercise an activity of the imagination—and therefore to experience the pleasures and the pains of a Hereafter that belongs to the realm of imagination.[109]

The way the theme is approached by Ibn Ṭufayl deserves special treatment.[110] We are familiar with the overall schema of the *Ḥayy ibn Yaqẓān:* the eponymous hero is alone on a desert island, sheltered from all corruption, but also deprived of any education. Without any external help, and only by the strength of his natural abilities to reason, he is able to attain the highest metaphysical knowledge. Ḥayy ultimately possesses perfect knowledge of the structure of the world. He deduces its creation by God. He discovers he is called to imitate him, indeed, to assimilate himself to him. The penultimate stage of the process implies an imitation of the stars.

For him to know how to assimilate himself to God, the method employed up to then was no longer sufficient. Ḥayy seeks in the world an example of what he must do. The stars and the spheres seem to him to possess remarkable qualities, both as to their bodies and as to their intelligence. Their bodies are transparent (the spheres) and brilliant (the stars). *A fortiori* reasoning enables him to conclude that the stars also possess an intelligent essence that knows God: if he, a being plunged into the needs of the inferior world, possesses this essence, how much more so do the stars who escape that earthly servitude.[111]

That essence thus renders him similar to the celestial bodies.[112] Indeed, the most perfect of all animal minds is such that one might almost say that its form has no opposite and that it thereby resembles the celestial bodies, whose form has, and this time quite literally, no opposite.[113] That mind has properties that assure it a resemblance with the celestial bodies: if it were placed—a hypothesis that can't become real—midway between the center of the world (and of the earth) and the extreme end of that toward which the fire can climb, it would remain there at rest in perfect balance. "If it moved according to the place, it would move around the center, as the celestial bodies move; if it moved in place, it would move on itself; it would be of spherical shape, since anything else is impossible. Subsequently, it would strongly resemble the celestial bodies."[114]

The comparison with the animals enables Ḥayy to go from hypothesis to the statement of reality. It convinces him that he is himself the animal whose mind is balanced, and which resembles all the celestial bodies. Of the two parts of which he is composed, the coarser, the body, is in everything the more similar to the celestial substances that transcend the world of generation and corruption. As for the nobler part, it is that which knows God: "When it became clear to him how he had as an advantage, over the rest of the animal species, a resemblance to the celestial bodies, he saw [or: was of the opinion] that he had to take them as a model, that he must imitate their actions and that he assimilate his effort to them."[115]

Ḥayy becomes aware that his actions are divided into three groups, according to whether they imitate those of the animals, the celestial bodies, or God. He finds he is obliged to perform three sorts of actions that assimilate him respectively to these three levels of being. The first comes to him from his body; the second from his animal spirit; the third from his true essence,[116] following an implicit Platonic tripartition, that of the parts of the soul according to the *Republic* and the *Timaeus:* (a) The first comes from the body and corresponds to the diversity of desires *(epithumētikon).* In the world it corresponds to the sublunary world, compared elsewhere to the animalcules that are formed in the intestines.[117] (b) The second comes from the animal spirit lodged in the heart.[118] It is the Platonic *thumos.* In the world the celestial spheres, beginning with that of the fixed stars, the origin of movement, are classically compared to the heart, the source of movement in the organism.[119] (c) The third comes from that which, in Ḥayy, is his true essence, which coincides with that of God.

The first type of action is necessary only hypothetically. It is necessary in fact that the body survive for the animal spirit to continue to reside in it. That spirit is indispensable, because it is through it that the second imitation is accomplished, that of the celestial bodies.[120] This second imitation provides only an impure intuition *(mušāhada),* for in it one keeps an awareness of one's own essence. The third imitation is the only perfectly pure one.

Ibn Ṭufayl thus describes the way in which his hero undertakes the three assimilations: (a) The first involves the maintenance of his body. A rather brief passage is devoted to this. Ḥayy imposes a rule upon himself to consume only what will cause no risk to the survival of an individual plant or, if he is forced to feed on flesh, to the species. He eats as little as possible, and only when hunger forces him to.[121] (b) The second assimilation, to the celestial bodies, is the object of a somewhat longer passage,[122] and is above all more articulate: it is distinguished from the other two passages in that it includes three divisions itself—thereby reproducing on a smaller scale the structure of the entire passage with its three divisions. The celestial bodies can in fact be considered from three points of view: their attributes refer either to their relationship to what is beneath them, or to their own essence, or finally to their relationship to God. Their relationship to the inferior world of generation and corruption is the entirety of beneficial influences that emanate from them. Their essential properties are related, on the one hand, to the matter of which they are made, which communicates a perfect purity to them; and on the other hand, to the movement by which they are animated, which is circular, whether rotation or revolution. Their relationship to God is also double. Some of the attributes that express this arise in fact out of speculation: to have the constant intuition of God. But others arise out of practice and its motives: to desire him, to obey him, to rule his movement on his will.[123]

Ibn Ṭufayl's central idea is not exactly the one we have seen in Plato and in subsequent tradition. In that thinking it was only a question of imitating the action of the stars—more precisely, the perfect regularity of their movements. Here, more is at stake. On the one hand the imitation of the actions of the celestial bodies bears not only on their harmoniously regulated movements, but also on the beneficial influence that they exercise over the inferior world. This idea is encountered elsewhere, for example in a passage from the Brethren of Purity which recommends that man imitate the generosity of the sun.[124] On the other hand, and above all, its object is not only the actions of the stars, but something like the intent that animates and explains it: the stars demonstrate perfect obedience toward God and scrupulously carry out his will. Again, the idea is not new.

Ḥayy therefore strives to imitate these three different attributes. Regarding the first, he aims to exercise an influence over what is placed below him that is as beneficial as the stars'. Let us note that there is no indication that Ḥayy himself receives any influence whatsoever. This concern inspires in him a maximum of beneficence toward the plants and the animals. Among the second group of attributes, purity is achieved through taking care of the body. Circular movement is the object of a very literal imitation: Ḥayy circles around his island, his house, or a rock, and turns around on himself in a way that clearly evokes the practices of the Mawlawiyah who are called, for that reason, "whirling dervishes."[125]

The third set of attributes is the object of only partial imitation. The celestial bodies have theoretical activities, but practical ones as well. Now, Ibn Ṭufayl mentions only Ḥayy's efforts to be absorbed in the exclusive contemplation of God. The desire to serve that the celestial bodies are supposed to feel, their obedience, the movements that result from it, do not have a counterpart in Ḥayy's activity. Ibn Ṭufayl hides the imperfection of the parallelism between Ḥayy and his model by later mentioning the circular movement which, through the vertigo that it provokes in Ḥayy, helps his hero to abstraction from the sensible world.[126] But two points are noteworthy: on the one hand, the rotation is no longer set in relation to the stars, and there are other ways to achieve vertigo. On the other hand, it was not the circular movement as such that Ibn Ṭufayl attributed to the celestial bodies. They are supposed "not to turn away from him [God], but to be besotted by him, to conduct themselves according to his decree, to bend to the accomplishment of his plans, not to move except through his will and under the power of his hand."[127]

Now, this aspect of things is of the very essence, since it gives the imitation of celestial movements all its value. This imitation must not be a simple conformity; there must be inward adherence. If we may repeat a distinction—elementary, moreover—observed by Kant, one must imitate the stars not through legality but through morality. In less anachronistic terms, the "duties of the members" are nothing without the "duties of the heart."

This is moreover what is implied by the program that Ḥayy sets for himself at the beginning of the last phase of his intellectual and spiritual ascension: "There was thus also obligation for him to work to acquire himself his [God's] qualities from every point of view wherever possible, to take his character, to imitate his acts, to apply himself zealously to accomplish his will, to abandon himself to him, to give in to all the decrees with all his heart, internally and externally, etc."[128]

We can note in particular that these two passages have an essential notion in common—the will of God. The last one quoted, appearing first in the text, accomplishes a decisive but tacit shift: one goes from a God endowed with properties to this same being possessing character traits, actions, and indeed a will—which had never been said until then. The idea of divine will poses quite specific problems: How can that will be expressed so that one might follow it with a full understanding of it?

Here, will is attributed to God only following a consideration of the celestial bodies. It therefore seems that such consideration legitimizes the application of the idea of will to God. But contemplating the movements of the stars does not enable one to go from a factual statement of their actions to the idea that those actions are the expression of an obedience—any more than seeing someone conduct himself honestly is enough to convince us that he does so out of respect for the Moral Law.

The third assimilation is the loftiest. It assumes the previous consideration of the attributes of God.[129] It therefore rests on a reversal. Ibn Ṭufayl stresses this very clearly in noting that Ḥayy had become aware of all that while he was still involved in purely theoretical speculations and had not yet reached the practical *(šurū‘ fī ’l-‘amal)*.[130] It is thus no longer a question of God's "conduct," of his "actions," or of his "will." A problem appears to have been raised, which comes out of the comparison between the last two assimilations: the third has the advantage over the second of possessing total purity due to the complete disappearance of self-consciousness. But, on the other hand, it represents a certain regression. Ḥayy, plunged into direct contemplation and a recluse in his cave, is totally inactive. There is no longer any question of his spinning around, or of his being concerned with the world below him: finished "his care *(i‘tinā’)* for animals and plants, his compassion *(raḥma)* for them, his concern with ridding them of shackles."[131] There was something like a providence there; one can note the proximity of *i'tinā'* and *'ināya*, and the inevitable echo in the word *raḥma*, that is, the attribute of mercy, so basic to the god of Islam. At the highest level of the mystical union, all of that is struck down. What becomes then of "practice"? It was a question, where Ibn Ṭufayl repeated this classic distinction, of a "passage to practice" for which he employed the word *šurū'*. Its root is the same as in *šar'*, *šarī'a*, etc. Should we see here an allusion to the role of the religious Law, as a determination of what is to be done? As it happens, at this moment in the narrative the character Asāl intervenes and, with him, reference to positive religion. Subsequently it will no longer be a question of celestial bodies as rules for action. The practices exposed by Asāl will be those of the Muslim religion.

In this way we catch a glimpse of the structure of the *Ḥayy ibn Yaqẓān*, as well as of a problem that it raises. Let us raise it again: the highest stage of the mystical union, that is, direct identification with God, causes the disappearance of what the preceding stage had brought, the imitation of celestial bodies. The first imitation enabled the formation of negative precepts—to abstain from doing harm. With the second, one can form positive precepts—to do good, to intervene in nature. With the third assimilation, however, no practice can be formed. To repeat a classic distinction, Ḥayy's ultimate religion no longer consists of anything but "opinions"; "actions" have disappeared.

This raises another problem: is God generous, provident, and so on? If assimilation to God excludes the attitudes equivalent to those qualities, must one conclude that imitation and assimilation, indeed absorption into God, exclude each other? Would the celestial bodies teach us something about God that direct assimilation to him cannot teach us? Is this supplement provided by the revealed religions? It is of a "political" nature, in the broad sense, in that it concerns relationships with others. The imitation of the stars is more "political" than pure mysticism. It permits concern for others, since the spiritual level in which it is located maintains an awareness of self: I need that awareness so that I can know there is something else outside me.

In this way, the structure of the work gains coherence. That the overall movement is one of ascension is useless to note. That after the highest summit only a descent can occur, again, this is obvious. But one can note, in addition, that the descent, or its first step, that is, Islam in its purest form, the "spiritual" Islam of Asāl, corresponds quite exactly to the penultimate step of the ascending movement, that is, the imitation of the stars. Both establish a practice, which, moreover, boils down to similar actions. The astral religion of Ḥayy has the same result as the Islam of Asāl.

As for the celestial bodies, they reappear later, in a different form: they are no longer models for a practice. They henceforth belong to the objects of the contemplation of God: the divine to which it is a question of assimilating is not an undifferentiated One, it is also a world, in the circumstances the Farabian/Avicennian architecture of the spheres layered in decreasing order to the sublunary. Providence, which seemed lost with the "abandonment of works" which was brought by the highest stage of the union, is regained once one understands that the cosmic edifice and the reciprocal action of the parts of the universe are themselves an integral part of the object to be contemplated and to which one is to assimilate. In this way, cosmological mysticism also opens up onto a mystical cosmology.

D. Jewish Thought

Finally, the theme is encountered in Judaism as well. But, to my knowledge at least, it did not appear very early on. Granted, one of the Talmudic rabbis, Bar Qappara, recommended studying the stars, in which he sees the wisdom by which Israel could be rendered respectable in the eyes of the pagan nations, according to Deuteronomy 4:6.[132] But this wisdom is not yet an imitation of the stars. All the less so, no doubt, in that the verse that stresses the identification of wisdom with astronomy bears, in its obvious meaning, on the Divine Law itself. I have not found it to occur before the eleventh century.

Rashi (d. 1105), in his commentary on Deuteronomy 30:19 ("I call heaven and earth to witness against you"), assumes that celestial movements could serve as examples of obedience: "The Holy One Blessed Be He said to Israel, Gaze upon *(histakkelû)* the heavens which I have created to serve you: have they ever changed their ways *(middah)?* Has the sphere of the sun ever failed to rise in the East to give light to the entire world?, as it is stated (Eccl. 1.5): 'The sun riseth and the sun goeth down.' Gaze upon the earth which I have created to serve you: Has it ever changed its ways? Have you ever sown it and (the seed) did not sprout? Or have you ever sown wheat and it yielded barley? If these, which were made not for reward and not for loss, (i. e.,) if they are found worthy, they do not receive a reward, and if they commit sin, they are not punished, (nevertheless) they did not change their ways, (then) you, who if you are found worthy, you will receive a reward, and if you commit sin, you will be punished, most certainly (you should not change to evil ways). *Therefore choose life.*"[133]

An Egyptian Jew, probably Hananael b. Shmuel (d. ca. 1249), explains a verse in which God says: "I say, 'You are gods *(elohim)*, . . . nevertheless, you shall die like men'" (Psalm 82:6): "I desired that your souls *resemble those of the stars* which are perfect and noble souls, which suffer no influence but on the contrary influence others. Yet you did not desire your souls to be thus, and therefore they have become truncated and lifeless, devoid of action, motion, and influence, but [on the contrary] passively influenced by others, incapable of attaining the elevated stations. They thus resemble the most abject of the human species. . . ."[134]

Nachmanides (d. 1270) explains the significance of the tree of knowledge of good and evil. Before eating the fruit, "Man did by nature what he should have done according to generation *(kefî ha-tōledet), as the skies and all their hosts do,* 'true workers because their work is truth and they do not change their role,' without having in their actions either love or hate. On the other hand, the fruit of that tree is that which causes to be born in them that eat it the will and the desire to choose something or its opposite, for good or for evil."[135] The fall is like a degradation, a passing from the level of natural obedience to the level of deliberate choice, a choice that includes the possibility of a preference for evil. The highest level is illustrated by the way in which the skies in their ordering fulfill the mission that is assigned to them.[136]

THE DISOBEDIENT ANIMAL

If, in this perspective, nature obeys its Creator, man appears conversely as an exception compared to the rest of nature. He is distinguished from the other animals by distancing himself from the laws of nature.[137] Modern thinkers frequently see in this transgression a reason to be proud, indeed an occasion for silly Promethean tirades. For ancient and medieval thinkers it was not for that reason that man surpasses the animals, but rather through his obedience to superior laws. Inasmuch as he is the disobedient animal, for them man is less well endowed than the animals that are thus proposed to him as a model. Francis of Assisi referred to all of creation: "All the creatures under the sky serve and know their Creator and obey him, in their way, *better than you.*"[138] This is why man's disobedience must inspire the disapproval of all of creation. God's anger is also that of all creation.[139]

One can uphold animals, not only as able craftsmen, thereby proposing them as examples of the ingenuity by which man might be inspired,[140] but also as moral examples. Thus their eagerness for work must shame the lazy. In the Bible, Proverbs invites the lazy one to consider the ant and to learn a lesson of wisdom from it; Marcus Aurelius was encouraged by and invoked the example of little industrious animals.[141] The wisdom of the world can thus also be that of an animal. A Talmudic rabbi, Yohanan, even makes a general statement, in a perhaps partially ironic declaration that implies something like a notion of a natural law: if the Law had not been revealed, that the animals could have given men lessons in moral virtue: the cat would have taught us modesty, the ant honesty, the dove chastity, the cock manners.[142] Among the pagans, animals encourage scorn for death: the fear of death does not exist for them. Their example was already proposed by the Ancients, and by Râzî.[143]

Conversely, man shows proof of an exceptional sensuality; he alone can be bestial, a paradox already found in Aristotle.[144] A recurrent example is his sexuality: man is not limited to a season of lovemaking, and the male continues to seek out females even when they are pregnant. A fifteenth-century English poet expresses this idea at the end of a brief description of all of nature, from the sea and the stars to the flowers: "Ac that most meved me and my mood changed / That Reson rewarded and ruled all beestes / Save man and his make."[145] The idea would persist until at least the eighteenth century.[146]

. . .

According to this model, human action is therefore related to the structure of the cosmos. This relationship is expressed in several images and, above all, dominant in the tradition of Platonic influence, that of the imitation of celestial regularities. This is hardly more than an image, since this "imitation" does not consist of following directives that emanate from the stars. The very constancy of their revolutions prohibits them from providing rules adaptable to the infinite diversity of cases that must be confronted by concrete moral life. Ancient and medieval man, just as much as we, had to put practical wisdom to work, what Aristotle called *phronēsis*, whose choices in no way rest on the structure of the physical universe. One can indeed build a morality without taking that structure into account and without making the slightest allusion to "wisdom of the world." This is the case, I will repeat, of modern moralities; and, in Antiquity, it was indeed the case with Aristotle.[147] It would therefore seem that cosmology is indifferent to morality and, consequently, to how man achieves his own humanity.

And yet the cosmos, such as ancient and medieval man represented its structure, did not provide human action with anything like an indifferent framework, a stage that would in no way influence the play that was playing on it. The imposing mass of the cosmos hovered over the theater of human action. Granted, it risked crushing it, revealing its insignificance, as in the theme repeated a hundred times of the smallness of all empires.

But at the same time its all-encompassing presence was that of a Good. The battle for the good cause was not waged only in our "little hideout." It also unfolded in the majestic scenery of the sky. Or rather, it had been won from the outset, indeed, it never needed to be waged. The Good triumphed from the start, it coincided with Being. Man's moral effort toward the full blossoming of his humanity was in phase with the tendency of all things toward their perfection. The cosmos was the model for moral action only through metaphor; it remained the confirmation of it. If we might say so, the riskiest moral investments were guaranteed by a gigantic margin.[148]

To describe the whole situation I have just examined, one might propose the concept of *cosmonomy*. Cosmonomy is not to be ranked on either one side or the other of the distinction that has become popular, and borrowed from Kant,[149] between "autonomy" and "heteronomy." It it is not captured by the alternative thus posed—as, moreover, most concrete moralities are not. It is in fact the insertion into the cosmos that enables the moral subject to be authentically himself, to be truly an *autos*. This conformity in no way consists of bending to an exterior law, an other *(heteros)*. For ancient and medieval man, the *kosmos* was precisely not an external fact which it was necessary to obey. Or it was so as much as Kantian moral law is. For ancient man, "the starry sky above me and the moral law in me" were not distinguished by anything essential. For us, finite beings, explains Kant, the moral law must appear as an external pressure, that is, as duty, because we have a "pathological" side.[150] In the same way, according to ancient man, the order of the *kosmos* appears to us as something external, because our earthly situation does not permit us a favorable point of view. It is only our insertion into the *kosmos* where it is most fully itself—such as, as Kant would have it, obedience to the moral law—that confers authentic freedom upon us.

Chapter 11

Abrahamic Excess

I have characterized the cosmology of the Middle Ages as lying between "Timaeus" and "Abraham." I have described the medieval model along the lines of the *Timaeus*. I will now examine the other side, the Abrahamic model. More specifically, I will see how, among the elements that came from "Abraham," some qualified the synthesis to the point of bending it away from its original direction, whereas others went beyond it, to the point of threatening its coherence, indeed, of foreshadowing its dissolution.

If what has been described as the dominant model, the *Timaeus*, already existed in the pagan world in its main features, and above all in its germinal cell, the appearance of the revealed religions certainly had an influence on that model. After the irruption of biblical revelation into the Hellenized cultural scene, it was necessary to rebalance the concept of the world by taking the new factors into account. This is, for example, what inspired Origen to redefine his understanding of the world, in the process taking stock of the biblical contribution over against the ancient "pagan" concept of *kosmos*.[1]

The Timaean model was not so radically questioned in every medieval religious context. It was without a doubt in the Christian world that it was subjected to the greatest scrutiny. It is there, in fact, that the subversive elements of Abrahamism developed their most virulent form. Let us recall a few of them: creation occurred *ex nihilo*. God alone is the creator, without anything limiting his free will.[2] The world had a beginning in time. The creation of our visible world was preceded by that of an invisible world of forms or angels, who are the intermediaries of a continuing cre-

ation. The visible world is ruled by a teleology focusing on man that reca-
pitulates all of creation in sin, but also in the resurrection of the body, ultimately focusing everything on God alone.[3] It is not impossible that this
radical nature of Christianity explains, at least in part, that it was where it
exercised its influence that the ancient cosmography could be contested.

NEW PROXIMITY

According to "Abraham," as we have seen, the way the world manifests
God is authentic. Unlike what occurs in Gnosticism, nature, even if it
only lets us guess that God is and who he is, does not disfigure him. This
manifestation does however remain burdened by a double inferiority. On
the one hand, by means of direct knowledge, which does not need to
go through the intermediary of nature. That is how the angels know God,
without "needing to raise their eyes toward this firmament and reading it
there."[4] On the other hand, even if one limits oneself to knowledge accessible to man, nature is no longer how God reveals himself the best. The revealed Law or the incarnate Word say much more about God than does the
world. Consequently, the study of the physical universe, without necessarily being ill advised, much less prohibited, loses a good part of its interest. Augustine sums up well the attitude I am attempting to trace here: it
is not necessary to know the structure of the created world, as soon as one
knows the Creator of it. He was consequently considered a "cosmoclast."[5]

The imitation of an order, or one's insertion into that order, must then
give way to the obedience to an "order"—the word itself changes meaning.[6] Ancient Judaism expresses this devaluing in a plastic sense: creation
trembles at the presentation of the gift of the Law, for it feels called upon
to lose its relevance.[7] Revelation circumvents other modes of access to God,
and those become provisional and, at best, almost superfluous. Such is the
case with nature. The Talmudic rabbis did not forbid its study, but their
knowledge of nature relates to more precise fulfillment of the command-
ments of the Law.[8] To be concerned with nature for other reasons becomes,
at best, a waste of time, at worst a virtual apostasy. Thus, he who interrupts
his study (of the Law) to admire a tree or a field commits a sin.[9] The importance, and thus the interest, of natural facts do not come from their dimensions, but from the capacity they have to be involved in the application
of a commandment: birds' nests or the onset of menstruation are central, astronomy and geometry merely dessert. From this angle even the "Timaean"
idea can be found, but through other means. Judaism represents creation

as itself having as its model a Wisdom identified with the Law. To live in accordance with the Law—but while circumventing nature—is thus to achieve the Stoic ideal of an "ordered" life *(homologoumenōs)*.[10]

In Christianity the proximity of God acquired through the gift of the Law is replaced with an even more direct intervention, the incarnation of Christ. This irrevocable event relegates natural regularities to a subordinate level. The relativization of the cosmos is illustrated by events within it, which are the deposits of a definitive suspension of its authority, a suspension that is still awaited. The Incarnation is thus conceived as having had cosmic consequences: the star of the Magi, according to a rather ancient legend, eclipsed the other stars. According to Ignatius of Antioch, "the prince of this world *(aiōn)* was unaware of Mary's virginity and the birth of her child, as well as the death of the Lord, three resounding mysteries that were carried out in the silence of God. How, then, were they manifested to the centuries? A star shone in the sky more brightly than all the others. Its light was unspeakable. Its novelty *(kainotēs)* was shocking *(xenismon pareikhen)*. All the other stars, and the Sun and the Moon, formed a choir around the star, and it projected its light more than all the others. They were disturbed *(tarakhē ēn)*, wondering where this novelty *(kainotēs)*, so different *(anomoios)* from themselves, came from. Then all magic was destroyed, and every connection of malice abolished, ignorance was dissipated, and the ancient kingdom ruined, when God appeared in the form of a man, for a new type of eternal life: what had been decided by God began to come about. And everything was disturbed, for the destruction of death was being prepared."[11] This tale fundamentally only continues a reinterpretation undertaken in Matthew's Gospel itself. In fact, the star observed by the magi was very probably an astral configuration, readable according to an astrological code; it is transposed into a historic event when it begins to guide them toward the manger (2:9)—like the column of smoke that guided Israel. The imagery is akin to Gnosticism, which contains a similar idea, for example in a text cited above.[12] The symbol is rather clear: the Incarnation has cosmic consequences. The logic of the world, as it is expressed and concentrated in magic, is put out of commission. The eternal return of cosmic configurations gives way to the novelty of the event. The legend that the star of Bethlehem obscured the light of the other stars is also found in apocryphal literature.[13] It is found again in Shakespeare: the birth of Jesus stripped magic of its efficacy. Around Christmastide: "No planets strike, / No fairy takes, nor witch hath power to charm."[14]

THEOLOGICAL HEIGHTENING

The entrance of the revealed religions into the sphere of ancient thought (a phenomenon that one might also describe as the reverse, the injection of ancient elements into those religions) had an impact on cosmology.

A. God above the World

Higher than the visible world one finds its Creator,[15] who has absolutely no need of what he has created. Several apologist Fathers, beginning with Athenagoras, then Tertullian and Minucius Felix, even hazarded formulations that God, before creating the world, was his own world.[16] There can therefore be no question of granting the visible world the honors that God alone deserves, even less of allowing the created to direct human life, which should be ruled by God alone. The idea echoes the Old Testament criticism of idolatry, with the qualification that the cult of the stars is assumed to be of greater dignity than the deities of wood or bronze; to adore the work of God is less objectionable than to worship something made by the hand of man. The attitude was already in the Greek Old Testament, which the Christians accepted.[17] It is found again in the Church Fathers and sometimes, as in Origen, with an interesting parallel between the cult of celestial bodies and philosophy, both of which were considered to be sins, but less serious: the one, better than the cult of false gods which are in no way divine; and the other, better than an attachment to absurd and "atheistic" legends.[18]

In any event, the polemics against the cult of the stars was continual, and often tiresome due to its repetitive nature. I will cite only one fairly early text here, by Tatian. It has the advantage of allowing us to detect the central theme of the *Timaeus:* "Such are those demons who defined fate. To become animals *(zōōsis)* was for them to be changed into constellations *(stoikheiōsis)*. Things that crawl on the earth, things that swim in the waters, and fourfooted creatures on the mountains, among whom they lived after the life of heaven was closed to them, to these they paid celestial honours so that they might themselves be thought to dwell in heaven, and might also make rational *(eulogos)* by arrangement of the stars *(astrothesia)* the irrational ordering of life *(alogos . . . politeia)* on earth."[19] The interesting point is the analysis that exposes a desire for self-immortalization underlying the astral cult, in a style akin to the "critique of ideologies." The demons banished from the sky and reduced to living among the animals suggest to men that there are animals in the sky, as well—Aries, Leo, etc. Thus, to lead the life of an animal ceases to be dishonorable. In addition, the stars are believed to confer a rational order on earthly disorder. The fundamental idea of the passage from the *Timaeus* which serves as a unifying thread is discretely suggested and critiqued. The irrational life of demons who became similar to animals lacking reason receives a semblance of order through the intervention of celestial powers.

Origen responds in detail to the accusation of Celsus that the Christians refuse to adore the visible and tangible gods. His argument gathers together several themes that would become classic. He begins by recalling the commandment of Deuteronomy (4:19) that we looked at above.[20] A people who were promised that they would become like the stars (Genesis 15:5, Deuteronomy 1:10) is not about to adore that to which they are to become similar. The perceptible light of the stars is very little next to the eternal intelligible light, all the less so next to the light that is God. It is not a question of disparaging the stars, but of conceiving, above them, a transcendent God to whom the stars themselves pray. The gifts of God descend not only from the stars, but, more decidedly, into the incarnate Son. The stars too, like all creation, aspire to the revelation of the sons of God.[21]

The skies cease to be the highest region of being and are demoted to second rank by the introduction of a higher level. The name Augustine gives this level, a name which is originally biblical, expresses the idea of intensification: the "heavens of heavens" are those compared to which everything, even the visible sky, becomes an earth.[22] All that the flesh perceives is called "earth."[23] The skies are not fundamentally interesting: "We must except these superior heavens that are unknown to us, we who are in the trial of the earth, and who seek them for better or worse through completely human conjectures; except, I say, those heavens, find how they are piled up, what is their number, in what way they differ from each other, of what inhabitants they are peopled, through what organization they are governed, how above it is a sort of continuous hymn in which are harmonized the songs of all who proclaim God, is for us an immense thing *(multum est ad nos)*, let us strive however, to achieve this."[24] Classical cosmology is summed up here in broad strokes: Augustine evokes the question of the number of skies, their distribution, their souls (or angels), as well as his version of the idea of the music of the spheres. But, in the rest of the text, astronomical knowledge, without being exactly dismissed, is avoided in favor of an allegory in which the skies are in fact the holy apostles of God, who cause the words of truth to rain down so that the harvest of the Church might grow.

The descriptions of ascension are crowned, in their classic version, by the accession to the highest in the world. They are henceforth completed by a final breakthrough: no longer beyond the walls of a world, toward a space where an infinite number of other worlds float around, as in Epicureanism, but in the direction of The One who transcends every possible world, God. A practical version of this attitude is provided in the description of the ascension of the supposed author of Psalm 61, Jeduthun: "This Jeduthun, thus, going beyond them [the men through whose intermediary God had spoken], went beyond through the acuity of his valiant mind *(acies mentis),* hardy and sure of himself, he went beyond the earth and everything found on the earth, the air and the clouds whence God spoke. . . . He went beyond, indeed, without being content with the things on the earth, but like an eagle whose flight transports it, every cloud with which every land is covered. . . . He reached something liquid *(aliquid liquidum)* while passing by every creature, in his search for God and spread his soul out over himself; he reached the Principle."[25] In Augustine's personal experience, we have the famous "ecstasy in Ostia." Augustine and Monica also transcended the stars: "Raising ourselves with a more ardent heart toward being itself, we traversed, degree by degree, all the corporeal beings, and the sky itself, whence the sun, the moon, and the stars cast their light on the earth."[26]

We have in a sixth-century Syriac author a perhaps falsely naive description of the ability of the first Adam, before his fall, to climb into the sky and to travel all the paths that are above the upper skies: "So that this other inferior part would not be sad and would not envy the glory of the superior part . . . God . . . gave [Adam] the strength to climb into the sky and to the higher vaults; and there as in the palace of the kingdom and in the celestial vestibules he traveled along all the paths and vast streets which are above the superior skies. Sometimes, for amusement, he descended into the spacious intermediary space between the firmament and the sky, as if he were all alone in a royal palace. He launched himself from there, when he wanted to, toward that terrestrial place, which is below the firmament. He flew in that fiery region, without being burned, he walked above the stars, as on stones in a river, without drowning. He opened himself up, with a true love, within the bosom of his spiritual brothers and all the choirs of the angels. And since from time to time he fixed the gaze of his thoughts on the course of the sun, and on the phases of the moon and the theory of the stars, he did so by means of his brothers [the angels], out of fear that he would cause their envy."[27] The author repeats the common Hellenistic theme of the human spirit's ability to escape the limitations of its body to travel in the blink of an eye over the most distant spaces.[28] But he subjects it to a double transposition: on the one hand, he neutralizes the distinction between the inferior and superior faculties of the soul: between the senses and the intellect, as between man and angel, it is a matter of avoiding envy; on the other hand, and at the same time, he also minimizes the distinction between the different levels of creation: Adam goes from one to the other as if playing a game.

All of creation appears as something tiny compared with the Creator. A more ancient theme, that of the smallness of the tangible compared to the intelligible,[29] is transposed to henceforth bear on the difference between the created and the uncreated. This smallness is illustrated by several images: Saint Benedict is supposed to have grasped the whole of creation in a single ray of sun *(quasi sub uno solis radio collectus);* and all of creation appears, according to a vision of Julian of Norwich, like a little marble in the hand of the Creator.[30]

The devaluing of the created compared to the Creator leads to a relativization of the differences in value within Creation. The most noble of beings are thus vile in relation to God. Thus the new relevance of two verses from Job 15:15 and 25:5: even the sky and the stars are not pure before God. The exegetic tradition is varied. Origen cites the passage within the framework of a discussion on the incorruptibility of the stars.[31] Gregory the Great has a purely moral interpretation: the skies designate the saints, the stars designate the elect.[32] Saadia Gaon explains that only the Creator of souls can know their secret sins, how souls are more noble than the stars and the spheres, and God knows the defects of those bodies, thus, and so on.[33] For Thomas Aquinas, material beings are in any case inferior to spirits, and the brightness of the stars is like darkness compared to the immensity of divine light.[34] And Gersonides, repeating an old argument against the divinity of the stars, mentions the eclipses that prevent the stars from spreading their influence over the world below.[35]

The distinction between the supralunary and the sublunary is relativized. The distance that separates them is small compared to that which separates all of creation from the Creator. Thus a Muslim author, the theologian of the Kalâm al-Bāqīllānī (d. 1012), insists on the fact that the celestial bodies do not have a specific dignity compared to sublunary beings: they are created the same as the others, neither more nor less.[36] One notes a diffuse tendency to refuse the stars the privilege of being animate. The stars, as Albertus Magnus concludes, are inert instruments, they are "deaf and mute."[37]

B. The Equality of Providence

Patristic thought often recalls that God the creator extends his benevolence in the same way over all of creation. The internal differences within creation are thus relativized. This is the case, for example, of the perceptible and the comprehensible. The principle receives a clear formulation from Gregory of Nyssa: "There occurs, through an effect of divine wisdom, a mixture *(mixis)* and a combination *(anakrasis)* of the perceptible and the comprehensible, so that everything can participate *equally (kata to ison)* in the good, and that nothing that exists is excluded from the higher nature. Also, although the sphere associated with comprehensible nature is the subtle and mobile essence, which, through the place that it occupies above the world, derives from the specific character of its nature a profound affinity with the comprehensible, there is produced, by virtue of a superior wisdom, a mixture *(sunanakrasis)* of the comprehensible with perceptible creation, so that nothing in creation is rejected, following the words of the Apostle, nor deprived of participation in divine favors."[38] The text is important in that it sets forth the principle as a nuance applied to a hierarchical cosmology that was otherwise accepted in its entirety.

Within the perceptible world, the same providence is at work in the supralunary as in the sublunary. The Fathers never tired of criticizing Aristotle who, in their opinion—or more likely in the opinion of their sources—excluded providence from the world in which we live, reserving it for the supralunary realm.[39] For them, on the contrary, providence is at work everywhere. Augustine insists on this on several occasions: one must not think that God is involved in celestial things and neglects earthly things.[40] In itself the theme is not originally Christian. It is no doubt of Stoic origin and is also found in Plotinus: "The art [of nature] is wonderful which appears, not only in the divine beings [the stars] but also in the things which one might have supposed providence would have despised for their smallness, for example, the workmanship which produces wonders in rich variety *(hē poikilē thaumatourgia)* in ordinary animals, and the beauty of appearance which extends to the fruits and even the leaves of plants, and their beauty of flower which comes so effortlessly, and their delicacy *(rhadinos)* and variety."[41] However, it is amplified through faith in creation, as seen in Origen: "We know that in its work of creation the divine skill is displayed not only in the heavens and in sun and moon and stars, as it pervades the whole of their mass, but also on earth it operates in the same way in any common substance, so that the bodies of the tiniest

animals have not been neglected by the Creator. Far more is this true of
the souls that exist in them, each soul receiving some special property, the
saving element in the material. It is so in the plants of the soil; in each is an
element of design, affecting its roots and leaves and the fruit it can bear and
the characteristics of its qualities."[42] For Tertullian the smallest flowers, the
tiniest insects display providence as much as do the elements of the world.[43]
Augustine applies the same idea to the flea, as al-Ghazâlî would later do in
the example of the spider.[44] Gregory of Nyssa points out in his *Hexameron*
(written in 380) that beauty designates the internal perfection of every natural being: "Since all that God has done is 'very good,' I assert that one must
see in each being the perfection of the beautiful. The addition of 'very,'
which is an intensifier, clearly shows that the perfection is lacking nothing.
As in the generation of the animals we can see thousands of differences in
the types that they include, whereas we say about each one that the fact of
being 'very beautiful' is applied equally to the universal formula that ap-
proves *(apodokhē)* each being, it is not for all that according to appearance
that approval is given, for otherwise the scolopendra, the toad and the animals that exist in the rotting bogs would benefit from the 'very beautiful.'
In fact, it is not because the divine eye watches the charm of creatures that
the beautiful is defined by the harmony of colors and forms."[45]

This extreme leveling of the gradients within creation has the effect
that the contents of the world are placed on the same level. Each place in
the world being at the same distance from God, the place where man is
found, or might through the impossible be found, is irrelevant: "There is
no difference whether a man is at the centre of the earth or in the highest
reaches of the encompassing sphere, were that possible; the former would
not be distant from God, nor would the latter be any closer."[46]

The final reason for this state of things is given only rarely. It is possible
that it is related to the fundamental fact of man's being-in-the-world.
This is what seems to me to be the foundation of a passage by a Byzantine
monk and theologian, Symeon the New Theologian (d. 1022): "He who
has been able to understand and to see that, drawn out of nothingness *(ek
tou mē ontos parakhtheis)*, he entered naked into the world *(eis ton kosmon
eisēlthen)*, he will recognize his creator; he will fear and love only him, he
will serve him with all his soul and will prefer over him no visible thing;
on the contrary, knowing with a complete certainty *(plērophoria)* that he is
foreign *(xenos)* to all things of the earth and even, it must be said, to those
that are in the sky, he devotes all the intention *(prothesis)* of his soul to the
service of the one who created him. For if he is foreign *(xenos)* to the things
of which he was formed and where he passes his life, how much more

would he be compared to those beings from which he is so distanced by his nature *(phusis)*, by his essence *(ousia)* and his type of life *(diagōgē)!*"[47]

We will not linger here on the consequences deriving from spirituality, to be precise from a certain type of spirituality of affliction *(penthos)* and compunction *(katanuxis)*, that Symeon derives from his description of the human condition; nor on the parallels of the fundamental ideas of the text that his work contains;[48] nor, finally, on the sources of those ideas: the idea of nakedness upon entering and leaving the world comes from Job (1:21); that of the world as a theater, from Hellenistic philosophy. What appears unique and fundamental in the text just quoted is the way in which Symeon derives consequences from man's being-in-the-world, with which he begins his sermon: we enter into the world and we enter it naked. Nakedness is not just an absence of clothing. It symbolizes foremost the fact that we bring nothing into the world and take nothing out of it—and therefore, that nothing in the world belongs to us; above all it seems to me that it symbolizes the fact that the world provides nothing to us—and therefore, that nothing of us belongs to the world. Because all that we might bring to the world would come from "another" world, would be the remains of another stage of the world, so that our coming into the world and our leaving it would not be radical events. But we do not fall from a superior level of the world to an inferior level. We enter into the world by coming out of nothingness, and thus from nowhere. This relativizes a potential belonging, through kinship *(sungeneia)*, with any part whatsoever of the contents of the world, even the most elevated. One can henceforth renounce any natural connection with the stars. It is not from them that we have fallen, but from higher up and outside the world, to which we are therefore fundamentally foreign. The difference between our proximity with the earth, from which our body is drawn and on which we live, and our distancing with regard to the stars is thus, in the end, without meaning. The only distance that counts is that which, separating us from the Creator, also enables us to cross it through spiritual life.

C. The Dignity of Man

According to the Abrahamic religions, the powers held by celestial realities over man are relativized. In Judaism this is true above all for the people of Israel. This people, unlike pagan nations, is not placed under the dominion of celestial bodies, but is under the direct jurisdiction of God. And further, one might say that those celestial powers are completely obliterated, since non-Jews are not men in the strictest sense of the term.[49] Consequently, no constellation exercises any influence over Israel *(eyn mazzal le-Yisra'el).*[50] There is a midrash that illustrates this superiority strikingly. Scripture says "And he [God] brought him [Abraham] outside and said, 'Look toward heaven!'" (Genesis 15:5). The midrash understands "outside" to mean "above the celestial vault." In this way, Abraham, who is rendered larger than the stars, watches them from above, looking down on them.[51]

For Christianity, man is ipso facto of greater dignity than the world. And even, than the world where it is most sovereignly cosmic, namely, the celestial bodies. In the modern era the role played by Christianity is seen well by Francis Bacon: "And therefore therein the heathen opinion differeth from the sacred truth; for they supposed the world to be the image of God, and man to be an extract or compendious image of the world; but the scriptures never vouchsafe to attribute to the world that honour, as to be the image of God, but only 'the work of his hands'; neither do they speak of any other image of God, but man."[52] Origen demotes the stars as compared to human freedom.[53] The polemic against astrology, begun by the pagans, takes a new turn. The accent is no longer on the uncertainty of its predictions or, assuming they are accurate, on the uselessness of the acquired knowledge. It is henceforth on the one hand on the idolatry of the stars that it assumes, and, on the other, on the fact that nothing can control man except God.[54] Gregory of Nyssa rises up against the idea of a microcosm: man is not in the image of the physical world, but of God alone. Being the image of the universe is equally true for the mice and the mosquitoes; man is as unknowable as the God on whose model he is created.[55]

Leo the Great formulates the idea of human dignity by contrasting it to the idea of the world: "Wake up, then, man, and recognize the dignity of your nature! Remember that you were created in God's image, an image that, although corrupted through Adam, has been restored through Christ! Use as you must the visible creatures, just as you use the land, the sea, the sky, the air, the springs and rivers, and all that in them is beautiful and admirable, bring it in praise of the glory of the Creator. Do not devote yourself to that shining star that causes the joy of the birds and the snakes, the wild beasts and tame animals, flies and worms. . . . If, indeed, we are the temple of God, and if the Spirit of God lives in us, what every faithful one carries in his soul has more value than what one admires in the sky *(plus est quod fidelis quisque in suo habet animo, quam quod miratur in caelo).*"[56]

In the twelfth century an anonymous Cistercian wrote: "This entire world cannot be valued at the price of a single soul." The idea was repeated later by John of the Cross, among others: "A single thought by man is worth more than the entire world; this is why God alone is worthy of him."

And by Pascal: "All the bodies, the firmament, the stars, the earth and its kingdoms, are not worth the least of the spirits; for it knows all that, and itself; and the bodies know nothing."[57]

This accent placed on the dignity of man has already been noted many times, and has had consequences in all realms of culture. Notably, it made possiblewhat is called "Western realism." In the realm of literature, prosaic reality, from the simple fact that it is human, becomes interesting in itself and thus worthy of being dealt with in higher style. In the visual arts, the most humble objects, in that they bear the mark of a human activity or need, become worthy of interest. A loaf of bread, a drop of milk spilt from a jug, or a peeled lemon can shine with a light that one might believe was reserved for the supralunary, "taken from the holy hearth of primitive rays." Finally, "particular attention is given to the body of man, without that body, in order to be beautiful, needing to be idealized (as the Greek fashion) or stylized (in the Asian, African, or Mesoamerican fashion)."[58]

D. A Microcosm Reversed

This superior value is sometimes translated into grand images relating to the grandeur of space. Hellenistic thinkers, as we have seen, had insisted on the rapidity of the human mind which in an instant travels over unimaginable distances.[59] The idea is repeated by al-Ghazâlî, who concludes that the human heart is larger than the world, for it contains it all: in the human heart, the entire world is nothing more than an atom in the sea.[60]

It happens that Christian authors reversed the notion of the correspondence between two worlds, one large and one small, in favor of man. Whereas usually man is the smaller of the two worlds and he is lodged, as one might expect, within the larger one, a deeper relationship is expressed through the paradox stating that it is man who is the bigger world. The formula is attempted, perhaps for the first time, by Gregory of Nazianzus. God created man "like a large world in the small one."[61] The rest of the passage multiplies the contrasts and oxymorons employed to express the double nature of man, leaving one to guess the source of the "grandeur" of man, grandeur being the ability he has to introduce the comprehensible into the perceptible, the superior into the inferior, thus causing the sensible to burst, incapable of containing what transcends it. In this way, we leave the physical idea of the world. The paradox holds only at this price: it is necessary to change the "order" (in Pascal's sense) so that the small can appear as such and it can become the location of the large—or of its bearer, man.

After Gregory, the formula was adopted by writers such as Nicetas

Stethatos: using a play on words that is difficult to translate, the author explains that man, in his original state before the fall, is "another world, the ornament of the world *(kosmou kosmos heteros)*, better and more elevated, visible and comprehensible, mortal and immortal, an intermediary between greatness and baseness. . . . One must also consider how, as a new world, man was created better and more elevated than the world and how, in a small world, he appears big."[62] Nicetas explains this through a parallel between the constituents of the visible world and ethical and intellectual virtues: the intelligible "world" is not that of ideas, but, the word maintaining its original sense of order, the harmonious edifice of a virtuous soul. "It is thus that the world was built by God—the big world—in the midst of this visible and small [world]; in it . . . the reasonable was established in the non-reasonable; the comprehensible in the apparent and the perceptible; the divine, the immortal and the most elevated, in the corruptible and the base."[63] Nicetas recognizes the influence of Gregory, whom he cites: "Isn't it true that this world is considered small by Gregory . . . , as we ourselves think with truth, and that we, in this world, we are big, we who have been created in God's image, and that, in both, paradoxically, the same elements compete in the formation and constitution of a body that is specifically one."[64] This faithfulness is all the more remarkable in that others reproduced the passage of Gregory, but while believing they were correcting the paradoxical expression. They thus fall within the traditional doctrine. This is what John of Damascus did, for example.[65]

THE HISTORICIZING OF COSMOLOGY

The concept of world until the revealed religions belonged in the realm of nature.[66] With those religions it entered into the realm of history.[67] Consequently, it was henceforth no longer a pleonasm to speak of the "natural world." Conversely, it was no longer absurd to apply to the world the determination that was classically contrasted to that of nature, that of "position" *(thesis)*, to speak of a "positive" or conventional world (in the sense that one speaks of positive laws). This is what the Isma'ili thinker Abū Ya'qūb al-Sijistānī (d. ca. 972) does when he mentions the existence, between the two worlds of nature and the intellect, of what would have been an oxymoron for the Ancients: a "world of position" or "positive world" *('ālam al-waḍ'* or *'ālam wad'ī).*[68]

Indeed, the way in which man attains the good (or wisdom) is henceforth in history. The intervention of God in history is considered more interesting, more "admirable" than creation, and, in any case, as having cost

God greater effort.[69] Man's salvation occurs in history; the question of man's salvation has no analogy in nature: nothing in nature needs to be "saved."[70] The idea of harmony, which was synchronic in the beginning, underwent a transposition into the diachronic; thus Augustine conceives of the history of salvation on the model of a poem, that is, a song. The harmony that governed the regular return of celestial phenomena is henceforth that of an irreversible history.[71] A change in the vocabulary is the sign and the seal of this: the world can henceforth also be called by a temporal name, that of *saeculum*.[72] The world thus shares the rhythms of the history of salvation. Cosmic wisdom becomes a secular wisdom.

A. The Fall

Biblical and rabbinic Judaism conceive of a certain participation of the phenomena of the universe in the events of history, at least wherever the destiny of Israel is concerned.[73] But it does not seem, for all that, that nature changes its status as being. In Christianity, on the other hand, the physical world is supposed to have been led along with man into the process of the fall and redemption.[74] Alongside the tendency to raise the terrestrial to the level of the celestial by showing that the same providence is at work there, another tendency appears, which one might consider the opposite movement. The idea comes from a literal interpretation of Paul's passage mentioning the impatient awaiting *(apokaradokia)* of Creation which, subjected to vanity, also awaits deliverance (Romans 8:20f.). The word "creation" *(ktisis)* is understood as meaning the totality of the physical universe, including the celestial bodies. To that end the passages from Job cited above enable those bodies to be encompassed in the common lot, and, consequently, to relativize the difference that raises them above our terrestrial world.

The idea is very clear in Origen: the entire physical universe, and at its head the celestial bodies, is brought into the history of Salvation. Christ did not suffer death only for man, but for all rational creatures. Among these are the celestial bodies which one might think also sinned, since the Scriptures say that they are not pure before God (Job 25:5). The stars are in fact endowed with a freedom that enables them to praise God; they can therefore also sin. What the stars must be redeemed from is the captivity of their soul in a body.[75] Whence this extraordinary conclusion, which opposes the ancient way of seeing things: we must *pray for the stars*.[76]

The Alexandrians were not the only ones to support this idea. Theophilus of Antioch held it with regard to the wild animals who were believed to have sinned at the same time as man. They are similar to slaves who imitate the depraved life of their master. When man is restored, they will rediscover their peaceful nature *(hēmerotēs)*.[77] Ambrose of Milan explains in detail how the celestial bodies are also subject to vanity.[78] In particular he explains what that subjection consists of: their light is obscured by the clouds, indeed are periodically subject to eclipses. They, too, will pass. But it will be to finally rest in the glory of the sons of God.

The consequence is that nature is led into the same adventure as man. These ties of solidarity makes man and the higher creatures "brothers." Francis of Assisi does not hesitate to call the sun "brother" in his famous *Canticle*.[79] We are equally distant from the Gnostics, who refused to worship the sun and called the vilest men "brothers," and from Plotinus, who was shocked by that.[80]

B. The End

This inversion is even clearer in what concerns the end: nature is perhaps destined to be relieved by a mode of being that will render it superfluous. Its history will have an end. Apocalyptic literature, recapitulated in the New Testament, says that the world "passes."[81] The first Christians even prayed: "Let grace *(kharis)* come and let this world pass *(pareltheto)*."[82] But the nature of what was thus to pass remained ambiguous: was it a matter of a mode of being or of all of creation? The question was disputed throughout the Middle Ages.[83] Augustine seems literally to repeat the New Testament's assertions on the final conflagration.[84] He distinguishes between the external form of the world, which passes, according to Paul, and its nature, which will never pass. Its elements will change their qualities and will adapt them to those of our bodies, which will henceforth be immortal.[85] Maximus the Confessor speaks of a renewal of the entire universe: like man, the macrocosm will have to pass through a death and a resurrection.[86] Anselm discretely suggests the necessity of a complete renovation.[87] Bonaventure imagines a Christian version of the Stoic conflagration: the terrestrial world will be transformed by the fire that will eliminate all that is provisional, leaving only the definitive.[88] Dante posits as a principle that all that is made by God without an intermediary is eternal, thus repeating a distinction taken from the *Timaeus*.[89] Thomas Aquinas and Bonaventure explain that, once the number of the elect has been reached, the movement of the celestial spheres will cease. Bonaventure has a superb image: the celestial revolutions will stop the way one stops the grinding stone once the knife is sharpened.[90] Here we have a wonderful example of the way in which the cyclical temporality of cosmic regularities is placed, in relation to the linear course of history, in a situation of subordination that is not only theoretical but also practical: the astronomical mechanism is the instrument of a plan for salvation. Bonaventure is not the first writer where we find an idea of this kind, since it is also in Robert Grosseteste.[91] In any case, the idea of the stopping of celestial revolutions is found again later, in the sixteenth century, for example in Rabelais.[92]

In Judaism, the idea of the end of the world is neutral. The Bible speaks emphatically about its creation, but is much less clear about its possible end. On the contrary, Ecclesiastes asserts that what God does persists throughout eternity (3:14). The Jewish philosophers are also ambiguous.[93] Greek philosophy unanimously assumes that all that has a beginning must also have an end. Plato has a model for the eternity of what has come into being: the derivative, willed eternity of what has been well fitted together and which the Demiurge could not wish to destroy.[94] Philoponus assumes that each being tends to slide *(exolisthainein),* experiencing a deviation *(parektropē)* toward nothingness when the force that maintains it is relaxed.[95] Saadia Gaon follows him. Maimonides has a doctrine akin to that of the *Timaeus:* the universe being perfect, it contains no internal cause of corruption.[96] Gersonides attempts to prove philosophically that the indestructibility of the universe is not only the result of divine will, but is a necessity that comes out of it. The world cannot be destroyed naturally, because the sublunary participates in the indestructibility of the celestial bodies that influence it; nor by the will of God, who would have no reason to do so.[97] For Crescas, if it is impossible for the world to be annihilated, it is possible that it makes way for another world, if that world represents a passage to the most perfect. It seems that this change affects only the world below, as the celestial bodies remain immutable.[98] Abravanel defends a strong version of destructibility, perhaps linked to his Messianism. The celestial bodies are corruptible because they are composite. Their destruction can occur suddenly, and it is rendered plausible by signs of senescence: the average duration of human life is becoming shorter; certain medicines, once all-powerful, have lost their effectiveness. The reason compatible with divine goodness for a destruction could be to prove that God is not identical to the universe.[99]

Islam asserts without hesitation that the world will end. The Koran, above all in the initial Meccan suras, multiplies eschatological descriptions. In a word, very frequently cited: "All things shall perish except [His face]" (28:88). The power of Allah is seen best in his ability to annihilate. Theologians do not question Koranic assertions. At the very most they qualify them, by drawing up increasingly lengthy lists of exceptions. These even include the tailbone (the sacrum), which was believed to survive the destruction of the human body and constitute something like the seed of its resurrection, according to a tradition that has already been noted in Judaism.[100]

C. Incompleteness

While awaiting this transfiguration, nature appears botched and incomplete. An Epicurean theme can be recognized, which has already been pointed out.[101] But that which, according to Epicurus, was related to the natural can be reinterpreted within the historicization of the whole: the world was seen as *imperfect;* it henceforth appears as *temporary.* In addition, the tone of this incompleteness changed: what was a sign of fragility, indeed, the announcement of an imminent decomposition, is henceforth the promise of progress, indeed, of redemption. This implies that the world is incomplete in a positive sense, in that it is open to human activity, which it calls upon and awaits. Marcus Aurelius had already indicated in passing that the activity of laboring insects such as ants or bees contribute to putting their little worlds in order, or—the text is ambiguous—to putting the larger world, that which relates to them, in order *(to kath 'hautas sunkosmousas kosmon).*[102] In Christianity the role of man in creation appears in a new way. One can interpret in this sense the fact that the biblical God places Adam in the garden of Eden "to till it and keep it" (Genesis 2:15). The Church Fathers were thus at the origin of a valuing of work; this was new compared to a certain aristocratic sensibility in pagan Antiquity, which reserved work for slaves and associated liberal activity to leisure alone. Some derived from this valuing of work a renewal of the anthropology that sometimes went as far as an implicit redefinition of man's essence: for man, to be the mediator between the sensible and the intelligible is no longer only the static definition of a degree of being, but, in a dynamic perspective, an activity, a task, a job. It is thus that Maximus the Confessor, in a formula that was cited several times by Johannes Scotus Eriugena, speaks of man as a workshop *(ergastērion, officina)* in which the synthesis of the opposites that divide creation is effected.[103]

However, the incompleteness that this view presupposes as regards reality is not clearly stressed. I have found an example of the notion only in the modern era, where it has primarily a more somber tone. Thus Malebranche writes: "The present world is a neglected work. It is the dwelling of sinners, it was necessary that disorder obtain there. Man is not such as God made him: it was thus necessary that he inhabit ruins and that the earth that he cultivates is only the debris of a more perfect world. Those points of rocks in the middle of the seas, and those rocky coasts that surround them show enough that now the Ocean is flooding the broken land. . . . Thus the present world considered in itself is not a work where God's wisdom appears as it truly is."[104] Malebranche bases his thinking on ancient observations, already found in Aristotle, on the mutability of the sublunary. Epicureanism saw it as an argument against teleology. Instead of repeating the classical response, Stoic, for example, Malebranche accepts the factual premise but transposes it onto another register. It is first that of the sensibility of the classical age, which rejects anything that is "neglected"—the word signifies here "made without care": we are before the English garden and the cult of nonchalant spontaneity. This was above all a biblical sensibility, and it is as if Malebranche were generalizing the curse of Genesis (3:17ff.) which was only concerned with agriculture. In this way he enters into a debate that was raging in seventeenth-century England.[105]

And a century later we again find the idea in Schelling: "Doesn't everything announce a life that has foundered? . . . Who would believe that the floods that . . . have traced these valleys and have in this way left in our mountains so many marine creatures, that they all act following an inner law? Who will agree that it is a divine hand that has piled up heavy rocky masses on slippery clay, so that they then slide down and bury the peaceful valleys, scattered with human habitations, or with happy strollers, in a horrifying ruin? Oh! It is not these ruins of an ancient human glory, for which the curious explore the deserts . . . , that are the true ruins; *the entire earth is a huge ruin*, where beasts live like ghosts and men like spirits, and in which many forces and hidden treasures are held as if by invisible powers or by a sorcerer's charm."[106] Schelling adds new, indeed contemporary, elements to the ancient file. It is possible that the emphasis on fossils exhibits a trace of the paleontology of the time. One might think for example of Georges Cuvier. Cuvier, born in Montbéliard, a town that belonged to Württemberg until 1793, was, moreover, in the seminary at Tübingen with Schelling and his two famous co-disciples. He developed his idea on the revolutions of the globe beginning in 1812. The allusion to archaeology perhaps refers to Volney, whose *Ruines* dates from 1791. The end of the text, through its contents as well as through its overall approach, recalls a famous passage from *Werther* to which I will return.[107] The overall context is different, however: it is foremost a question of a meditation on original sin and on the resulting subjugation of all creation, with a clear and repeated allusion to Romans 8:19–21, a meditation itself oriented toward magic. The final image of hypnotic lethargy invites one to seek the means of removing the spell and putting nature back in motion. We will later see how this was able to be imagined.[108]

CONTEMPLATION AS A THEOLOGICAL EXERCISE

All these revolutions in cosmography induced a new way to use the world. The world ceased to be the most elevated object of contemplation. One could *descend* to the contemplation of nature.[109]

A. Knowledge

The study of the skies does not lead directly to imitation of the skies, but to knowledge of their Creator. The Church Fathers knew of the contemplation of nature *(theōria phusikē)*. In Islam, the idea, already Koranic, was amply developed by al-Ghazâlî.[110] In Judaism, Bahya ibn Paquda devotes a chapter of his treatise on spirituality to it, a treatise that, moreover, has the same sources as Ghazâlî.[111] In Christianity, Albertus Magnus has a formula of magnificent concision: "The entire world is a theology for man *(Totus ... mundus theologia est homini)*."[112] The idea is illustrated by the recurrent metaphor of the book that enables one to know the mind of its author.[113] A living book whose interpretation has more value than do books written on parchment: "The trees and the rocks will teach you more than you could ever learn from professors."[114] Meister Eckehart insists on the progressive aspect of this knowledge. The world is a training ground: "If the soul were capable of knowing God completely, as the angels are, it would never have entered into bodies. If it were able to know God without the world, the world would not have been created for it. It is for that reason that the world was created for the soul, so that the eye of the soul is exercised *(geü-bet)* and reinforced, so that it is capable of enduring the divine light."[115]

In Islamic lands and the Judeo-Arabic literature, the theme enters into a complex strategy that is also intended to legitimate the practice of philosophy in the eyes of religious law. It is a matter of showing that religious sources recommend, indeed, order the practice of philosophy.[116] Thus Averroes, in the *Decisive Treatise*, interprets a certain number of Koranic passages in this way. Elsewhere he does not hesitate to give them a scientific content. And here too, the figure of Abraham renders good service: "To contemplate *(ițțilā')* the various actions of the heavenly bodies is contemplating the kingdom of heaven, which Abraham [!] contemplated, according to the words of the Koran: Thus did we show Abraham the kingdom of heaven and of the earth, that he should be one of those who are sure."[117]

Among the Jews, Maimonides expresses this idea in the *Mishneh Torah:* "And what is the way that will lead to the love of Him and the fear of Him? When a person contemplates *(hitbōnen)* His great and wondrous works and creatures and from them obtains a glimpse of His wisdom which is incomparable and infinite, he will straightway love Him, praise Him, glorify Him, and long with an exceeding longing to know His great name."[118] The *Guide of the Perplexed* posits the principle: "There is, moreover, no way to apprehend Him except it be through the things He has made *(maṣnūʿāt);* for they are indicative of His existence and of what ought to be believed about Him."[119] The doctrine of his earlier talmudic work is recalled: "We have already explained in *Mishneh Torah* that this *love* [required in Deuteronomy 6:15] becomes valid *(taṣiḥḥu)* only through the apprehension of the whole of being as it is and through the consideration of His [God's] wisdom as it is manifested in it."[120] "It is therefore indispensable *(ḍarūra)* to consider *(iʿtibār)* all beings as they really are."[121] We can note an important addition: whereas the *Mishneh Torah* spoke of considering the creatures, here it is a question of considering all that exists. This consideration encompasses the most subtle details of the science of nature, above all astronomy, in the knowledge of the Creator: "As for the matters pertaining to the astronomy of the spheres *(al-hayʾat al-falakiyya)* [the celestial phenomena] and to natural science, I do not consider that you should have any difficulty in grasping that those are matters necessary for the apprehension of the relation of the world to God's governance as this relation is in truth and not according to imaginings."[122] Maimonides thus legitimizes the practice of physics by making it equal to a meditation on the Law. Indeed, he devalues the level of knowledge of God attained by specialists in religious law, comparing them with those "who direct all the acts of their intellect toward an examination of the beings with a view to drawing from them proof with regard to Him, so as to know His governance of them in whatever way it is possible."[123]

Within the framework of his point of view, which is very original, indeed, atypical, to the point that it attracted the sarcasm of Crescas, Gersonides attributes to physics a sort of beatifying function: the more we know the world, the more we realize the concepts contained in the active intellect, the more we enlarge that part of us that will know immortality.[124]

The problem is not raised in exactly the same way in Christianity. The overall context is inverted here: it is rather a question of justifying theology before the tribunal of philosophy. But as for the content, Thomas Aquinas develops the same doctrine. The issue is worked out in a question presented quite formally at the beginning of the second part of the *Summa contra gentiles:* "That the consideration *(consideratio)* of creatures is useful for the instruction of the faith."[125] It enables us, in fact, positively, to have a just idea of the attributes of God. Chapter 2 thus lists his wisdom, his power, his goodness. In addition, consideration of the created renders us in some way similar to God, insofar as we acquire knowledge that resembles his. Chapter 3 considers the same issue in a negative sense. Eliminating the errors about creatures enables us to avoid errors about God: to mistake him for a body, to attribute to creatures effects that God alone can produce, to take away from God effects that are his responsibility. A fourth reason is particularly interesting: ignorance of the nature of things, and consequently of his own place in the universe, leads man to be mistaken about himself and to believe himself inferior to creatures to which he is in reality superior. Knowledge of nature thus makes human dignity rest upon a solid foundation; physics and anthropology communicate directly: "Man, who through faith moves toward God as toward his ultimate end, by the fact that he is unaware of the nature of things and subsequently the rank that he occupies in the universe *(gradus sui ordinis in universo)*, thinks that he is subject to certain creatures to which he is in fact superior, as is manifest in those who submit the wills of men to the stars . . . , in those who assume that the angels are the creators of the souls, that the souls of men are mortal, and all that deviates from human dignity *(hominum derogant dignitati)*."[126] In conclusion, Thomas rejects the beliefs of those for whom knowledge of creatures is unnecessary.

Here we see the development of an original model for using the world. It is remarkable that Thomas constructs this model by overturning the authorities he invokes, such as Augustine. Augustine, however, in a famous passage, had implicitly excluded the physical universe from subjects deserving an authentic interest, these being reduced to two, God and the soul.[127] And, as the editors indicate in a note, Thomas refers to a passage in the book on the origin of the soul.[128] Augustine says in fact that there are things about which not only is it not a sin to ignore them, but that it is one to investigate them, and that among them is not only that which concerns God, but that which concerns our soul—such as, indeed, its origin. If the text that Thomas was reading was the same as ours, he then demonstrates, with the greatest discretion, a nonchalance toward its "authority" that is ultimately rather typical of true Scholasticism (as distinguished from the dark legend attached to that adjective): a citation by the great figure of patristic literature, taken quite exactly in its opposite meaning, serves to hide a new attitude. This attitude comes much less from the Latin tradition than from Greek knowledge, having come from the Arab world. It happens, moreover, that Thomas cites the true sources from which he borrows, among them Maimonides, who holds an important place.[129]

The goal of knowledge of the world is not the technical transformation of the world, as in Francis Bacon or Descartes. Nor does it aim to imitate it, as in the dominant Platonic (or Timaean) model. Nor, finally, is the world questioned, as by Thomas's master, Albertus Magnus, to learn about its Creator. The theological element is indirect here. It is a question rather of keeping one's distance with regard to the world and of eliminating one's fear of the stars, as is indicated by the biblical quotation: "Nor be dismayed at the signs of the heavens because [the pagans] are dismayed at them" (Jeremiah 10:2)—which connects Thomas Aquinas to Epicurus—strange bedfellows! However, the error that is to be eradicated here is not the ethical relevance of the world, but the confusion of one of its parts with another. This is why it is not a question of creating an interworld for oneself and, even less, of course, of dreaming of an evasion of it in the Gnostic fashion. It is a question of inhabiting the world correctly. We can see this by taking the opposite of the three errors that Thomas indicates. The world is inhabited rightly by the one who knows how to orient himself there—through his freedom, without being held on a leash by the stars; where he comes from—from God, not the angels; and where he is going—toward God, not nothingness. To be mistaken about the structure of the world is therefore also to be mistaken about the nature of the one who inhabits it. "Physics" is therefore not only an indirect theology, but even more decidedly, perhaps, an indirect anthropology.

B. Imitation

The object of imitation of the world is no longer the regular movement of the world, but the obedience to divine will to which the world bears witness. The idea that the relationship of created to creator is a relationship of obedience is a biblical idea, found in the book of Baruch.[130] It is repeated by an apostolic Father, Clement of Rome: "The heavens that move under his government obey him in peace. The day and the night accomplish the course that God has assigned to them, without disturbing each other. The sun, the moon, and the choirs of stars evolve according to his order, in agreement, within the limits that are fixed for them, without ever going beyond them. The earth, filled with fruit, submissive to his will, raises up food in abundance in favorable seasons . . . ; it does not protest, it changes nothing of the rules he has set. The same rules maintain the unfathomable laws that govern the abysses and the indescribable laws that govern the subterranean world. The cavity of the sea . . . does not cross the barriers by which it has been surrounded, but it acts according to the orders that it has received. . . . The ocean . . . and the worlds that are beyond are directed by the same orders of the Master."[131] The context is an exhortation to concord, as in a passage by Dio Chrysostom cited above.[132] Clement repeats the common theme, attested in particular in Stoicism, of the harmony of the world. But the emphasis, at least in the part of the text I have just quoted, is changed from the horizontal to the vertical: it is much less about the harmony of the parts of the world with each other than about what renders it possible, that is, the obedience of creatures to their Creator. It is their common obedience to a single and sole God that assures the harmony of relationships that they form among them.

The same idea is found in Ignatius Loyola: "Just as, in the celestial bodies, so that the inferior receives the movement or influence of its superior, it is necessary that it be subject and subordinate to it in such a way that a body be with another in a relationship of conformity and order; similarly, when a rational creature is placed in motion by another (which is done through obedience), it is necessary that the one that is moved be subject or subordinate, for it to receive the influence and the virtue of the one that moves. And this submission does not occur without conformity to the superior of the understanding and will of the inferior."[133] A decade after Copernicus, the model remained the celestial bodies and the influences that cascaded from one sphere to another, then from the supralunary to the sublunary.

The idea is also found in the Islamic realm, as in the first of the Falāsifa, al-Kindī, who devotes a treatise to explain the way in which the most distant body (the First Moved) bows down before God and is subject to him. Or in Avicenna, for whom the stars move in order to imitate the First. The notion assumes that all of nature is conceived as being dependent on divine will and acting "in the mode of servitude" *('alā sabīl al-tashīr)*.[134]

The Abrahamic model entails a shift in the idea of imitation, which thus changes its object: the world being the work of God, imitation of the world leads to imitation of divine attributes, to the point that the first imitation is no longer an end in itself. The idea is already in al-Kindī, who continues the definition of philosophy given in the *Theaetetus:* "[the Ancients] also defined it [philosophy] by its action. Thus they said: philosophy is the imitation of the *actions* of God . . . insofar as man is capable of doing so. They meant that man be perfect in virtue."[135] Comparison of the texts of the "Philosopher of the Arabs" with those of the Neoplatonic commentators Elias and David show an interesting shift in the definitions of philosophy that they provide. Four are common: "love of wisdom," "concern about death" *(meletē thanatou),* "art of arts or wisdom of wisdoms," "knowledge of divine and human things." On the other hand, an important nuance separates two versions of the same definition: where Elias, copying Plato, mentions the imitation of God, Kindī speaks of the imitation of God's *actions.* Finally, in the place of a "knowledge of things that are" of which Elias speaks, Kindi substitutes a "knowledge of self."

The idea is found in Saadia Gaon. It is implicit in Farabi, in the texts cited above: the perfect legislator imitates the work of the Creator by instituting a city that resembles that work. Finally, it is very probably found, again only implicitly, in Maimonides.[136]

C. Knowledge of Self

The point of departure for knowledge of God henceforth changes. Basil of Caesarea places knowledge of the external world and knowledge of self on the same level: "The sky and the earth are no more *(ou mallon)* able to make us know God than is our own constitution, for him who studies himself with intelligence."[137] We can also go further and clearly favor the knowledge that the soul has of itself in relation to that of nature. We saw the development of this idea above in Philo.[138] According to a Neoplatonic formula, which also passed into the Arab world: "He who knows himself knows all things."[139] In the Middle Ages this was sometimes modified on an essential point. Indeed, the object of which knowledge passes through knowledge of the soul is henceforth God.[140] Clement of Alexandria had introduced the formula into Christianity.[141] Islam even attributes it to Muhammad: "He who knows himself [or: who knows his soul] knows his Lord *(man 'arafa nafsahu fa-qad 'arafa rabbahu)."*[142] Judaism adopts the formula, which it perhaps borrowed from al-Ghazâlî.[143] This is the same Ghazâlî who traces the progress of ascension. One must begin below, with oneself; one must then consider the earth and raise oneself while passing through the air, the atmosphere, the seven skies, the throne, the angels, to Allah.[144]

But it was almost only in Christianity that a Socratism developed. There naturally resulted a critique of curiosity, of an eagerness to know without discernment *(curiositas).*[145] This critique does not bear on knowledge as such, since there exists a legitimate desire to know what deserves to be known *(studiositas).* But it condemns the forgetting of the most necessary knowledge, that which alone enables moral reform. Knowledge of the mysteries of nature is not equal to knowledge of oneself.[146] And this critique is also encountered almost exclusively in the Christian domain, to such a degree that the very term "curiosity" does not have an equivalent with a pejorative connotation in Hebrew or Arabic.[147]

COSMOLOGICAL CONSEQUENCES OF THEOLOGY

The new faith did not have a direct cosmological consequence. To assert that the world is created is not to decide on the structure of that which is created. One can however assume that the idea of creation was, indirectly, to induce those who admitted it to think of the way the world *is* made as a function of the way it *was* made. One has been able to note certain places where theology has exercised an influence on cosmography. But in some cases the modifications brought to the image of the world did not truly relate to cosmography, but rather to theology. Such is the case with the empyrean.[148] To the edifice of the stacked spheres, accessible to sight or to astronomical reasoning, the Christian theologians added the sphere postulated by faith. This sphere appears in the Pseudo–Hugh of Saint-Victor and again in Alain of Lille, Thomas Aquinas, and Dante. But the reasons for admitting it are exclusively theological and do not relate to the relationship to the physical universe that concerns us here. The same is true of considerations such as those of Sohravardi, who abandons the distinction between sublunary and supralunary because he moves the principal barrier: it is henceforth the sphere of the fixed stars that separates the world of pure light from that of darkened light.[149]

A. A Single Matter

The clearest example of the new influence is no doubt the distinction between two matters, supralunary (ether, *quinta essentia*) and sublunary (the four elements). The sublunary served above all, as we have seen,[150] to resolve a purely cosmographic problem: how is it that the stars follow a circular motion whereas heavy bodies fall and light bodies rise on a straight trajectory? Aristotle's response, which indeed invokes this difference between two matters, each endowed with its own motion, won out at the beginning of the period we are looking at here. But it never totally eliminated other hypotheses. This is even more so among independent thinkers who pay little attention to Aristotle's authority. Thus Râzî, a free-thinker in philosophical as well as religious matters, explains the heaviness and the lightness of bodies by the greater or lesser quantity of empty intervals between the atoms, thus breaking with the traditional explanation. Furthermore, he draws attention to the presence, even within the sublunary domain, of mo-

tions that spontaneously take on a circular form, whereas they nevertheless affect well-known elements, such as boiling water or molten gold.[151]

The earliest representative of the medieval protestation against Aristotle
is no doubt John Philoponus,[152] who is perhaps also its historical source, as
was believed in the Middle Ages in any event by Aristotelians of strict ob-
servance such as Farabi, Avicenna, Ibn Bājja, or Maimonides, who made
him their *bête noire*.[153] Philoponus was Christian by birth, it seems. Granted,
he does not draw a specific cosmography directly from biblical texts whose
authority he recognizes. And Xenarchus, who seems to have been the first
to undertake a systematic critique of the notion of ether, predates Christianity.[154] But we have no difficulty identifying the religious background that
influenced the critique: the idea of creation places the sky on the same level
as the rest of the created. "God is present in an equal way in all things and
substances in nature, in the heavens and on the earth. The heavens no longer
have any favored position."[155] Philoponus even asserts, against Theodore of
Mopsuestia, that the stars are not guided by the angels. He thus brings to
its end the critique by the prophets of Israel of the worship of the stars and
completes a radical desacralization of the world. The sky is in no way eternal. It is simply very durable. Moreover, sublunary beings can also last for
a very long time, such as precious stones, mountains, and . . . elephants.[156]

A view of the world that considers it a single entity fits well with the
leveling introduced by the idea of creation that is then transposed from the
ontological to the physical. Philoponus seems not to have understood this
from the outset, since a critique of the fifth element is not present at the
beginning of his writings, but for the first time in his book against Proclus,
which probably dates from 529. It forces a global attack against the physics
of Aristotle which, itself highly coherent, could not be amended on certain points of detail alone. If one dispenses with the fifth element, one
must still provide alternative explanations for the phenomena it explained.
It would therefore be necessary, for example, to explain the movement of
projectiles, and, already, the heat that emanates from the stars and, in first
place, from the sun. Ancient physics explained this only by the rubbing of
the sphere that carries it, not by the properties of the sun itself. It was
henceforth necessary, once again, for the stars to be made of fire.

The adversaries of Philoponus sensed the influence on his thought of a
Christianity that they sometimes considered a pure façade, one intended
to mislead the Christian power of the time. They also sensed that the new
world view was not only unorthodox as compared to Aristotle, but as compared to something like a sentiment of the world that indeed had to be
called religious. Thus Simplicius notes that renouncing the fifth element

led to placing celestial light and glowworm light on the same level, since both shine without burning or being consumed. According to him, this is nothing less than a profanation, a blasphemy *(blasphēmein).*[157]

In the Middle Ages, we have noted, the question remained disputed. Several authors defend the unity of the two matters: Grosseteste assumes a single principle, light; Roger Bacon relies on the results of optics.[158] But Ockham is interesting because he connects the discussion to the idea of an axiological worth: "I say that in the heavens and in these lowly things, matter is of entirely the same ratio. While admittedly this statement cannot be demonstrated, neither can its negation. Yet one can give persuasive arguments. In the first place, if they were not of the same ratio, it would be because of the nobility of the form of the heavens or because of their incorruptibility. It is not because of the former, for—according to those who hold the contrary opinion—the form of heavens is less noble than the intellective soul [of man], as in general—according to them—the inanimate is less noble than the animate; yet notwithstanding this, the matter informed by the intellectual soul is of the same ratio as the matter informed by all the corporeal forms; thus the nobility of form is not an impediment. Nor is it because of the latter. . . . The incorruptibility of the heavens is not incorruptibility simply and absolutely, but relatively. God can certainly destroy the heavens, and cause them simply to pass out of existence. They are incorruptible only in that they cannot be corrupted by a created agent."[159] The physical question is envisioned in its own order, and in it alone. The axiological ranking of realities is placed in parentheses: the physical is only the physical. Man is not made of a more noble matter than other sublunary realities. Now, it seems to go without saying that his dignity wins out over that of the sky. The dignity of the parts of the world, beginning with that of man, thus has nothing to do with their physical status. Would it simply be conferred upon them by an act of divine will?

B. Divine Omnipotence and the Plurality of Worlds

There is a point on which theology perhaps exercised direct influence concerning the conception of the physical universe. It indeed prepared or, at the very least, made possible a move from the Aristotelian view of the world by causing it to lose part of its legitimacy, the part it owed to the unique character of the world. The idea of a plurality of worlds is ancient; it was found in Epicurus.[160] Aristotle was able to exorcise it, through arguments adopted a hundred times after him.[161]

The idea did not, however, disappear in the patristic era.[162] It also survived in the Middle Ages, where it appeared in several forms. First of all, it appeared in a form that is not related to cosmography; it involved the representation of a hierarchical layering of levels of being whose nature can vary, but which one can call "worlds." Neoplatonism uses "world" in this sense, in its Greek origins as well as in its Colloquial Arabic version, in which the Koranic naming of Allah as "Lord of the 'worlds'" was an excellent loophole for the idea.[163] Sufi authors did the same. Avicenna reflects on this usage and integrates into his definition of the word "world" *('ālam)* the fact that it might be a plural form: "'world' is also used for the entire assembly of related realities, as one says: 'world of nature,' 'world of the soul,' and 'world of the intellect.'"[164] Among Jewish thinkers, Ibn Ezra, perhaps following Avicenna, distinguishes three worlds: the sublunary, the supralunary, and the superior world, that of the angels or the spirits separated from matter.[165] The Kabbala, borrowing from Gnosticism and from Neoplatonism as transmitted by Isaac Israeli and Abraham bar Hiyya, asserts the idea of a layering of worlds. It interprets the words of the Canticle: "The young girls *('alāmōt)* love you" (1:3) as in fact designating worlds *('ōlāmōt)*. It represents a creation in stages, each one being made concrete in a world, the whole forming a layering from high to low to the material world.[166] In this way, a first step is taken: the idea of world is detached from its identification with "our" world, the world we see here.

To the spatial coexistence of worlds is added the idea of temporal succession. Our present world would be the last in a series of created universes, a series that can be long. This idea appears among the talmudic rabbis, but it does not find favor among Aristotelian philosophers such as Maimonides. For the Sages, it was perhaps a question of proving to the Gnostics that the current world, if it is the result of a choice—God having destroyed all the worlds that did not please him, must be the best one possible.[167] This idea also reveals the ultimate conclusion of the historicizing of cosmology. As a result, and no doubt contrary to the intention of the proponents of the idea, our present world is once again relativized. It is only a specific stage in a vaster history.

But the plurality of worlds takes a particular turn when it leans directly on the idea of an all-powerful God. In the Middle Ages, it takes on several forms. One of them remains in the realm of the possible: God could have created as many worlds as he wanted. This idea is found in Islam among authors of different sensibilities: a theologian of the Kalam such as al-Naẓẓām, a mystic such as Nasafī, and even the great scientist al-Biruni.[168] Most of the time, thinkers remain in the realm of suppositions, even the Christians of the fourteenth century, who thought most about the question.[169]

There is also the question of knowing whether there could have been a more perfect world, and therefore, supposing this were possible, why God would not have created it. Al-Ghazâlî raises the question and answers it in the negative: if God had discarded the real possibility of a more perfect world, he would have done so either through lack of power, which his omnipotence excludes, or through avarice, which his goodness excludes.[170] The argument has the form of a recurrent objection drawn from the existence of evil. Ockham relies as a physicist on a view of the world that is classically Aristotelian, but, as a theologian, he can take into account the omnipotence of God by disregarding the orientation of the world toward the economy of Salvation. Nothing then opposes the fact that God might produce another world.[171]

In any case, the thought of other worlds, at least possible ones, relativizes the observable facts in our own world. Some historians saw in this hypothesis, precisely because it is a possibility, a destablizing element in the consciousness of the waning Middle Ages, a source of disquiet worse than that of the ancient atomists.[172] Whatever the case may be, the hypothesis relativizes man's judgment of his world. The thought experiment of looking at things from the point of view of some "other," an extraterrestrial or a "savage," had become commonplace in, and indeed almost the signature of, the eighteenth century. Now it is encountered in the middle of the fourteenth century: according to the Cistercian Peter Ceffond, if moles gathered in the center of the earth to wonder whether there were a surface, they would respond in the negative, since the surface would seem useless to them for their well-being.[173]

The plurality of worlds, even if it remains a pure hypothesis, has an ontological consequence. The real is reduced to being nothing more than the factual. The being and the good are in this way dissociated: the being of this real world which is ours has its source in a good that does not coincide with it but is external to it, namely, the benevolence of God, who chose it among other possible worlds.

. . .

Thus, the medieval model superimposed elements emerging from the religions acknowledging Abraham onto a Platonically inspired cosmology. Those elements had an influence over "pagan" motives, enriching them or limiting them. But on many points, it also went farther than they did. Consequently, Abraham does not boil down to Plato. When the Greek model lost the cosmographic foundation that made it possible and crumbled, that which came from Abraham did not have to follow it in its fall.

Part Four

The New World

Chapter 12

The End of a World

The way of conceiving and experiencing the world that I have discussed at length in this study so far is no longer our own, and henceforth cannot but appear foreign or frankly strange to us. What for some of the authors I have cited involved a quickly rejected hypothesis or a deviant doctrine has for us become a fact that must be accepted.

The domination of the model that I have described belongs to a delimited period in time, a period we can now envision as a whole. This period in the history of human thought, which, from the point of view of the link between cosmology and anthropology that I wanted to explore, is of very specific interest, extends from Late Antiquity to the end of the Middle Ages. Indeed, it represents a remarkable instance, an encounter between cosmology and cosmography, if not a quasi-coinciding of the two. Over more than a millennium, scholarly thought was dominated by a cosmography that, on the one hand, was broadly shared by virtually all, and, on the other hand, could easily be connected to an ethics. It was indeed a period in time, for it had a beginning and an end. For that connection, as we have seen, did not always exist. Subsequently—that is, for the most part in the modern era—the cosmography that could be agreed on was no longer associated with ethical concerns, either negative or positive. The modern cosmos is ethically indifferent. The image of the world that emerged from physics after Copernicus, Galileo, and Newton is of a confluence of blind forces, where there is no place for consideration of the Good.

I will now trace the history of the destruction of the model the absence, indeed the impossibility, of which has placed us in our present position. Due to lack of space and above all of competence, I will now undertake no more than a sketch of what more knowledgeable scholars have presented in detail.[1] I will therefore be even more schematic than I have been up to now, and I will sketch a picture with a few broad strokes.

THE NEW COSMOGRAPHY

The first factor in this history is found outside philosophy (in the modern sense of that word, in any event), since it concerns new data relating to knowledge of the physical universe. Until the modern era, the cosmography commonly admitted by scientists coincided for the most part with the representation of the world shared by most educated people. At the very least, it could be transposed into the arsenal of notions and images through which that representation was expressed. After the Middle Ages this was no longer possible. New observations and the theories forged to account for them ended up in a vision of the physical universe that could no longer be reconciled with the ancient and medieval image of man's place in the cosmos. I do not mean, using a positivist explanation, that facts had (so to speak) been spontaneously presented for observation and, also automatically, had inspired theories capable of accounting for them. Phenomena became significant only when theories, at least potential theories, had rendered them acceptable: for example, the earliest recorded meteorite fall, that of Ensisheim (Alsace), on November 10 of a significant year—1492.

This is the case for certain facts that rendered the revision of astronomical theories inevitable—*new* facts, with all the symbolic weight attributed to that adjective at the time of the discovery of the "New" World[2] and the development of "new sciences."[3] These facts, of an astronomical nature, were named for nothing but their novelty: the new [stars] *(novae)*—as it happens, they were *super*novas, no less—which Tycho Brahe observed beginning on 11 November 1572 in the constellation Cassiopeia and Kepler in October 1604 in Ophiuchus.[4] Since Antiquity the Chinese had observed the appearance of new stars, for the first time no doubt around 1300 B.C.E., and as late as 1054.[5] But, as this phenomenon in no way disturbed their view of the world, they would not, or could not, "see" them. The same is true of the alterations noted by Hipparchus and Varro.[6] Their observations became relevant because they were disturbing in an Aristotelian cosmos where they showed that the skies were not immutable. Philosophers immediately saw the consequences of this, men such as Justus Lipsius, who because he was a Stoic could do without a clear distinction between the terrestrial elements and celestial quintessence.[7]

In 1577, Tycho Brahe established that the comets, which Aristotle had classified among the meteorites, thus situating them in the sublunary, moved in orbits beyond that of the Moon.[8] A boundary that was believed to be impenetrable thus found itself crossed. David Fabricius (d. 1617) noted, on 3 August 1596, with his naked eye, variations in the luminosity of Mira in Cetus.[9] The supposed celestial matter was therefore not immutable and thus lost the property that had previously been assumed for it. Later, the discovery of sunspots by the Jesuit Christoph Scheiner (d. 1650), in March 1611,[10] constituted a more significant novelty, for only new optical instruments made the discovery possible. It showed that the skies and the earth were made of the same impure and corrupt matter. Galileo explicitly abandoned the Aristotelian division between the sublunary and the supralunary.[11]

A second, symmetrical revolution took place at the same time. Optical instruments that made it possible to enlarge objects were applied not only to distant things but also to things close up that were too minute for the naked eye to see. After the telescope there came the microscope.[12] Roger Bacon pointed out the importance of magnifying glasses in reading,[13] and the first depiction of a person wearing eyeglasses appeared in a 1404 painting by Conrad of Soest (Westphalia), in the church of Nieder-Wildungen. The theoretical use of optics had to await the invention of the microscope, in the first decade of the seventeenth century. But the need for such an instrument was felt well before that, and no doubt encouraged its invention. Indeed, a text written by Gersonides, completed in January 1323, contains an evocation of the help that such an instrument would provide for the observation of insects.[14] Descartes envisioned the same use.[15] The microscope enabled discoveries in biology and pathology, which are not within the scope of the present study, but it is relevant to note here that that instrument led to a revolution in the notion of the world, which was formulated a few years afterwards, when what had thus been revealed in fact received the name of world. Pascal, who was probably inspired by a letter from the Chevalier de Méré (1654) and who in turn influenced the *Logique* of Port-Royal (1662), formulated as a simple intellectual experiment the idea of worlds stacked inside each other ad infinitum.[16] The microscope made it possible to pass into the realm of the concrete. This occurred beginning with Robert Hooke (1665).[17] Philosophers took up the idea: Fontenelle speaks of a "little world," Leibniz says "an imperceptible world," Berkeley "a new world," and for Hume microscopes "open up a new universe in miniature."[18]

The story I have told so far, up to the end of its medieval journey, has unfolded within three civilizations. Henceforth, it would be confined to

Europe, and primarily within a Christian milieu. Jewish thinkers were not particularly interested in questions of cosmology; beginning in talmudic times, they were reluctant to deviate from the Mesopotamian view of the world in favor of "Greek" ideas which they perceived as contradicting that view. They had a mixed attitude toward the science of the beginning of the modern era, from enthusiastic reception to rejection, including pure and simple unawareness of it.[19] Thus Salomon Maimon mentions astronomical discoveries as novelties in a text published as late as 1791 in which he corrects the Master—Maimonides—whom he is commenting on.[20]

The Muslim world quite simply bypassed the astronomical revolution. The first mention of Copernican hypotheses dates to an Ottoman author from the end of the seventeenth century and is limited to a single sentence. Worse, those hypotheses are pointed out as a pure curiosity.[21] The same is true of the Byzantine world: a physics manual whose cosmology is that of Aristotle and Ptolemy was still being copied, in manuscript, until the eighteenth century.[22]

DEATH OF THE COSMOS

The new astronomy, following Copernicus and his successors, had consequences for the modern view of the world. It is remarkable that in the modern era we find a phenomenon similar to what was observed above:[23] the need for studies written for non-specialists, indeed, by them, on the view of the world that had become common. But there was a significant difference: ancient and medieval thinkers presented a synchronic schema of the structure of the physical world, which erased the traces of its own genesis; the Moderns, on the other hand, remembered the past and in addition provided a diachronic view of astronomy—as if the evolution of ideas about the cosmos was even more important than the truth about it. Indeed, "the progress [of astronomy is] the most incontestable monument to the success to which the human mind can raise itself through its efforts."[24] We can cite the example of Adam Smith, the author of a history of astronomy that saw it as a vast illustration of the influence of curiosity on the acquisition of knowledge and remained incomplete, published only in 1795;[25] or Leopardi, who, scarcely fifteen years old, wrote for his own use a long and erudite recapitulation of the historical journey of astronomy up to his time (1813).[26]

The very concept of "world" was repositioned by modern, post-Galilean physics. It was first granted a new relevance. Kepler entitled a treatise *Mysterium cosmographicum* (1596).[27] Descartes wrote (without publishing it) a

Traité du monde (1633), wherein the idea of order is determining: world is contrasted with chaos.[28] For Leibniz, a world—several are possible, and God chose the best of them all—is an assembly of co-possibles. But is the concept of world thought out as such? Descartes, perhaps without being aware of it, uses the expression "alone in the world" at the moment when he nevertheless exhibits the most extreme doubt concerning the existence of external things: it is as if the world were the horizon of presence that is in fact assumed by all absence.[29] On the other hand, the concept of world was then used in the plural to designate inhabited planets or systems like the Solar System. But these worlds no longer made up a "uni-verse" in the strict sense of the term. Can we then still speak of cosmology? It seems that the West ceased to have a cosmology with the end of the world of Aristotle and Ptolemy, an end due to Copernicus, Galileo, and Newton. The "worlds" then no longer formed a whole. We again see the beginnings of a cosmology with Eddington, starting with whom we have a unified, henceforth dynamic, model of the unity of the cosmos.[30]

The first revolution in the way the world was viewed is global and is reflected in the very name of the thing in question. Seen through the eyes of the Moderns, the collection of physical phenomena could no longer strictly bear the name of world. The passage "from the bounded world to the infinite universe" (Alexandre Koyré) is also reflected in a change in vocabulary, which ends up in the situation referred to above: "The long use of *world* to mean an object so patterned and unified as the geocentric *kosmos* went so far as to disqualify it as a name for what we now call 'universe.' When once the old model is broken, we become aware that a detailed knowledge of the Region of all regions will be forever unattainable. We now need a word not for some specific and imaginable object but for 'whatever the totality may be,' and *universe* is such a word. Furthermore, the same process which broke the old model threw a new meaning on *world* [that of 'inhabited realm'] which, while it lasted, made it impossible without grave inconveniences, to call the totality the *world*."[31] And in fact, after the anticipations of Nicholas of Cusa, we see the appearance of terminological distinctions such as Giordano Bruno's between universe, levels of being (intelligible, natural, rational), and dwellings.[32]

This change at the terminological level inaugurated a loss of legitimacy at the conceptual level. It was no longer possible to call what ancient and medieval cosmology presented and what modern physics reveals by the same name, "world." Nietzsche perhaps saw and expressed the phenomenon most clearly. He proceeded in fact to the successive destruction of the principal metaphors that enabled one to conceptualize the world. According to Nietzsche, the world is not an organism; we do not have the right to transpose onto the whole of the world a state that is valid only for an exception. Nor is it a mechanism, for it has no purpose. As for the cyclical order of the movements of the solar system, it is a temporary exception. This is the polar opposite of the Greek view of the world as an order *(kosmos)* inserted into the wide opening of an original void *(chaos)*. The world is no longer *kosmos* but, indeed, chaos: "The general character of the world, on the other hand, is to all eternity chaos; not by the absence of necessity, but in the sense of the absence of order, structure *(Gliederung)*, form, beauty, wisdom, and whatever else our aesthetic humanities *(Menschlichkeiten)* are called."[33] This is not, perhaps in spite of certain formulas by Nietzsche, a scientific statement that might be refuted by the discovery of new laws or more refined regularities—discoveries that continue to be made. The passage deals with the consequences of man's uncoupling, of the radically inhuman, because amoral, nature of the world.

I will focus here, however, only on the consequences of the new cosmography within the anthropological, and thus ethical, realm. Those consequences did not occur abruptly. In any event, they did not consist, as is too often believed, of man's ceasing to feel he is at the center of the world and having been humiliated by this. This is a legend whose genealogy we should now reconstruct. In Ptolemaic cosmology, the central place was a place of shame rather than a place of honor, and the earth, a trash can rather than a throne.[34] What strikes thinkers *(certain* thinkers) is that once the universe is assumed to be infinite, any point of reference must henceforth be lacking. The end of the Aristotelian cosmos provided John Donne, in a text that has been quoted too often for me to reproduce it here once again, with a whole arsenal of images.[35] Basically, the poet only repeats one of the most classic processes of metaphorization of the human experience: a historical event of great consequence, in this case a death, is supposed to be accompanied by cosmic upheavals. Thus the birth of some great personage coincides with an eclipse, and so on. But here, what was only metaphor seems to be corroborated by a revolution in realities themselves.

THE DEATH OF THE SKY?

The astronomical revolution did not take place in the realm of astronomy alone. It also had consequences in what must indeed be called "metaphysics"—a term that was hazarded in this context, for the first time to my knowledge, by Leopardi.[36] At the very least, it was perceived as occurring alongside a metaphysical revolution. The effect cosmology had on anthropology and ethics is my chief concern here. But it is not always easy to dissociate the effects of the cosmological revolution from those of the metaphysical revolution, for the latter, even if it has its own domain, always occurred in phase with the former.

I will not discuss the metaphysical aspects of the passage into modern times here. I will confine myself to pointing out the consistency with which metaphors borrowed from the new cosmology were invoked to render the obsolescence of classical metaphysics believable. It was as if, taking the biblical euphemism designating God at its word,[37] there was a veiled attempt to assimilate the Sky to the sky. In this way, the proclamation of the "death of God" occurred with the help of astronomical illustrations.

First an absence is noted: the libertine presented by Pascal—and above all not, according to a mistake that has been repeated a hundred times, Pascal himself—was already afraid in the face of "the eternal silence of these infinite spaces."[38] Using the same image, Adam Smith expresses the nightmare of a world without God: "To this universal benevolence, on the contrary, the very suspicion of a fatherless world, must be the most melancholy of all reflections; from the thought that all the unknown regions of infinite and incomprehensible space may be filled with nothing but endless misery and wretchedness. All the splendour of the highest prosperity can never enlighten the gloom with which so dreadful an idea must necessarily over-shadow the imagination."[39] The world appears once again as incomplete. The theme, we have seen, predates the astronomical revolution.[40] But the revolution gave it a new tone. This is the case in particular with Hume, Smith's mentor. Hume envisioned a world that was only the first attempt of a still young god, which was abandoned by him as imperfect; or that, on the contrary, was the work of an already senile god who had since died.[41] The world was no longer considered provisional as compared to being in the definitive state that it might assume only eschatologically. The provisional was now definitive, as the principle of order which could have retrieved it and given it its complete form no longer existed.

The idea sometimes took an extreme turn. The sardonic excessiveness of Hume, or the dark nightmare depicted by Smith, became a hypothesis worthy of serious consideration. Thus in a letter written in his youth (4 June 1790), Benjamin Constant proposes the parable of a god who died before he could complete his work: "A Piedmontese, a man of wit whom I met in The Hague, one Chevalier de Revel, envoy from Sardinia, . . . claims that God, that is, the author of us and of our surroundings, died before having finished his work; that he had the most beautiful and vast projects for the world and the greatest means; that he had already put many of those means to work, as one raises scaffolding to build, and that in the middle of his work he died; that everything at present is in a condition with a goal that no longer exists, and that we, in particular, feel destined for something about which we haven't the slightest idea; we are like watches without dials, whose gears, endowed with intelligence, turn and turn until they are worn out, without knowing why, telling themselves always: since I turn I therefore have a goal."[42] We can note that this text was written close to when Jean Paul (d. 1825) put down on paper the first sketches of his famous "dream of Christ dead," which he published in 1796 in *Siebenkäs*. Thus Constant's letter is perhaps, after Hume, the oldest occurrence of the modern, not Christological, meaning of the statement "God is dead."

In a text written toward the end of his life, Gérard de Nerval dreams that the earth has come undone: "The stars shone in the firmament. All of a sudden it seemed that they had just been extinguished all together. . . . I thought that time had come to an end and that we had reached the end of the world as announced in the Apocalypse of St. John. I thought I saw a black sun in the deserted sky and a globe of red blood above the Tuileries. I said to myself: 'The eternal night is beginning, and it is going to be terrible. What will happen when men realize there is no more sun?' . . . Through the clouds rapidly being chased by the wind, I saw several moons going by very fast. I thought that the earth had left its orbit and that it was wandering in the firmament like a dismasted ship, approaching or leaving the stars that were growing bigger or smaller in turn. I contemplated this disorder for two or three hours."[43] The images come from many sources: one, the Apocalypse, is noted. Others are cited without references, but it is not difficult to find the convergence of several sources here: the black sun, already evoked in an earlier poem, *El desdichado,* as is the image of Dürer's Melancholia.[44] But here, black is the sign of a void, not of a negative ray of light. The sun is not just hidden, it is no longer there; thus the consequence: the earth is detached from its orbit and wanders without a destination. The sky is compared to the sea, and the wandering to that of a dismasted ship, also a classic image.[45] The passage ends with the implicit paradox: "contemplating the disorder." Ancient contemplation derived its meaning from what it viewed as an order on which the subject contemplating it was to model himself. Here, the situation is worthy of contemplation precisely because it is disordered.

The passage continues with the nightmare in which "there is no more Christ." Nerval suddenly places himself midway between two famous texts: Jean-Paul's, in which Christ is resurrected only to announce that he did not find God, and Nietzsche's, which has his "madman" *(toller Mensch)* announce the "death of God." Whereas the first text does not use cosmological images, Nietzsche orchestrates his idea with the strong support of astronomical metaphors: "How were we able to drink up the sea? Who gave us the sponge to wipe away the whole horizon? What did we do when we loosened this earth from its sun? Whither does it now move? Whither do we move? Away from all suns? Do we not dash on unceasingly? backwards, sideway, forewards, in all directions? Is there still an above and below? Do we not stray, as through infinite nothingness? Does not empty space breathe upon us? Has it not become colder? Does not the night comeon continually, darker and darker?"[46] As in Nerval, who was shocked that no one was aware of what he had seen in his dream, it is a matter here of the delay that occurs between the fact and one's awareness of it. Elsewhere, Nietzsche refers explicitly to the new astronomy: "Since the time of Copernicus man distances himself from the center and moves toward X."[47] The Copernican turning point, we should note, receives a completely paradoxical interpretation here, since heliocentric cosmology resolutely chains the Earth and the Sun together.

The end of the ancient and medieval cosmos was not perceived without some regret. We are aware of the tenacious legend that Freud popularized, but which he only borrowed from writers before him: the new heliocentric cosmography constituted a "blow to human narcissism."[48] It in no way corresponded to reality and had itself to be explained.[49] Now, I am inclined to think that his sources are none other than expressions of an unavowed regret. The oldest text I have been able to locate is by Fontenelle (1686).[50] The idea is again found in a comic dialogue by Leopardi written in 1827.[51] But the clearest avowal of regret is perhaps to be found in early German romanticism, in an essay by Novalis on Christendom and Europe. This text was written in 1799 but was published only in 1826, or one year before Leopardi wrote his dialogue. In it Novalis mentions a prohibition that the pope was supposed to have instituted against the divulging of astronomical results that would make the earth "an insignificant planet" *(ein unbedeutender Wandelstern)*. He places the prohibition, in his fantastic historical schema, before the Reformation. It confirms the positive image that he had of medieval Christianity, for there is a salutary measure there: "He [the pope] knew well that men, with the respect for the place that they inhabited and their earthly fatherland *(Vaterland)*, would also lose respect for the celestial fatherland *(Heimat)* and for their species, that they would prefer limited knowledge to infinite faith, and would get used to scorning everything that was great and worthy of admiration, to consider it the effect of dead laws."[52]

INDIFFERENCE

[JEEVES] "'All that befalls you is part of the great web.' . . ."
[BERTIE WOOSTER] "He said that, did he?"
"Yes, sir."
"Well, you can tell him from me he's an ass."[53]

The new cosmography had moral consequences. First, as we have seen, through the intermediary of metaphysics. But also more directly. To clarify the issue, two points of view may be distinguished. Cosmology had an anthropological and ethical relevance that can be highlighted as follows: the order of the cosmos was the framework to which it was necessary to adapt oneself, and it was also presented as an example to be followed. Subsequently, cosmology lost its relevance in two ways, each corresponding to one of those two aspects: on the one hand, its ethical value was simply neutralized as the cosmology was considered amoral; and on the other hand, it was more seriously discredited as being immoral.

We are aware of the idea, which has become trite, that the modern world is the era of the "disenchantment of the world."[54] What I am attempting to describe is expressed more adequately by a formula that has been presented as an equivalent, the "neutralization of the cosmos."[55]

The first tenet of the early, Stoic-style, cosmology, adaptation to the order of nature, assumed a benevolent nature—psychoanalysts would say it was perceived through the fantasy of the "good mother." Rival schools in Antiquity contrasted the theme of the wicked stepmother nature, who abandons her children.[56] It reappeared in the modern era with a diametrically opposite tone: nature is cruel, it is the executioner of its children.[57]

However, the cruelty of nature would still imply interest in us; to wish us evil is still to wish something for us. This is why it is perhaps more unbearable to think that nature is indifferent. It is difficult to know how early this idea was encountered. It is possible that it is implied in a Homeric simile, when Patroclus, reproaching Achilles for failing to intervene, imagines that he might not be the son of humans, but of "the grey sea and the towering rocks."[58] It is also possible that the idea is in the background of a biblical passage: "the almond tree blossoms, the grasshopper drags itself along and [the caper-bush yields its fruit, while] man goes to his eternal home" (Ecclesiastes 12:5). The author perhaps chose to place a burial scene in a setting that evokes summer, with flowers that, under the burning sun and in the deafening concert of grasshoppers, exhale their heady odor. One translator explains the passage thus: "Here again . . . , indifferent nature forms the backcloth for human death. The old man dies at the very moment that nature revives with the spring."[59] But this interpretation, and also the textual choices it assumes, are far from unanimously shared.

It thus seems that the idea did not appear clearly before the modern era. Granted, ancient and medieval thinkers knew how to distinguish the mineral from the vegetable, and the vegetable from the animal. But the Moderns turned the idea that nature is insensitive into a central theme of their polemics against ancient physics.[60] Another step was taken when the inability to perceive was combined with an inability to feel, and this at the time when, following Rousseau, the moral value of sensibility was being promoted. Thus Goethe writes: "Because unfeeling *(unfühlend)* / Is nature: / The sun shines / On the evil and the good."[61] He gives a gospel phrase a negative tone. The phrase illustrates the goodness of the Creator, which is offered as an example to emulate. Applied to nature, it becomes a sign of indifference. Another "Spinozist," Flaubert, as Proust noted somewhere, derives sinister pleasure in situating sad scenes in full sunshine and happy scenes in the rain. And Henry Adams derives from the horrible death of his sister, under an Italian summer sun, that God can only be a substance, not a person.[62]

Nature appears indifferent to human activities. This is not at all new, but what is new is that the indifference is henceforth considered unacceptable, as something that should not be. Indignation constitutes something like the opposite of a regret—the feeling of not being able to respond with similar apathy: the Stoic attitude was clothed in global confidence in the providence of god-nature. To compensate for the absence of god-nature there is a call to revolt before the silence of nature. Thus the American Stephen Crane: "When it occurs to a man that nature does not regard him as important, and that she feels she would not maim the universe by disposing of him, he at first wishes to throw bricks at the temple, and he hates deeply the fact that there are no bricks and no temples. Any visible expression of nature would surely be pelleted with his jeers.

"Then, if there be no sensible thing to hoot, he feels, perhaps, the desire to confront a personification and indulge in pleas, bowed to one knee, and with hands supplicant, saying, 'Yes, but I love myself.'

"A high cold star on a winter's night is the word he feels that she says to him."[63] The star, which was once the response, has become the paradigm of the absence of any response.

In a poem no doubt written around 1844, Matthew Arnold rises up against those who preach a harmony with nature. The qualities of nature contrast term by term with those that are expected of man: Nature is "strong . . . , cool . . . , cruel . . . , stubborn . . . , fickle. . . . Nature forgives no debt, and fears no grave." In sum: "Man hath all which Nature hath, but more, / And in that *more* lie all his hopes of good." The conclusion goes from description to exhortation: "Man must begin . . . where Nature ends."[64]

EVIL WITHOUT APPEAL

There is a second way in which the anthropological and ethical relevance of cosmology is consumed by modern cosmography. Modern cosmography shows in fact that the sky is ruled by the same laws as the world below; in Newton, the moon and the apple are equally subject to them. Now, these laws are not precisely those of exemplary moral conduct. One can, of course, see in gravity an image of reciprocal love.[65] But in the final analysis, only force matters. In the Cartesian cosmos, then the Newtonian one, the large stars attract the small. Everything occurs in the same way as in the Dutch proverb that Spinoza cites: "The big fish eat the little fish."[66] Fontenelle, popularizing the Cartesian theory of vortices, presents celestial equilibrium as the result of a struggle of influences: "Each world . . . is like a balloon that would get bigger if we let it; but it is immediately pushed aside by neighboring worlds and it goes back into itself, after which it begins again to expand, and so on. . . . I like these balloons that inflate and defend themselves at every moment, and those worlds that always *battle*."[67] For Newton, the celestial bodies do not fall on each other only because their speed enables them to escape the attraction that they exercise over each other, nothing more. Newton himself, who carefully avoided speaking of the "force" of gravitation out of fear that he would be accused of resorting to occult properties, was even more reluctant to speak of celestial equilibrium as a struggle. But it is tempting to take the step. Other literary figures did so without hesitation. Thus Restif de la Bretonne uses the image of the fish devouring each other with regard to a comet.[68] The "big" would get even bigger from the bulk of the "little," unless they managed to escape.

From this it can be deduced that the same battle that opposes animal species and individuals on earth also characterizes the celestial mechanism. We see the reappearance of the Epicurean idea that worlds are not linked through harmony but are opposed in a struggle that allows only the most able to survive.[69] Schopenhauer continues this interpretation of the Newtonian system when he mentions: "The constant tension between centripetal and centrifugal force . . . that maintains the edifice of the world in movement and which itself is already an expression of that universal combat, essential to the representation of will."[70] Alfred de Musset, in a work written in 1836, well before the ideas of the German thinker became known, endows the hero of his autobiographical novel with a similar view of nature as perhaps overseen by a cruel God. Nature condemns us always to be born and always to die. Then even the perfect regularity of celestial phenomena takes on a serious aspect: "This great law of gravity that holds the world in its place, wears it out, and eats it up in endless desire; each planet carries its miseries while groaning on its axis . . . ; they ardently carry out their empty and useless labor . . . not a disorder—all is regulated, marked, written in lines of gold and in parables of fire; everything marches along to the sound of the celestial music on the pitiless paths, and forever; and all of that is nothing."[71] Newton's world and his fundamental law are associated with the ancient idea of the music of the spheres. Order is linked to beauty. But everything changed its sign: the absence of disorder, which dazzled the Ancients, is now experienced as an inescapable form of slavery. It is no longer "love that moves the sun and the other stars," but desire. Consequently, the world is such that evil exists in each of its parts, on the earth as in the sky, and no less in the sky than on the earth. Thus Leopardi writes: "Evil is a thing common to all the planets of the universe."[72]

Even if it were agreed to classify beings according to their relative value, the celestial bodies would no longer be at the very top, but at the very bottom of the scale. Hume, after inviting the reader to cast his gaze on the entire circle of the universe, to admire its prodigious variety and fertility, writes in an aside that the "living existences" are *the only beings worth regarding.*"[73] Hegel wrote that the stars were only an eruption of luminous blemishes and that they thus deserved as little admiration as blemishes on a man's face, or a swarm of flies—a comparison with which he commits the very same blasphemy for which Simplicius reproached Philoponus.[74] For Marx, the most criminal thought of the worst assassin is worth more than the entire world.[75] It is amusing to see that the comparison of the stars with pimples, in favor of human dignity, was reversed a few decades later: man is now compared to dermatitis of the earth.[76]

The examples of the "crimes" of nature (volcanoes, earthquakes, tidal waves, etc.) were known from the beginning of time. But a gulf separates the Ancients and the Moderns: the Ancients could appeal and refer to the supralunary to show that in the overwhelming majority of cases nature is governed by the Good. For us, on the other hand, that path has become a dead end. We no longer recognize the distinction between the sublunary and supralunary domains. For us, the universe is a totality, a seamless garment. We no longer have the right to differentiate between levels of the world that would have more or less value. This was recognized by an

English moralist at the end of the nineteenth century. Arguing to restrict the qualities "good" or "bad" to the human, Henry Sidgwick writes: "No doubt there is a point of view, sometimes adopted with great earnestness, from which the whole universe and not merely a certain condition of rational or sentient beings is contemplated as 'very good': just as the Creator in Genesis is described as contemplating it. But such a view can scarcely be developed into a method of Ethics. For practical purposes, we require to conceive some parts of the universe as at least less good than they might be. And we do not seem to have any ground for drawing such a distinction between different portions of the non-sentient universe, considered in themselves and out of relation to conscious or sentient beings."[77] What for Sidgwick was an obvious fact that did not need to be established, that is, the conviction, expressed at the end of the text, that no part of the world is "better" than another, would have been unthinkable in Antiquity and the Middle Ages.

In the same spirit, Wittgenstein writes near the end of the *Tractatus Logico-Philosophicus:* "The sense of the world must lie outside the world. In the world everything is as it is, and everything happens as it does happen: in it no value exists. And if it did exist, it would have no value."[78] The formula is prefigured by a note taken down during the War: "Ethics doesn't deal with the world." And in a conversation, he confides: "In the exhaustive description of the world, no ethical sentence ever occurs."[79] The world is amoral. The world is the realm of what is, in which "all is as it is," nothing more. We can note the phrase: if there were a value in the world, it would have no value. To put this in Nietzsche's terms, the world is the very devaluation of values. The world is, by itself, nihilistic. This is why ethics must be situated outside the world. Now, to arrive at this so-called evidence required the efforts of scientists to destroy the earlier evidence, which argued the contrary. This is the result of a movement that was underway at the dawn of the Modern era.

AN EXTRA-MORAL MORALITY

The new cosmography had a moral consequence of even greater, although only indirect, importance. Once the barrier that had separated the sublunary from the celestial had been removed, nature was presented as perfectly homogeneous. It had long been felt that man, although he lived in the sublunary, was associated with the sky in one way or another: through the presence in him of a divine element similar to that of the stars, through the orientation toward the above imposed upon him by his erect posture, through the regulation of his behavior according to the regularities of the above, and so on. Once this reference had lost its celestial anchor, it became tempting to insert man into the seamless fabric of nature and to eliminate the exception that made him an "empire within an empire."

Since man was not an exception, what distinguished him from the rest of the world was conceived on the model of the world itself. Morality was seen in an "extra-moral" way, to borrow Nietzsche's word. The tendency was centuries old, beginning with thinkers from the dawn of the Modern era. Machiavelli recommends that we do what we are, that we duplicate with an "ought" what in any case "is."[80] This tendency spread in liberalism: it is by pursuing self-interest (the very concept was forged to avoid the classical and Christian reproach of selfishness) that we contribute to the common good. This idea is found in Spinoza, then in Bernard Mandeville. I have not found among these authors and in this context a reference to the cosmographic revolution. However, Montesquieu connects honor, as a principle of the monarchy, to the way the "system of the world" is governed by centrifugal force and weight, so that "each person is drawn to the common good, believing he is moving toward his individual interests"; and the influence of the Newtonian model, no doubt badly understood, moreover, on people such as Adam Smith is well known.[81]

One example of this influence is particularly revealing. It is the famous parable of the porcupines in Schopenhauer: in the den where the animals hibernate, they get close to each other to keep warm, but then they prick each other; they end up finding the optimal distance that allows them not to be too cold, while not hurting each other too much.[82] This scene is meant to provide an image of a moral issue. The allegory is interesting in that it implicitly confirms the directive role of cosmology for a view of the world in its entirety. One has the impression in fact that it transposes into zoology a situation that had already been observed in celestial mechanics: morality has nothing moral about it; it is concerned with neither good nor evil. It simply seeks a certain distance, a certain equilibrium. The problem is to find the point where opposite forces are canceled out, as in the Newtonian cosmos. Rather than dismissing nature in favor of a superior instance, it is a question of negotiating a compromise or, literally speaking, a *modus vivendi*, with nature.

A good portion of modern thought thus seeks to enter into a flexible, not to say contradictory, relationship with nature: it is a matter, on the one hand, of accepting nature's sovereignty which is assumed to be salutary, and on the other to arm oneself against what is destructive and overwhelming about it. Through this, attempts have been made to explain the domination of two paradigms in nineteenth-century philosophy: aesthetics and therapeutics. The first tames nature as a source of artistic genius; the second, after the failure of aesthetics, becomes the only way to present nature while taking the edge off its roughness.[83] It still remains to be explained why it was felt that nature was adequately described through its "black definition." And this is exactly what the history I am attempting to recount here explains.

Chapter 13

An Impossible Imitation

We have just seen how the Modern era introduced a process by which man thought of himself as being a part of nature and governed by the same laws as nature. Ancient and medieval cosmology proposed that part of nature which seems to behave with perfect regularity and which consequently constitutes what is most "cosmic" in the world—the sky—as a model for human behavior or, at the very least, as a guarantee of that behavior. The modern view of the universe robs that model of its relevance. To imitate the sky no longer has any meaning.

A fundamental consequence of this reality is a certain change in paradigm. For ancient and medieval man, nature revealed itself above all in the guise of the celestial world. For modern man, the realm of the living is the new paradigm. And for us, "nature" designates above all the vegetal world. Astronomy gives way to biology as the exemplary field of knowledge. Nevertheless, the regulating function is no longer carried out in the same way. To imitate the sky becomes impossible; to attempt to do so is ridiculous. Any attempt to imitate the rest of nature is just as shocking for the Moderns as it would have been for the Ancients. But at the same time, in a certain way it becomes necessary.

IMMORALITY

In his famous *Essay on Man* (1732–34), Alexander Pope parodies the Platonic (or Timaean) idea of the imitation of celestial revolutions. It would be absurd to ". . . tread the mazy round his [Plato's] follow'rs trod, / And quitting sense call imitating God; / As Eastern priests in giddy circles run, /

And turn their heads to imitate the Sun."[1] Plato of the *Timaeus* is ridiculed by a comparison, rather out of place, moreover, with the "Eastern priests" who are no doubt the "whirling dervishes"—one might wonder how Pope knew of them.

But there is more. An imitation of nature would not only be ridiculous. It would be sinful. One might certainly "imitate nature." But that would have amoral, indeed, immoral, consequences. We can no longer take anything in the world as a model for moral action. Let us cite the example of Schiller's famous distich, "Das Höchste": "Do you seek what is highest, greatest? The plant can teach it to you. That which it is without wishing *(willenlos)*, be so by wanting—there you have it!"[2] The central idea of the text—be through will what nature is spontaneously, rediscover through conscious work unconscious grace[3]—is not new. It recalls a passage by Farabi cited above.[4] Except that for the medieval philosopher the undertaking would sometimes be condemnable, sometimes praiseworthy, depending on the part of nature that was to be imitated. For the Moderns, who gave up the right to distinguish between different parts or levels of nature, there can be no more moral imitation of nature. Beauty, in the best of cases, is only a subjective invitation to morality, of which it is the "symbol."[5] It is henceforth in no case the expression of a Good into which it might be "converted," in the sense of the Scholastic doctrine of transcendentals. Schiller had already determined the consequences of this. A material imitation of the plants would of course be unthinkable: aren't flowers fundamentally sexual organs, exposed in full daylight at the center of a brilliantly colored skirt, hiked up provocatively? The imitation can only be formal. It is not the activity of the plant, but only its beauty that can be imitated. In addition, in order to do this, one must forget what that beauty is in fact used for, to wit, to attract insects that transport pollen. In a word, one must forget that the plant is nothing less than *willenlos*. One must be blind to the display of force and to the victory it demonstrates over its neighbors, which is represented by the simple fact that it grows—like the tree that Barrès says Taine came to visit.[6]

Finally, such imitation would not only be ridiculous, not only immoral, but quite simply absurd. Indeed, since we are subject to the same laws as the rest of nature, and since we thus do consciously or unconsciously what nature dictates to us, the proposal for imitation would be purely redundant.

The clearest formulation of why it is impossible for modern man to base his behavior on an imitation of nature is no doubt the essay for which John Stuart Mill chose the very simple title, *Nature*. It was published posthumously in 1874, as the first in a collection of three essays on religion. The editor, his daughter-in-law Helen Taylor, points out in her preface that the first two essays had been written between 1850 and 1858, noting that Mill could therefore not have been influenced by Darwin or by Sir Henry Maine.[7] And in fact, *The Origin of the Species* is dated 1859, and *Primitive Law*, 1861. It is not in any case impossible that Mill wrote his essay shortly after the publication of the poem by Matthew Arnold mentioned above,[8] although I do not claim that he must have read it. Mill's purpose is to show that nature cannot serve as a model for moral action. To do this he distinguishes two meanings of the word "nature": the first designates all the powers that exist in either the outer or the inner world and everything that takes place under the influence of those powers; the second designates what takes place without the voluntary and intentional agency of man. Once this dichotomy is set forth, it is easy to show that obeying nature in the first sense does not need to be required or recommended, since it is something we cannot *not* do.[9]

As for the second meaning, its rejection is the object of a more in-depth demonstration: "The order of nature, in so far as unmodified by man, is such as no Being whose attributes are justice and benevolence would have made with the intention that his rational creatures should follow it as an example. If made wholly by such a Being, and not partly be beings *of very different qualities,* it could only be as *a designedly imperfect work* which man, in his limited sphere, is to exercise justice and benevolence in amending."[10] Mill quickly conjures up the possibility of a plurality of creators who exhibit no justice or benevolence—demoniac demiurges, therefore. Good can only be a human endeavor. He repeats the idea of an uncompleted world, as already mentioned above, but with an optimistic slant that we have also seen: an imperfect world leaves the field open for human action.[11] But in this world, man has nothing to imitate and, in particular, no longer anything that would obviously exhibit the attributes of God. To be sure, Mill distinguishes the sky and the earth, as Plato would have done, but he does not claim that the sky is the realm of the good and the earth the realm of evil. Celestial nature, "the solar system and the great cosmic forces which hold it together," can only inspire a feeling of the sublime in us. Terrestrial nature, which Mill sees above all as a biological force, acts with "perfect and absolute recklessness," out of pure wantonness, with "the most callous indifference." As with Sade, nature is criminal: "nearly all the things which men are hanged or imprisoned for doing to one another are nature's everyday activities."[12]

Nature is therefore something to be corrected, not imitated. Mill points out that we are still tempted to take as an example a certain part of nature as most clearly expressing the intentions of the Creator. But this favored part of nature is not external to man—as are the celestial bodies. It is only a certain part of man, that is, "the active impulses of human and other animated beings."[13] Mill has no trouble showing that good conduct is the result of the correction or the training of instincts, a very righteous idea, but one that no longer concerns us here.

It is remarkable that nature is completely leveled. The astronomical, the biological, and the human are not distinguished by any essential feature. The idea of order does not come from observable or calculable regularities in natural phenomena. Mill does not deny the existence of these regularities, but he denies them any relevance as to how we should govern our actions: "Even the love of 'order' which is thought to be a following of the ways of nature is in fact a contradiction of them. All which people are accustomed to deprecate as 'disorder' and its consequences is precisely a counterpart of nature's ways." The order must be completely artificial: "This artificially created or at least artificially perfected nature of the best and noblest human beings is the only nature which it is ever commendable to follow."[14]

Nietzsche, who we know read certain texts by Mill, explains the same idea in a famous passage criticizing the Stoic ideal of "living according to nature."[15] And during the same period, we see the appearance of the idea that nature would be not only bad, but also ugly, because it is raw, not corrected, or incomplete.[16]

NATURAL VIOLENCE
A. Excuse

The world appears increasingly as a battleground where blind powers confront each other. Hume generalizes Hobbes's idea—the war of all (men) against all—and extends it to all living beings: "A perpetual war is waged among all living creatures."[17] Later, the idea underlies scenes in Africa in Céline.[18] Carl Zuckmayer describes a year in the lives of the fauna of a swamp as governed by the most pitiless struggle for life. He thus takes literally the "warm little pond" from which Darwin assumed that life might have emerged.[19] The moral of this story, if there is one, is that of natural selection. The final sentences express this: "Among the larvae and the small ones of this year, few became adults. But these were large and strong and lived for a long time"—a harsh parody of the traditional end of fairy tales.[20]

This point of view is ancient, at least as regards the idea of a struggle against natural elements. Plato, and in the *Timaeus* itself, already described the relationship between the elements using the metaphor of a sort of "chemical war." But in the Renaissance the idea assumed the appearance of a general law. Thus Pico della Mirandola states that natural philosophy (physics) can only teach relative peace, since its principle is Heraclitean: War, the father of all things.[21]

It is remarkable that the idea of imitation is again found in this context, no longer the sublunary's imitation of the supralunary, but transposed entirely into the heart of the terrestrial domain. Thus Shlomo Ibn Verga (beginning of the sixteenth century) has the pope who was supposed to have justified the expulsion of the Jews from Spain say: "It is well known that we are composed of four elements and that the nature of simple [bodies] is [present] in what is composite. We note that each element [is concerned] with dominating and seeks to absorb the other and to transform it into its own substance; thus we note that fire burns everything if water does not prevent it. . . . The same is true of the animals, birds and fish: the strongest swallows the other. And also for people: the dominant nation seeks to transform the others into its own substance. And if I had the possibility that no one else in the world would rule except me, I would devote all my abilities and all my power to that."[22] The underlying reasoning is the same we have seen above among the anonymous thinkers whom al-Farabi criticized: that which *is* is also that which *ought to be*.[23]

Several decades after Sade, but in a play set close to the time when the "divine marquis" wrote his works, Georg Büchner has Saint-Just deliver a speech to the Convention in which he justifies the Terror. Ostensibly taking his adversaries for over-sensitive types whom the word "blood" alone causes to swoon, he repeats the philosophical gesture that consists of rising to general considerations about nature. "Nature follows quietly and irresistibly her laws; Man is destroyed, wherever he comes in conflict with them. An . . . epidemic, a volcanic eruption, a flood bury thousands. What is the result? A meaningless, on the whole, scarcely noticeable alteration of physical nature, which would have passed by scarcely leaving a trace, if corpses did not lie in its path. I ask you: shall moral nature be more considerate than physics in making her revolutions? Shall not an idea, just as well as a law of physics, annihilate that which opposes it? Above all, shall an experience which alters the whole configuration of moral nature, which means humanity, not dare to wade through blood? The spirit of the world uses our arms in the spiritual sphere just as in the physical it uses volcanoes and floods. What difference does it make whether one dies now through an epidemic or through the Revolution?"[24] Granted, Büchner's Saint-Just assumes what must be proven, that the fact can establish a right. The gist of the argument nevertheless remains interesting: in an extreme way man is seen as a part of nature; he is not an exception to it and has ceased to be "an empire within an empire." Physical nature and spiritual *(geistig)* or moral nature are placed on the same level. In the second type of nature, the principle at work is displaced from concrete, responsible man onto a "Mind of the world" *(Weltgeist),* the evocation of which recalls the Hegelian philosophy of history.

B. . . . Model

If there is one author who placed crime at the center of his view of the world, it is Sade. Now, he grounds the necessity, indeed the legitimacy, of destruction—in short, of what was later called "sadism"—on a theory. That theory is meant to formulate what nature is. Sade thus leans, or believes he is leaning, on what the science of his time knew or believed it knew to be true.[25] Crime has a double role: synchronically, it is a factor of equilibrium. "Wolves that eat lambs, lambs devoured by the wolves, the strong that sacrifice the weak, the weak victim of the strong—this is nature, these are its views, these are its plans: a perpetual action and reaction, a crowd of vices and virtues, a perfect balance, in a word, resulting from the equality of good and evil on the earth, a balance essential to the maintenance of the stars, the vegetation, and without which everything would be destroyed in an instant. . . . A completely virtuous universe could not survive for a minute; the knowing hand of nature creates order out of disorder, and, without disorder, it would achieve nothing: such is the deep equilibrium that maintains the course of the stars, that suspends them in the immense plains of space, that makes them move periodically."[26] Sade's view of the animal world is classical. On the other hand, it is remarkable that the same principles are extended to the stars. In that, Sade is probably only following Robinet, who had resuscitated the Greek hypothesis of exhalations upon which the luminous stars were fed.[27] Thus, the almost sacrificial necessity of terrestrial crimes was built on an anachronistic physics: "If war, discord, and crimes were to be banished from above the earth . . . , all the celestial bodies would stop, influences would be suspended through the overwhelming power of one of them."[28]

The other justification of crime, this one diachronic, sees it as a way for nature to clean up and give itself the ability to produce anew. Nature allows massacres "because it desired the complete annihilation of existing creatures, in order to enjoy the its ability to relaunch new ones."[29] This is the ancient theory of cataclysms, the cyclical return of which rids humanity of its surpluses or purges it of its vices.[30] But for the Ancients, nature aimed in the long run for the good of humanity; for Sade, it no longer seeks anything but its own enjoyment. Nature practices a large-scale libertinage so that nature is a model for the rake. Ideally, then, crime must exist in the entire expanse of nature, without being limited to that which surrounds us immediately: just as stars maintain themselves only through crime, the libertine dreams of extending his misdeeds to the cosmic order: "I would like to upset its [nature's] plans, thwart its progress, stop the course of the stars, upset the globes that float in space."[31] An imitation of nature is thus an encouragement to crime: "It is only through crimes that nature is maintained and reconquers the rights that virtue takes from it. We obey it then by giving in to evil; our resistance is the only crime that it must never pardon us."[32]

In another work, the chemist Almani expresses the paradox of such an imitation: "I will imitate it, even as I detest it; I will copy it, as it wants this, even as I curse it; and, furious to see that my passions serve it, I am going to reveal its secrets so well that I will be able, if it is possible for me, to become even more evil, to throw my entire life at it."[33] It is amusing to see a theme here that would flourish in popular literature and even into comic strips: the madman who wants to blow up the world. The paradox it expresses is ancient, since it is already found in Ockham: if God commanded us not to love him, we should obey him; but we could not, since to obey him is to love him.[34] Sade's position continued to foment a similar antinomy: to do evil to avenge oneself on the wicked stepmother nature is at the same time to be the accomplice of her criminal plans. But we are now after the modern plan for the scientific conquest of nature, and we have a parodistic version of Francis Bacon's famous adage on nature which says that one cannot rule nature without obeying it. A "ruse of reason" is at work here, except that its goal is destruction more than edification (in both meanings of the word).

C. . . . Necessity

The same perspective is found throughout modern literature. Here, it is all the more untamed because it is no longer counterbalanced by anything: in the eighteenth century it is found in Goethe's first novel, *Werther.* During a mood swing that occurs following the sentimental misfortunes of the young man, nature appears in a completely different light. It had seemed bursting with fertility, as if animated by a spirit that never ceases to create and rejoices in all that lives, as if offering to the one who is contemplating it the possibility of joining the joy of the Creator. It implies a Stoic or Spinozan god. Then a curtain goes up, and the theater of infinite life changes into the abyss of the eternally open tomb. The young Werther concludes: "There is not a moment but preys upon you, and upon all around you,—not a moment in which you do not yourself become a destroyer. The most innocent walk deprives of life thousands of poor insects: one step destroys the fabric of the industrious ant, and converts a little world into chaos. No: it is not the great and rare calamities of the world, the floods which sweep away whole villages, the earthquakes which swallow up towns, that affect me. My heart is wasted by the thought of that destructive power which lies concealed in every part of universal Nature. Nature has formed nothing that does not consume itself, and every object near it: so that, surrounded by earth and air and all the active powers, I wander on my way with aching heart; and the universe to me is a fearful monster, forever defouring its own offspring."[35] The fundamental idea is clear, but we can note a few details that had enormous consequences: on the one hand, the sky and the earth are placed on the same level, without the monstrosity of nature, a new Chronos devouring its children, being limited to the world below; on the other hand, it is not only what in nature destroys man in a sudden and spectacular way that incites horror. Goethe is certainly thinking—the allusion is too clear—of the famous earthquake of Lisbon. That event, which occurred scarcely twenty years earlier (1755), had stricken Enlightenment Europe with horror and had inspired the reflections or many thinkers, from Voltaire to Kant. In the face of that type of catastrophe, one could assert one's dignity as a thinking being against the background of cosmic indifference. In the face of nature that destroys him, man retains his nobility, for he alone knows he will die: "But when the universe will crush him, man will be even more noble than that which kills him, since he knows that he will die and the advantage the universe has over him, the universe knows nothing about it."[36] This attitude is no longer possible: a change in scale occurred, due to observations through the microscope, which seemed to open up a new world. Now, in that world a war of all was being waged which was as implacable as the one on our own scale.[37] And it happens that we ourselves are implicated in the destruction: our very existence assumes the death of other living beings; we cannot take a step without causing the deaths of thousands of animalculae. We are to those creatures what the earthquake is to man. The sky and the earth, but also man and nature, are in the same predicament. We are a part of nature and, as such, we must play the same game.

Literature written later took up the theme but transposed it. What we have just read related above all to the unhealthy subjectivity of the young Werther. Goethe was far from identifying with his hero. Quite to the contrary, to tell his story was a sort of therapy for Goethe. We also know that the mature Goethe saw nature in an entirely different way. On the other hand, later thinkers, often in the wake of Schopenhauer, drew extreme consequences from this type of experience, by turning it into a general notion. The world as it appears in the dark panel of the diptych is the world as it is. To see the world as beautiful and good results from illusion or myopia; its profound reality is terrible. The contrast is formulated in different ways by different writers. Thus Hugo von Hofmannsthal employs the same reversal as the one in *Werther:* the noise (!) of a spider devouring its prey is enough for a young man to cease seeing the world through rose-colored glasses, and for him to discover the horror of it.[38] Dino Buzzati takes up the idea but substitutes a change of mood with a simple change in scale: the same scene, a garden at dusk, is first viewed by humans who contemplate it from the balcony of a bedroom, and then lived by insects and creatures that devour each other in it; it appears either as a haven of peace or like a slaughterhouse.[39] A similar idea is perhaps implied in a painting by Gustave Doré where, in a clump of grass amidst the humming of insects, a scythe hs been placed, for the moment at rest.[40]

TECHNOLOGY AS MORALITY

Modern cosmology neutralizes the world. The difference between good and evil nevertheless remains. Ancient and medieval nature, inasmuch as it was offered up for contemplation in celestial phenomena, was the reign of the good; modern nature, present above all in biological facts, appears to be the kingdom of evil. But the good comes back to nature: since good is not in nature, it is thus necessary to introduce it into nature. And by force, by taking nature against the grain. This can only be done, of course, inside the only realm of nature that is within the scope of human action—foremost, on the earth. Modern technology defines itself through an undertaking of domination, through a plan to become, according to the famous epigram of Descartes, the "master and possessor of nature."[41] Technological activity was considered up until the modern era as a perfection of nature. It was a matter of delivering nature of that which it could not produce by itself. One then appealed on behalf of effective nature to a superior jurisdiction, which might be seen as the not completely accomplished intent of nature, or the plan of the Creator. Henceforth it was a question of imposing external order upon nature. If technology could set out to ameliorate nature, it was because nature left a lot to be desired. Modern technology thus accepted a fundamental premise of Gnosticism.[42]

Concern with alleviating human suffering is not associated only with the lazy quest for comfort. It has an ethical importance that governs it and gives it increased power. The ancient and medieval thinkers were not unaware of technology; the medieval West invented or incorporated agricultural processes that improved the human condition, beginning with population increase. But such results were not considered to lead to a good that went beyond usefulness or convenience. For the Moderns, on the other hand, to battle nature was to battle evil and spread good. Thus, technical production assumes to itself the strength of moral practice. The Aristotelian term *praxis* was applied to that practice, and to it alone, while manufacturing was called *poiēsis*. Primarily in the modern era, but not exclusively in Marxism, it became commonplace to designate the technical transformation of nature by the term *praxis*. This was not a simple misuse of language: technology was a form of morality, and perhaps even true morality.

In contrast, the technological transformation of nature, through compensation, enabled another neutralization of nature. The ancient and medieval model aimed to make the earth a sky and have the order and good that reigned in the sky descend to earth. Similarly, in the modern era the axiological neutrality of the sky passed onto the earth. This neutrality, as applied to terrestrial phenomena, is the loss of their threatening character. Nature, ceasing to be evil, does not for all that become good. The only way that it keeps being a good is its being the contradictory of evil: nature is a non-evil. Nature enters into the realm of the beautiful, which is no longer convertible into a Good in the sense of one of the Transcendentals, but only as identified with the "weak" version of Good, pleasure. The beautiful that is henceforth identified with a weakened good is the aesthetic. The nature of the Moderns is not so much beautiful than it is "aesthetic."

Ancient and medieval thinkers, up to a certain point, did not consider nature other than as a setting that never turned into a theme, a background that never became a foreground.[43] It appeared within various literary *topoi*, for example the pleasant place *(locus amoenus)* in which man feels good.[44] The modern landscape, on the other hand, is nature as it deserves to be observed in and of itself. Its appearance, unusual in Antiquity, is clear at the dawn of the modern era. It is possible that the first medieval thinker to profess a "modern" feeling for nature was Ramon Lull.[45] It is also possible that Petrarch's ascension of Mount Ventoux on 26 April 1336 represents a watershed.[46] I will leave aside here the interpretations of the letter in which Petrarch recounts the event; there have been particularly controversial interpretations ever since Burckhardt (1860). The landscape represents the terrestrial as a possible object of contemplation, rendered capable of withstanding the gaze that ancient and medieval man reserved for the sky.

The aestheticizing of nature caused it to turn into a landscape. But that passage into aesthetics was itself made possible by the technical conquest and the objectification that it enabled. Only a nature that can be reached only by "going out," "for a walk," beyond the mastered space of culture can appear with a beauty that relates only to itself.[47]

THE METAPHORIZATION OF COSMOLOGICAL REFERENCES

Ancient and medieval cosmography, once it was replaced by the post-Copernican model or models, was not purely and simply forgotten. Its elements survived in an isolated state, and as images which were not to be taken seriously. This is true, for example, of the idea that the earth was made of the solidification of debris that fell from the spheres that encircle it.[48] The same is true of cosmological references through which man defined his humanity. They survived, even when their anchoring point in an outdated cosmography had been destroyed. No doubt it could not have been otherwise, since certain data cannot disappear: either because they belong to the very constitution of the human being—erect posture, for example; or by dint of inevitable illusions, such as the height of the sky. But with modernity they took a metaphorical, indeed ironic, turn.

A. Ascension

Classical literature presented its view of the world in a plastic fashion in tales of *post mortem* ascension or of ecstasies. We have seen a few examples of these already.[49] With Christianity the same theme endured, in the context of a metaphysical theory of love. This is the case with Dante, in the last poem of the *Vita nova:* "Besides the sphere which larger turns / Passed the sigh issued from my heart: / New intelligence, that Love / Crying put in it, toward above pulls it / When it arrives where it desires." John of the Cross, despite the extreme apophatism of his theology, is also sure of his deed. His way of reaching his goal can be very paradoxical, since the extreme height coincides with extreme humility. But he does not doubt that he has reached his prey: "I flew so high, so high / That I reached what I was hunting"—the last line constituting a sort of refrain.[50] Both reach their objects, Beatrice for the one, and for the other, nothing less than God. This is also the case for authors who choose to displace themselves through the imagination into a pre-modern universe; thus Goethe transposes Zeus's raising of Ganymede, who rises and indeed reaches "Upwards! / Embraced and embracing! / Upwards into thy bosom / O Father all-loving!"[51]

In the modern era we see the appearance of the idea that the sky is empty. It is haunting in Musset, who writes with a lower case letter what he nevertheless considers to be the dwelling place of God. The vacuousness of the sky is the symbol of despair, and it does not fail to fill itself in moments of joy.[52] In Joseph Conrad, it is first of all a question of the visible sky, clear, free of clouds, but all the less serene, the image of the abandonment of man in his earthly voyage.[53]

Consequently, ascensions are transformed into a gliding flight in which the subject floats between two levels of being, without ending up on a superior level. The takeoff, far from directing the gaze toward the superior world, has no other effect than to allow the earth to be seen from higher up. Petrarch already explains his ascension of Mount Ventoux by his desire to see from on high. Among the Ancient and Medieval thinkers, the experience ends up with the earth being devalued, because of its tiny dimensions, which make it laughable. An example of the new sensibility is found in Baudelaire's "Elévation."[54] The poet takes flight. His flight is situated with reference to traditional cosmology, to which a discrete allusion is made: nine levels are crossed, corresponding to the nine spheres of ancient astronomy, finishing with "the confines of the starry spheres." But the flight is cut short and ends up on what has been called an "empty transcendence." The poet drinks from the "clear fire that fills the limpid spaces" only to acquire "the language of flowers," that is, to become capable of understanding the lowest category of living things, "the mute." The *logos* that defines man is no longer transcended toward the mystical silence, which rests on the superiority of the intuition of the ineffable, but is subverted by the silence of the vegetative.

The Chilean surrealist poet Vicente Huidobro (1893–1948), using the pretext of a celebration of the first balloon flight by a Cuban aeronaut, celebrates the dissolution of the self in an empty sky, mirrored by the progressive dissolution of the poetic form.[55]

B. Erect Posture

Modern thinkers retained the theme of man's erect posture. But they saw something else in it. It was primarily the sign of domination. Man is upright, not in order to look at the sky, but in order to be able to watch the rest of creation from above. This is true in Buffon or Herder.[56] Or in Marx: man in the world is "the real, corporeal, man standing on the solid and well rounded earth, the man who inspires and exhales all the forces of nature."[57] In which case the cosmological gaze toward the above is associated with a historicist and progressivist gaze toward the future. This is expressed well in a song from the *Wandervogel* movement in turn-of-the-century Germany, which was later taken up by the pioneers of the Communist youth movement in East Germany: "Brother, don't let your head hang down, for you can't see the stars, look upwards, rush forwards."[58] Freud gives a grating version of the same idea in explaining that standing upright, by distancing the head from the ground, brings a weakening of the sense of smell, and, because it exposes the sexual organs, the development of modesty.[59] It can also be the condition for a completely immanent confrontation: standing upright enables the face to be confronted. The theme of standing upright is transposed in this way in Feuerbach in his considerations on the human head.[60] Finally, it can be a matter of a purely theological elevation. Thus the idea of the height of God is found in Lévinas, who, moreover, cites Plato.[61]

THE RETURN OF ALTERNATIVE THINKING

In Antiquity and the Middle Ages, thinking was dominated by the Platonic model. But that is no longer the case today, and the modern distancing from that model invites reconsideration of the rivals it supplanted at the time when it was the winner on the battlefield, or that it forced into coexistence while influencing them.

A. Epicureanism

First, we can note the strong return of an atomist influence, sometimes called by its name,[62] for example, in Gassendi. Thanks to Quevedo, Epicurus was freed of the charges of immorality that were brought against him.[63] And, true, he even became an honorable reference for some courageous types. Thus Spinoza claims to place more importance on Democritus and on Epicurus than on Plato and Aristotle.[64]

Epicureanism might be considered to be one of the most "modern" of the ancient doctrines, precisely because it loosens the connection between physics and morality.[65] Conversely, regarding the basics, one can find modern equivalents of the Epicurean attitude. First, relating to the physical underpinnings of the system, it is increasingly said that our existence is the result of chance. Modern physics has chosen Epicurus's mechanism over Aristotle's teleology. We have been lucky, that's all. Life was lucky enough to appear on our planet, man was lucky enough to evolve from certain primates, that is, to have won the biological lottery several times in a row. In a successful book that was published some thirty years ago, *Le Hasard et la nécessité* [Chance and Necessity]—a title derived from a fragment by Democritus—the French biologist J. Monod uses the image of the Monte Carlo roulette wheel. It is not important here that the image is not very rigorous, as chance cannot, strictly speaking, be considered a cause. It remains interesting as a symptom of a diffuse sensibility which, having come from philosophy, was taken up again by the popular philosophy of scientists. This is also the case with the tendency to avoid speaking of truth as an object of philosophy in order to assign it a role that is above all therapeutic. Truth is presented today with a great deal of self-assurance by Richard Rorty: the agreement between men, which Epicurus called "friendship" *(philia)*, to which he prefers to give the modern name of "democracy," is more important than inaccessible truth.[66]

There is also evidence, generally speaking, of a certain "Epicureanism" in which the popular meaning of the adjective is, for once, relatively legitimate. The Fourth Gospel sums up the authentic mode of a presence in the world in the form of "tribulation" *(thlipsis):* "In the world you have tribulation" (John 16:33). This is henceforth replaced by "comfort"—a comfort whose meaning has itself changed from what it signified in Thomas More's famous text in which it conversed with tribulation. This comfort is no longer that which, feeding courage, enables us to endure tribulation as such; it is henceforth assumed to be a substitute for tribulation. Man's task is to construct an island of order in the heart of an infinite ocean which he is also meant to forget: the equivalent of the "garden" of Epicurus is the conclusion of Voltaire's *Candide* or Leopardi's "bower" *(siepe).*[67]

B. Gnosticism

In the modern era, Gnosticism is above all the object of historical rehabilitation, most often within the framework of an "enlightened" polemics against the Great Church. It is so in Bayle, under the name of Manichaeism.[68] Gibbon considers the Gnostics the most acceptable among the first Christians.[69] Others, Voltaire, for example, recognize a certain currentness in it: Voltaire makes the Manichaean Martin one of the few sympathetic characters in *Candide;* and Hume, who makes the dualist solution an at least respectable hypothesis; or John Stuart Mill, who is surprised that in his time no one has attempted to revive Manichaeism.[70] But more generally, a certain sensibility touched with Gnosticism appears, a phenomenon regarding which several works have been written.[71] The boldest is probably Schopenhauer, followed by an entire series of more or less conscious disciples, who made him the inspiration of almost all European literature of the second half of the nineteenth century, until World War I, at least.[72]

The elements of the Gnostic image of the human condition are found, separate or joined together, in various authors of the eighteenth and nineteenth centuries. Thus there is the idea of existence as a propulsion into the world, in the words of a character in Kierkegaard: "Where am I? What does it mean: the world? What does that word signify? Who played this trick on me to plunge me into the great all and to leave me here now? Who am I? How did I come into the world? Why wasn't I consulted, why didn't anyone tell me what to do instead of throwing me into the ranks, as if I had been indentured by a ship's pressgang?"[73] This point of view is the reverse of the Epicurean view that we have just seen: chance *(cadentia, from cadere),* has become decadence; chance *(Zufall)* has become the fall *(Fall).* This explains the consonance of these models with the most contemporary scientific sensibility, including that of Wittgenstein: "*How* things are in the world is for the Higher a matter of complete indifference. God does not reveal himself *in* the world." It has been pointed out that this sentence, with others that I have already quoted, not to mention the very first one of the *Tractatus,* could belong to a Gnostic or Manichean text.[74] On the other hand, the concept of *Geworfenheit,* as Heidegger develops it, does not seem to me to be found on that plane. Attempts have been made to connect Heidegger to Gnosticism, without awareness of what truly separates the two perspectives: the Heideggerian "thrownness" has no point of departure in any other world than that into which we are thrown.[75]

Cosmic anguish is evoked by Hamann: "Anguish in the world is the unique proof of our heterogeneity. For if we lacked nothing, we would be lost in the contemplation of nature *(sich . . . in die Natur vergaffen),* no yearning would grip us."[76] After the enthusiasm of Giordano Bruno before the infinite universe there followed a return of the impression of confinement under the celestial vault.[77] The paradox is only apparent: nothing encloses better than the infinite, which is impossible to leave behind you.

We find the idea of an evil or stupid Demiurge in the famous line in which A. E. Housman invites us to curse "whatever brute or blackguard made the world."[78] A character in a novel by Joseph Conrad associates two Gnostic ideas, man's foreignness with regard to the world, and the dementia of the creator, in an interesting way: "'Man is amazing, but he is not a masterpiece. . . . Perhaps the artist was a little mad. Eh? What do you think? Sometimes it seems to me that man is come where he is not wanted, where there is no place for him; for if not, why should he want all the place?"[79] A few years later in the novelist E. M. Forster, who, moreover, recognized Housman's influence on some of his chapters, we read the following sentence: "The world has been built slapdash, and the beauty of mountain and river and sunset may be but the varnish with which the unskilled artificer hides his joins."[80]

. . .

For us, there is no longer any connection between cosmology and ethics, no longer any relationship between what we know of the structure of the physical universe and the way man thinks about himself and feels what he is and what he ought to be. Such is the common opinion of the modern era, which institutes such an extreme separation between the two realms that the question of their relationship is no longer even raised. This fact has been formulated in various ways, for example by saying that man has "lost the world," or that he is "alienated" from it: for myself, I will repeat the distinctions I made at the outset: the fantastic progress of astrophysics or of the earth sciences enable an increasingly exact *cosmography;* they end up in more and more likely conjectures concerning *cosmogony.* It is only that much more obvious that, strictly speaking, *we no longer have a cosmology.*[81]

What we have, on the other hand, and in abundance, are *Weltanschauungen,* "world views"—what we might hazard to call, by taking up a word that is already well established in Spanish, *cosmovisions.*[82] In a famous text from 1938, Heidegger was able to see our era as being "the time of the image of the world."[83] The essential thing for him is to grasp that the importance of "world views" is only one aspect of the process that reveals the world in its entirety as an image. But at the same time we should learn to see that the rise and reign of "world views" are perhaps only intended as compensation, in the heart of an intellectual economy itself, for the now-abandoned dominance of what I have called cosmonomy.

So that morality can be detached from cosmonomy and begin to be conceived exclusively as "autonomy," the cosmos must already have lost its constitutive function with regard to the human subject. It must no longer appear as anything but the indifferent setting in which human activity, which is fundamentally foreign to it and which owes it nothing of what makes it achieve its humanity, can continue. And this is exactly what has happened to the concept of nature in the modern era. The idea of a moral imitation of nature became impossible because our concept of nature changed. *The world can no longer help us to become men.* We are, taking the adjective literally, *un-worldly.*[84]

Chapter 14

The Lost World

I have been seeking to show the impact of various conceptions of the world on the humanity of man. Man's humanity is not simply an immutable given; man must achieve his excellence by developing what he begins with. He achieves this through an activity that is entrusted to him: for man, to be a man is a task; his humanity must, literally, be brought to perfection. The impact of cosmology on anthropology will thus also, and inseparably, be an ethical impact. I must first recall an obvious fact: it cannot be demonstrated that any of the upheavals in cosmography that we have discussed have ever prevented anyone from behaving correctly; any more than, conversely, the pre-modern model of the world ever turned anyone away from vice. Sherlock Holmes does not have to know how the solar system works to respect and defend a very Victorian morality; and Professor Moriarty, a brilliant mathematician who must have had some insight into astronomy, is no less evil for all that. We have no statistics for real men; and, even if we did have them, who could try the hearts and minds of men? Furthermore, it is quite clear that one can "found" morality (assuming it needs to be founded) without referring to the issue of the structure of the physical world. This is the case, for example, in Epicurus or, very differently, in Kant. And Aristotle, who despite having marked both ancient and medieval cosmology and Western morality more than any other figure, almost never mentions cosmological phenomena in his ethics, and at best very allusively and indirectly.[1]

THE COSMOLOGICAL DEMANDS OF ETHICS

And yet, the modern view of the world has important consequences for man's experience with his moral dimension. An entire aspect of man—namely, his presence in the world—remains lacking in ethical relevance. It is important to understand precisely why this situation is of concern. It is not disturbing that ethics cannot be established on a cosmology and the anthropology deduced from it, since, in any case—to recall an obvious commonplace—one can never derive a norm from a description. A certain modernist rhetoric can even derive facile effects from man's derelict situation in nature; a very sober passage from Marcus Aurelius has shown us that there was nothing new in that.[2]

What is troubling, on the other hand, is that we can no longer determine what relationship there is between ethics and the fact that man is in the world. Granted, in practice, we can establish a livable domain within a hostile, or simply mute, nature—or, at least we should be able to do so. But it is man's very existence in the world that, for us, no longer has a moral dimension. We can perhaps define the rules that enable men to coexist more or less peacefully. We can even give these rules a minimum of plausibility by connecting them, in fact, to the requirements of coexistence: what is good, in this perspective, is what eliminates friction with the least amount of residue possible. We can finally raise to the rank of supreme principle the conditions that make such a coexistence possible. But what we no longer know is whether or why it is morally good that there are men in the world; and, for example, why it is good that there continue to be men: is their existence worth the sacrifices it entails—for the biosphere, for their relatives, indeed, for themselves? The fact that ethics no longer has a cosmological or anthropological foundation is basically not really a very serious matter; what is more serious is rather the opposite; that, if we may say so, cosmology and anthropology no longer have an ethical foundation.

This notion of an ethical foundation of the world is found again in Wittgenstein. He continues a sentence cited above with: "Ethics must be a condition of the world, like logic."[3] It is perhaps this status as a condition of possibility that explains why Wittgenstein elsewhere describes ethics using the Kantian term "transcendental." The expression is all the more interesting in that it seems to be the result of a deliberate choice; the first formulation in fact said "transcendant."[4] On 17 December 1930, Friedrich Waismann asked him: "Is the existence of the world consistent with what is ethical *(das Ethische)*?" Wittgenstein did not reply directly, but recalled that this relationship was felt by people who gave it a theological expression that was nothing less than the Christian dogma of the Trinity: "God the Father has created the world, God the Son (or the Word that procedes from the Father) is what is ethical. The fact that God is considered both divided and as one shows that there is consistency within Him."[5] There is no question of making Wittgenstein a Church Father. It is, however, interesting that he seems to have been content to answer such a question using a theological image. One might wonder how much he was trying to evade the question, or to indicate that it can only have a metaphorical or narrative response.

Why is man both ethical and in the world? Ancient thinkers never asked that question. In Antiquity the answer was given from the outset with the ethical nature of the world; the question did not have to be asked. The implicit response was that wisdom is not achieved against the structure of the world, but if it is not required it is at least encouraged by it. Plotinus most clearly raises this question, to my knowledge, in his treatise against the Gnostics. This is not, moreover, accidental, since the Gnostics in fact protested that basic presupposition of classical Greek thought, that the world is "good." Plotinus thus writes: "But if this All *(todo to pan)* is of such a kind that it is possible to have wisdom in it and to live *(bioun)* according to things above *(kat' ekeina)*, when we are here, how does it not bear witness that it depends on the realities There?"[6] Plotinus agrees with his adversaries on at least one point: there is wisdom in the world. Perhaps he even chooses, by employing the word *sophia* here, which is rare in his writings, to speak like the Gnostics who tell about the misfortunes of Sophia. Sophia, a divine hypostasis, is indeed present in the world, since she fell into it. The question implicitly raised is transcendental. It can be formulated thus: "What must the world be for wisdom to be possible in it?"[7]

A question of this sort remains fundamental for us, as well. And the issue of the ethical foundation of the world is not purely academic. It has taken on a new and burning aspect with Modernity and the plan for the technological "conquest" of nature made possible by the mathematicized science of nature. For, as a result, it is the very question of Being that is raised in a different way. It is possible, in fact, that our existence did in fact come about by chance. I concede this, without committing myself completely. But even if this were true, it no longer is so. Our very existence is the result of the scientific knowledge and technological mastery of nature. Granted, man has never been able to survive without artifice. But today, technology is not only that which enables man to survive; it is increasingly that which enables us to live.

We have seen how classical thinking sought to bring the moral quest for good into accord with the massive presence of good in nature, which was conceived and perceived as a beautiful order, as a *kosmos*. We have seen how the physical pillar of the bridge between man and the world has crumbled. We must now, to answer the same question, seek another concept of the world, which will no longer be physical, but which will explain the very way in which man is present and lives "in the world."

THE HUMANIZED WORLD

An initial attempt consists of noting the presence, alongside the natural or created world, of a human world. The idea that man possesses creative power imitating God's is medieval; Antiquity had recoiled before the equivalence, or had explicitly refused it, as Dio Chrysostom had done. The idea is encountered first in the theory of art, in the Middle Ages, in Nicholas of Cusa, and flourished in the theory of painting in the Italian Renaissance, especially in Leonardo da Vinci.[8]

But it does not go without saying that one can call what man creates, through analogy with the object of divine creation, by the name of world. The step is only taken when one ignores the difference between the real and the imaginary, either by putting the intellectual reconstruction of the structure of the world and its actual production on the same level, or by speaking of a world of poets, the *mundus fabulosus* of Baumgarten.[9] The idea of the poet as creator, a cliché that we have grown accustomed to, is made possible only at the price of many conceptual decisions made in the modern era. It reached its highest point in the Romantic era, especially in Shelley. In his poetry we find the idea of the poem as a second world, or as "heterocosm," an idea that would find a place in the visual arts.[10]

Language had used the word "world" for a very long time to designate the community of men. But that was not enough for that usage to have been raised to a concept or for it to have been said why the human community constitutes a world. That had to wait for Vico, who established a strict parallel between human history and the physical universe. He conceived of the historical activity of man as constituting a "world of the city" *(mondo civile)*. Man is its creator as God is the creator of the physical universe. Consequently, man, who creates it, and because he creates it, knows this world the way God knows the world of nature: "This civil world *(mondo civile)* has certainly been made by men. As a result, principles can, because they must, be found again in the modifications of our human spirit itself. Here is what must plunge whoever thinks about it into astonishment: all philosophers have quite seriously put it into their heads to attain the science of the natural world that God alone possesses, because it is he who made it, and they have neglected to meditate on this world of nations, or civil world a knowledge of which men can attain, since it is men who made it."[11]

In Vico's wake, and citing his central idea at least once, Marx widens the perspective to make man in his work the creator of what he calls a world: "the practical engendering of an objective world *(gegenständliche Welt),* the fact of working non-organic nature, is the way in which man proves *(Bewährung)* he is a conscious generic being, that is, a being who is related to his species as to his own essence, or to the self as a generic being."[12] He criticizes Feuerbach for not having seen "how the perceptible world that surrounds him is not a thing immediately given for all eternity, always equal to itself, but is the product of the industry and the state of society, and in this sense that it is a historical product, the result of the activity of a whole series of generations." According to Marx: "This activity, this constant way of working and acting perceptibly, this production [is] the foundation of the entire perceptible world." The perceptible world must be conceived "as all the living and concrete activity of the individuals that make it up." We can note, however, that "world" thus designates nature, or simply the earth: what is called production of the world is also elsewhere called "production of the entire earth."[13] Marx can conceive of the relationship between man and nature, perceptibility, work, etc., in an original and fertile way; on the other hand, he does not seem to have wondered about the worldliness of the world as such.

This attitude has consequences for those who claim, legitimately or not, to follow Marx's thought. A so-called "materialism," which proclaims its "realism," ends up in fact in a practical "idealism" (the word "idealism" also being taken in a very fluid sense). The revolutionary mind has a tendency to consider that man is capable of remaking the world, and sees in this capacity to destroy the existing order what is needed to compensate for the impression of being only a negligible presence in the universe. There is a wonderful example of this attitude in German expressionism, in particular in Ludwig Rubiner (1881–1920): "Whereas in the era of artistic and spiritual impressionism man considered himself defenseless *(hilflos)* and unredeemable, an infinitely tiny being oppressed by the monstrous and dark walls of nature, man recognizes himself today as a creator. He knows he is the center of the world around which he always creates anew the world that surrounds him in a circle. This periphery of the world, which he creates for himself, he must also answer for it. . . . We never have the right to let the most terrible warning fall into oblivion: Being itself does not exist; that which subsists *(das Bestehende)* does not exist. It is we who make everything *(Wir machen alles erst)*!"[14] As we can see, Rubiner does not hesitate to plead for a very literal anthropocentrism.

This is what George Orwell expresses, but through a caricature of it. The central character in his masterpiece is questioned by O'Brien, the functionary the Party put in charge of reeducating him, who asserts the Party's absolute power over all things. He puts forth the argument that the world is only a speck of dust, man tiny and helpless, a newcomer on an earth much older than he. Here is the response: "Nonsense. The earth is as old as we are, no older. How could it be older? Nothing exists except through human consciousness. . . . Before man there was nothing. After man, if he could come to an end, there would be nothing. Outside man there is nothing.

"But the whole universe is outside us. Look at the stars! Some of them are a million light-years away. They are out of our reach forever.

"What are the stars? . . . They are bits of fire a few kilometers away. We could reach them if we wanted to. Or we could blot them out. The earth is the center of the universe. The sun and the stars go round it."[15] What Orwell is expressing here, while pushing it to the extreme, in spite of the emphatic denials of the Leninists, represents the meaning of revolutionary practices. Those practices must consider the existence of natural, and thus unreformable, realities to be an unbearable limitation. One solution is an outrageous idealism, which can only appear in spite of the official doctrine, in the margins of that doctrine, as in the capacity of a Freudian slip. Was Orwell thinking of specific doctrines when he had the torturer say that the stars are within the reach of human intervention? We have the example, among the vague cosmologies of Nazi Germany, of the theory of the hollow world *(Hohlweltlehre)* according to which the world is a bubble in a rocky infinity and the stars nothing more than luminous sparks in the gassy mass that occupies the center. It is interesting to note something found throughout the history of thought, that is, resorting to the stars as the ultimate guarantee of the existence of an independent reality.[16] Scorn for the celestial bodies is only the ultimate consequence of an attitude already noted in Hegel and Marx. O'Brien's attitude leads to revolt against the Copernican revolution. The price to be paid for this attempt is the willing ignorance of all that is not connected to the "world" that one thus claims to create.

THE INTELLIGIBLE WORLD

Up to now we have not noted any attempts to rethink the very notion of world. It is no doubt Kant who once again made it an object of inquiry.[17] Beginning in the precritical period, the world appeared problematic. The *Dissertation of 1770* sees the concept of absolute totality as the cross of philosophers.[18] For that totality can never be given: progress toward the greatest or the smallest, regression toward the cause, joins through the series of effects cannot be completed. With awareness of this, the concept of world is displaced into another realm, leaving the realm of contemplation in which it had been established since Antiquity: the world can no longer be the object of an experience, but only of a thought.

The first *Critique* proceeds to the destruction of rational cosmology, in the form that Wolff had given it in 1731, by showing that it ends up in antinomies. The world presumes absolute totality. It is, moreover, not the only thing to demand it: all transcendental ideas do the same. This is why they all have the right to the name "cosmic concepts" *(Weltbegriffe);* and what we call "the world," which can be distinguished even more finely as world and nature, is only one specific case of the cosmic character that in general characterizes every idea. Ideas belong to reason. Reason cannot find a field on its level in the theoretical realm. Ideas, with reason, are restricted there to purely regulatory use.[19]

But Kant distances pure reason from its theoretical foray only to refer it to its authentic domain, which is practical/ethical. There he rediscovers in another modality that which he had banished from the theoretical. The ideas of reason, which, in their theoretical usage, were limited to a regulatory role, again became legislative.[20] And this is, in fact, what occurred with the idea of world. The true world is the world of minds. One senses this in everyday language, which speaks of "knowledge of the world" whereas by that it means only the experience of men.[21] Kant develops this intuition by establishing it on the analysis of that which makes man what he is—freedom.

The physical world is incapable of sufficiency as a concept of world; it is not "worldly" enough. Kant thus carries out an essential uncoupling: *the idea of world is liberated from physics.* The world enters into the ethical realm in the guise of the intelligible world. In itself, the idea of an intelligible world is ancient. It is not found in Plato, who indeed speaks of a "supracelestial place," in the myth of the *Phaedrus,* but who does not make this place a "world"; and reciprocally, the "other world" spoken of in

Christianity is not the place of Platonic ideas, as Origen points out.[22] But the idea appears with Philo, and in Plotinus it is accompanied by this assertion, essential for the link of the idea of world with subjectivity, that the intelligible world is found in us and, even, that we *are* that world.[23] However, if the idea of "intelligible world" is ancient and ambiguous, as Kant knows very well,[24] it is only after him that we are able to think in a rigorous way of the "worldly" nature of the edifice of ideas.

The three ideas that the transcendental dialectic banished from the speculative use of reason reclaim their rights from the moral perspective. This is not true only for the ideas of the Self and of God, but also for the idea of world: "Thus the fact that respect for the moral law necessarily makes the *summum bonum* an object of our endeavours, and the supposition thence resulting of its objective reality, lead . . . to that of which speculative reason contained nothing but *antinomy*, the solution of which it could only found on a notion problematically conceivable indeed, but whose objective reality it could not prove or determine, namely, the *cosmological* idea of an intelligible world and the consciousness of our existence in it."[25]

The physical world is not solid enough to provide a base enabling access to God, for we cannot know whether the real world is the best of all possible worlds without knowing those other worlds, which would require continual, interminable exploration.[26] On the other hand, the moral world is presented at one go as the only possible one. The true world is the reign of ends. This is implicit in the conclusion of the *Critique of Practical Reason.* The presence of the moral law in me "exhibits me in a world which has true infinity, but which is traceable only by the understanding, and with which I discern that I am not in a merely contingent but in a universal and necessary connexion."[27]

Taking up the ancient image of the amphibian, indeed his youthful reflections on Swedenborg, Kant writes that we belong to two worlds.[28] How can they be reconciled? The gulf between the harmony of the physical world and the disorder of human history seems enormous.[29] Kant can only sketch a reconciliation between the moral world and the physical universe from a philosophy of history and aesthetics. The beauty of the world can serve only as a "symbol of morality" *(Symbol der Sittlichkeit).*[30] A magnificent formula, which recaptures, perhaps unconsciously, the Greek meaning of *symbolon,* the sign of recognition enabling travelers who shared ties of hospitality to identify themselves over the generations. The simple fact that we are sensitive to beauty shows that, without having a permanent dwelling in the world, we are not purely strangers in it; we are guests.

The new determination of the concept of world resolves, in any case, the question of our presence in the world. We can indeed perceive in the "contingent" (*zufällig,* "fallen like that") nature of our presence in the physical universe a final trace of ancient images: the Gnostic image of being thrown, or the Epicurean image of a shipwreck.[31] But to say that we are "in the world" is only fully true if we mean thereby the intelligible world. Indeed, if our presence in the physical universe is contingent, our belonging to the moral world is necessary. At the same time, the anthropological aspect of the concept of world assumes a new dimension. Indeed, the very concept on which anthropology rests, the concept of man, thus, is determined at new costs: morality does not deal with man as a certain type of animal, but every rational being in general,[32] to the extent that, if it is finite, a being of that type will experience the law as something external.

After Kant, German idealism wanted to go further than he did by attempting a devaluation, no longer only of the world as a moral world, but of nature. Fichte shows that nature is called upon by human freedom as a condition for its action. For Hegel, the mind lays down nature, and lays it down as *its* world.[33]

THE PHENOMENOLOGICAL CONCEPT OF THE WORLD

A similar deepening of the concept of world is proposed in another style by Heidegger.[34] He does not begin with a relationship of perception with things, which in his opinion is not foremost but is supported by a relationship between use and utensils; the world is then indeed the object of an experience, but that experience is not perceptual, it is that of an inhabiting. It is that of a total presence, of an all or nothing. The concept of world thus becomes subjective; rather it constructs subjectivity.

Heidegger's analysis of the idea of world extends over a period of around ten years. He begins with the idea of "surrounding world" *(Umwelt),* of what "worlds"—to say this Heidegger creates a verb, "to world"—*(es weltet).*[35] He isolates the idea that life is essentially marked by the fact that we live in the world *(Weltcharakter des Lebens):* "Our life is the world in which we live, in the direction of which and each time inside which the tendencies of life run. And our life does not exist as a life except insofar as it lives in a world. . . . Our factical life is our world. . . . The factical experience of life is literally "worldly" *(weltlich gestimmt),* it always lives in the direction of a world, it exists in a world of life *(Lebenswelt).* . . . The world is the fundamental category of that whose meaning is to be contained *(das Gehaltsinnliche)* in the phenomenon of life."[36]

The master work of 1927, *Being and Time,*[37] provides an initial synthesis with its analysis of "being-in-the-world" *(in-der-Welt-Sein)*. This is not a category, a characteristic of what is available *(vorhanden)*, but an "existential," a characteristic of *Dasein*. A distinction must be made between the world and nature. All previous ontology sidestepped the phenomenon of the world: it confused the world with nature, which it took as its guiding thread.[38] But nature is not the world; instead it is a being that is encountered within the world. On the other hand, "ontologically, 'world' is not a way of characterizing those entities which Dasein essentially is *not*; it is rather a characteristic of Dasein itself."[39]

The Essence of Ground (1929) develops the analysis further, by adding a few notes on the history of the concept: "It is therefore the case that Dasein is a being-in-the-world not because, or only because, it factically exists, but the converse: it *can be* as existing, i.e., as Dasein, only *because* its essential constitution lies in being-in-the-world. . . . It is therefore equally erroneous to appeal to the expression world either as a designation for the totality of natural things (the natural concept of world), or as a term for the community of human beings (the personal concept of world). Rather, what is metaphysically essential in the more or less clearly highlighted meaning of *kosmos, mundus*, world, lies in the fact that it is directed toward an interpretation of human existence [*Dasein*] *in its relation to beings as a whole*. . . . To selfhood there belongs world; world is essentially related to Dasein."[40]

It is perhaps in the winter semester 1929–30 course that Heidegger pushed his analysis of the phenomenon of the world furthest, and that analysis connects explicitly to his reflections developed in *The Essence of Ground*. He does so with a comparison between mineral, animal, and human and develops a triple thesis: "1. the stone (that which is material) is without a world; 2. the animal is lacking in world; 3. man is such that he constitutes a world *(weltbildend)*."[41] The last point was not developed in as much detail as the second, and, it seems to me, remains programmatic. Heidegger's later thought returned to the question of the world only indirectly and on a different level.

I will therefore limit myself to noting that, also in this perspective, and almost as radically as in Kant, the concept of man is rethought and rid of all "anthropology." And it is the presence in the world that enables the humanity of man to be thus reconsidered. Once it is conceived as *Dasein*, as being-there, the world is conceived beginning with the "there" of man. But to be-"there" is the object of an invitation addressed to man, by the fact that "existence *(Dasein)* as such is assigned to man . . . he receives the task of existing *(Dasein)*. . . . Man, if he is to become what he is, must indeed at all times endorse existence. . . . It is a matter of liberating the humanity in man, the humanity of man, that is, the essence of man, to see to it that existence becomes essential in him. This liberation of existence in man does not mean leaving him to his whims, but imposing existence on man as his most personal burden."[42] One thus notes that Heidegger is closer to Kant than he first appears—and to an unexpected aspect of Kantism: morality. One might interpret the Heideggerian concept of world as a generalization of the Kantian concept. In both cases the world belongs to the practical realm.

THE SUBJECTIVE WORLD

Thus the concept of world toward which contemporary philosophy is directed is, in a sense, already there. There is nothing original about it, since it corresponds to what we more or less explicitly mean when we say, without too much reflection, that when a child is born he "comes into the world," or that to die is to "leave the world." These expressions did not appear, moreover, until after a particular period in the history of thought, and quite specifically at the time when Jewish and Christian representations entered into the culture of the Hellenized world. Heidegger noted that it is with Christianity that "the world of the self *(Selbstwelt)* as such enters into life and is lived as such."[43] Certain languages borrow their word for "world" from that experience, deriving it from the idea of duration of life (Greek *aiōn*), of "age of man": thus we see in Germanic languages which form *world, Welt, vereld* on the roots of "man" (Latin *vir*) and "age" (English *old*, German *alt*). This etymology is mentioned by Schelling, who, moreover, connects *Welt* to *währen*, "to endure."[44]

In conclusion, let us attempt a very elementary look at the implications of this concept of world. We understand today by "come into the world" or "leave the world," most of the time, to enter into the company of men or to leave it. But we still perceive that our coming into the world leads us to a totality, and conversely it is a totality that death makes us leave. And there are thinkers such as Montaigne who elevate this sentiment to an explicit formulation: "As our birth brings us the birth of all things, then too will our death bring the death of all things."[45] And Pascal: "Everyone is an entirety for himself, for, once dead, the entirety will be dead for him."[46] Pascal situates himself here, as he often does, in the wake of Montaigne, even if he only envisions mortality and does not mention the "natality" (Hannah Arendt) of man. But his formula, in addition to having a greater stylistic terseness, has the merit of passing the idea of totality onto the subject. Montaigne speaks of "all things"; Pascal speaks of the whole that we are and that causes all things to be a totality for us. The complete character of things, which turns them into the world that they form, is connected to our mortality, or to an anticipation of it.

In order to get a world, you must have totality. But the totality in question is not obtained through a synthesis. It is given at the outset. It is not quantitative. The unity is not the result of the course of multiplicity, or the exhaustion of it. It precedes and makes all courses possible and subsists in every point of them. The complete character of the presence in/of the world has nothing to do with the quantity of objects we are experienced with, which is quite obviously an infinitesimal part of everything the world contains. In this way, the world is not a world by itself; its "worldliness" does not come from it, but from us.

If this is true, forming a relationship between the idea of world and anthropology does not consist of rejecting the infiniteness of the universe in favor of the warm intimacy of the environment. By entering into the world, at our birth, we enter into that which, just as decidedly, but also indifferently, contains both our cradle and the most distant galaxies. More important, nor is it a question of taking refuge in subjectivity by abandoning the world of "concrete" objects. The opposite is true: it is a matter of showing that the true world is situated on the side of the subject and that what we call "the world"—or the universe of objects—is not capable of satisfying the requisites of the concept of world—in a word, it is not yet "worldly" enough for man.

Thus we have seen first how the idea of world, beginning with its Greek formulation as *kosmos,* implied a particular anthropology. We then saw how what remained virtual developed in Antiquity and the Middle Ages into a cosmological anthropology or an anthropological cosmology. Then we saw how the connection was broken in the modern era. Finally, we have seen how it could be reestablished, indeed, with an even tighter bond. But this would be at the price of a dual reformulation of the ideas of world and man, as conceived in their reciprocal association.

Notes

Abbreviations are taken from the *Oxford Classical Dictionary,* 2d ed., wherever possible. Other abbreviations are provided in the bibliography or reflect entries for primary sources listed there. Citations in the form 1.2.3.4.5 denote book.chapter.section, etc. down to line number(s); citations in the form 6: 7 denote volume and page; citations in the form 8:9 denote chapter and verse (Bible and Koran). Page numbers are preceded by a comma and line numbers may be added to them.

Introduction

1. Sir Arthur Conan Doyle, *A Study in Scarlet* [1887], ch. 2, "The Science of Deduction," ed. H. Greene (London: Murray and Cape, 1974), 26.

2. See Arist., *Pol.* 1.5.1254b36–37.

3. *Kosmogonia* is in Cleomedes; *Kosmographia* might have been the title of a work by Democrites (LSJ, 984b).

4. *Oxford English Dictionary,* s.v., cites a text from 1656. Wolff published his *Cosmologia generalis* in 1731 in Frankfurt and Leipzig, Maupertuis his *Essai de cosmologie* in 1750 in Berlin, and Lambert his *Kosmologische Briefe über die Einrichtung des Weltbaues* in 1761 in Augsburg.

5. Galileo, *Dialogo* 1, pp. 53/64.

6. Arist., *Cael.,* 1.9.279b32ff. or Speusippe, frag. 54a L; Xenocrates frag. 54 Heinze or 153–58 Isnardi Parente. See Tarán 1971; Sorabji 1983, 268–75; Plotinus 4.3 [27], 9.15, generalized 6.7 [38], 35.28–29. See Baltes 1976, 1978.

7. On "universe" see pp. 188–89; "cosmos" was reintroduced by A. von Humboldt, who makes it, moreover, not the title, but the "pre-title" of his master work, see *Kosmos,* 1: 52 and 2: 12.

Chapter 1: Prehistory

1. See Pl., *Ti.* 22b4, p. 107.

2. Voegelin 1956, part 1, "The Cosmological Order of the Middle East," 13–110, bears directly on our subject.

3. See J. Wilson 1949, 54–55, and Lambert 1975, 62, who, in passing, shows that the idea that the Babylonians represented the sky as a vault is without basis.

4. See p. 87.

5. See J. Wilson 1949, 53, 59; J. Assmann 1990, 166; Hornung 1992, 33; the collection of texts in Allen 1988.

6. See *RlA,* s.v. "Kosmogonie" (Lambert); Egypt does not connect cosmogony and theogony, see Bickel 1994, 206.

7. Text in *ANET,* 60b–72b; Bottéro and Kramer 1989,604–653.

8. See Bottéro and Kramer 1989, 603; Jacobsen 1949, 183.

9. See J. Wilson 1949, 64; Plumley 1975, 32; Hornung 1992, 41.

10. See the text cited in Lambert 1975, 58, and also Psalm 115:16.

11. See *A Dialogue about Human Misery* (the Babylonian *Theodicy*), VIII line 82, in *ANET,* 439b–40a; cf. W. G. Lambert, *Babylonian Wisdom Literature* (Oxford: Clarendon, 1960), 77. See also Isaiah 54:9.

12. *Gilgamesh and the Land of the Living* (Sumerian), in *ANET,* 48b; repeated in *A Pessimistic Dialogue between Master and Servant* (Akkadian), in *ANET,* col. 438b, or Bottéro 1987, 309 and commentary p. 317; cf. Lambert, *Babylonian Wisdom Literature,* 149.

13. K. Jaspers, *Vom Ursprung und Ziel der Geschichte* (Munich: Piper, 1949).

14. See Malamoud 1989, 307–9.

15. See Jenni (1953). See also Barr 1969, 86–109. The only suspect text, Ecclesiastes 3:11, is in any event late. Ibn Ezra remarks ad loc. that "in all of the Holy Writ, we find the word *'olām* only in the sense of time and eternity" (MG, p.87b).

16. See W. Helck et al., eds., *Lexikon der Ägyptologie, s.v.* "Weltbild," col. 1212 n. 1 (W. Westendorf), and J. Assman 1990, 174.

17. See Brague 1989, 107–8. See also Houtman 1993, 75–84; I am not convinced by the reason given on p. 77: the Hebrews, persuaded that only God was one, would have refused any unity for the created. It is already in M. D. Cassuto, on Genesis 1:1, *From Adam to Noah*, 3d ed. [Hebr.] (Jerusalem: Magnes, 1959), 10. This does not explain why the same expression is encountered in decidedly polytheistic civilizations.

18. Translated in *ANET*, 417b. See also, for Mesopotamia, Jacobsen 1949, 153.

19. See Brunner-Traut 1992, 124.

20. See *RIA, s.v.* "Kosmologie," col. 222a (Hunger). On the formula, see *CAD, s.v. šamû* A, esp. 342a–43b. We also have *kibrāt arba'*, "the four regions," see *CAD, s.v. kibrātu.*

21. See Brague 1988, 28 n. 38; Mansfeld 1992, 405 n. 24. See for example Augustine, *Against Academics* 3.11.24, BA, 4: 160.

22. Brunner-Traut 1992.

23. See Bickel 1994, 37–38.

24. Cited in Brunner-Traut 1992, 130.

25. The phrase "configuration of the universe" in *Enuma elish* I 61b, according to Jacobsen 1949, 188, is rendered completely differently in *ANET*, 61b (Speiser); *RPOA*, 40; and Bottéro and Kramer 1989, 607.

26. See *CAD, s.vv.*

27. *Enuma elish* iv 14, trans. Bottéro and Kramer 1989, 625; see also *ANET*, 66a; *RPOA*, 50. Akkadian in R. Labat, *Le Poème babylonien de la création* (Paris: Maisonneuve, 1935), 122.

28. See J. Wilson 1949, 71–72.

29. I borrow the expressions in quotes from Brunner-Traut 1992, 2, 60.

30. See Collingwood 1945, 43ff.; Strauss 1953, 97–99; Lambert 1975, 49; Cormier 1994, 20.

31. See E. Cassirer, *Philosophie der symbolischen Formen*, 2: *Das mythische Denken* (Berlin: B. Cassirer, 1925), 2.2.3, pp. 132–49; E. Voegelin, *Order and History*, 4 (1974), 76, quoted in J. Assmann 1990, 30 n. 42.

32. Voegelin 1956, 38–39.

33. Jacobsen 1949, ch. 5: "The Cosmos as a State," 137–99

34. H. Schmid 1968, 30, 46.

35. See H. Schmid 1966; Broadie and McDonald 1977a,b.

36. See Cassirer, *Das mythische Denken* [n. 31 above], 141.

37. See H. Schmid 1968, 61, 50, 51, 55. See also Plumley 1975, 36–37; Indian analogies in Malamoud 1989, 312–13.

38. See Assmann (1990), respectively pp. 34, 218, 35, 176, 37, 34, 33, 37, 89, 283, 163, 195, 220, 218. Synthesis in French in Assmann (1989).

39. See J. Assmann 1990, 163, 174, 186, 197, and already J. Wilson 1949, 53; see also Cormier 1994, 46, 63. It is interesting that the concept that has been characterized as earlier than the emergence of the idea of nature *(phusis)* is that of "path" or "way," see Strauss 1954, 99–100; 340 n. 3; 1989, 253–54—to which we will add Arist., *Meta.* N4.1091a35, and *SVF*, 2: 774 (or Diog. Laert. 7.156).

40. Here we have a meaning opposite to the valuation of the stability which has become a given for Greek, then Western, thought. See Averroes, *Epitome of Physics* 3, p. 44.12–13, ed. Puig; trans. esp. p. 145, and Bergson: "There is more in the motionless than in the moving" (*L'Evolution créatrice*, 4, (Paris: Alcan, 1907), 315–16). See its inversion by Galileo, *Dialogo*, 1: 83.

41. See Assmann 1991, 65.

Chapter 2: The Birth of the Cosmos in Greece

1. This is a summary of Brague 1988, 28–31.

2. Hesiod, *Theog.* 738.

3. Heraclitus, DK 22 B 1, 7, 53, 64, 66, 80, 90.

4. Empedocles, DK 31 B 13, 14.

5. See pp. 12–13.

6. Jeremiah 10:16 and Isaiah 44:24, and see Brague 1989, 108–10.

7. See Costantini 1992, 110–11, on the passage from parataxis to syntax.

8. Respectively Hom. *Il.* 4.145 and 14.187; on the etymology, see, following A. von Humboldt, *Kosmos,* 1: 52–55; Puhvel 1976; Casevitz 1989.

9. See, for example, "Hermes Trismegistus," *CH* 9.8, 1: 99.

10. Pliny, *HN* 2.3.4.

11. Tert., *Adv. Hermogenes* 40.2, *Apol.* 17; Isidor of Seville, Bede, Paulinus of Nola, cited in Kranz 1955, 130–32.

12. Johannes Scotus Eriugena, *On John* 3.6.21–22, ed. E. Jeauneau, SC 180: 232; see also J. de Saint-Amand, *Concordanciae,* ed. J. L. Pagel (Berlin, 1894), 206, cited in Biard 1984, 70; Leibniz, Theses on Metaphysics, in, *Opuscules et fragments inédits,* ed. L. Couturat (1903, repr. Hildesheim: Olms, 1961), 535.

13. Goethe, *Faust Part II* 5.5.11297 (Türmerlied); A. von Humboldt, *Kosmos,* 1: 52ff., 62.

14. Aëtius, *Placita,* 2.1.1, p. 327, DK 14 A 21.

15. Diog. Laert. 8.48.

16. See Kerchensteiner 1962, 227–32.

17. Empedocles, DK 31 B 134.5; Anaxagoras, DK 59 B 8; Diogenes of Apollonia, DK 64 B 2 or 4 Laks.

18. J. Bollack and H. Wismann, *Héraclite ou la séparation* (Paris: Minuit, 1972), 234, 262–63.

19. Heraclitus, DK 22 B 30.

20. In H. Diels, *Doxographi Graeci* (Berlin: De Gruyter, 1879), 475–76, or DK 22 A 5, and Diogenes Laertius 9.8, or DK 22 A 1.

21. Plutarch, *De animae procreatione in Timaeo* 5.1014a, ed. Hubert-Drexler, BT, p. 148.

22. Kirk 1962, 311. Borrowed by Marcovich in his edition of Heraclitus (Merida, 1967).

23. Aristophanes, *Aves,* 193–94, 1515ff.

24. Xen., *Mem.* 1.1.11–12, 15.

25. Empedocles, DK 31 B 111.

26. Arist., *Div. Somn.* 2.463b14.

27. Xen., *Mem.* 4.3.13, and *Cyr.* 8.7.22.

28. Pl., *Ti.* 92c7–d3, p. 359. [All quotations from the *Timaeus* are taken from Francis M. Cornford's English translation, *Plato's Cosmology: The "Timaeus" of Plato* (Indianapolis: Hackett, 1997). Trans.]

29. Ibid., 31b3–4, p. 42.

30. Arist., *Cael.* 1.9.278b11–21; for the discussions that resulted among Greek commentators as to the unique object of the treatise, see Mansfeld 1992, 398. The synonymy of "all," "sky," and "world" is again noted by Avicenna, *Al-Mabdā' wa-'l-Ma'ād,* 1.52, ed. Nûrânî (Teheran, 1984), 74.

31. See Hesiod, *Theog.* 585, and Buchner 1965, 46–49; Pindar, *Pyth.* 2.40; Arist., *Metaph.* M.3.1078a31.

32. Posidonius, ed. Edelstein-Kidd (2d ed.), frag. 18 (Meteorological), p. 44; or Simplicius, *In Phys.* 2.2, ed. H. Diels, CAG 11: 291–92. For the interpretation of the sentence that concerns us here, see Commentary p. 131: "on the basis of the preliminary acceptance . . . that it takes from philosophy." See also Themistius, *Orationes* 8.23.119a.

33. Pl., *Phlb.* 28c6–8; the verb most often signifies "to take oneself seriously"; I am translating with the aim of having the etymology stand out. See Brague 1991, 288 n. 29.

34. Nietzsche, Fragment of autumn 1887, 10 [90], *KSA,* 12: 507, or *The Will to Power,* §677.

Chapter 3: Socrates' Revolution; Plato's Restoration

1. Nietzsche, *Ecce homo*, "Why I am a Destiny" 3, *KSA,* 6: 367.

2. See for example Heraclitus, DK, 22 B 94; Spitzer 1963, 66–67; Vlastos 1995, 57–88.

3. Pl., *Gorg.* 507e6–508a4. The Dodds edition, pp. 157–58, gives references for ancient citations. See Mattéi 1989, 188–89; Lloyd 1991, 363. [English trans. by W. R. M. Lamb, LCL (1925), 469–71. TRANS.]

4. Ibid., 506e2–4, pp. 156–57 Dodds.

5. The phrase as a whole does not appear to be older than E. Dupréel's *La Légende socratique et les sources de Platon* (Brussels, 1922), 122; but the word "revolution" is found in the translation by É. Boutroux of the manual by E. Zeller, *La Philosophie des Grecs considérée dans son développement historique* (Paris: Hachette, 1877–94), 172 (the German simply says *Umkehr*). I owe this information to M. B. Castelnérac.

6. See Goldschmidt 1953, 51.

7. Arist., *Metaph.* A.6.987b2.

8. Arist., *Part. Anim.* 1.1.642a28–30. It is through this passage that Arabic-language authors learned of the "Socratic revolution." See Mas'ūdī (d. 956), *Kitāb al-Tanbīḥ wa-'l-Išrāf,* ed. De Goeje (Leiden: Brill, 1894), 116–17, and Ṣā'id al-Andalusi, *Tabaqāt al-Umam* (1068), ed. H. Boualouane (Beirut: Dār al-Ṭalī'a li-'l-ṭabâ'a, 1985), 95. See also Themistius, *Orationes* 26.9.317d–318a and 26.5, p. 994.

9. See Xen., *Mem.* 1.1.11, 4.7.2–8. Xenophon suggests elsewhere that Socrates in fact engaged in, or had engaged in, "physical" studies, see *Mem.* 4.6.1, and Strauss 1972, 7, 116. See also the curious passage in which Seneca assumes that Socrates would have been able to teach physics to King Archelaus: *Ben.* 5.6.3, ed. F. Préchac, CUF, p. 7.

10. See Strauss 1966.

11. Cic., *Tusc.* 5.4.10, ed. M. Pohlenz, BT, p. 409; ed Fohlen-Humbert, CUF, p. 111.

12. Cic., *Acad.* 1.4.15, ed. H. Rackham, LCL, p. 424; see also *Brut.* 8.31, ed. J. Martha, CUF, p. 11.

13. Pl., *Phd.* 97c8–d3. I am reading *hautou* against L. Robin's first translation (CUF, p. 69), but with Schleiermacher (p. 60), G. Stallbaum (p. 188), M. Wohlrab (p. 118), L. Robin's second translation (Pléiade, 1: 825), and M. Dixsaut (p. 274).

14. I quote several texts in Brague 1988, 48 no. 86; to which may be added Strabo 16.2.35, ed. H. L. Jones, LCL, p. 282.

15. Cic., *Rep.* 1.10, ed. C. Appuhn (Paris: Garnier, 1954), 23.

16. Pl., *Phdr.* 270a4–5; see Szlezák 1996, 28.

17. Pl., *Leg.* 7.821c7ff., 10.892a ff., and 12.967e1 (reading *hēgemona* with Des Places).

18. Cornford (1937). See also L. Brisson, introduction, 12: "The *Timaeus* is without question a work of cosmology, since it proposes a model of the physical universe." On the *Timaeus* in its entirety see Benardete 1971, Hadot 1983, Kalkavage 1985, and Cropsey 1989–90.

19. See Mittelstrass 1962, 111–12.

20. Pl., *Ti.* 27a, p. 20. See also 90e2, p. 356. [All citations of *Timaeus* are taken from the Cornford translation. TRANS.]

21. Brague 1985.

22. Pl., *Ti.,* respectively 43a–b, p. 148; 44b–c, p. 150; 44d, pp. 150–51.

23. Ibid., 47b6–c4, p. 158.

24. This point was seen very well by Chalcidius, *in Tim.* 263, ed. Mullach, *FPhG,* p. 237b.

25. See Pl., *Leg.* 7.818a5.

26. Pl., *Ti.* 68e6–69a5, p. 279.

27. Ibid., 90c7–d7, p. 354.

28. Ibid., 88d1.7–8, p. 351.

29. A link between *sophia* and *kosmos,* in early times, is indicated by Gladigow's title (1965) and formulated on his p. 140; it rests only on weak connections (pp. 107, 118, 122).

30. See Festugière 1973, 125–28.

31. See chapters 8–10.

Chapter 4: The Other Greece

1. As noted by Philostratus; he sees there an essential difference between old and new sophism. See *VS* 1.481, trans. Cassin 1995, 537, commentary 455, 458.

2. Protagoras, DK 80 B 1.

3. Diog. Laert. 6.39 (Diogenes) and 103 (Menedemus).

4. Diog. Laert. 2.92 (Aristippus).

5. Eusebius of Caesarea, *Praep. Evang.* 15.62; PG 21: 1405b.

6. Sextus Empiricus, *Pyr.* 1.18, ed. R. G. Bury, LCL, 1: 12.

7. See Diogenes of Oenoanda, *The Fragments,* translation and commentary by C. W. Chilton (London: Oxford University Press, 1971), frags. 3–4, p. 4; frags. 4–5 Smith (1993), Greek pp. 153–55, English p. 369.

8. C. Bailey. *Contra,* see Vlastos 1995, 328–50; nuances in Salem 1996, 306ff., 325ff.

9. Cic., *Fin.* 5.29.87, p. 199.

10. Leucippus, DK 67 A 22.

11. Democritus, DK 68 B 34 and 135.

12. See for example Epicurus, *Kuriai Doxai* 25; *Gnomologium Vaticanum* no. 21, trans. Bollack, pp. 337, 449.

13. [Philodemus], [*On choices and avoidances*], 13.13–21, ed. G. Indelli and V. Tsouna-McKirahan, *SE* 15: 93, trans. p. 106.

14. Polystratus, *Sul disprezzo irrazionale delle opinioni popolari* 4.18–19, ed. G. Indelli, *SE* 2: 118–19, trans. p. 136.

15. Cic., *Fin.* 1.19.64, p. 28.

16. Epicurus, *Gnom. Vat.* no. 27. *HPh,* p. 156, cite it as rendering impossible the idea that knowledge would be only a means; careful discussion in Salem 1989, 25ff.

17. Epicurus, *To Pythocles* 85, 87, 96, then 97; *Gnom. Vat.* no. 14, ed. Bollack, pp. 88, 188–89.

18. Ibid., 85, trans. Bollack-Laks, p. 76; *K.D.* 11, or Diog. Laert. 10.142; trans. Jean Bollack, *La Pensée du plaisir: Epicure, textes moraux, commentaires* (Paris: Minuit, 1975), 277.

19. Hermarchus, in Porph., *Abst.* 2.8.4.

20. Epicurus, *Peri physeōs* 1.16, in H. Usener, *Epicurea* (Leipzig, 1887), 128. See also the critique of Pl. *Ti.* 27c1–3, p. 115, in Hermarchus, *Frammenti,* frag. 48, ed. F. Longo Auricchio, *SE* 6: 79, trans. pp. 104–5.

21. Pl., *Ti.* 40d2, p. 135—some manuscripts omit the negation; then Epicurus, *Peri telous,* in Usener, frag. 68, p. 121, after Plutarch, *Quod non potest suaviter vivi* 4.1089d, ed. M. Pohlenz and R. Westman, BT, p. 132. The connection is made by DeWitt 1954, 233–34.

22. Pl., *Ti.* 47c1, p. 158, and see p. 33.

23. See Epicurus, *K.D.* 11, 13; Lucretius 5.1204–40.

24. *Etna* 272–78, ed. J. Vessereau, CUF, p. 22.

25. K. Marx, *Differenz der demokritischen und epikureischen Naturphilosophie,* 1, in *Marx Engels Werke,* Ergänzungsband, 1 (Berlin: Dietz, 1968), p. 276.

26. See Polystratus, *Sul disprezzo* 8.29.15–19, p. 127, trans. p. 140.

27. Epicurus, *To Herodotus* 79–80; *To Pythocles* 87, 113; Diogenes of Oenoanda, frag. 8.3, p. 6 Chilton; frag. 13.3, pp. 1–13 Smith (1993), Gk. p. 171, Eng. p. 374.

28. Lucretius 5.526–33.

29. Epicurus, *To Herodotus* 73, 74.

30. Cicero, *Nat. D.* 1.10.24, p. 26, and the response of the Stoic Lucilius in 2.18.47, p. 168; Epicurus, frag. 300 Usener. Compare with Achard de Saint-Victor, *L'Unité de Dieu et la pluralité des créatures* 1.45, ed. E. Martineau (Saint-Lambert des Bois: Authentica, 1987), 118.

31. Epicurus, *To Herodotus* 45, etc.

32. Epicurus, *To Pythocles* 89.

33. Cic., *Div.* 2.17.40; *Nat. D.* 1.8.18, p. 20; *Fin.* 2.23.75, p. 66; Hippolytus, *Haer.* 1.22, p. 42.

34. See Blumenberg 1988, 187.

35. Philodemus, *On piety,* first part, critical edition with commentary by D. Obbink (Oxford: Clarendon, 1996), 71.1.2043–50, pp. 246–47.

36. Lucretius 5.200–203; Cicero, *Nat. D.* 1.10.24, pp. 26–27; *Acad. Pr.* 2.38.120, p. 622. The same argument is found in the writings of the most diverse authors. Thus, in the eleventh century in the Ismaili Nasir-i Khusraw: "If this world were the kingdom of God, thousands of deserts, where no plant grows and no animal lives, would not be found; it would not be endowed with thousands of deserts with dry sand, salt deserts, many mountains without plants, without water and without precious stones. One notices that on this land there flow destructive watercourses that cause serious damage to all that man has built, that wild animals take shelter there who kill other, more useful ones. In the kingdom of God, there is no place for all that" (*Goshâyesh va Rahâyesh,* q. 23, trans. P. Filippani-Ronconi, *Il libro dello scioglimento e della liberazione* [Naples: IUO, 1959], 75). Diogenes of Oenoanda mentions the very interesting example of the Dead Sea, see frag. 21.2.10–3, p. 8 Smith (1993), Greek p. 183, English p. 377.

37. Lucretius 5.95–96.

38. Ibid., 2.1144–45.

39. Ibid., 5.104–6.

40. Ov., *Met.* 1.256–59; *Tr.* 2.426; *Am.* 1.15.23—see C. Bailey's ed. of Lucretius ad loc., p. 1335; *Octavia* 391–94.

41. *Etna* 173–74, ed. J. Vessereau, CUF, pp. 14–15.

42. *HPh* 46 G, p. 276; 52 C, p. 309.

Chapter 5: Other than Greece

1. See *DS,* s.v. "Monde, 1. Le Monde dans l'Écriture sainte" (P. Grelot, 1980).

2. See Stadelman 1970.

3. *ANET,* 369b–71a.

4. The fact was already recognized by John Philoponus: the author of Genesis—for Philoponus, Moses—targeted the religious instruction and moral edification of his readers and thus wanted them to know God and to have the highest morals. In particular, Moses says nothing about the question of knowing "what is the substance of celestial realities, and if [it is] something other than that of [substances] below the moon, and if the substance changes with the movements of those [realities]" (*De opificio mundi* 1.1, ed. Reinhardt, BT, p. 3.12–14, cit. 6–8). The notion is enunciated by Giordano Bruno, *La cena delle ceneri* 4, Fr. trans. Y. Hersant (Combas: L'Éclat, 1988), 89–90, and by Spinoza, *Tractatus Theologico-Politicus,* preface, *Opera,* 2: 89.

5. See *ThWAT,* s.v. *kôkab* (R. E. Clements), col. 89.

6. See p. 12.

7. See Pidoux 1954; McKenzie 1952, 135–36.

8. See Rashi and Qimḥi ad loc., MG, p. 14b.

9. Proverbs 3:19–20, 8:22–23, Psalm 104:24; see Robinson 1946, 9–10; McKenzie 1952, 30–31.

10. See Beauchamp 1969; Strauss 1981.

11. For sculptural representations see Zahlten 1979, 175.

12. On 1:16, "and [God] made," MG, p. 7a; and see Commentary on Ibn Ezra, no. *'ayn.* Ibn Ezra takes for granted here the astronomy of his time, which was not that of the sacred writer. But his observation remains pertinent.

13. See *ThWAT,* s.v. *mô'ed* (K. Koch, 1984), esp. col. 747, which cites Psalm 104:19, Sirach 43:7, and 1QS 9:26–10:8 ("Manual of Discipline").

14. See Beauchamp 1969, 172–86; in Jeremiah 23:9 the word is in the simple form.

15. Deuteronomy 4:19. "all the host of heaven" translates *kol ṣeba' haš-šamayim;* Onqelos: *kol ḥeyley šemaya';* of note is the Greek version in the Septuagint: *panta ton* kosmon *tou ouranou.*

16. This is the understanding since talmudic times, see b*Megilla* 9ab; see Houtman 1993, 204–5; Fascher 1964.

17. b*Šabbat* 156a, and see Daniélou 1953, 49–55; Urbach 1979, 277, 809 n. 66.

18. Ibn Ezra ad loc., MG, p. 15a.

19. He assumes a play on *ḥālaq*, "to share," and *heḥliq*, another form of the same root, "to cause to slide" (MG, p. 14b).

20. Tov 1984, 70, 80, 82.

21. Arist., *Eth. Nic.* 5.7.1134b25–26, and Polystratus, *Sul disprezzo* 6–8.

22. See Plutarch, *De Is. et Os.* 67.377F.

23. Halevi, *Kuzari* 1.27, p. 12.5–7; Fr. trans. p. 11; see his question to Ibn Ezra in Ibn Ezra's commentary on Exodus 20:2, MG, p. 82a.

24. Respectively Psalm 102:27; Isaiah 51:6, 65:17.

25. See Bietenhard 1951, 19–42.

26. See Ego 1989, 125–68.

27. Jubilees 12:16–18, p. 62 Kautzsch, p. 31 Charles; Johannes Scotus Eriugena, *Div. Nat.* 3.23.689d, 35.724a; see Liebeschütz 1926, 98–99.

28. 2 Esdras 4:26 RSV, or: *Die Esra-Apokalypse* (IV. Esra), 1. Teil, *Die Überlieferung,* ed. B Violet, GCS 18: 36–37; *Esdrae Liber Quartus arabice,* ed I. Gildemeister (Bonn, 1877), 7; *Die Apokalypsen des Esra und des Baruch in deutscher Gestalt* (Leipzig, 1924), 16. Another passage (7:12) is cited by Heidegger, *Die Grundbegriffe der Metaphysik: Welt-Endlichkeit-Einsamkeit,* ed. F.-W. von Herrmann, *GA* 29/30: 396.

29. See Volz 1934, 155; Bietenhard 1951, 49–52.

30. Matthew 6:26, 28; Luke 12:24, 27 (*katanoein);* see Betz 1984, 156–60; an interesting connection with the Cyclops of Hom. *Od.* 9.108 in Cormier 1994, 29.

31. See p. 151.

32. Matthew 24:35; Mark 13:31; Luke 21:33; based on Isaiah 51:6.

33. Matthew 5:34, and see 23:22.

34. b*Šebu'ot* 4.13 and 35a in Strack and Billerbeck, ad loc., pp. 332–33.

35. *Spec. Leg.* 1.5, ed. Daniel, p. 238.

36. See the recent synthesis of Bosch i Veciana (1979).

37. See Heidegger, *Vom Wesen des Grundes* (1929) 2, in *Wegmarken* (Frankfurt, Klostermann, 1967), 39–41; among the reflections most akin to philosophy, see Bultmann 1954, §42, pp. 361–63, and Schlier 1968, 281–94. See also M. Henry, *C'est moi la vérité: Pour une philosophie du christianisme* (Paris: Seuil, 1996). See pp. 226–27.

38. See Brague 1988, 34.

39. See Bultmann 1954, §26, pp. 249–55.

40. See Taubes 1996, 122.

41. On the meaning of "elemental spirits," see Pépin 1964, 307–13.

42. Regarding the chronological order of the suras, I am following the hypotheses of Blachère, which are for the most part those of all philologists. [All citations from the Koran are taken from the English translation by N. J. Dawood (New York: Penguin, 1999). TRANS.]

43. I prefer to keep the Arabic word here, which is distinguished from the proper name we use, "God," by the presence of the article *(al-(i)lah),* so that it should be translated: "*The* (one and only) God."

44. See Masson (1976), which is above all a synopsis of biblical parallels, and Speyer (1931) for the Midrash.

45. 29:9/10, p. 279, and see Paret 1977, 12.

46. 22:72–73, p. 240; 50:14/15 [i.e. verses numbered differently in different editions], p. 365; 46:32, p. 356, then 6:72, p. 99; 2:111/117, p. 21.

47. 50:37, p. 367; 25:60, p. 256; 32:3, p. 291; 11:9, p. 157; 7:52/54, p. 113; finally 41:8, p. 335.

48. 32:3, p. 291; 10: 3, p. 147; 7:52/54, p. 113; 13:2, p. 175; 57:4, p. 381.

49. 35:1, p. 305; then 10:3, p. 147; 32, p. 150.

50. 35:40, p. 308, and see 22:64/65, p. 239.

51. 6:100, p. 102; then 6:110, p. 103; 13:17/16, p. 176; finally 39:63/62, p. 326; 40:64/62, p. 332.

52. 32:6/7, p. 291, and Genesis 1:31.

53. 31:9/10, p. 288; 21:30 and 34, p. 229.

54. 71:14, p. 407; 67:3–4, p. 399; 23:17, 88, pp. 241, 244; 41:11, p. 335; 17:46, p. 200; 2:27/29, p. 13; then 65:12, p. 397.

55. 15:16–17, p. 184; 37:6–7, p. 312. The presumed myth here is parallel to that of the *Ascension of Isaiah*, see pp. 52–53.

56. 91:1–6, p. 426, and see 81:15–18, p. 419; then 99:1–2, p. 430, 82:1–3, p. 420; finally 81:1–6, p. 419; 84:1–3, p. 422; 77:8–10, pp. 413–14.

57. See Matthew 16:2 and p. 52.

58. 86:6–8, p. 423; 80:18–22, p. 419; 75:37–40, p. 413; 53:47–48, p. 373; 36:79, p. 312; then 43:10, p. 343; 35:10, p. 305; 7:55, p. 113; finally 79:27–33, p. 418; the theme is extensively developed in 50:6–11, p. 365.

59. 80:24–32, p. 419; 88:17–20, p. 425; 78:6–16, p. 416; 55:1–24, p. 376; 15:16–23, p. 184; 27:60–65, p. 269.

60. 53:18, p. 372; see 51:20, p. 368.

61. 20:56, p. 222, and see 128, p. 226; then 55:2–4, p. 350, and see 12, p. 351; see also 2:159, p. 25; 3:187/90, p. 59; finally 29:43, p. 281.

62. Respectively: *(a)* 39:22, p. 323; *(c)* 20:56 and 128, pp. 222 and 226; then 39:22, p. 323; *(d)* 16:67, p. 191; then 16:71, p. 192; finally 16:81, p. 193.

63. 7:184, p. 124; 6:75–79, p. 99; see Speyer 1931, 124–28, and see p. 51.

64. 16:3–8, 10–11, 12, 13 (and see 35:25–26, p. 306), 14, 15, pp. 187–88; 67–71, pp. 191–92; similarly 30:19–24, p. 285. See also 41:37–38, p. 331.

65. This archaic trait is also found in Egypt, see *Instruction for Merikare*, in *ANET*, 417b.

66. 26:7, 67, 103, 121, 139, 158, 174, 190.

67. 36:33–44, p. 310; 51:24, p. 368; 54:15, p. 374.

68. 51:47–48, p. 369; 26:6–7, p. 257; then 38:42/43, p. 319; 39:50/51, p. 282.

69. See for example 2:159/164, p. 25; 14:37, p. 182; 31:30, p. 290; 10:23/22b, p. 149.

70. See Saint Ephraem, *Sermon on Resurrection*, Op. Gr. 3.119, in Andrae 1955, 179.

71. 45:12, p. 351; then 30:46, p. 287, and 17:66, p. 202; finally 42:31/33, p. 341.

72. 64:3, p. 395; then 31:19, p. 289; finally 14:37/33, p. 182.

73. 91:7, p. 427; then 51:20–21, p. 368. See also 41:53, p. 338; analogy in 9:119/118, p. 145.

74. 33:72, pp. 299–300; see Paret 1977, 402.

75. 22:18, p. 235; 16:50–51, p. 190; then 38:17, p. 318.

76. 44:38–39, p. 349; then 21:16, p. 228; finally 38:26, p. 319.

77. 45:21, p. 351; 16:3, p. 187; 30:7, p. 284; 14:22, p. 181; 39:7, p. 322; 29:43, p. 281; 10:5, p. 147; 46:2/3, p. 353.

78. See for example, with various meanings, Proverbs 8:30; Pl., *Leg.* 7.803c; Proclus, *In Ti.* 2, vol. 1, p. 334.1–2, and see Deichgräber 1954; Rāmanuja, *Commentary on the Bhagavadgita* 7.12. On the popularity of this image in the second century see Dodds 1979, 22–25.

79. 30:7/8, p. 284; 46:3, p. 353.

80. See Lane, *Arabic–English Dictionary*, s.v.

81. 2:27, p. 13; see Paret 1977, 16; Al-Qāḍi (1988).

82. 2:29/31, p. 13. See Brague 1993b, 120; Speyer 1931, 51–54, stresses the similarities more than the differences.

Chapter 6: The Other Other

1. This word was most probably coined by Pétrement 1984; see Dewitte 1989.

2. These are the titles of Dodds 1979 and of chapter 4 in Murray 1925.

3. See Stroumsa 1984, 9, 14, and Couliano 1990, 150–51 (and see also pp. 95–96, 122).

4. Dodds 1979, 29, follows M. Burrows in citing a text that speaks of the world as "the dominion of fear and terror, the place of distress with desolation"; but the original, the *Manual of Discipline* (1QS 10:15), in *Die Texte aus Qumran: Hebräisch und deutsch . . .* , ed. E. Lohse (Munich: Kösel, 1964), 36–38, is generally understood differently.

5. See Mansfeld 1981; Taubes 1996, 107.

6. Plotinus, 2.9 [33], 6.10–12; Elsas 1975, 75–76; Alt 1990, 22–23; Taubes 1996, 110–13.

7. *NHL*, 319–20, viz., *Resp.* 9.588a–89b.

8. See Mansfeld 1981.

9. See Alt 1993; O'Brien 1993.

10. See Benardete 1971, 41–42.

11. See *La Sagesse de Jésus-Christ*, 92, pp. 21–22, ed. C. Barry, BCNH 20: 119, or *The Sophia of Jesus Christ* in *NHL*, 223; *L'Ecrit sans titre*, 97* (145), ed. L. Painchaud, BCNH 21: 147, or *Fragments* in *NHL*, 171; *Traité tripartite*, 109.5–6, ed. E. Thomassen, BCNH 19: 191, or *The Tripartate Tractate* in *NHL*, 90; *Traité sur la résurrection*, 46.8–9, ed. J. E. Ménard, BCNH 12: 49, or *The Treatise on the Resurrection* in *NHL*, 55.

12. See Jonas 1933, 1954; Puech 1978.

13. Tertullian, *De praescr. haeret.* 33.

14. Text in Ort 1967, 140–41. The beginning (up to "hell") is translated in Couliano 1990, 217. Not knowing Pehlevi, for the next paragraph I am translating from the German of Andreas and Henning, loc. cit. (*Mitteliranische Manichaica aus Chinesisch-Turkestan von F. C. Andreas aus dem Nachlass hrsg. von W. Henning* [Berlin: De Gruyter, 1932–34]).

15. H. H. Schaeder, in Reitzenstein and Schaeder 1926, 301. See also Puech 1979; Couliano 1990, 206.

16. Hippolytus, *Haer.* 8.17.2, pp. 432–33; ed. Wendland, GCS, 236.18–237.1, or Tert., *Adv. Herm.* 40.2–3, pp. 430–31 Kroymann.

17. Ptolemy, in Irenaeus, *Adv. haer.* 1.7.5, ed. A. Rousseau, SC 264: 111.

18. See Couliano 1990, 19, 132 (the world as half-light), 165.

19. See Couliano 1990, 131, 217.

20. *Évangile selon Philippe*, Introduction, text, translation, commentary by J. E. Ménard (Paris: Letouzey et Ané, 1967), §99 [p. 77], p. 95.2–3, or *The Gospel of Philip* in *NHL* 2, 75:3, p. 154. See Couliano 1990, 100.

21. *Traité sur la résurrection*, 48:15, ed. J. E. Ménard, BCNH 12: 55, or *The Treatise on the Resurrection* in *NHL*, p. 55.

22. See Couliano 1990, 112–70; Basilides, in Hippolytus, *Haer.* 7.23, p. 366.

23. Ptolemy, *Letter to Flora*, ed. G. Quispel, SC 24bis: 68–70.

24. See p. 23.

25. "Hermes Trismegistus," *CH*, respectively 10.10, vol. 1, p. 118; 6.2, vol. 1, p. 73; 6.4, vol. 1, p. 74; Kranz 1955, 87.

26. Heracleon, frag. 20, p. 77 Brooke, or Origen, *On John*, 13.16; VEP, p. 127.

27. See Jonas 1954, 146–99, 223–33, 251–55.

28. *Ascension d'Isaïe*, Translation of the Ethiopian version with the principal variants of the Greek, Latin, and Slavic versions, Introduction and notes by E. Tisserand (Paris: Letouzey et Ané, 1909), 10:29, p. 201, and Légende grecque, 2:9, p. 220.

29. *Évangile selon Marie*, 15:21–16:1, ed. A. Pasquier, BCNH 10: 39–41, or *The Gospel of Mary* in *NHL*, p. 526.

30. See Jonas 1954, 148.

31. Reported by Augustine, *Enarrationes* 140.12, p. 2034.

32. Plotinus 2.9 [33], 13.7–8, vol. 1, pp. 242–43; Alt 1990, 31.

33. *Authentikos logos*, 26.26–33, ed. J. E. Ménard, BCNH 2: 17, or *NHL*, p. 307.

34. *Papyri Graecae Magiae*, ed. K. Preisendanz, 1: 118, lines 1345–80, in J. Smith 1978, 162. It would be interesting to compare this text with the poem by Ingeborg Bachmann of the same title, "Anrufung des grossen Bären," in *Gedichte* (Munich: Piper, 1956), 21.

35. In R. C. Thompson, *Semitic Magic* (London, 1908), 47–50, cited in J. Smith 1978, 139; see Dodds 1979, 28–29.

36. *Ginzâ,* Right side, 11th book, ed. M. Lidzbarski (Göttingen: Vandenhoek & Ruprecht; Leipzig: Hinrichs, 1925), 261–62. Not knowing Mandaic, I must translate from the German of the editor and translator.

37. Basilides, in Clem. Al., *Strom.* 4.12, 88.5, ed. Stählin, GCS, p. 287, §8; Quispel 1974, 126.

38. *The Gospel of Truth,* 1.17.5–21, in *NHL,* p. 40. Cited in Couliano 1990, 118.

39. Clement of Alexandria, *ET,* 48.3, p. 160. The editor assumes that this is a reference to the four classical elements; Irenaeus, *Against Heresies,* 1.4.2, in Couliano 1990, 95.

40. *Lettre de Pierre à Philippe,* ed. J. E. Ménard, BCNH 1, pp. 17–18, or *The Letter of Peter to Philip* in *NHL,* p. 434.

41. *The Gospel of Truth,* 1, 29.1–30.12, in *NHL,* p. 45; Dodds 1979, 23 no. 2.

42. Basilides, in Hippolytus, *Haer.* 7.26, p. 374; Quispel 1974, 118.

43. See Jonas 1954, 108; Puech 1978, 207–13, 257 n. 2.

44. Clem. Al., *ET* 78.2, p. 202. The parallel formula in Porphyry, *Abst.* 1.27.1, ed. J. Bouffartigue, CUF, p. 61, indeed does not include the idea of "propulsion"; on the context see Norden 1913, 102–3, to which we might add *Pirqey Abhoth* 3.1.

45. *Pistis Sophia,* trans. J. E. Ménard, pp. 176, 215.

46. *Hymn of the Naassenes* 7, in Hippolytus, *Haer.* 5.10, p. 174.

47. *Ginzâ,* Right side, 11th book, p. 254. See also pp. 176, 242, 393, 454, 457–58, 461.

48. Lucretius 5.222–24; Lactantius, *De opificio Dei* 3.1, ed. M. Perrin, SC 213: 116. See Pascal, *Discours sur la condition des grands,* 1; ed. L. Lafuma (Paris, Seuil, 1963), 366a. On the theme, see Blumenberg 1979.

49. *Der Kölner Mani-Kodex: Über das Werden seines Leibes,* critical edition ed. and trans. by L. Koenen and C. Römer (Bonn: Westdeutscher Verlag, 1988), 52.

50. See Couliano 1990, 131, 162–63.

51. See Puech 1978, 206; Brague 1988, 37–38 n. 63; Couliano 1990, 315. "Heidegger's cosmology is anti-gnostic": Depraz 1996, 640.

52. *Epître apocryphe de Jacques,* 5, 29–30, ed. D. Rouleau, BCNH 18, p. 49, or *The Apocryphon of James* in *NHL,* p. 32.

53. Heracleon, frag. 23, p. 80 Brooke, or Origen, *On John,* 13. 20; VEP, pp. 130–31.

54. Clem. Al., *ET* 80, p. 202; Quispel 1974, 51.

55. Tertullian, *Adv. Marc.* 1.14.

56. Clem. Al., *ET* 33.3, p. 130.

57. See frag. 23, cited just above.

58. Frag. 11, p. 66 Brooke, or Origen, *On John,* 11.9, VEP, p. 75; frag. 40, p. 93 Brooke, or Origen 13.59, VEP, p. 173.

59. Marcus Aurelius 4.29, p. 62.

60. *Der Kölner Mani-Kodex,* 72.

61. See *Hymne de la Perle des Actes de Thomas,* Introduction, text, translation, commentary by P.-H. Poirier (Louvain-la-Neuve, 1981), 344 (line 23b).

62. See G. Stroumsa 1980–81.

63. Clem. Al., *Strom.* 3.3.12.3; see Puech 1978, 209; then 4.26, 165.3–4 [p. 321.27–33], and see 2.3, 10.3 [p. 118.17–20 Stählin].

64. *Hymn of the Naassenes* 16–17, in Hippolytus, *Haer.* 5.10.2, p. 176; *Ascension d'Isaïe,* 6:9, p. 138.

65. Clem. Al., *ET* 74, p. 196.

66. See 1 Corinthians 1:20, and see pp. 54–55.

67. *Ecrit sans titre: Traité sur l'origine du monde* 122* (170), 1.24–26, ed. L. Painchaud, *BCNH* 21 (1995), 205. [*On the Origin of the World* in *NHL,* p. 186, replaces "the wisdom of the world" with the personified "Sophia." Trans.]

Chapter 7: Marginal Models

1. Lucian, *Icaromenippus* 4, in *Die Hauptwerke von Lukian: Griechisch und deutsch,* ed. K. Mras (Munich: Heimeran, 1980), 286–87. See Helm 1906, ch. 3, then p. 103 n. 3.

2. Xen., *Mem.* 1.1.11, and see p. 21.

3. See Descartes, *Lettre à Mersenne* 10.5.1632, Oeuvres, 1: 250–51; Nicolson 1960, 167–68; "Morris Zapp," in David Lodge, *Changing Places: A Tale of Two Campuses* (London: Penguin, 1978), 10.

4. Heraclitus, DK 22 B 124; see p. 20.

5. Galen, *De usu partium* 3.3 end, ed. Helmreich, pp. 133.6–134.7; the quotation is from Empedocles, DK, 31 B 44; the fish is the *Uranoscopes scaber* of Linnaeus; the allusion is to Pl. *Resp.* 7.529b. On the legacy of the text, see for example Lichtenberg, *Aphorismen,* F 638, ed. Leitzmann, 3: 238, cited by Blumenberg 1966, 123. Eng. trans. by Margaret Tallmadge May (Ithaca: Cornell University Press, 1968), 160.

6. See p. 99.

7. Avicenna, *Al-Mabda' wa-'l-ma'ād,* 1.46, ed. Nûrânî (Teheran, 1984), 62.18. The passage is repeated verbatim in subsequent works, where the name of Alexander is replaced by "the best of all predecessors *(fāḍil al-mutaqaddimīn)*" (*Metaphysics* 9.3, p. 393.16; *Najāt,* p. 304.4). See Gutas 1988, 290–91.

8. Alexander of Aphrodisias, *On the Cosmos,* ed. C. Genequand (Leiden: Brill, 2001), §91, p. 90; for the Greek Alexander see Alex. Aphrod., *Quaestiones* 1.25, ed. I. Bruns, pp. 40.34–41.4; but this work seems not to have been translated into Arabic, see Fazzo and Wiesner 1993, 124.

9. Avicenna, *Najāt,* ed. al-Kurdî (Cairo, 1938), 271.17; the Fakhry edition, p. 308, omits the proper name.

10. Ibn Ezra, *Commentary to the Torah,* ed. A. Weiser (Jerusalem: Mosad Rav Kook, 1976), Preface to Genesis, pp. 7–8; on Genesis 1:1, vol. 1, p. 12, *Reader,* p. 147; on Exodus 23:25, vol. 2, p. 164, *Reader,* p. 179; see also *YM,* p. 48.

11. Wallace-Hadrill 1968,101–2.

12. Marcus Aurelius 4.27, p. 62; commentary, pp. 614–17, then 9.28, p. 182; commentary, p. 809; see Goldschmidt 1970, 257; nothing in Rutherford 1989.

13. See Schuhl 1953.

14. See Furley 1989, 2.

15. Galen, *On the Doctrines of Hippocrates and Plato,* 9.7.9–14, ed. Phillip De Lacey (Berlin: Akademie-Verlag, 1978), 588.7–27.

16. Julian the Apostate, *To Heraclius the Cynic* 7.24.237bc.

17. Galen, *Compendium Timaei Platonis,* ed. P. Kraus and R. Walzer (London, 1951), §§7, 23, pp. 12/55 and 33/94; in Bādāwī 1980, 97, 118.

18. See Nazzaro 1969–70, pp. 67–74.

19. See p. 51. In his time, see Josephus, *AJ* 1.8.2.167; b*Yoma* 3:28b; b*Baba Bathra* 16b.

20. Philo, *De gigantibus* 60–62, trans. Mosès, p. 48.

21. Ibid., *Quis rerum divinarum heres sit* 97–99; Eng. trans.: *Who Is the Heir,* tr. F. H. Colson and G. H. Whitaker, LCL, 1934.

22. Ibid., *De migratione Abrahami* 136–38; Eng. trans.: *The Migration of Abraham,* tr. Colson and Whitaker, LCL, 1932.

23. Isaiah 40:13; Job 38:4.

24. Philo, *De somniis* 1.53–58; Eng. trans.: *On Dreams,* tr. Colson and Whitaker, LCL, 1934.

25. Pind., *Pyth.* 3.60; see Blumenberg 1987.

26 See Exodus 23:21; Deuteronomy 24:8; Exodus 34:12; see Nazzaro 1970.

27. Philo, *De migratione Abrahami* 185–87.

28. See for example Xen., *Mem.* 1.4.8; Pl., *Phlb.* 30a; Cic., *Nat. D.* 3.11.27, p. 310.

29. Seneca, *QNat.* 7.32.2, p. 335.

30. Julian the Apostate, *Letter to a priest,* 301cd.

31. Alain de Lille, *De planctu naturae* 8, prose 4.

32. For details see Jones 1989, ch. 5, pp. 135–41, with references to which might be added the two preceding.

33. See Urbach 1979, 29–30.

34. See Liebeschütz 1926, 132 n. 100; Pabst 1994, 125.

35. Obolensky 1948, 113, 180; Borst 1953, 147.

36. Cited in Puech 1978, 211.

37. Fahr ad-Dīn ar-Rāzī, in Razi, *Opera*, 206; and see Goodman 1975.

38 Respectively, Razi, *Opera*, 284–85; Ger. trans. in Schaeder 1925, 232–33, and Meier 1991, 10; then *Opera*, 308–9.

39. See Stern 1983, 7.19, trans. p. 18; 12.5–6, trans. p. 25; Halm 1978, 75–90 and 115–27, esp. 77.

40. See p. 68.

41. On Islam: Nicholson 1921, 90–92.

42. See Stroumsa 1992, 145–62, and pp. 54–55.

43. See Bultot 1963, 40; 1964, 69; and *DS*, s.v. "Fuite du monde" (Z. Alszeghy).

44. See Guillaumont 1968, 111, 114.

45. See Dewitte 1989, 168–72; Walker Percy, *Lost in the Cosmos: the Last Self-Help Book* (New York: Farrar, Straus & Giroux, 1983). I learned of this book from S. Maddux.

46. See Bultot 1963, 112–13.

47. See Guillaumont 1968, 114.

48. See H. Ritter 1978, 45–53.

49. *CTM*, 1: 377a, or Muslim, *Ṣaḥīḥ*, book 53 (Zuhd), no. 1, §2956(n.p., 1955), 4: 2272; and *CTM*, 4: 473b, or al-Bukharī, *Ṣaḥīḥ* 81 (Riqāq), 3; Fr. trans. D. Houdas (1914, repr. Paris: Maisonneuve, 1977), 4: 272.

50. *Logion* in J. Jeremias, *Les Paroles inconnues de Jésus* (Paris: Cerf, 1970), 109–15; Ritter 1978, 45.

51. Hans Peter Rüger, *Die Weisheitschrift aus der Kairoer Geniza* (Tübingen: Mohr, 1991), 1.10a, p. 82, and 2.18, p. 89; Bahya ben Joseph ibn Paquda, *Hidāja 'ilā Farā'iḍ al-Qulūb*, 3.2 no. 2, p. 131.16; 8.3 no. 30, p. 346; *Der Mikrokosmos des Josef ibn Saddik*, ed. S. Horovitz (Breslau: Schatzky, 1903), 1.1, p. 8.25; 2.B,.3, p. 43.14; 4.B, p. 77.18; Vajda 1954, 11 n. 1.

52. See for example Yedaya Bedersi, *Bekhinat ha-ʿolam*, 8.1–5, ed. D. Slotzky (Warsaw, n.d.), 7b.

53. See Shahar 1971; Scholem 1974, 45.

Chapter 8: The Standard Vision of the World

1. Johannes Scotus Eriugena, *Div. Nat.* 1.31.76c; see Chenu 1966, 118–19.

2. See Le Roy Ladurie (1975), ch. 19: "Le sentiment de la nature et du destin," pp. 446–51, and Ginzburg (1976); on the popular feeling toward nature, see Steinen 1967, 92–96.

3. See Grant 1994, 40–44; for the iconography, see Zahlten 1979, 149–51.

4. See Lloyd 1991, 141–63; on the mythical image of the world, see Ballabriga 1986.

5. See Grant 1978.

6. Ocellus Lucanus, *De universi natura*, in *FPhG*, 1: 388–406.

7. Pseudo–Apollonius of Tyane, *Buch über das Geheimnis der Schöpfung und die Darstellung der Natur* (Buch der Ursachen), ed. U. Weisser (University of Aleppo, 1979).

8. See Langlois 1911.

9. See Zahlten 1979, 178–84.

10. Averroes, *Tahāfut* 1.76–78, pp. 44.15–47.7; trans. pp. 26–27.

11. Maimonides, *Guide*, 1.72, p. 127.10ff.; pp. 354ff.—the commentary, or rather the *companion Ruaḥ Ḥēn*, also contains a summary of cosmology—as does *Mishneh Torah*, Madda', Yesodey ha-Torah, chs. 3–4; trans. *The Book of Knowledge*, ed. M. Hyamson, 2d ed. (Jerusalem: Feldheim, 1981), 36b–40a; on its status, see Kellner 1991.

12. See Rutherford 1989, 155–61.

13. See *Eine Mithrasliturgie,* ed. A. Dieterich, 3d ed. (1923, repr. Stuttgart: Teubner, 1966), 6–7, and commentary, 78–79.

14. See Etana, C-5 and C-6, in *ANET,* 118. The same scene appears in the legend of the ascent of King Alexander; see Jerusalem Talmud, *'Avoda Zara,*3:1, p.42c; Tabari, *Tafsir* (Cairo, 1957), 16: 6–7.

15. *Le Livre de l'échelle de Mahomet (Liber Scale Machometi),* new ed., trans. by G. Besson and M. Brossard-Dandré (Paris: Le Livre de Poche, 1991).

16. In Granada 1988, 79.

17. Cervantes, *Don Quixote,* 2.41, trans. J. Cassou (Paris: Gallimard, 1949), 818, 822.

18. Marcus Aurelius 8.52, p. 166—I will not enter into the textual problems of the passage.

19. See C. S. Lewis 1964, Grant 1978, quite recently the superb synthesis by Lerner 1996.

20. Pl., *Ti.* 69c, pp. 280–81; Plotinus 2.1 [40].5.

21. Arist., *Cael.* 1.2–3.268a–269b. See PW, s.v. "Quinta essentia" (P. Moraux, 1963).

22. Ibid., cols. 1232–36. See especially Cic., *Acad. Post.* 9.39, ed. H. Rackham, LCL, pp. 446–47; *Fin.* 4.5.12, pp. 124–25; Goldschmidt 1953, 84.

23. Grant 1983, 164–65, repeated for the most part in Grant 1993, 244–70.

24. See Johannes Scotus Eriugena, *Div. Nat.* 3.32, *PL* 122: 715ab; Liebeschütz 1926, 124.

25. Saadia Gaon, *Beliefs* 1.3, p. 61/70; Bahya ben Joseph ibn Paquda, *Hidāja 'ilā Farā'id al-Qulūb,* 1.6, p. 47; *De l'âme,* ed. I. Goldziher, *Kitâb Ma'âni al-Nafs: Buch vom Wesen der Seele, Von einem Ungenannten* (Berlin: Weidmann, 1907), 56.18, 65.29; see Vajda 1949, 110–11.

26. Bonaventure, *In Sent.* 2.14.1.1.2c, *Opera,* 2: 339b–40a; see Schaefer 1961, 318.

27. Ibn Ezra, on Exodus 33:23; *Reader,* 184; Isaac Albalag, *Tiqqūn ha-de'ōt,* ed. G. Vajda (Jerusalem, 1973), 33.15–17; Fr. trans. in Vajda 1960, 139—who omits the last sentence.

28. Maimonides, *Guide* 2.26, pp. 231.22, 232.3–4, 8–11, trans. pp. 330–32. See also 2.19.

29. *Avencebrolis (Ibn Gabirol)* Fons Vitae *ex arabico in latinum translatus ab Johanne Hispano et Domenico Gundissalino,* ed. C. Bäumker (Münster: Aschendorff, 1892–95), 1.17, Lat. pp. 20–21, trans. J. Schlanger (Paris: Aubier Montaigne, 1970), 54.

30. Bahya b. Asher, *Commentary on the Torah,* on Genesis, ed. H. D. Chavel (Jerusalem, Mosad Rav Kook), 15; Nachmanides, *Commentary on Genesis,* 1.1, in MG, p.3b, col. a, end; ed. Chavel, p. 12.

31. Gersonides, *Wars* 6.17 end, p. 40c; p. 368.

32. Averroes, *De substantia orbis* ch. 3 end, ed. A. Hyman (Cambridge, Mass.: Medieval Academy of America; Jerusalem: Israel Academy of Sciences and Humanities, 1986), Hebr. p. 42, 1.110–11 (1st version) and p. 47, 1.116–17 (2d version); Eng. p. 111; compare *Tahāfut* 8.9, p. 396.9; Eng. trans. p. 239; *Commentary on Plato's "Republic,"* 2.15.2, 4, ed. E. I. J. Rosenthal (Cambridge: Cambridge University Press, 1969), p. 75.25, 28–29; J. Lay, "*L'Abrégé de l'Almageste:* Un inédit d'Averroès en version hébraïque," *Arabic Sciences and Philosophy* 6 (1996): 52–53.

33. See for example Xenophanes, DK 21 A 33; Herodotus 2.12.1; Strabo in A. von Humboldt, *Kosmos* 2: 170 n. 153, and see ibid., pp. 329–30; Avicenna, *De congelatione . . . lapidum,* ed. E. J. Holmyard and D.C. Mandeville (Paris: Guethner, 1927), Eng. p. 28, Lat. p. 49, Ar. p. 78.7–8.

34. Arist., *Mete.* 2.1.353a34–b5; Cic., *Somnium Scipionis,* and Macrobius, *In somn. Scip.* ad loc., 2.9; Boëthius, *De Consolatione* 2.7, p. 216, etc.; see Festugière 1949, 449–56.

35. Lucan 9.1–14; Dante, *Paradiso* 21.133–35, p. 833; Chaucer, *Troilus and Criseyde* 5.1814–19; see C. S. Lewis 1964, 32–33; North 1988, 11–12.

36. See Brague (1997c), pp. 202–3; add the expressions attributed to the Aristotelian Simplicius in Galileo, *Dialogo* 1, p. 84, and 2, p. 292.

37. See *Etna* 250–52, ed. J. Vessereau, CUF, p. 20; see Bernath 1988, 190.

38. Kant, *Logik,* Introduction, 3; *Werke,* 3: 448.

39. Pl., *Tht.* 174b4; Albinos, *Introduction à Platon,* ed. P. Louis (Paris: CUF, 1945), 7; *Altercatio Hadrian . . . et . . . Secundi philosophi* 8, *FPhG,* 1: 518a.

40. Augustine, *Confessiones* 4.4.9, p. 422; slightly reworded by Heidegger, *Augustinus und*

der Neuplatonismus, Summer Semester 1921, *Gesamtausgabe* 60: 178; Tawḥīdī, in Miskawayh, *al-Hawāmil wa-'š-Šawāmil,* ed. A. Amīn (Cairo, 1951), 180; Arkoun 1973, 112.

41. *Poimandres* 15, "Hermes Trismegistus," *CH* 1: 11; Plotinus 4.8 [6].4.32, 2: 238; Hierocles, *Commentary on the Golden Words* 24, *FPhG* 1: 471b.

42. Thomas Aquinas, *Summa contra gentiles,* 4.55, p. 515a; Dante, *Monarchia* 3.15.3. The expression comes no doubt from the *Liber de causis,* 2.22, Arabic in Bādāwī 1954, 5—where it is applied to the universal soul.

43. See Pliny, *HN* 7 preface 1–4, and Pöhlmann 1970,301–11. See also Ronsard, *Amours de Cassandre,* "Mignonne, allons voir. . . ."

44. On the controversy regarding the ultimate goal of creation—men or angels, understood most often as the intellects of celestial bodies—see Malter 1921, 212–13 n. 485.

45. Sura 2:31ff., pp. 13ff.

46. Ephesians 3:10.

47. See for example William of Saint-Thierry, *De natura corporis et animae* 2; *PL* 180: 721d; Thomas Aquinas, *Summa theologica* 1, q. 93, a. 3; Dante, *Convivio* 4.19.6.

48. Xen., *Mem.* 1.4.8; Pl., *Leg.* 10.903cl–2.

49. Arist., *Eth. Nic.* 6.1141a21–22, and see Plotinus 2.9 [33].13.18–19, vol. 1, p. 243; Dunash Ibn Tamîm, *Commentary on the Sefer Yetsira* 1.13, ed. G. Vajda, *Revue des études juives* 113 (1954): 45.

50. Hierocles, *Commentary on the Golden Words* 23, on 52–53; *FPhG,* 1: 468b.

51. See for example Plotinus 3.2 [47].8.9–10; Theophilus of Antioch, *To Autolycus* 2.24, ed. Grant, OECT, p. 66; see Lubac 1974, 184–204. One can add Novalis, *Heinrich von Ofterdingen* 2 (Munich: Goldmann, n.d.), p. 157.

52. Maimonides, *On the Management of Health* 3.18, Arabic in Kroner, *Die Seelenhygiene des Maimonides* (Stuttgarter Ausstellung der Gesundheitspflege, 1914), 8.7–11; Hebr. trans., Rambam, *Hanhagat ha-beri'ūt,* in *Ketavim Refū'iyyim,* ed. S. Muntner, 4th ed. (Jerusalem: Mosad Rav Kook, 1989), 1: 63; Eng. trans. R. L. Weiss and C. Butterworth, eds., *Ethical Writings of Maimonides* (New York: Dover, 1975), 110.

53. Maimonides, *Guide* 1.2, p. 16.6–7, trans. p. 25.

54. Marsilio Ficino, [Letter to the human race], in *Lettere,* 1: *Epistolarum familiarium liber I,* ed. S. Gentile (Florence: Olschki, 1990), no. 110, p. 194; see Blumenberg 1966, 121.

55. Ibn Abī Usaybi'a, *'Uyūn al-anbā' fi' ṭabaqāt al-aṭibbā'* (Beirut: Dar maktabat al-hayat, n.d.), 608.

56. See Ṣā'id al-Andalusî, *Ṭabaqāt al-Uman,* ed. H. Boualouane (Beirut: Dâr al-Tali'a, 1985), 177.

57. Ibn Bājja, *Letter of Farewell,* in *Opera metaphysica,* p. 121; analogous expression in Jalāl ad-Dīn Rūmī, cited in Bausani 1971, 207.

58. See Allers 1944; Altmann 1969, 19–28; Kurdzialek 1971; Chiesa 1989, 68–80; Rico 1988; Brague 1997b.

59. See G. Widengren 1980; Tardieu 1984, 300–308. Let us note a curious resurgence of the archaic idea of the *Adam Qadmon* in Islam: the primitive body of which the world is made is none other than . . . the Prophet's. See the Bengali poet quoted in Schimmel 1989, 121.

60. Pseudo-Hippocrates, *Peri hebdomadon* chs. 2 and 8; Democritus, DK 68 B 34, mentioned in Arist., *Ph.* 8.2.252b26.

61. Brethren of Purity, *Rasā'il* 2.12 [26], 3.3 [34].

62. See Albertus Magnus, *In Physicam Aristotelis,* 8.1.9.17, ed. Borgnet, 3: 540, cited by Kurdzialek 1971, 46.

63. Hildegarde von Bingen, *Liber divinorum operum simplicis hominis* 1.2.1, *PL* 197: 752a.

64. See d'Alverny 1953, 79; Kurdzialek 1971, 50. Pl., *Ti.* 36b8, p. 72; Justin, *First Apology,* 60.1–7, ed. L. Pautigny, TD, pp. 124–25.

65. See Hommel 1943.

66. *Aboth de-Rabbi Nathan,* version 1, ch. 30, ed. S. Schechter (Vienna, 1887), 46a ff.; the

idea is attributed to R. Josi the Galilean: Qirqisani in Chiesa 1989, 54–55. For the Talmud, see Urbach 1979, 233, etc.

67. Yahyâ Ibn 'Ady, in Platti 1982; Honorius Augustodunensis, *Lucidarium* 1.11, *PL* 172: 1116bc, etc.

68. Al-Kindī, *Prosternation of the Last Sphere*, in *Rasā'il*, 1: 259–61; Miskawayh, *Le Petit livre du salut*, 3.2, ed. S. Udeyma, ref. Ar. pp. 118–22, Fr. trans. R. Arnaldez (n.p.: Maison arabe du livre, 1987), 74–77; Nasir-e Khosraw, *Le Livre réunissant les deux sagesses* ch. 28, Fr. trans. by I. de Gastines (Paris: Fayard, 1990), 295–301, etc.

69. Galen, *De usu partium* 3.10, ed. G. Helmreich, BT, p. 177.

70. Judah Halevi, *Kuzari* 4.3, pp. 156, 156–57; Maimonides, *Guide* 1.72, pp. 132–33; trans. pp. 184–94.

71. Manilius, *Astronomica* 4.893–95; see also Johannes Scotus Eriugena, *Div. Nat.* 2.4.530cd; 4.5.755b, etc.

72. *Der Mikrokosmos des Josef ibn Saddik*, ed. S. Horovitz (Breslau: Schatzky, 1903), 23, 39; see Idel 1992, 199.

73. Pl., *Ti.* 41d–e, p. 142.

74. *Genesis Rabbah* 24:2, p. 231 (parallels in the note); see Idel 1992, 93, 170.

75. Sura 7:171–72, p. 123.

76. Brethren of Purity, *Rasā'il* 2.12 [26], "That Man is a Small World," 2: 462. The quotation is from Sura 95:4.

77. *Risāla Jāmi'a*, ed. M. Ghalib (Beirut: Dar al-Andaloss, 1984), 119, 153, 180, 226, 261, 359.

78. See Gaiser 1961 for Plato's texts. See also Polybius 6.5.5, CUF, p. 73.

79. Philo, *De aeternitate mundi* ch. 24 (and *SVF* 1.106a, pp. 31.29–32.2); Gersonides, *Wars* 6.1.15, pp. 58c–59a, pp. 356–58, see Touati 1973, 187–93.

80. See for example al-Biruni, *Epistle . . . Razi*, p. 28.5–6; *Gärten*, 37, or Machiavelli, *Discorsi* 2.5, pp. 247–48 Flora-Cordié. Hume, *Dialogues* 6, pp. 74–75, uses a similar hypothesis to render the eternity of the world plausible. But the flood henceforth has only metaphorical value: it is the arrival of the barbarian nations.

81. See for example Marsilius of Padua, *Defensor Pacis* 1.17.10, ed. R. Schulz, Monomenta Germaniae Historica, Fontes, 7: 118.

82. Al-Birunī, *India*, ed. E. Sachau (London, 1887), 200; ed. A. Safa, 2d ed. (Beirut: Alam al-kutub, 1983), 305; Eng. trans. Sachau, *Alberuni's India*, 2 vols. (London, 1888), 1: 400–401; *Gärten*, 226.

83. *Chronologie orientalischer Völker von Albêrûni*, ed. C. Eduard Sachau (Leipzig: Brockhaus & Harrasowitz, 1878), 298.20; *Gärten*, 227.

84. See C. S. Lewis 1964, 102–12; North 1986, and, summing up, North 1987, Grant 1987. For the Muslim and Jewish worlds, for lack of a synthesis, a few indications in Freudenthal 1993, 77–84.

85. Arist., *Gen. Corr.* 2.10. See Brague 1988, 406–9.

86. Arist., *Mete.* 1.2.339a21–23.

87. Elijah del Medigo, *Behinat ha-dath* [3.3], ed. J. J. Ross (Tel-Aviv University, 1984), 99; on magic see Scholem 1974, 140–44; a similar idea already in Pl., *Menex.* 238a4–5; see Kranz 1955, 17.

88. On the two images of the circle and the line, see Syrianus, in Goldschmidt 1953, 52 (in n. 3 read vol. VI, not IV); E. Young, *Night Thoughts* (1742), 6.692, ed. S. Cornford (Cambridge: Cambridge University Press, 1989), 166.

89. See Pomian 1986; on the example of Machiavelli, Parel 1992.

90. See p. 164.

91. A long list of ancient texts in Dickerman 1909, 15–20, esp. 93–101; synthesis in Thomas Aquinas, *Summa theologica* 1a, q. 91, a. 3, ad 3m.

92. See Wlosok 1960–62, 8–47; Silverstein 1948, 97 n. 28.

93. See Verhaeghe 1980, 71–74; Brague 1988, §28c, pp. 237–38.

94. Gregory of Nyssa, *The Creation of Man* 8, *PG* 44: 144bc, 148c–49a, and 10, *PG* 44: 152b; Leroi-Gourhan 1964, ch. 2: "Le cerveau et la main," pp. 40–89.

95. Pseudo-Apollonius, *Sirr al-Xaliqah*, ed. Weisser (Aleppo, 1979), 6.1.2, p. 424, and summary in Weisser 1980, 135. See also 6.2.6, pp. 431–32, Weisser 1980, 136; 6.6.3, p. 446, Weisser 1980, 138; 23.1, p. 497, Weisser 1980, 148; 25, pp. 500–501, Weisser 1980, 149; *Picatrix* 3.5; Pseudo-Magriri, *Das Ziel des Weisen*, 1, ed. H. Ritter (Leipzig: Teubner, 1933), Ar. 178–79, Ger. trans. 188. See also al-Muqammis, *Išrūn maqala*, ed. S. Stroumsa (Leiden: Brill, 1989), ch. 7, p. 132; Aiyūb al-Abras ar-Ruhawī, *Book of Treasures*, ed. A. Mingana (Cambridge, 1935), 2.14, pp. 94–95.

96. See p. 75.

97. Pl., *Cra.* 399c. Long list of other authors in Dickerman 1909, 23–26. The true etymology is unknown, see Chantraine, *Dictionnaire étymologique de la langue grecque* (Paris: Klincksieck, 1980), s.v.

98. Isidore of Seville, *Etymologies* 11.1.5; Abelard, *Expositio in Hexaemeron* 6th day, *PL* 178: 775ab.

99. Pl., *Ti.* 90a7, p. 353. Philo, *Quod deterius* 84–85, ed. I. Feuer (Paris: Cerf, 1965), 72; for the twelfth century (Alain de Lille, etc.), see Edsman 1966, 94–97; for Islam, see Masʿūdi, *Golden Meadows*, cited in Tardieu 1986, 13; for Judaism, see Löw 1934, 4: 370ff.: "Der Mensch ein umgekehrter Baum."

100. Philo, *De gigantibus* 31, ed. Mosès (Paris: Cerf, 1963), 34–35; see also *Praemiis* 124; *De plantatione* 16, ed. Pouilloux, pp. 30–31.

101. Cicero, *Nat. D.* 2.56.140, pp. 256–57, and *Leg.* 1.11.26, ed. C. Appuhn (Paris: Garnier, 1954), 242.

102. Ov., *Met.* 1.84–86.

103. Seneca, *De otio* 5.4, ed. R. Waltz, CUF, p. 117; Juvenal 15.146–47; Prudentius, *c. Symm.* 2.260–69; Firmicus Maternus, *Mathesis*, 8.3–4, ed. C. Sittl (Leipzig: Teubner, 1894), 281–82.

104. Pl., *Ti.* 44d, pp. 150–51; Macrobius, *In Somn. Scip.* 1.14.9, ed. J. Willis (Leipzig: Teubner, 1963), 5; Kurdzialek 1971, 54, 56.

105. *Letter to Diognetus* 10.2, ed. H.-I. Marrou, SC 33bis: 76; Minucius Felix, *Octavius* 17.2, ed. B. Kytzler (Stuttgart: Reclam, 1977), 48–50. See Pellegrino 1964.

106. Lactantius, *De Opificio Dei* 8.2–5, ed. M. Perrin, SC 213: 148–49; see also *De ira Dei* 7.5.

107. See Pseudo-Dionysius, *On the Celestial Hierarchy* 15.3, ed. M. de Gandillac, SC 58: 171.

108. Augustine, *De Gen. contra Manichaeos* 1.17.28, *PL* 34: 186–87; see also Bede, *In Hexaem.* 1, *PL* 91: 29cd; *Gen. Lit.* 6.12, ed. Zycha, CSEL 28.1: 187.

109. See for example Bernard of Clairvaux, *Sermon on the Feast of St. Martin* 4, 14, in *Opera*, 5: 402, 409; *PL* 183: 492b, 496d.

110. Cassiodorus, *De Anima* 9: "De positione corporis" beginning, *PL* 70: 1295ab.

111. Augustine, *De Trinitate* 12.1.1, BA 16: 212, then *De diversis quaestionibus LXXXIII* no. 51.3, *PL* 40: 33.

112. See Pl., *Resp.* 6.509d2–3; see also *Cra.* 396b8–9; Philo, *De opif. mundi* 10.

113. Basil of Caesarea, *In Hex.* 9.2.5–7, *PG* 29: 192a; ed. Naldini (n.p.: Fondazione L. Valla/Mondadori, 1990), 274–75.

114. Gregory of Nyssa, *Op. hom.* 8, *PG* 44: 144ab; trans. J. Laplace, SC 2: 106; Dionysius, *Cael. hier.* 15.3, ed. M. de Gandillac, SC 58: 171; Ibn al-Tayyib, *Commentary on Genesis*, ed. J. C. J. Sanders (Louvain, 1967), 18.10–11, cited in Chiesa 1989, 63.

115. Persius 2.61, ed. W. Kissel (Heidelberg: Winter, 1990), 32; commentary p. 352.

116. Pl., *Ti.* 91e–92a, p. 358. The idea is in Sall., *Cat.* 1.1, ed. A. Ernout, CUF, p. 54; Horace, *Sat.* 2.2.77–79; Seneca, *Ep.* 90.13, p. 335; *QNat.* 5.15.3, p. 229.

117. Clem. Al., *Strom.* 4.163.1; Bernard of Clairvaux, *In Cant.* 24.2.6–7, *Opera*, 1: 157–58; *PL* 183: 897a–d.

118. Saadia Gaon, *Beliefs* 4 introduction, pp. 150–51; pp. 180–81. The same idea is found in the general introduction, but no reason is given there. See §5, p. 21; p. 24, and ch. 9.1, p. 261;

p. 323. I have reproduced the text elsewhere; this is why I am only summarizing here, see Brague 1994a, 8–9.

119. Nāsir-i Khusraw, *Goshâyesh va Rahâyesh* q. 24, trans. P. Filippani-Ronconi, *Il libro dello scioglimento e della liberazione* (Naples: Istituto Universitario Orientale, 1959), 82.

120. Hildegarde von Bingen, *Scivias* I, vision 3, *PL* 197: 408a; Ibn al-ʿArabī, *The Production of Circles* I, trans. P. Fenton and M. Gloton (Paris, L'Éclat, 1996), 3.

121. See Freudenthal 1991; Touati 1973, 185–87; Ehrard 1963, 118.

122. Samuel Ibn Tibbon, *Maʾamar Yikkawu ham-Mayyim*, ed. M. L. Bisseliches (Bratislava, 1837, repr. Jerusalem, n.d.); analysis in Vajda 1962, 13–31.

123. Strabo 17.1.36; Johannes Scotus Eriugena, *Div. Nat.* 3.30.708a, p. 215; Brethren of Purity, *Rasâ'il* 2.5 [19], 2: 91–92; al-Biruni, *Taḥdīd* 4, p. 143.3, Eng. trans. pp. 107–8; *Gärten*, p. 86.

124. Miskawayh, *Petit livre du salut* 2.10, ed. R. Arnaldez (n.p.: Maison arabe du livre, 1987), Ar. p. 100.7, Fr. trans. p. 60.

125. Averroes, *Epitome of the De generatione et corruptione* on 2.10.337a8–15, ed. G. Jehamy (Beirut: Dar al-Fikr al-Lubnani, 1994), 121.2–7; ed. J. Puig Montada (Madrid: CSIC, 1992), 53.13–54.4; Span. trans. p. 68; *Epitome of Meteorology* ch. 2, ed. G. Jéhamy (Beirut: Dâr al-Fikr al-Lubnânî, 1994), 62.23–63.7. See also Dante, *Quaestio de terra et aqua* 69–73.

126. Al-Biruni, *Taḥdīd*, Eng. pp. 23–25; *Gärten*, p. 84.

127. See Fontaine 1995.

128. William of Conches, *Notes on Boethius' De consolatione philosophiae*, in J. M. Parent, *La Doctrine de la création dans l'école de Chartres: Etude et textes* (Paris: Vrin; Ottawa: Institut d'Etudes médiévales, 1938), 129.1–13, and see Werner 1873, 327; Bonaventure, *In Sent.* 2.14.2.2.1c, *Opera*, 2: 358b.

129. Grosseteste, *Hexaemeron* 1.17, pp. 75–76; see McEvoy 1982, 397.

130. Gersonides, *Wars* 5.2.3, pp. 32b–33a, 194–97. Quotation from pp. 32b, 196.

131. See Tuzet 1965, 56.

Chapter 9: An Ethical Cosmos

1. See Brague 1991.

2. Abd al-Latif al-Baghdadi, *Metaphysics* 18, MS. Istanbul, Carullah 1279.173b–75a. I am translating from F. Rosenthal, *Das Fortleben der Antike im Islam* (Zurich: Artemis, 1965), 219. [Eng. trans.: F. Rosenthal, ed., *The Classical Heritage in Islam*, tr. Emile and Jenny Marmorstein (Berkeley: Univesity of California Press, 1975), 159 TRANS.].

3. See Pl., *Ti.* 34b8–9, p. 58; Alexander of Aphrodisias, *On Fate* 25, ed. P. Thillet, CUF, p. 50.4. R. W. Sharples translates "the happy state of the universe" (London, 1983, 75). His commentary does not discuss the expression (pp. 158ff.); that of P. Thillet is not yet available.

4. See for example Pl., *Resp.* 10.617b; Cic., *Somn. Scip.* 17–18; Montaigne, *Essaies* 1.23, 1: 202; Shakespeare, *Merchant of Venice* 5.1.60ff.; Milton, "On the Harmony of the Spheres" (2d Prolusion), 1.1624–42, in *Complete Prose Works.*, ed. D. M. Wolfe (New Haven: Yale University Press, 1953), l234–39. All the texts are in Spitzer 1963; contemporary reflections in Proust 1990. Regarding the music, I am thinking of Monteverdi, "Laetatus sum" for chorus, soloists, and orchestra, in *Missa e salmi* (1650).

5. See the parallel in Nietzsche, *The Dawn of Day* 2.100, *KSA*, 3: 89–90.

6. Arist., *Part. An.* 1.1.641b18–20. [Eng. Trans. by A. L. Peck, LCL, 1955. TRANS.]

7. Ocellus of Lucania, *De universi natura* 2.2, *FPhG*, 1: 394.

8. August., *De genesi contra Manichaeos* 2.21.32, *PL* 34: 213[a]; Eng. trans., pp. 127–28.

9. "Hermes Trismegistus," *CH*, frag. of Strobaeus 11.18, 3: 55.

10. "Hermes Trismegistus," *CH*, 9.4, 1: 98.

11. Alexander of Lycopolis, *Against the Doctrine of Mani* ch. 13, ed. Brinkmann (Leipzig: Teubner, 1895), 20; Fr. trans. A. Villey (Paris: Cerf, 1985), 73, commentary 262–63. Eng. trans. by P. van den Horst and J. Mansfeld, *An Alexandrian Platonist against Dualism: Alexander of Lycopolis* (Leiden: Brill, 1974).

12. See Brague 1994a.

13. Seneca, *Phaedra* 959–88, ed. F.-R. Chaumartin, CUF, pp. 241–42; details in Rosenmeyer 1989, 72.

14. Arist., *Metaph.* G.5.1010a25–32; the parallel in K.6.1063a10–17 is clearer, but its Aristotelian authenticity is less certain. [Eng. trans. *The Works of Aristotle*, vol. 8, "Metaphysica," 2d ed., trans. by W. D. Ross (Oxford: Clarendon, 1928) TRANS.]. See Happ 1965; Brague 1988, 410–11. The idea of course is found in the commentators ad loc., Averroes, *Tafsīr* C 23, pp. 428–30 (back translation from the Hebrew and the Latin); Thomas Aquinas, *Expositio* 4 lectio 13.689, ed. R. Spiazzi (Turin: Marietti, 1950), 191.

15. Theophr., *Metaphysics* 9.32.11a18–26, trans. Laks and Most, CUF, p. 21; Eng. trans. Ross and Fobes (Oxford: Clarendon, 1929), 34–36.

16. Alexander of Aphrodisias, *De anima* 2 *(Mantissa)*, ed. I. Bruns, in: *Supplementum Aristotelicum* 2/1 (Berlin: Reimer, 1887), 170.11–12, 20, then 171.28–34.

17. Hippolytus, *Haer.* 1.20, p. 38.

18. Themistius, *Discorsi* 6.4.73ab, p. 294.

19, August., *Enarrationes* 102.10.18, p. 1468.

20. Brethren of Purity, *Rasā'il* 4.1 [42], 3: 463; Ital. trans. C. Baffioni, *L'epistola degli Ihwân al-Safâ' "Sulle opinioni e le religioni"* (Naples: Istituto universitario orientale, 1989), 138.

21. Here I follow Michot 1986, 61. I have merely verified the citations and completed the references.

22. Avicenna, *Ta'līqāt*, ed. Bādāwī (Qom and Teheran, 1984), 62.9–10.

23. Avicenna, *Epistle of the Throne*, in *Rasā'il*, ed. Bidar (Qom, 1400 A.H.), 256.15; Ger. trans. E. Meyer, "Philosophischer Gottesglaube: Ibn Sînâs Thronschrift," *ZDMG* 130 (1980): 270; "Notes sur la 'Théologie d'Aristote,'" in Bādāwī 1947, 65.4–5; Fr. trans. G. Vajda, *Revue thomiste* (1951): 393.

24. Avicenna, *Metaphysics* 9.6, Ar. p. 417.4–5; for the context see Fr. trans., p. 151. See also p. 422.9–13; trans., p. 155. Repr. in *Najāt*, pp. 321–22.

25. Maimonides, *Guide* 3.12, pp. 318.24–29, 319.4–6, 9–12; Eng. trans., pp. 442–43. Echo in Spinoza, *Tractatus Theologico-Politicus* 16, VL, p. 259.

26. Thomas Aquinas, *De veritate*, q. 5, a. 4c, in *Quaestiones disputatae*, vol. 1, ed. R. Spiazzi (Turin: Marietti, 1949),96b. The reference is to Avicenna, *Metaphysics* 9.6 (see n. 24); Leibniz, *Théodicée* 3.262, in *Oeuvres philosophiques de Leibniz*, ed. P. Janet (Paris: Alcan, 1900), 2: 257–58.

27. See Hdt. 3.108.2. Despite the sarcasm of Aristotle (*Hist. An.* 7.31.579b2), the legend is still found, for example in St. Basil, *In Hexaemeron* 9.5, ed. S. Giet, SC 26bis: 502–3.

28. Lucr. 5.871–77.

29. See Thuc. 1.76.3, 4.61.5, then 5.85–111; see also Arist., *Pol.* 1.9.1258a1, 2.7.1267b3–4.

30. See Arist., *Hist. An.* 9.2.610b17–18; August., *Enarrationes* 38.11, p. 413; Shakespeare, *Pericles* 2.1.30, etc.; see Parsons 1945.

31. See Lingat 1967, 231 and n. 3; Drekmeier 1962, 137ff., 200–201, 249.

32. See Hes., *Op.* 277–78. The verse is cited in Porph., *Abst.* 1.5.3; see also Farabi, *Philosophy of Plato* 24, in Bādāwī 1973, 22.7; or 7.30, in *Alfarabi's Philosophy of Plato and Aristotle*, Eng. trans. by M. Mahdi (Ithaca: Cornell University Press, 1969), 64; on the background see Arist., *Eth. Nic.* 6.7.1141a23, and Rupert Brooke's poem "Heaven" (1913). On the Bible, see Robinson 1946, 5 n. 4.

33. Theoph, *Ad Autol.* 2.16, ed. R. M. Grant, OECT, pp. 52–54; Basil, *Hexaemeron* 7.3.1–2, ed. M. Naldini (Milan: Mondadori, 1990), 218.

34. Nemesius, *De natura hominis* 1, ed. T. Morandi, BT, pp. 12.17–13.1; the same issue is perhaps at the basis of the Egyptian text stating that fish live on the water of the Nile; see Bickel 1994, 132.

35. *Pirqey Abhoth* 3:2; see Urbach 1979, 596.

36. Exodus 20:13; Deuteronomy 5:17, then Genesis 9:4; b*Hullin* 101b.

37. Al-Farabi, *Perfect State* 6.18.2b–4, pp. 286–90, commentary 482–84; ch. 34, pp. 131–32; trans., 113–14. See Galston 1990, 139–40.

38. Pl., *Grg.* 484d3, ed. E. R. Dodds, 2d ed. (Oxford: Clarendon, 1966), and the parallels cited p. 267 (Hdt. 2.64; Ar., *Nub.* 1427ff., *Av.* 757ff., 1347 ff.); *Leg.* 3.690b7.

39. For a parallel between Farabi, who considers the city on an astronomical model, and Ibn Khaldun, who considers history on a sublunary physical model, see Maróth 1994, 247.

40. See for example Arist., *Gen. An.* 2.1.731b30; see Preus 1990, 490.

41. See Heidegger, *Einführung in die Metaphysik* (Tübingen: Niemeyer, 1953), 151.

42. Machiavelli, *Prince* ch. 15, in *Tutte le opere*, ed. F. Flora and C. Cordié (n.p.: Mondadori, 1949), 48.

43. Hume, *Treatise on Human Nature* 3.1.1. See contemporaries in Macklem 1958, 119 n. 4. For prefigurations of this distinction, see, in addition to the passage by Seneca cited on pp. 128–29, Ibn Bajja: "What is always right [to do] is always in view of something else, different from action. For that is found in its definition, and it is by this that there subsists that which designates what it is right [to do] insofar as it is what it is right [to do]. And this is why the action of natural men subsists by that which is right [to do]" (*Risāla al-widāʿ*, 1, in *Opera metaphysica*, 118.17–19).

44. Arist., *Ph.* 1.9.192a16–25, and see Landau 1972.

45. For example, Bonaventure, *In Sent.* 2.15.1.2, ad. 6; *Opera*, 2: 378b; see Schaefer 1961, 319; Legrand 1946, 1: 238.

46. Meister Eckhart, *Sermons*, no. 38, "In illo tempore," in *Werke*, 2: 228; see also no. 51, "Hec dicit dominus," 474; Fr. trans. p. 346.

47. See for example Cic., *Fin.* 5.15.41, p. 176, and see Heinemann 1926, 15.

48. See *SVF* 2 §§38–40; see Descartes, Letter-Preface to the *Principes*, in *Oeuvres*, 9/2: 14–15.

49. Chrysippus, *Phusikai theseis*, in Plutarch, *Contradictions of the Stoics* 9.1035c, ed. Pohlenz-Westman, BT, p. 7, or *SVF* 3 §68; for the context, see Striker 1991, 1–13.

50. Cic., *Fin.* 4.5.11–12; Eng. trans. by H. Rackham, LCL, 1914, p. 313.

51. Simpl., *in Phys.*, ed. H. Diels, *CAG* 9: 4.17–5.21.

52. Ibid., 4.23–26.

53. Anaximander, DK 12 B 1.

54. Farabi, *al-Siyāsa al-madaniyya*, ed. F. Najjâr, RDAM, p. 59.13–60.2. See also *Perfect State* 3.9.2, p. 146, and 6, p. 158; ch. 19, p. 72 (trans., pp. 55–56) and pp. 74–75 (trans., p. 58).

55. Pl., *Grg.* 508a6.

56. Averroës, *Commentary on the Physics*, preface, p. 2A–H Juntes.

57. Ibid., p. 2C; Hebr. in S. Harvey 1985, 66.22–23; see also *Der Mikrokosmos des Josef ibn Saddik*, ed. S. Horovitz (Breslau: Schatzky, 1903, 69; Heinemann 1926, 59.

58. *The "Glosae super Platonem" of Bernard of Chartres*, ed. and introduction by P. E. Dutton (Toronto, 1991), 140.32ff., and see the texts cited by Gregory 1958, 59–73; 1992, 113–14.

59. Abraham ibn Daud, *The Exalted Faith*, trans. and commentary by N. M. Samuelson (Cranbury, N.J.: Associated University Presses, 1986), 3.1, p. 210a, 2 (p. 302), Eng. trans. p. 260a.

60. Cited in Kranz 1955, 219–20 and n. 107.

61. See for example de Champeaux and Sterckx (1966).

62. See d'Alverny (1953); Kranz 1955, 153.

63. Nietzsche, *Thus Spake Zarathustra* 1.15, *KSA*, 4: 75.

Chapter 10: A Cosmological Ethics

1. Irenaeus, *Adv. Haer.* 4.20.7, ed. A. Rousseau, SC 100: 648; Plotinus 3.8 [30].1.2; 1: 395.

2. Arist., *Protrepticus* frag. 11 Ross; §20 Düring. See J. Ritter 1953; Verhaeghe 1980, 243ff.

3. Arist., *Eth. Nic.* 10.7–8, *Metaph.* A.9.1074b32–33, *Part. An.* 1.5.644b22–645a4.

4. Arist., *Eth. Eud.* 8.3.1249b16. There is controversy about how the passage should be interpreted.

5. See Arendt 1961, 24.

6. Christiaan Huygens (1629–1695), Κοσμοθεωρος, *sive de terris celestibus, earumque ornatu, conjecturae* (The Hague, 1698); in *Oeuvres complètes*, vol. 21: *Cosmologie* (The Hague: Nijhoff,

1944), 680–842. One reads in Fontenelle, in a work on the same subject that appeared earlier (1687): "It is simply necessary to be a spectator of the world, and not an inhabitant" (*Entretiens* 2, p. 40). The expression appears again in Kant, *Opus posthumum*, Akademie-Ausgabe, 21: 31; Fr. trans. F. Marty, PUF, 1986, p. 219; and M. Merleau-Ponty, *Le Visible et l'Invisible* (Paris: Gallimard, 1964), 152. Note also the title of the astronomy of Jean Fernel, *Cosmotheoria, libros duos complexa* (Paris: S. Colinaeus, 1528), fols. (10)–46.

7. Anaxagoras, DK 59 A 30.

8. Chalcid., *in Tim.* 264, p.237b Didot; §266, ed. J. H. Waszink (London: Warburg; Leiden: Brill, 1962), 271.

9. Bernard of Tours, *Cosmographia*, 151; p. 103 above.

10. See Pines and Harvey 1984.

11. Arist., *Ph.* 2.4.196a33; *Cael.* 2.12.292b32.

12. Pliny, *NH* 2.1.1, p. 128.17–20.

13. [*Mund.*] 1; Festugière 1949, 460–61.

14. Menander, *Hypobolimaios* or *Agroikos* frag. 481, in *Comicorum Atticorum Fragmenta*, ed. K. T. Kock (Leipzig, 1888), 3: 138.1–7; in Festugière 1949, 165, 169; Hadot 1995, 319–20. For the pessimistic theme, see Theognis 425–26; Sophocles, *OC* 1225–26; Arist., *Eudemus* frag. 6, ed. W. D. Ross, OCT, p. 19.

15. Cic., *Luc.* 11.127, ed. Rackham, LCL, pp. 630–31; Fr. trans. Bréhier-Goldschmidt, Pléiade, 246–47.

16. See Lessing, *Eine Duplik* 1 end, in *Werke*, ed. K. Eibl et al. Munich: Hanser, 1979), 8: 33. See Brague 1992, col. 448.

17. See Chalcid., *in Tim.* 193, ed. J. H. Waszink, p. 216.8; Bernard of Clairvaux, *De consideratione* 2.2.5, *Opera*, 3: 414; *PL* 182: 745b.

18. Pl., *Phdr.* 246e1–2.

19. Alex. Aphrodisias, *Commentary on the Prior Analytics I*, prologue, ed. M. Wallies, *CAG*, 2/1: 3.15–29; Eng. trans. J. Barnes et al., *The Greek Commentators of Aristotle* (London: Duckworth, 1991), 44–45.

20. Seneca, *De Otio* 5.3–6, 8, ed. R. Waltz, CUF, pp. 117–19; see André 1977, 180.

21. Plotinus 3.8 [30].4.39–40; 1: 400.

22. Arist., *Metaph.* A.1.980a21; *Protrepticus* frag. 5 Ross; ed. Düring, 53.

23. See Blumenberg 1988.

24. See p. 99ff.

25. See Brague 1994a, 8.

26. Lucretius 1.72–73; [Longinus], *Subl.* 35.3, ed. H. Lebègue, CUF, p. 50.

27. See Blumenberg 1966; *HWPh*, s.v. "Spectator caeli" (P. Probst).

28. Aristotle, see pp. 121–22. Commentaries have little to say about this, see Michael of Ephesus, *CAG* 12: 22–23; Averroës, ed. Juntes (Venice, 15??), 126K–127B.

29. Gersonides, *Wars* 5.2.24, in B. Goldstein, *The Astronomy of Levi ben Gerson (1288–1344): A Critical Edition of Chapters 1–20 with Translation and Commentary* (New York: Springer, 1985), 301.[10] Hebr., 26 Eng.

30. Proclus, *In Republicam*, ed. W. Kroll, BT, 2: 234.22–26; see Festugière 1949, 189. See Samburski 1962, 59–60.

31. See Idel 1992, 249, 262.

32. Maximus of Tyre, *Orations* 37.8, ed. F. Dübner (Paris: Didot, 1877), 148.

33. See p. 116.

34. See Pl., *Resp.* 7.529c7–d5; *Ti.* 91e, p. 358.

35. *Claudii Ptolemaei Opera quae extant omnia*, vol. 1: *Syntaxis mathematica*, ed. Heiberg, BT, 1: 7.17–24. On the context see Kranz 1955, 82; Taub 1993, 135–53. The same idea is also found in the Taḥrīr of Ṭūsī (d. 1274), Bib. Nat. Fr., MS. ar. 2485, f. 2v. Then, more than a century later, Gersonides again alludes to the passage: *Wars* 5.2, ed. B. Goldstein, *The Astronomy of Levi ben Gerson (1288–1344): A Critical Edition of Chapters 1–20 with Translation and Commentary* (New

York: Springer, 1985), Hebr. p. 8, Eng. p. 24. The commentary by Abu Ja'far al-Hâzin (early tenth century), Bib. Nat. Fr. 4821, fols. 47–68 does not include the preface; nor does the Taḥrîr of Avicenna, Bib. Nat. Fr. 2484, 2, fols. 1–143. I have not seen Farabi's commentary nor that of Ibn al-Haitham (d. 1041) [F. Sezgin, *Geschichte des arabischen Schrifttums*, vol. 6 (Leiden: Brill, 1978), 259]. Bar Hebraeus, ed. F. Nau, *Le Livre de l'ascension de l'esprit sur la forme du ciel et de la terre: Cours d'astronomie rédigé en 1279 par Grégoire Abulfarag dit Bar Hebraeus* (Paris, 1900), includes nothing about it, except perhaps the allusion implicit in the title.

36. *Anth. Pal.* 9.577, and see Boll 1950, 143–55; Brethren of Purity, *Rasā'il* 1.3 [3], 1: 138; see Augustine, cited in Blumenberg 1987, 44.

37. Aratus, *Phaen.* 100–136, and see B. Effe, in *Hellenismus* (Stuttgart: Reclam, 1985), 135; Schwabl 1972, 342–43; Greek sources of the idea of the departure of the gods in Hes., *Op.* 197–201; Theognis 1.1135–50; for a Jewish parallel on the rising to the sky of the *shekhina* at the Flood, see Aptowitzer 1921, 80.

38. Virgil, *Ecl.* 4.6 *(jam redit et virgo)*, *G.* 2.474.

39. Sen., *QNat.* preface 1–17, pp. 6–12.

40. Kant, *Critique of Practical Reason* 1.2.2.3; pp. 138–39.

41. See Cic., *Leg.* 1.23, ed. C. Appuhn (Paris: Garnier, 1954), 270.

42. Euripides, frag. 910 Nauck. The passage is cited by Themistius, *Discorsi* 24.10, 307d–8a, p. 834, and Clem. Al., *Strom.* 4.25, 155.1.

43. Pl., *Resp.* 6.500b8–c7 [English Translation with Notes and Interpretive Essay by Allan Bloom (New York: Basic Books, 1968), 179–80. TRANS.]

44. Ibid., respectively 6.486a and 9.592b2.

45. Poseidonius, ed. Kidd-Edelstein, 2 vols. (Cambridge: Cambridge University Press, 1972–88), frag. 186, p. 169; commentary pp. 670–74.

46. See Epictetus, *Discourses* 1.6.19, ed. J. Souilhé, CUF, p. 26; cited and commentary in Goldschmidt 1953, 79.

47. Cic., *Nat. D.* 2.14.37, p. 158, or *SVF* 2.1153.

48. Sen., *Prov.* 6.5; then *De vita beata* 8.4.

49. Sen., *Ep.* 104.23, pp. 439–40.

50. *Asclepius* 11, "Hermes Trismegistus," *CH*, 2: 310.13; Heinemann 1926, 28. See Groethuysen 1928, 61; Hadot 1989.

51. Sallustius, *De deis et mundo* 4.10, ed. Rochefort, CUF, p. 8; see also Clem. Al., *Excerpta* 41, p. 149; Proclus, *In Ti.* 1: 6.5.

52. Elias, *In Categorias* preface, 6th point, ed. A. Busse, *CAG* 18/1: 121.23–28; *On the Isagoge*, ed. L. G. Westerink (Amsterdam, 1967), ch. 14.18–20, p. 22; ch. 23.8–9, p. 47.

53. David, *Prolegomena* 12, ed. A. Busse, *CAG* 18/2: 38.18, then 28.31.

54. Procl., *In Ti.* 1: 5.7–6.6; trans., 1: 28–30; the citation is *Ti.* 90d4–5.

55. See Dodds 1979, 20–21.

56. Sen., *Clem.* 1.7.2.

57. Sen., *De Ira* 3.6.1, ed. Bourgery, CUF, pp. 71–72.

58. Sen., *Ep.* [6].59.16, p. 116.

59. Philo, *De Abrahamo* 13.61. [Eng. trans. LCL, 1935. TRANS]

60. See Simson 1988.

61. Pl., *Leg.* 6.771b5–6; see L'Orange 1953, Schabert 1997.

62. See Taub 1993, 146.

63. Eur., *Phoen.* 543–45; Kranz 1955, 42.

64. See pp. 31–33.

65. Cic., *Sen.* 21.77, ed. K. Simbeck, BT, p. 39.6–8.

66. Plutarch, *On the Delays of Divine Justice* 5.550ce, ed. R. Klaerr et al., *Oeuvres morales*, vol. 7/2, treatises 37–41, CUF, p. 135.

67. Iambl., *De vita pythagorica* 33.229 end.

68. Dio Chrys., *Or.* 40.35–39, ed. J. W. Cohoon et al., LCL, 4: 140–44. Other examples in

Christian writers: Gregory of Nazianzus, *On Moderation* 8–9, *PG* 36: 181c–85a; following him, Nicetas Stethatos, *Letter added to the Treatise on Paradise* 7.6, ed. J. Darrouzès, SC 81: 278.

69. See *FPhG*, 2: 176b.

70. [Chalcidius], *Timaeus a Calcidio translatus commentarioque instructus* 263, *FPhG*, 2: 237b; William of Conches, *Glosae super Platonem* 151, ed. E. Jeauneau (Paris: Vrin, 1965), 254–55.

71. See Chenu 1966, 142–58; Zonta 1996, 262–67.

72. See Rémi of Auxerre, in Courcelle 1967, 284 (on 2.8, p. 226), 262, 272 (on 3.9, p.270), 237, 314 (on astronomy).

73. Respectively: Boethius, *Consolatione* 3.9, p. 270; see Brinkmann 1980, 318–47; Gruber 1978, 277–78; *Consolatione* 4.2, p. 326; 3.8, p. 260.

74. Ibid., 4.6.1–5, p. 372; Gruber 1978, 364–65.

75. Ibid., 1.4, p. 146; Gruber 1978, 115–16.

76. Ibid., 1.5.26–27, p. 160; see Sen., *Phaedra* 974–75; Gruber 1978, 138, 141.

77. Ibid., 2.8.28–30, p. 226; cited by Dante, *Monarchy* 1.9.3, and implicit in *Paradiso* last verse; Klingner 1921, 26–27; Gruber 1978, 230.

78. Respectively, *Consolatione* 2.7, p. 216; 2.5, p. 200; 5.5, p. 420; 4.4, p. 346.

79. Ibid., 4.7.34–35, p. 382; Gruber 1978, 376.

80. Bernard of Tours, *Cosmographia* 2.11, p. 142; p. 114. On how the work was received, see Liebeschütz 1926, 134 n. 104.

81. Ibid., 2.12.13–14, p. 145; p. 117.

82. Ibid., 2.13.10, p. 148; p. 121.

83. Ibid., 2.4.31–32, p. 127; p. 98; see Pl., *Ti.* 41e, p. 143.

84. Ibid., 2.10.29–32, p. 141; p. 113.

85. Alain of Lille, *Anticlaudianus* 7.325, p. 166.

86. On the history of the notion, missing from Adolf Berger's *Dictionary of Roman Law, Transactions* of the American Philosophical Society (Philadelphia) 43 (1953), see Hering 1954, 107, then Miethke 1969, 479–80 n. 179.

87. August., *Sermons* 355.4.5, *PL* 39: 1572 [d].

88. Gratian, *Decretum* c. 43.117, q. 4.

89. Rupert of Deutz, *De glorificatione Trinitatis et processione Sancti Spiritus* 9.5, *PL* 169: 184b.

90. Gerhoh of Reichersberg, *Libellus de ordine donorum Sancti Spiritus, Opera Inedita*, 1, *Tractatus et libelli*, ed. D. van den Eynde et al. (Rome: Pontificium athenaeum antonianum, 1955), 104.15–20, and see p. 100.26–32. The passage is quoted by Blumenberg (1966, 120), from a book in which I have not found the quoted passage and without noting that the source is Rupert.

91. Dante, *Monarchy* 1.9.1; English trans., p. 13.

92. Arist., *Ph.* 2.2.194b13.

93. See Boyde 1981, 250ff.; it is possible that the expression generalizes a term in astrology: some men are, according to their characters, "sons" of a certain planet; see North 1988, 291.

94. Petrus Ramus, *Dialecticae Institutiones* (Paris, 1543; repr. Stuttgart: Frommann-Holzboog, 1964), 40b; this text was pointed out to me by M.-D. Couzinet. See also Schmidt 1938, 27.

95. Lucretius 1.79; *Etna* 250–53, ed. J. Vessereau, CUF, p. 20.

96. Johannes Scotus Eriugena, *Div. Nat.* 5.20.893d.

97. Alain of Lille, *Anticlaudianus* 1.62–63, p. 59.

98. Ibid., 9.392–95, p. 196.

99. Meister Eckhart, *Expositio Libri Exodi* [on 20:24], *Werke*, vol. 2, ed. K. Weiß, §242, p. 198. See also *Sermons* 14 ("Surge, illuminare"), *Werke*, vol. 1, ed. J. Quint, p. 233.5ff. and parallels.

100. See p. 78.

101. Pseudo-Majrîtî, *Das Ziel der Weisen*, ed. H. Ritter (Leipzig: Teubner, 1933), 78.2.3.

102. Respectively Farabi, *As-Siyāsah*, ed. F. Najjâr, RDAM, 84.2–6; *Taḥṣīl as-Saʿadah* 19–20 G. Yā Sin / 20 M. Mahdi, p. 63.13–64.7 Yā Sin. See also *Kitāb al-Millah*, ed. M. Mahdi, RDAM, p. 65.3–6; trans. D. Mallet (Damascus: Institut Français de Damas, 1989), 143; Galston 1990, 140, and see 197.

103. Avicenna, *Risāla fī 'l-kalām 'alā al-nafs al-nāṭiqah*, ed. el-Aḥwānī, *Majallat al-Kitāb* 11 (April 1952): 419–23, quotation from p. 422.7–19; Eng. trans. in Gutas 1988, 78, whose interpretations I have followed in several places.

104. Avicenna, *Metaphysics* 9.7, pp. 425.15–426.4, Fr. trans. p. 159; Lat., pp. 510–11. The passage is repeated with a few minimal variations in *Nijāt*, Metaphysics 2.38, p. 328.17–24.

105. Plotinus 3.4 [15].3.22, 4.7 [2].10.35. See Beierwaltes 1985, 273. Leibniz points out the interest of this, see Letter to Hanschius, 23 July 1707, §3, in *God. Guil. Leibnitii Opera philosophica quae exstant Latina Gallica Germanica omnia*, ed. Erdmann (Berlin: Eichler, 1839–40), 445b: "Porro quaevis mens, ut recte Plotinus, quemdam in se mundum intelligibilem continet, imo mea sententia et hunc ipsum sensibilem sibi repraesentat."

106. *Theology of Aristotle* 8.161, in Bādāwī 1955, 117; Eng. trans. by G. Lewis, in *Plotini Opera*, ed. H.-R. Schwyzer and P. Henry (Brussels: L'édition universelle; Paris: Desclée De Brouwer), 2 (1959): 403. Avicenna does not comment on the passage in his notes.

107. Miskawayh, *Tahdīb al-Axlāq*, ed. H. Tamîm (Beirut: Dâr maktabat al-Hayât, 1398 A.H.), 58; Fr. trans. M. Arkoun, p. 66.

108. See the parallel in *Al-Mabdā' wa-'l-Ma'ād*, 3.5, ed. A. Nûrânî (Tehran: Institute of Islamic Studies, 1984), 97–98; repeated with a few minimal variations in *Metaphysics* 8.7, p. 370.1; finally repeated in *Najāt*, Metaphysics 2.17, p. 282.21; *Epistola sulla vita futura* ch. 7, ed. F. Lucchetta (Padua: Antenore, 1969), 197–98.

109. See Michot 1986, 179–89.

110. For a fuller discussion see Brague 1997a.

111. Ibn Ṭufayl, *Ḥayy b. Yaqdhân*, p. 99.4–12; p. 73.

112. Ibid., p. 99.13, p. 74, and see Ibn Bājja, *Tadbīr al-mutawaḥḥid*, 3.17, *Opera metaphysica*, 94.19.

113. Ibn Ṭufayl, *Ḥayy b. Yaqdhân*, p. 103.8–9; pp. 75–76.

114. Ibid., p. 104.2–5, p. 76.

115. Ibid., p. 105.10–12, p. 77.

116. Ibid., p. 106.12–107.7, p. 78.

117. Ibid., p. 80.10–12, p. 61.

118. Ibid., p. 107.4–5, p. 78, and see p. 103.3, p. 75.

119. See Maimonides, *Guide* 1.72, p. 129.10–16; trans. pp. 361–62.

120. Ibn Ṭufayl, *Ḥayy b. Yaqdhân*, p. 108.4, p. 79.

121. Ibid., pp. 107.12–113.7, pp. 79–82.

122. Ibid., pp. 113.7–117.9, pp. 82–84.

123. Ibid., pp. 113.10–114.8, p. 82.

124. Brethren of Purity, *Rasā'il* 2.8 [22], 2: 222; on Matthew 5:45, see p. 66.

125. The practice existed before Ibn Ṭufayl; see Schimmel 1985, 254ff.

126. Ibn Ṭufayl, *Ḥayy b. Yaqdhân*, p. 116.10–11, p. 84.

127. Ibid., p. 114.6–8, p. 82.

128. Ibid., p. 106.2–5, pp. 77–78.

129. Ibid., p. 117.10–11, p. 84.

130. Ibid., pp. 117.11–118.1, p. 85.

131. Ibid., p. 119.6–7, pp. 85–86.

132. b*Shabbat*, 7:75a.

133. Rashi, commentary on Deuteronomy 30:19, MG, p. 88a; Fr. trans. Gugenheim, *Le Pentateuque . . . accompagné du commentaire de Rachi traduit en français* (Paris: Fondation O. S. Levy, 1968), 205; Eng. trans. from *The Pentateuch and Rashi's Commentary: A Linear Translation into English*, by Rabbi Abraham ben Isaiah and Rabbi Benjamin Sharfman et al. (Brooklyn, N.Y.: S. S. & R. Publising Co., 1950), 5: 276 [emphasis in original]. Ibn Ezra knows only the first explanation: "because they are permanent" (MG, p. 90a).

134. In P. Fenton, "A Judeo-Arabic Commentary on the Haftarot by Hananael ben Semuel(?), Abraham Maimonides' Father-in-law," *Maimonidean Studies* 1 (1990): 27–56, quotation from p. 41.22ff.; Eng. trans. p. 43; see also *YM*, pp. 79, 259.

135. Nachmanides, *Commentary on the Pentateuch,* Genesis 2:9, ed. Chavel, p. 36; the quotation is from b*Sanhedrin* 42a.

136. The idea seems to appear again in Jonathan Eibschütz (d. 1764); see Levine 1983, 214.

137. Alain of Lille, *De planctu naturae, PL* 210: 448c, 449c. Examples in medieval German poetry in Brinkmann 1980, 69–73.

138. Francis of Assisi, *Admonitions* 5, in *Oeuvres;* Fr. trans. by A. Masseron (Paris: Albin Michel, 1959), 99.

139. See August., *Confessiones* 7.7.11, p. 606; Bonaventure, *Soliloquium* 3, in *S. Bonaventurae Opera omnia,* ed. A. C. Peltier (Paris: Vivès, 1868), 12: 114b; Martin Luther, *The Seven Psalms of Penitence* (1517) 6, in *Werke, Kritische Gesamtausgabe* (Weimar: Böhlaus), 1 (1883): 207; *Resolutiones disputationum de indulgentiarum virtute* (1518) concl. 15, ibid., p. 557.37–39; and see Martineau 1977, 202; Ignatius Loyola, *Ejercicios espirituales* 60, ed. I. Iparraguirre, BAC, p. 212. In a non-religious context, see Dante, *Vita nova* 15.7–8.

140. On this theme of the atomists, see Salem 1996, 278–81.

141. Proverbs 6:6; Gersonides ad loc., MG, p. 194b; nice story in *YM,* p. 129; Marcus Aurelius 5.1.1; see also Hor., *Sat.* 1.1.33.

142. b'*Eruvin,* 10:100b; see Urbach (1979, 323. The passage is cited by Bahya ben Joseph ibn Paquda, *Hidāja 'ilā Farā'iḍ al-Qulūb,* 2.2.

143. Epictetus, *Discourses* 1.16.1–5, and see Dierauer 1977, 180–93; for the case of tranquility, see Pyrrho, in Diog. Laert. 9.68; Râzî, *The Spiritual Physick* ch. 20, *Opera,* 95.

144. Arist., *Eth. Nic.* 7.3.1147b4–5.

145. W. Langland, *The Vision of Piers Plowman* [version B], ed. A. V. C. Schmidt (Everyman), 11.368–70, p. 131; see also Juan Ruiz [Arcipreste de Hita], *Libro de buen amor* 74; Swift, *Gulliver's Travels* 4.7 (World's Classics), p. 328. For a positive assessment of the same fact, see Xen., *Mem.* 1.4.12.

146. See Macklem 1958, 59.

147. On this point I distance myself from Aubenque 1976, 87, 90—who, moreover, does not truly insist on it. See Brague 2000, 189–93.

148. This financial metaphor can be attributed to Pl., *Resp.* 6.506e–507a, and Plotinus 3.7 [45].5.26, 2: 375; and see Kranz 1955, 11.

149. Kant, *Practical Reason* 1.1.1.8, p. 39; n. II, p. 43 (demands a "knowledge of the world"); 1.1.1.1, p. 51; 1.1.2, pp. 75–76. On the "other law" *(heteros nomos),* see Romans 7:23.

150. Kant, *Practical Reason* 1.1.1.7, p. 37.

Chapter 11: Abrahamic Excess

1. See Origen, *De principiis* 2.3.6, pp. 314–22; *Commentary on Matthew,* 13:20, *PG* 13: 1148ff.

2. Dihle 1982, 1–19, 159–74, emphasizes the abyss that separates this notion of will from the Greek view.

3. On the cosmology of the Fathers, see the study, which is more systematic than historical, by Marcus (1956).

4. August., *Confessiones,* 13.15.18, p. 456.

5. August., *Enchiridion* 3.9, ed. E. Evans, CCSL 46: 52–53; Mittelstrass 1962, 188; Sloterdijk 1993, 93.

6. Unless an etymology that we are unaware of is discovered; see Haebler 1967, 116–17.

7. See Aptowitzer 1921, 166.

8. See Lieberman 1950, 180–93 (botany and zoology). While several compilations of the *knowledge* of nature (fauna, flora, medicine, etc.) implicit in the Talmud exist, as for example Löw 1928–34, I am not aware of any on the *conception* of the nature that underlies them. The *Entisqlopedia Talmudit* does not include an entry for *ṭebha'.* Sketches in Sarfatti 1965–66 and Wewers 1972.

9. *Pirqey Abhoth* 3:9 (7), then 3:23 (18).

10. See Philo, *De opificio mundi* 1.3; see Weiss 1966, 283–304; on Philo, Früchtel 1968,172–75.

11. Ignatius of Antioch, *To the Ephesians* 19, ed. Camelot, SC 10: 74–75. See Schlier 1929, 5–32, and Schoedel 1985, 87–94. Similar tale on the subject of the Ascension in Synesius of Cyrene, cited in Kranz 1955, 119.

12. Clem. Al., *Excerpta* 74, p. 196; see p. 69.

13. "Protevangelium Jacobi" 21:2, in *Los Evangelios Apócrifos,* ed. A. de Santos Otero, BAC 148, 6th ed. (1988), 165.

14. Shakespeare, *Hamlet,* 1.1.158–64, esp. 162–63.

15. Pépin 1964, 278–83.

16. Athenagoras, *Leg. pro Christ.* 16.3, PG 6: 920d; Tert., *Adv. Praxean* 5; PL 2: 160a; Minucius Felix, *Octavius* 18.7, p. 56 Kytzler.

17. Wisdom of Solomon 13:1–5.

18. Clem. Al., *Strom.* 6.14.110.3; Origen, *Commentary on John* 2.3.25, ed. C. Blanc, SC 120: 222; see Fascher 1964, 120–21.

19. Tatianus, *Ad Gr. and Fragments,* ed. and trans. by M. Whittaker, OECT (1982), 16–17; what I render as "to become animals . . . constellations" is there translated as "their basic principle was the giving of life."

20. See p. 49.

21. Origen, *contra Cels.* 5.10–13, ed. M. Borret, SC 147: 34–47.

22. August., *Enarrationes* 113.24.11, pp. 1646–47; same idea later in al-Ghazâlî, *The Niche of Lights,* trans. D. Buchman (Provo, Utah: Brigham Young University Press, 1998), 11; Bernard of Clairvaux, *On the Canticle* 27.2.4; *Opera,* 1: 184.

23. August., *Enarrationes* 166.6.13, p. 2131.

24. Ibid., 32.6.6, p. 259.

25. Ibid., 61.13.18, pp. 786–87.

26. August., *Confessiones* 9.10.24, p. 117.

27. Barḥadbšabba 'Arbaya, *Cause of the Foundation of Schools,* Syriac text published and translated by Mgr A. Scher, Patrologia Orientalis, 4: 346–47. Not knowing Syriac, I am quoting the French translation [English translation rendered from the French. Trans.].

28. See Brague 1988, 40–41.

29. See for example Ibn Gabirol, *Fons vitae* 3.57, ed. Bäumker (Münster: Aschendorff, 1892–1895), 205; Ar. in Pines 1977, 48.

30. Gregory the Great, *Dialogues* 2.35.5, ed. A. de Vogüé and P. Antin, SC 260: 238–39; Julian of Norwich, *Revelations,* 5, 1st vision, in *A Book of Showings to the Anchoress Julian of Norwich,* ed. E. Colledge and J. Walsh (Toronto: Pontifical Institute of Medieval Studies, 1978), brief text ch. 4, pp. 212–13, long text ch. 5, Revelation 1, pp. 229–30; iconography in Zahlten 1979, 130–31. See also Honorius Augustodunensis, in Kranz 1955, 165.

31. Origen, *De principiis* 1.7.2, p. 236; see also *On John* 1.35 (40), VEP 11: 281.

32. Gregory the Great, *Moralia in Job* 12.33.38 [on 15:15], CCSL 143A: 650–51, 17.16.22 [on 25:5], pp. 864–65.

33. Saadia Gaon, *Beliefs* 5.1, pp. 170, 206–7.

34. Thomas Aquinas, *Expositio super Iob ad litteram,* ed. A. Dondaine, in *Opera Omnia* (Rome: Commissio Leonina), 26 (1965): 97b, 143ab.

35. Gersonides, *Commentary on Job* 25:5; MG, p. 207b; see Tertullian, cited in Blumenberg 1987, 48.

36. Al-Bāqillānī, *Kitāb al-Tamhīd* ch. 5 [Against the astrologers] 85, ed. R. J. McCarthy (Beirut: Librairie orientale, 1957), 48.3–9; see Bausani 1971, 203.

37. See Dales 1980; Albertus Magnus, cited in Zambelli 1991, 1112.

38. Gregory of Nyssa, *Oratio catechetica* 6.2, trans. P. Méridier, TD, p. 36.

39. See Festugière 1932, 221–63; Wallace-Hadrill 1968,109 n. 1.

40. August., *Enarratione* 9.12.29, p. 71; 32.2.2.5, p. 251; 148.8.10, p. 2172.

41. Plotinus 3.2 [47].13.20–25, 1: 286–87; Eng. trans. A. H. Armstrong, LCL, pp. 83–85.

42. Origen, *Select., in psalm:* Philocalia 2 preface, VEP 15: 256, cited by Wallace-Hadrill 1968, 121.

43. Tert., *Adv. Marcionem* 1.13–14.

44. August., *Enarratione* 148.8.10, p. 2172; and *De civ. D.* 5.11, col. 204: Spitzer 1963, 178–79 n. 33; extensive discussion in Ghazâlî, *Iḥyā* 36 Love 7, 4: 336–37; see also 39 Meditation, 4: 467.

45. Gregory of Nyssa, *On the Hexameron* 1, *PG* 44: 92cd.

46. Zachary the Doctor, *Midrash ha-Hefes* (1430), in *YM* 9.6, pp. 162–63; I did not have access to the original Arabic.

47. Symeon the New Theologian, Ethical Treatise no. 14, "On Feasts" 1–16, in *Traités théologiques et éthiques,* ed. J. Darrouzès, vol. 2, *Ethics* 4–15, SC 129: 422–23. The translation has been slightly modified.

48. The passage from nothingness to being: *Catéchèses,* ed. B. Krivochéine and J. Paramelle, 17.47–48, 36.1–2, 183 (SC 113: 258, 330, 344); the tears of the newborn: *Cat.* 6.90 (SC 104: 92), 29.218 (SC 113: 184); entering the world naked: *Cat.* 36.244 (SC 113: 350); leaving the world naked: *Cat.* 9.177 (SC 104: 118); man's superiority over the stars: *Cat.* 2.401 (SC 96: 274), which were created for him: *Cat.* 5.160 (SC 96: 388), and see 35.11 (SC 113: 304).

49. See Brague 1990a, 221–22.

50. See p. 45. See Ibn Ezra, On Exodus 33:23, *Reader,* 184–85.

51. *Midrash Tanḥumah,* Šofṭim 11, cited by Langermann 1993, 50; see also *YM,* p. 116.

52. Francis Bacon, *Of the Advancement of Learning* 2.6.1, in *Works,* ed. J. Spedding, R. L. Ellis, and D. D. Heath, vol. 3 (London, 1876), 350; cited by Löwith 1960b, 325–26.

53. See Origen, *De principiis* 1.7, pp. 232–36; more distant references in Lubac 1946, 192 n. 6.

54. See Bonaventure, *Breviloquium* 2.4, *Opera,* 5: 221b.

55. Gregory of Nyssa, *On the Creation of Man* 16, ed. J. Laplace, SC 6: 151–52; Johannes Scotus Eriugena cites the passage (*Div. Nat.* 4.12.793c–94a) having taken up the idea a bit earlier, in 4.7.771bc; William of Saint-Thierry quotes the work at length in his *De natura corporis et animae* but omits this passage. He in fact defends the idea of microcosm (prologue, *PL* 180: 695–96).

56. Leo the Great, *Sermons for Christmas* 7.6, ed. R. Dolle, SC 22bis: 160; echoed by Bernard of Clairvaux, *Sermon on the Nativity* 2.1, *Opera,* 4: 252; see also *Sermon on Advent* 1.7, ibid., 166–67.

57. *Meditationes piissimae de cognitione humanae conditionis* 3.8, *PL* 184: 490c; see also Johannes Scotus Eriugena, *Div. Nat.* 4.10.784d; John of the Cross, *Dichos de luz y amor* 34, in *Obras completas,* ed. L. Ruano de la Iglesia, BAC 15: 46; Fr. trans. Maximes no. 51, in *Oeuvres complètes* (Paris: Desclée De Brouwer, 1967), 980; Pascal, *Pensées,* Br. 793, p. 233, and see Br. 347, p. 262.

58. Besançon 1994, 356; on literature, we acknowledge Erich Auerbach's idea, initially formulated in *Dante als Dichter der irdischen Welt* (Berlin: De Gruyter, 1929), 18ff.

59. See pp. 159–60.

60. Al-Ghazâlî, *Das Elixir der Glückseligkeit,* trans. H. Ritter (Jena: Diederichs, 1923), 36.

61. Gregory of Nazianzus, *Oratio* 38, On Theophany ch. 11, *PG* 36: 324a; ed. C. Moreschini and P. Galley, SC 358: 125; "a second universe, great in its smallness."

62. Nicetas Stethatos, *On the Soul* 16, in *Opuscules et lettres,* ed. J. Darrouzès, SC 81: 78— the translation "other world in the world," though correct, does not capture the wordplay; then 27, p. 88.

63. Ibid., 30, p. 92.

64. Nicetas Stethatos, *On the limits of life* 25, pp. 388–89.

65. John of Damascus, *On Orthodox Faith* 2.12; *PG* 94: 921a; *contra,* Kranz 1955, 129 n. 33.

66. See pp. 20–21.

67. The fact has been noted many times, to repletion. The earliest formulation I have been able to find is Schelling, *Lessons on the Method of Academic Studies* (1803) ch. 8, "On the His-

torical Construction of Christianity" 5.1, p. 287; Fr. trans. J.-F. Courtine and J.-F. Rivelaygue, in *Philosophies de l'Université* (Paris: Payot, 1979), 108.

68. See Walker 1993, 110–11. Around the same time, Saadia Gaon (d. 942) places a "middle world" between the macrocosm and the microcosm which is the temple, *Commentary on the Sefer Yetsira* 3.6, ed. J. Qafih (Jerusalem, 1972), p. 103; trans. M. Lambert (Paris: Bouillon, 1891), 89. See also the text of "Jâbir" cited in Kraus 1942, 47 n. 1.

69. Implicit in August., *De civ. D.* 7.31, col. 302ab; explicit in Leo the Great, *Sermon XV on the Passion* 1, in *Sermons****, ed. R. Dolle, SC 74bis: 184—the formula passed into the Catholic liturgy, Oratory of the offertory of the ordinary of the Roman mass; Bernard of Clairvaux, *On the Canticle* 20.2, *Opera*, 1: 115.7–11; *PL* 183: 867cd.

70. See Groethuysen 1928, 91.

71. August., *Epistolae* 136.1.5, *PL* 33: 527 [b] and see 166.5.13, *PL* 33: 726 [d]; compare de civ. *D.* 11.18, p. 459; see Spitzer 1963, 28–31; Bettetini 1994, 110–13.

72. See Löwith 1960a.

73. See Aptowitzer 1920–21.

74. See for example Bonaventure, *Breviloquium* 7.4, *Opera*, 5: 285a.

75. Origen, *Commentary on John* 1.35.253, ed. C. Blanc, SC 120: 188, 1.18.98, 112.

76. Origen, *De oratione* 7, *PG* 11: 440cd; VEP 10: 245–46.

77. Theophilus of Antioch, *Against Autolycus* 2.17, ed. Grant, OECT, p. 54.

78. Ambrose, *Letter XXXIV* (to Horontianus, ca. 387), *PL* 16: 1119b–23a, esp. 7, 1121b, and 9, 1122b.

79. Francis of Assisi, *Cantico di frate sole* 2.1.

80. Plotinus 2.9 [33].18.17–18; 1: 252; Elsas 1975, 84.

81 See pp. 52, 55–56.

82. *Didache* 10.6, in *Padres apostolicos*, ed. D. Ruiz Bueno, BAC 65: 88.

83. See Grant 1994, 77–82.

84. August., *Enarratione* 17.2.3, p. 197; 101.2.28.13, p. 1448.

85. August., *De civ. D.* 20.14, col. 950a; 20.16, col. 953b.

86. Maximus the Confessor, *Mystagoge* 7, *PG* 91: 685bc; ed. and Ital. trans. R. Cantarella (Florence: L.E.F., [1929] 1990), 164; see Balthasar 1961, 146.

87. Anselm, *Cur Deus homo* 1.18, ed. R. Roques, SC 91: 296–97.

88. Schaefer 1961, 377–80.

89. Dante, *Paradiso* 7.67–68, p. 676; see Boyde 1981, 246–47.

90. Texts in Litt 1963, 242–52. One might add *De spir. cr.* 6c (cited ibid., 107); Bonaventure, *In IV Sent.* d. 48, q. 2, a. 2, c, in *S. Bonaventurae Opera omnia*, ed. A. C. Peltier (Paris: Vivès, 1868), 6: 562; *Opera* (Quaracchi), 4: 991b. See Schaefer 1961, 379. For the background of the image of the whetstone, see Bultot 1963, 36; 1964, 90.

91. See pp. 103–4.

92. Rabelais, *Pantagruel* ch. 8 (Pléiade), 203. See Gilson 1955, 234.

93. See the synthesis by Feldman 1986.

94. Pl., *Ti.* 41ab; pp. 139–40.

95. Philoponus, *De aeternitate mundi* 8.1, ed. H. Rabe (Leipzig: Teubner, 1899), 302–3; 9.6, p. 336. See also Themistius, *Discorsi* 32.12.363d, p. 974.

96. Maimonides, *Guide* 2.28, pp. 234–35; trans. pp. 334–36.

97. Gersonides, *Wars* 6.1.16, cols. 59a–60a; pp. 359–61. See Feldman 1986, 61.

98. Crescas, *Light* 4, q. 1; p. 388.

99. Abravanel, *Mif'alot Elohim* 8.2 (Venice, 1592), 50a–51c.

100. See Gardet 1967, 262–66; see Leibniz, *New Essays* 2.27. 6, ed. Gerhardt (Berlin: Weidmann, 1880), 5: 216.

101. See pp. 42–43.

102. Marcus Aurelius 5.1.1.

103. Maximus the Confessor, *Ambigua, PL* 91: 1305a; Johannes Scotus Eriugena, *Div. Nat.* 3.37.733b, etc.

104. Malebranche, *Méditations chrétiennes et métaphysiques* (1683) 7.12, *Oeuvres Complètes,* vol. 10 (Paris: Vrin, 1959), 73. The passage is cited in Maupertuis, *Essai de cosmologie* (1750) 1, p. 16.

105. See *Dictionary of the History of Ideas,* s.v. "Cosmic Fall" (R. W. Hepburn, 1968).

106. F. W. J. Schelling, *Über den Zusammenhang der Natur mit der Geisterwelt: Ein Gespräch [Clara]* (1810), 2: *Schriften von 1806–1813* (Darmstadt: WB, 1976), 459–62. Romans 8:19–21 is cited pp. 458, 482.

107. See pp. 207–9.

108. See p. 221.

109. Palladius, *Lausiac History* 18 [Makarios of Alexandria] 18, ed. A. Lucot, TD, p. 132.

110. Al-Ghazâlî, *Iḥyâ'* 39 Meditation, 4: 466, 473.

111. Bahya ben Joseph ibn Paquda, *Hidâja 'ilâ Farâ'iḍ al-Qulûb,* 2.

112. Albertus Magnus, *On Matthew* 13:35, ed. Borgnet (Paris, 1890–99), 20: 571a; similar formula in Proclus, *In Ti.* 2, 1: 217.25.

113. Blumenberg 1983, chs. 5–6; Schaefer 1961, 329–30.

114. Bernard of Clairvaux, *Lettres* 106.2, *Opera,* 7: 266–67; *PL* 182: 242.

115. Meister Eckhart, *Sermons* no. 32, "Consideravit semitas," *Werke,* 2: 134–35; Fr. trans. pp. 333–34. The parallels cited in *Werke,* ibid. n. 1, leave aside what seems to me to be the immediate source, that is: "Tota . . . opera nostra . . . est sanare oculum cordis, unde videatur Deus," August., *Sermons* 88.5.5, *PL* 38: 542[a].

116. See Strauss 1989, 78–100; Davidson 1974; W. Harvey 1988.

117. Averroës, *Tahâfut* 1, p. 52.1–4; Eng. trans. p. 30; Catalan trans. by J. Puig Montada (Barcelona: edicions 62, 1991), 103; the citation is from Sura 6:75, p. 99. See also 10.6, p. 416, trans. p. 251, and *Tafsîr,* Lam 41, p. 1634.4–6.

118. Maimonides, *Mishneh Torah,* Yesodey ha-Torah 2.2, p. 7; Eng. trans. *The Book of Knowledge,* ed. M. Hyamson, 2d ed. (Jerusalem: Feldheim, 1981), 35b.

119. Maimonides, *Guide* 1.34, p. 50.8–9; Eng. trans. p. 74.

120. Ibid., 3. 28, p. 373.19–21; trans. pp. 512–13.

121. Ibid., 1.34, p. 50.10–111; trans. p. 74.

122. Ibid., 1.34, p. 50.14–17; trans. p. 74.

123. Ibid., 3.51, p. 456.6–8; trans. p. 620.

124. See Freudenthal 1992; Crescas, *Light* 2.6, p. 233.

125. Thomas Aquinas, *Summa contra gentiles* 2.2, pp. 93b–94b; ch. 3, pp. 94b–95a. The text has few close parallels. See, however, *In symbolum Apostolorum expositio* 1.879–86, pp. 196b–98a Marietti.

126. Ibid., p. 95a.

127. August., *Soliloquia* 1.2.7, ed. P. de Labriolle, BA 5: 36.

128. August., *De anima et ejus origine* 4.4, CSEL 60: 385.11–15.

129. Thomas Aquinas, *De potentia* q. 3, a. 17, p. 93a Marietti. The reference is no doubt to Maimonides, *Guide* 2.19, trans. p. 311.

130. Baruch 3:33–35; 6:59, 60a.

131. Clement of Rome, *First Epistle to the Corinthians* 20.1–8, ed. A. Jaubert, SC 167: 135–37.

132. See pp. 136–38.

133. Ignatius Loyola, *Letter 86 to the Brothers and Fathers of Portugal* (26 March 1553), in *Obras completas,* ed. I. Iparraguirre, BAC 86: 811.

134. Al-Kindî, *On the Prosternation of the Supreme Body, Rasâ'il,* 244–61; Avicenna, for example *Ta'liqât,* ed. A. Bâdâwî (Cairo: G.E.B.O., 1973), 102; *Metaphysics* 9.2, p. 382.10–11; see also Ghazâlî, *al-Munqid min adalâl* (error and deliverance), trans. F. Jabre (Beirut, 1969), Ar. p. 23, Fr. p. 79.

135. Al-Kindî, *Definitions* no. 73 s.v. "Philosophy" no. 2, *Rasâ'il,* 1: 172.

136. Saadia Gaon, *Commentary on the Sefer Yetsira,* introduction, ed. Qâfîḥ, p. 19: philos-

ophy is the imitation *(tašabbuh)* of the works of the Creator (or: "philosophy is compared to what is best among the works of the Creator," ed. Lambert (Paris: Bouillon, 1891), 1.15; trans. p. 14); Maimonides, *Guide* 2.52, and Berman 1961; on Farabi, see pp. 142–43.

137. Basil of Caesarea, *Sermons on the Hexaemeron* 9.6, ed. S. Giet, SC 26bis: 512; the argument is turned on its head in Montaigne, *Essaies* 2.12, p. 409; see Blumenberg 1987, 71.

138. See pp. 80–82.

139. Olympiodorus, *Commentary on the 1st Alcibiades of Plato* 125, ed. L. G. Westerink (Amsterdam: North-Holland, 1956), 199.5; Hermiae Alexandrini, *In Platonis Phaedrum scholia*, ed. P. Couvreur (Paris: Bouillon, 1901), 31.15–16; Photius cited in Kranz 1955, 88, 105; *Theology of Aristotle* 2.24, in Bādāwī (1955, 32.19–20).

140. See Altmann 1969, 1–40.

141. Clem. Al., *Pedagogy* 3.1.1.1. See also the text of an alchemist cited by Tardieu 1986, 38.

142. Absent from *CTM* 4: 189ab, but cited in the Brethren of Purity, *Rasā'il* 1.1, 1: 76; 4.7 [48], 4: 193; Avicenna, "Letter to Abu Saʿīd b. Abī 'l-Xayr," in *Rasā'il* (Qom: Bîdâr, 1980), 337.10; Ghazâlî, *Iḥyā'* 31 Conversion 2, 4: 27; 36 Love, 4: 318, 356; Masʿūdī, *Al-Tanbīh wa-'l-Išrāf*, ed. De Goeje (Leiden, 1894), 162.4; Averroës, *Epitome of Metaphysics*, ed. G. Jéhamy (Beirut, 1994), 147; Ibn Arabi, *The Production of Circles* 1, trans. P. Fenton and M. Gloton (Paris: L'Éclat, 1996), 20. See Schimmel 1985, 271.

143. See Bahya ben Joseph ibn Paquda, *Hidāja 'ilā Farā'iḍ al-Qulūb*, 2.5, p. 106.2–3; Joseph Albo, *Sefer ha-Iqqarim* 3.6, ed. I. Husik (Philadelphia: Jewish Publication Society of America, 1930), 3: 54; Simon b. Semach Duran, *Magen Avot* 1.53 (Verona, 1785; repr. Jerusalem, n.d.), 49a; Hebr. trans. by Ghazâlî, *Mozney Ṣedeq*, ed. I. Goldenthal [1939] (Jerusalem, 1975), 28.13–14.

144. Al–Ghazâlî, *Iḥyā'* 39 Meditation, 4: 472.

145. See Blumenberg 1988.

146. Bernard of Clairvaux, *De consideratione* 2.3.6, *Opera,* 3: 414.

147. See Brague 2001.

148. See *HWPh*, s.v. "Empyraeum" (Kurdzialek and Maurach); Lerner 1996, 215–21.

149. See Jachimowicz 1975, 151.

150. See pp. 88–90.

151. See Pines 1936, 41; then Moses b. Ezra, *Arugat ha-bosem,* cited by Pines 1979, 142–43.

152. See Böhm 1967 and Sambursky 1962, 154–78.

153. Farabi, in Bādāwī 1968, 108–15; Engl. trans. in Mahdi (1967); Avicenna, *Correspondence with al-Biruni,* q. 2, in al-Biruni, *Rasā'il,* 416; *Gärten,* 49–50; Ibn Bājja, *Commentary on Physics,* ed. Fakhry, 2d ed. (Dar al-Nahar, 1991), 153; Maimonides, *Guide* 1.71, p. 122; trans. p. 177.

154. See Sambursky 1962, 126–30.

155. Böhm 1967, 301, quotation p. 304, and see PW, s.v. *Quinta essentia,* 25, col. 1244.30–53 (P. Moraux).

156. Philoponus, *De opificio mundi* 1.2, then 6.2, ed. W. Reichardt, BT, p. 28.20ff., then 231.12.

157. Simplicius, *Commentary on the Treatise on the Heavens,* ed. Heiberg, CAG 7: 90.13, then 88.29.

158. See McEvoy 1982, 185; Grant 1983; Werner 1879, 493; Funkenstein 1986, 71 n. 1.

159. William of Ockham, *Quaestiones in Librum secundum Sententiarum* (Reportatio), q. 18, in *Opera theologica,* ed. G. Gál and R. Wood (St. Bonaventure, 1981), 5: 400.9–19. The reference to those of the opposite opinion might target Thomas Aquinas, *Summa theologica* 1, q. 40, a. 2, ad 4m. Eng. trans. in W. Harvey 1992, 90.

160. See pp. 40–41; on this theme, see Dick 1982, Crowe 1988.

161. Arist., *Cael.* 1.8–9; Saadia Gaon, *Beliefs* 1.1, pp. 36, 41–42; interesting astronomical arguments in Gersonides, *Wars* 6.1.19, pp. 62b, 379; summary in Touati 1973, 287–89.

162. See Pépin 1964, 76–78.

163 See for example, "*Book of Causes*" 21, in Bādāwī 1954, 23.3. And Farabi, *Aphorisms of the Statesman* 69, ed. F. M. Najjar (Beirut: Dar el-Mashreq, 1971), 78.

164. Avicenna, *Book of Definitions* 27.56, ed. A.-M. Goichon (Cairo, IFAO, 1963), 28; on Ghazâlî, see Wensinck 1933; Lazarus-Yafeh 1975, 503–22.

165. Ibn Ezra, *Commentary on Exodus 3:15, Reader,* 172–73; see also *YM,* p. 24.34.

166. See Scholem 1931, 416–19; 1974, 118–19.

167. *Genesis Rabbah* 3:5, p. 23, and 9:2, p. 68; see Urbach 1979, 211–12; Sèd 1981, 180–92; allusions in Halevi, *Kuzari* 1.67, p. 18.10, 17. Critique by Maimonides, *Guide* 2.30, p. 245.13–14; pp. 232–33.

168. Ibrahim Al-Naẓẓīm, in al-Ḥayyāt, *Kitāb al-intiṣār,* ed. H. S. Nyberg (Cairo, 1925), 52.4–5; ed. and Fr. trans. A. Nader (Beirut: Les Lettres orientales, 1957) §31, p. 44.16–17, trans. p. 47; 'Azīz ad-Dīn an-Nasafī, *Al-Insān al-Kāmil,* ed. M. Molé, pp. 346–47, both cited in Bausani 1971, 204–5; Al-Biruni, *Gärten* 8, p. 56.

169. See the texts gathered in Boulnois 1994. See Grant 1994, 150–68. Among Jewish writers, see Crescas, *Light* 4, q. 2, pp. 388–92, who also did not go beyond possibility.

170. Ghazâlî, *Iḥyā'* 35 Abandonment 1, 4: 275; a very similar doctrine is attributed to the philosophers in *Maqāṣid al-falāsifa, Metaphysics* 3, 7th claim, ed. Al-Kurdi (Cairo, 1936), 84.12–14; see Ormsby 1984.

171. See Maurer 1976; Biard 1984, 74–79; Bianchi 1984.

172. See Blumenberg 1957, 86, 88; 1988, 183–84.

173. Cited in Randi 1989, 322.

Chapter 12: The End of a World

1. See, after Koyré 1961, the recent work by Lerner 1997.

2. The formula did not appear until some time after Christopher Columbus's first voyage (1492); see A. von Humboldt, *Kosmos,* 2: 241, 280–81.

3. The idea, without the word, is in Dante, *Monarchy* (1311) 1.1.4–5; the expression *('ilm mustanbaṭu 'l-naš'a)* appears in Ibn Khaldūn, *Muqaddima* (1377), 1 preface, ed. Quatremère, pp. 61–62; trans. F. Rosenthal (Bollingen Series 43; New York: Pantheon, 1958), 1: 78. For Europe, see Machiavelli, *Discorsi* (1520) 1 preface, in *Tutte le opere,* ed. F. Flora and C. Cordié (n.p.: Mondadori, 1949), 89. In the title of works, see Galileo, *Discorsi* (1633–50), and Vico, *Scienza Nuova,* 1st ed. (1725); see Arendt 1961, 280 n. 1.

4. Tycho Brahe, *De nova et nullius aevi memoria prius nota stella anni 1572* (Copenhagen, 1573), see *DSB* s.v. (C. Doris Hellman), esp. 402b–3b; J. Kepler, *De stella nova* (1606), see *DSB* s.v. (O. Gingerich), esp. 297b–98a.

5. See Needham 1959, ch. 20.2, pp. 423–29.

6. Hipparchus in Pliny, *NH* 2.24.26.95, ed. J. Beaujeu, CUF, p. 41; Varro in August., *De civ. D.* 21.8.2, col. 1005d; see Grant 1994, 210.

7. See Justus Lipsius, *De constantia* (1572) 1.16, in J. Lagrée, *Juste Lipse. La restauration du stoïcisme* (Paris: Vrin, 1994), 132–33.

8. Tycho Brahe, *De mundi aetherei recentioribus phaenomenis* (Uraniborg, 1588); and see Tuzet 1965, 294.

9. See J. Poggendorff, *Biographisch-Literarisches Handwörterbuch zur Geschichte der Naturwissenschaften* (Leipzig, 1863), 1: col. 712.

10. C. Scheiner, S.J., *Tres Epistolae de maculis solaribus scriptae ad Marcum Velserum* (Augsburg, 1612). See Shea 1970.

11. Galileo, *Dialogo* 1, pp. 62ff. On the importance of this idea, see Hume, *Dialogues* 2, pp. 52–53.

12. See C. Wilson 1995.

13. Roger Bacon, *Opus Majus,* 5: *Perspectiva* 3a.2.4, ed. Bridges (Oxford, 1900), 2: 157; *Opus Tertium, De perspectiva* 7, ed. A. G. Little (British Society for Franciscan Studies 4, 1912), 40.

14. Gersonides, *Supercommentary on the "Book of the Animals,"* cited in Freudenthal 1992, 348. For the date, see Touati 1973, 73.

15. Descartes, *Dioptrique,* 10, in *Oeuvres,* 6: 226.

16. Pascal, *Pensées* 72, pp. 75–76; the letter from Méré is cited p. 76 n. 6; *Logique de Port-Royal* 4.1, ed. P. Clair and F. Girbal (Paris: P.U.F., 1965), 296; see Blumenberg 1988, 183.

17. R. Hooke, *Micrographia; or, Some Physiological Descriptions of Minute Bodies Made by Magnifying Glasses,* preface, cited in C. Wilson 1995, 66.

18. Fontenelle, *Entretiens* 3, p. 70; Leibniz, Table of definitions, in *Opuscules et fragments inédits de Leibniz,* ed. L. Couturat (Paris: Alcan, 1903), 224; Berkeley, *An Essay Towards a New Theory of Vision* (1709) 85 (Everyman), 53; see Blumenberg 1983, 156–57; Hume, *Dialogues* 2, p. 68.

19. See Levine 1983; Ruderman 1995; on the Talmud, see Sarfatti 1965–66, 147. Saadia Gaon is perhaps the first to notice the retrograde nature of rabbinical cosmography; see *Commentary on the "Sefer Yetsira"* 2.4, ed. J. Qafih (Jerusalem: Committee for the publication of the works of Saadia Gaon, 1972), 83.

20. Salomon Maimon, *Giv'at ha-Moreh,* on Maimonides, *Guide* 1.11, ed. S. H. Bergman and N. Rotenstreich (Jerusalem: Israel Academy of Sciences and Humanities, 1965), 46; Funkenstein 1993, 242. See also, in the commentary on 1.15, p. 52, awareness of the illegitimacy of the distinction between the heavy and the light.

21. See B. Lewis 1984, 151; see also Heinen 1982, 15.

22. See Lackner 1972, 160.

23. See pp. 86–87.

24. D'Alembert, *Discours préliminaire de l'Encyclopédie* (1751) 1, ed. F. Picavet [1894] (Paris: Vrin, 1984), 29.

25. Adam Smith, "The Principles which lead and direct Philosophical Enquiries; illustrated by the History of Astronomy," in W. P. D. Wightman and J. C. Bryce, eds., *Essays on Philosophical Subjects,* The Glasgow Edition of the Works and Correspondence, vol. 3 (Oxford: Oxford University Press, 1980), 33–105.

26. G. Leopardi, "Storia della astronomia dalla sua origine fine all'anno MDCCCXI" (1813), in *Tutte le opere,* 2: *Pensieri, discorsi e saggi,* ed. F. Flora (Milan: Mondadori, 1940), 723–1042, and "Dissertazione sopra l'origine, e i primi progressi, dell'astronomia" (1814), ibid., 1043–69.

27. Kepler, *Prodromum dissertationum cosmographicarum continens Mysterium cosmographicum* (1596).

28. Descartes, *Traité du monde,* ch. 6, "Description d'un nouveau Monde," in *Oeuvres,* 11: 34ff.; the opposition cosmos/chaos is not earlier than Ovid and Pseudo-Lucian; see Kranz 1955, 13.

29. Descartes, *Meditationes* 2, in *Oeuvres,* 7: 25; 3, 42–43.

30. See Merleau-Ponty and Morando 1971, 114, 184.

31. See C. S. Lewis 1967, 251.

32. G. Bruno, "Theses de magia" 5, in *Opera latine conscripta,* ed. F. Tocco and H. Vitelli (Florence, 1891), 457–58; cited in Blumenberg 1988, 183 n. 54.

33. Nietzsche, *Die fröhliche Wissenschaft* 3.109, *KSA* 3: 467–68. Eng. trans.: *The Joyful Wisdom,* trans. by Thomas Cannon, in *The Complete Works,* vol. 10, ed. Oscar Levy (London: Allen & Unwin; New York: Macmillan, 1910), 152.

34. See Brague 1994a.

35. John Donne, *The First Anniversary, Anatomy of the World* (1611) 205–14 (Everyman), 335. Koyré 1962, 32. See also: "As new Philosophy arrests the Sunne, / And bids the passive earth about it runne," To the Countess of Bedford, *Letters to Severall Personages* 37–38, ibid., 274.

36. Leopardi, "Il Copernico," *Operette,* 285; see also, less clearly, Goethe, "Materialien zur Geschichte der Farbenlehre" 4, Zwischenbetrachtung, in *Sämtliche Werke* (Munich: Hanser), 10 (1989): 618.

37. From 1 Maccabees 3:18–19; see Bietenhard 1951, 80–82.

38. Pascal, *Pensées,* Br. 206, p. 127, clarified by Br. 194, p. 106; among the examples of misunderstandings, Valéry, "Variations sur une pensée," *Oeuvres* (Paris: Gallimard, 1957), 1: 458–73. Correction in Koyré 1962, 47 n. 1.

39. Adam Smith, *Theory of Moral Sentiments* (1759) 6.2.3.2, Glasgow edition, vol. 1 (Oxford: Clarendon, 1976), 235.

40. See p. 42 and pp. 170–72.

41. Hume, *Dialogues* 5, p. 71. The text was not published until 1779 but circulated in manuscript form beginning in the 1750s. The passage is copied out by Nietzsche, frag. 29 [86], summer/autumn 1873, *KSA* 7: 667–68.

42. Benjamin Constant, Letter of 4 June 1790 to Mme de Charrière, cited in Rudler (1909, 376–77. On the chevalier Ignatius Thaon de Revel (Nice, 1760–Turin, 1835), see *Biographie universelle, ancienne et moderne. Supplément* (Paris: Michaud), 79 (1846): 1a–3a, which mentions his trips to England. Might he have encountered Hume's work there?

43. Nerval, *Aurélia* 2.4.

44. See Saint Girons 1993, 186ff.

45. Rimbaud, "Le bateau ivre"; Mallarmé, "Brise marine." See also Musset, *Confession* 1.4, p. 55; Tuzet 1965, 145, 181.

46. Nietzsche, *Joyful Wisdom* 3.125, *KSA* 3: 481; Eng. trans. pp. 167–68.

47. Nietzsche, frag. autumn 1885–autumn 1886, 2 [127], *KSA* 12: 127.

48. Freud, "Eine Schwierigkeit der Psychoanalyse" (*Imago* 5 [1917]), *Gesammelte Werke* (Frankfurt: Fischer, 1966), 12: 3–12, esp. 7. The same year, the same text, almost word for word, was reproduced in *Introduction to Psychoanalysis,* ch. 18. Finally, Freud cites himself again in *Die Widerstände gegen die Psychoanalyse* (1925), in *Werke,* 14: 109.

49. Refutation in Lovejoy 1936, 101–8; Collingwood 1945, 96–98; C. S. Lewis 1964, 62–63; and Brague 1997c. I reproduce the texts of Fontenelle, Leopardi and Freud there; this is why I am not quoting them here. See also Hallyn 1987, 299–300.

50. Fontenelle, *Entretiens* 1, pp. 26–28.

51. Leopardi, "Il Copernico," *Operette,* 284.

52. Novalis, "Die Christenheit oder Europa," *Werke und Briefe* (Munich: Winkler, 1962), 389–408, at p. 391.

53. P. G. Wodehouse, *The Mating Season* [1949], ch. 4 (London: Vintage, 1991), 39.

54. The first occurrence of "disenchantment" is in Musset, who proposes as synonyms *dénégation* or *désespérance* [disparagement or hopelessness] (*Confession* 1.2, p. 37). The phrase appears in Max Weber, for example in the famous lecture *Wissenschaft als Beruf* (1919), then in Rosenzweig, *Der Stern der Erlösung* (1921) 2.3 (Frankfurt: Suhrkamp, 1988), 246–47; finally as the title of a book by M. Gauchet (Paris: Gallimard, 1985).

55. See C. Taylor 1989, 148, and see pp. 206–7.

56. See p. 91.

57. Leopardi, "Dialogo della natura e di un islandese" (21–30 May 1824), *Operette,* 127.

58. *Il.* 16.34–35, Eng. trans. p. 331; Biese 1882, 18; see also p. 68 (example in a Greek romance).

59. R. Pautrel, in *La Sainte Bible,* translated into French under the direction of the École biblique de Jérusalem (Paris: Cerf, 1956), 855 note b; Eng. trans. *The Jerusalem Bible* (Garden City, N.Y.: Doubleday, 1966), 990 note d. For another interpretation, with bibliography, see Fox 1988.

60. See Descartes, *Principia Philosophiae* 3.56, in *Oeuvres,* 8: 108; Hobbes, *Leviathan* 4.46, ed. M. Oakeshott (Oxford: Blackwell, 1960), 444; Pascal, *Pensées,* Br. 75, pp. 96–97; Kant, *Metaphysical Foundations of Natural Science* 3 Mechanics, part 3, remarks; Fr. trans. by J. Gibelin (Paris: Vrin, 1952), 131.

61. Goethe, *Das Göttliche* (1783) 3, with an allusion to Matthew 5:45; see p. 53.

62. *The Education of Henry Adams,* ed. I. B. Nadel (Oxford, 1999), ch. 19, pp. 241–43.

63. S. Crane, "The Open Boat" (1899) 6, in *The Red Badge of Courage and Other Stories* (London: Penguin, 1983), 246–47; Blumenberg 1966, 123; 1997, 455. The last words are a near quotation of Heine, "Fragen," in *Die Nordsee* (1825–26), 2 n. 7.

64. M. Arnold, "In Harmony with Nature," in *The Strayed Reveler* (1849).

65. See Young's text cited in A. Assmann 1980, 28.

66. Spinoza, *Tractatus Theologico-Politicus* 16, VL, 258; see p. 111.

67. Fontenelle, *Entretiens* 5, pp. 105–6, and see 4, p. 86.

68. See Tuzet 1965, 90 n. 40; reference to Restif, p. 351.

69. Diderot, *Lettre sur les aveugles* (1749), in *Oeuvres philosophiques*, ed. P. Vernière (Paris, Garnier, 1964), 123; Hume, *Dialogues* 5, p. 69.

70. Schopenhauer, *The World as Will and Idea* 2.1.27, *Werke*, 1: 220.

71. Musset, *Confession* 5.6, p. 303; on love and gravity, see also 3.6, p. 160; on Hugo, see Tuzet 1965, 127.

72. Leopardi, "Dialogo della terra e della luna" (24–28 April 1824), *Operette*, 79.

73. Hume, *Dialogues* 11, p. 113.

74. Hegel, *System der Philosophie*, 2: *Die Naturphilosophie* 268 Zusatz, in *Jubiläumsausgabe*, ed. H. Glockner (Stuttgart: Frommann, 1927), 9: 118. See Heine, relating a scene from autumn 1822, *Geständnisse* (1854), ed. G. Heinemann (Hamburg: Hoffmann and Campe), 15 (1982): 34; clarifications pp. 507–8; the passage is cited by Blumenberg 1975, 85; on Simplicius, see pp. 179–80

75. Marx, according to Paul Lafargue; cited by Blumenberg 1975, 89.

76. Nietzsche, *Thus Spake Zarathustra* 2.18, *KSA* 4: 168; Lämmli (1962, 1: 20) compares Ovid's idea of man as the earth's garment.

77. Henry Sidgwick, *The Methods of Ethics*, 3d ed. (London, 1884), 1.9.4, pp. 109–10.

78. Wittgenstein, *Tractatus Logico-Philosophicus* 6.41, ed. B. McGuinness and J. Schulte (Frankfurt: Suhrkamp, 1989).

79. War note of 24 July 1916, then Conversation of 5 January 1930, in *Ludwig Wittgenstein und der Wiener Kreis, Werkausgabe* (Frankfurt: Suhrkamp), 3 (1984): 92.

80. Manent 1977, 10.

81. Montesquieu, *De l'esprit des lois* 3.7, and Ehrard 1963, 379; on Smith, see Marejko 1989, 18.

82. Schopenhauer, *Paralipomena* 31.396; *Werke*, 5: 765.

83. "Über einige Beziehungen zwischen Ästhetik und Therapeutik in der Philosophie des neunzehnten Jahrhunderts" [1963], in Marquard 1973, 85–106, 185–208. On the "black definition" of nature, see 92–93; see also Marquard 1986, 17–18.

Chapter 13: An Impossible Imitation

1. Alexander Pope, *An Essay on Man* 2.23–26; similar pleasantry in Grosseteste, *Hexaëmeron* 1.17.1, p. 76.19–24; see Dales 1980, 542.

2. Schiller, "Die Horen" (1795–96), in *Werke*, vol. 1 (Weimar: Nationalausgabe, 1943), 259.

3. See H. von Kleist, *Über das Marionettentheater* (1810).

4. See p. 112.

5. Kant, *Critique of Judgement* 59.

6. Barrès, *Les Déracinés* (1897), ch. 7; one might compare Claudel, *Tête d'or* (1894), part 1.

7. John Stuart Mill, *On Nature*, 371.

8. See pp. 195–96.

9. John Stuart Mill, *On Nature*, respectively pp. 377, 375, 379.

10. Ibid., 383 [emphasis added].

11. On the idea of an uncompleted world, see pp. 170–72; for his optimistic interpretation see F. Schlegel, quoted in Blumenberg 1960, 84–87; Koschorke 1989, 222.

12. John Stuart Mill, *On Nature*, 385. On Sade, see pp. 206–7.

13. Ibid., pp. 391–92.

14. Ibid., p. 386, then 396–97.

15. Nietzsche, *Beyond Good and Evil* 9, *KSA* 5: 21–22.

16. See Baudelaire, *Le peintre de la vie moderne* 11, "Eloge du maquillage," and O. Wilde, *The Decay of Lying*, beginning.

17. Hume, *Dialogues* 10, p. 96.

18. Céline, *Voyage au bout de la nuit* (1932).

19. Darwin, Letter to Joseph Hooker dated 1 February 1871.

20. C. Zuckmayer, *Die Geschichte vom Tümpel* (1926), in *Gedichte, Erzählungen* (Frankfurt: Fischer, 1960), 223–30.

21. Pl., *Ti.* 56c8–57c6, pp. 224–30; Pico della Mirandola, *Oratio de hominis dignitate,* ed. Boulnois-Tognon (Paris: Presses Universitaires de France, 1993), 22; see also references to Calderón in Souiller 1992, 151.

22. Shlomo b. Verga, *Shevet Yehuda,* ed. M. Wiener (Hanover, 1924), 79; see Funkenstein 1993, 214; Baer 1923, 1934.

23. See p. 113.

24. Büchner, *Dantons Tod* (winter 1835), 2.7; Eng. trans. by Stephen Spender and Goronwy Rees (London: Faber & Faber, 1939), 86f.; similar reasoning in La Mettrie, with pre-Sadean accents, in the texts cited in Ehrard 1963, 390–91.

25. This has been shown by Deprun 1968, whom I follow for the most part; on Sade in general see Shattuck 1996, 227–99.

26. Sade, *La Nouvelle Justine* 10, *Oeuvres,* 6: 343 (and *Justine, Oeuvres,* 3: 209), and *Histoire de Juliette* 1, *Oeuvres,* 8: 206.

27. See Deprun 1968, 143.

28. Sade, *Histoire de Juliette* 4, *Oeuvres,* 9: 172.

29. Ibid., 9: 169. The idea of creation as a launching is also found elsewhere in various aspects; it is in Gnosticism, but also in the Greek myth of Deucalion.

30. See pp. 96–99.

31. Sade, *La Nouvelle Justine* 16, *Oeuvres,* 7: 225.

32. Sade, *Juliette* 6, *Oeuvres,* 9: 578, and see *La Nouvelle Justine* 10, *Oeuvres,* 6: 344.

33. Sade, *La Nouvelle Justine* (1797) 11, *Oeuvres,* 7: 43–44.

34. Ockham, *Quodlibeta* 3 q. 13, in *Philosophical Writings,* ed. P. Boehner (London: Nelson, 1957), 147. See also Descartes, *Entretien avec Burman* 25, *Oeuvres,* 5: 160.

35. Goethe, *The Sorrows of Young Werther,* book 1, letter of 18 August; Eng. trans. by Thomas Carlyle (New York: Collier, 1917). An echo in Renan, *Dialogues philosophiques* 3, in *Oeuvres Complètes* (Paris: Calmann-Lévy, 1947), 1: 618.

36. Pascal, *Pensées,* Br. 347, p. 262.

37. See Kant, *Enquiry into the proofs for the Existence of God* [1763] 2.5.2, *Werke,* 1: 683 n.

38. Hugo von Hofmannsthal, "Der Jüngling und die Spinne," in *Gedichte und kleine Dramen* (Frankfurt: Suhrkamp, 1966), 41–43.

39. D. Buzzati, "Dolce notte," in *Il colombre* (Milan: Mondadori, 1966), 193–99; Fr. trans. "Douce nuit," in *Le K* (Paris: Laffont, 1967), 160–65.

40. Gustave Doré, *Été* (Boston, Museum of Fine Arts).

41. Descartes, *Discours de la méthode* 6, *Oeuvres,* 6: 62.

42. See Blumenberg 1988, 150ff.; Brague 1993b, 180.

43. See A. von Humboldt, *Kosmos,* 2: 6 (literature), 65 (painting); C. S. Lewis 1964, 101.

44. See Curtius 1953, 191–209.

45. See J. H. Probst 1936; possible exceptions in Biese 1884, 132.

46. The tale is conveniently accessible in F. Petrarca, *Die Besteigung des Mont Ventoux, Lateinisch/Deutsch,* trans. and ed. K. Steinmann (Stuttgart: Reclam, 1995). Synthesis of the preceding works in Groh and Groh 1992; against the notion of a Greek taboo on the ascension of the summits, see Jacob 1984.

47. See J. Ritter 1963, 158–63; context in Marquard 1986, 27–28.

48. One might compare the medieval references in Brague 1997c, 202–3, with Sterne, *Tristam Shandy* 1: 5 (1760), ed. I. C. Ross (Oxford: Clarendon, 1983), 9.

49. See pp. 87–90.

50. Dante, *Vita nova* 41, "Oltre la sfera che piu alta gira"; John of the Cross, "Tras de un amoroso lance," *Obras completas,* ed. L. Ruano de la Iglesia, BAC 15: 33; Fr. trans. *Oeuvres complètes* (Paris: Desclée De Brouwer, 1967), 922–23; see also Luis de León, cited in Spitzer 1963, 113.

51. Goethe, *Ganymede* (1774) 28–31; Eng. from *The Poems of Goethe, Translated in the Original Metres,* by Edgar Alfred Bowring (New York: Alden, 1883), 179.

52. Musset, *Confession* I, II and VII, III, 10, V, 6; pp. 28–29, 42, 78, 181, 302.

53. J. Conrad, *The Nigger of the Narcissus* (1897) 2 (World's Classics), 33, 35.

54. Baudelaire "Elévation," *Les Fleurs du mal,* and see Friedrich 1956, 35–36. See also A. Blok, "Dans la neige," *Masque de neige* [Sneznaja maska] (1907), 1.16—I owe this reference to J. Deprun.

55. V. Huidobro, *Altazor* (1931). I owe my knowledge of this work to A. Vallega.

56. Herder, *Ideen zur Philosophie der Geschichte der Menschheit* 5.6.5 (last words in the book), ed. B. Suphan (Berlin, 1909), 13: 201. The passage was rewritten four times.

57. Marx, *Ökonomisch-philosophische Manuskripte* (1844), 3d MS. 26, in *Marx Engels Werke,* supp. vol. 1 (Berlin: Dietz, 1968), 577; see Granel 1972, 217 n. 1. One can detect an echo of Goethe, *Grenzen der Menschheit* (1778) 3.

58. J. Brand, "Wir sind jung, die Welt ist offen."

59. Freud, *Das Unbehagen in der Kultur* 4, in *Studienausgabe* (Frankfurt: Fischer, 1982), 9: 229f. n. 1.

60. L. Feuerbach, "The *Essence of Christianity* in its relationship to *The Unique and its Property*" 13, in *Manifestes philosophiques,* trans. by L. Althusser (Paris: PUF, 1960), 232.

61. E. Lévinas, *Totalité et Infini: Essai sur l'extériorité* (The Hague: Nijhoff, 1961), 4, 90.

62. Jones 1989.

63. Francisco de Quevedo, *Defensa de Epicuro contra la común opinión* (1635), ed. E. Acosta Méndez (Madrid: Tecnos, 1986).

64. Spinoza, *Letters* 56, to Hugo Boxel (1674?), VL, 3: 192.

65. See Goldschmidt 1953, 173–74.

66. See R. Rorty, *Philosophy and the Mirror of Nature* (Princeton: Princeton University Press, 1979).

67. Leopardi, *L'infinito* (1819) 2; see Keats, *Endymion* (1818), 1.4 *(bower).*

68. Pierre Bayle, *Dictionnaire Historique et critique* (1696), s.v. "Manichéisme."

69. Gibbon, *The History of the Decline and Fall of the Roman Empire* 15, ed. D. Womersley (London: Allen Lane/Penguin, 1994), 1: 457.

70. Hume, *Dialogues* 11, p. 113; John Stuart Mill, *Autobiography* 2 (World's Classics), 33.

71. See R. Smith, in *NHL,* 532–49; Couliano 1984; 1990, 289–323.

72. See Henry 1989; for art, Besançon 1994, 406ff.

73 Kierkegaard, *Repetition* part 2, 11 October; Fr. trans. by N. Viallaneix (Paris: Garnier-Flammarion, 1990), 144.

74. Jacob Taubes, "Das stählerne Gehäuse und der Exodus daraus oder Ein Streit um Marcion einst und jetzt" [1984], in *Vom Kult zur Kultur* (Munich: Fink, 1996), 179, quoting Wittgenstein, *Tractatus Logico-Philosophicus* 6.432.

75. See Brague 1988, 37 n. 63; Couliano 1990, 315.

76. Hamann, cited by Eichendorff, "Zur Geschichte der neueren romantischen Poesie in Deutschland" 1, in *Sämtliche Werke, Historisch-kritische Ausgabe,* 8.1: *Aufsätze zur Literatur,* ed. W. Mauser (Regensburg: Habbel, 1962), 17–18; himself cited by Staiger 1939, 93.

77. Texts cited in Koschorke 1990, 253–81.

78. A. E. Housman, "The Chestnuts are Casting Their Flambeaux," in *Last Poems* (1922). See also, for example, F. Zorn, *Mars,* part 3: "Ritter, Tod und Teufel" (Frankfurt: Fischer, 1979).

79. Joseph Conrad, *Lord Jim* [1900] 20 (London: Penguin), 195. See Brague 1990b.

80. E. M. Forster, *Howard's End* [1910] 26 (London: Penguin), 229.

81. See Koyré 1962, 2—the formula is missing in the original English; Arendt 1961, 286; Marejko 1989, 125.

82. Alexander von Humboldt seems to have both reintroduced the word *kosmos* into modern languages and widely used the word *Weltanschauung,* which appears only once in Kant

(*Kritik der Urteilskraft*, §26, p. 99 Vorländer), see *Kosmos*, preface, 1: 7, and preliminary considerations, 1: 41; the two words are moreover linked: it is necessary that the world be grasped in its unity, as *kosmos*, for it to be the object of a *Weltanschauung* (*Kosmos*, 2: 183)—this is why the latter term does not have the meaning in Humboldt it has since assumed.

83. Heidegger, "Die Zeit des Weltbildes" [1938], in *Holzwege* (Frankfurt-am-Main: Klostermann, 1950), 69–104.

84. The author plays with the term "im-monde," which in French conveys both a negative, immoral sense ("immonde" literally means, "filthy, rubbish"), and, when the elements of the word are divided into im-monde, a separation from the world. Unfortunately, this wordplay is lost in the English. TRANS.

Chapter 14: The Lost World

1. See Arist., *Eth. Nic.* 6.7.1141a34–b2; *Metaph.* A.10.1075a19ff.

2. See p. 76.

3. Wittgenstein, 24 July 1916 [3].

4. Wittgenstein, *Tractatus* 6.421 and *Prototractatus* 6.422: compare 30 July 1916 [9].

5. Conversation dated 17 December 1930, in *Ludwig Wittgenstein und der Wiener Kreis, Werkausgabe* (Frankfurt: Suhrkamp), 3 (1984): 118.

6. Plotinus 2.9 [33].8.43–45; 1: 235; Alt 1990, 25 [Modified Eng. trans. by A. H. Armstrong, LCL, p. 255 TRANS.].

7. See similar considerations in Henrich 1990, ch. 7.

8. Dio Chrysostom, *Orations* 12.83; Nicholas of Cusa, *De beryllo* 7, ed. C. Bormann and J. G. Senger, in *Opera Omnia* (Hamburg: Meiner), 11/1 (1987), 9; see texts quoted in Panofsky 1924, 121 n. 303.

9. Ficino, *Theologia Platonica*, 13.4, ed. R. Marcel (Paris: Les Belles Lettres, 1964), 2: 226, cited in Hallyn 1987, 64; Baumgarten, *Aesthetica* 455, in Schweizer 1973, 188; for the prehistory of the idea, see Saloustios, *On the Gods and the World* 3.3, ed. G. Rochefort, CUF, p. 5.

10. See Curtius 1953, 400–1; Abrams 1953, ch. 10.3: "The Poem as Heterocosm," pp. 272–85; Kandinsky, in Besançon 1994, 448.

11. Vico, *Scienza Nuova* (1730) 1.3, Principles 331, ed. F. Nicolini (Milan: Ricciardi, 1953), 479.

12. Marx, *Ökonomisch-philosophische Manuskripte* (1844), 1st MS. 24, p. 517; *Das Kapital* 4.15.1 note; trans. by M. Rubel (Paris: Gallimard, 1963), 1: 915.

13. Marx, *Deutsche Ideologie* (Berlin: Dietz, 1960), 41–43, then 34.

14. Ludwig Rubiner, "Zur Krise des geistigen Lebens" (1916), in *Künstler bauen Barrikaden: Texte und Manifeste 1908–1919*, ed. W. Haug (Darmstadt: Luchterhand, 1988), 126–27; then "Der Kampf mit dem Engel" (1917), ibid., 145.

15. George Orwell, *Nineteen Eighty-Four* 3.3 (London: Penguin, 1954), 213. It is unfortunate that the texts of Rubiner and Orwell escaped the attention of Blumenberg (1975).

16. Since Arist., *Metaph.* Z.16.1041a1–2, and see Happ 1968, 87. Orwell perhaps borrowed the idea that the stars represent a limit inaccessible to all tyranny from a scene in Charlie Chaplin's *The Great Dictator* (1940).

17. See Unger 1924, Clavier 1997.

18. Kant, *De mundi sensibilis atque intelligibilis forma et principiis* 1.2.3, *Werke*, 3: 24.

19. Kant, *Critique of Pure Reason*, respectively A 407/B 434, A 418/B 446, A 684/B 712.

20. Ibid., A 328/B 384–85.

21. Kant, *Anthropology*, preface, *Werke*, 6: 399.

22. Plato, *Phaedrus*, 247c3; Origen, *PA*, 2.3.6, p. 316.

23. Plotinus 3.4 [15].3.22; 4.7 [2].10.35–36; see also "Hermes Trismegistus," *CH* 13.21, 2: 209; Kranz 1955, 91–92.

24. Kant, *Pure Reason* A 256/B 312.

25. Kant, *Critique of Practical Reason* 1.2.2.6, pp. 239–40; Eng. trans., p. 230.

26. Ibid., 1.2.2.7, p. 251.

27. *Ibid.*, conclusion, p. 289; Eng. trans., p. 260.

28. Ibid., 1.1.3, p. 155, and *Grundlegung zur Metaphysik der Sitten* 3 (Akademie-Ausgabe, 4: 451–52). See also *Träume eines Geistersehers* (1766) 1.2, *Werke*, 1: 940.

29. Kant, *Ideen zu einer allgemeinen Geschichte in weltbürgerlicher Absicht* 9, *Werke*, 6: 49.

30. See Kant, *Critique of Judgement* 59.

31 See pp. 67–70.

32. Kant, *Practical Reason* 7, p. 57, and see *Pure Reason* B 72.

33. Fichte, *Grundlage des Naturrechts* 5–6; Hegel, *Encyclopedia* 384, p. 314 Meiner.

34. See Biemel 1950.

35. Heidegger, *Zur Bestimmung der Philosophie*, Summer semester 1919, ed. B. Heimbüchel, *Gesamtausgabe* 56/57: 73.

36. Heidegger, *Grundprobleme der Phänomenologie*, winter semester 1919–20, ed. H.-H. Gander, *Gesamtausgabe* 58: 33–34, 96, 250; then *Phänomenologische Interpretationen zu Aristoteles*, winter semester 1921–22, ed. W. Bröcker et al., *Gesamtausgabe* 61: 86.

37. The path to this work was paved by all the courses of lectures that preceded it, but most specifically by *Ontologie*, summer semester 1923, ed. K. Bröcker-Oltmanns, *Gesamtausgabe* 63 §§16–26, pp. 79–104, and *Prolegomena zur Geschichte des Zeitbegriffs*, summer semester 1925, ed. P. Jaeger, *Gesamtausgabe* 20 §§18–26.

38. See Brague 1984.

39. Heidegger, *Being and Time* 14, p. 92.

40. *Vom Wesen des Grundes*, repr. in *Wegmarken*, pp. 35–55; quotes from pp. 37, 51–52, 53. First version in *Anfangsgründe der Logik*, summer semester 1928, §11, ed. K. Held, *Gesamtausgabe* 26: 203–52. Eng. trans.: *Pathmarks*, ed. William McNeill (Cambridge: Cambridge University Press, 1998), 97–135, at 110–11, 120–21, 122.

41. *Grundbegriffe der Metaphysik*, winter semester 1929–30, ed. F.-W. von Herrmann, *Gesamtausgabe* 29/30: 261–62, 263.

42. Ibid., pp. 246–48, and see p. 255.

43. Heidegger, *Grundproblem der Phänomenologie*, Winter 1919–20, ed. H.-H. Gander, *Gesamtausgabe* 58: 61.

44. Schelling, *Philosophie der Offenbarung* lesson 14 (Darmstadt: Wissenschaftliche, 1983), 308; Fr. trans. by J. F. Marquet et al. (Paris: Presses Universitaires de France, 1991), 2: 160–61.

45. Montaigne, *Essaies* 1.20; 1: 166.

46. Pascal, *Pensées*, Br. 457, p. 369.

Bibliography

Abbreviations

ANET   James B. Pritchard, ed. *Ancient Near Eastern Texts relating to the Old Testament,* 2d
       ed. Princeton: Princeton University Press, 1955.
BAC   Biblioteca de Autores Cristianos. Madrid.
BCNH   Bibliothèque copte de Nag-Hammadi, Textes. Quebec: Presses de l'Université
       Laval, 1977–.
BT   Bibliotheca Teubneriana. Leipzig.
CAD   I. J. Gelb et al., eds. *The Assyrian Dictionary of the Oriental Institute of the University
       of Chicago.* Glückstadt: J. J. Augustin, 1956–.
CAG   Commentaria in Aristotelem Graeca. Berlin: Reimer, 1882–1909.
CCSL   Corpus Christianorum, Series Latina. Tournai: Brepols, 1953–.
CTM   A. J. Wensinck. *Concordance et indices des traditions musulmanes,* 8 vols. Leiden:
       Brill, 1936–88.
CUF   Collection des universités de France. Paris: Les Belles Lettres, 1920–.
DK   H. Diels and W. Kranz, *Die Fragmente der Vorsokratiker* [Greek and German], 11th
       ed. 3 vols. Zurich: Weidmann, 1964.
DS   M. Viller et al., eds. *Dictionnaire de spiritualité ascétique et mystique.* Paris: Beau-
       chesne, 1932–95.
DSB   C. G. Gillispie, ed. *Dictionary of Scientific Biography.* New York: Scribners, 1970–
       80.
FPhG   A. Mullach. *Fragmenta Philosophorum Graecorum.* Paris: Didot, 1860–80.
GCS   Die griechischen christlichen Schriftsteller der ersten drei Jahrhunderte. Berlin:
       Hinrich, 1897–.
HPh   A. A. Long and D. N. Sedley, *The Hellenistic Philosophers,* vol. 1: *Translations of the
       Principal Sources with Philosophical Commentary.* Cambridge: Cambridge Univer-
       sity Press, 1987.
HWPh   J. Ritter et al., eds. *Historisches Wörterbuch der Philosophie.* Basel: Schwabe, 1971–.
LCL   Loeb Classical Library. Cambridge: Harvard University Press; London: Heine-
       mann, 1912–.
LSJ   H. G. Liddell, R. Scott, and H. S. Jones et al. *A Greek-English Lexicon,* 9th ed. Ox-
       ford: Clarendon, 1968.
MG   Miqrā'ōt gedōlōt [1859]. Jerusalem: Eshkol, 1976.
NHL   James M. Robinson, ed. *The Nag Hammadi Library,* 3rd ed. San Francisco: Harper-
       Collins, 1988.
OCT   Oxford Classical Texts. Oxford: Oxford University Press.
OECT   Oxford Early Christian Texts. Oxford: Clarendon.
PG   J.-P. Migne, ed. *Patrologia graeca.* Paris, 1857–66.
PL   J.-P. Migne, ed. *Patrologia latina.* 1841–64.
PW   A. Pauly and G. Wissowa, eds. *Realenzyklopädie der classischen Altertumswis-
       senschaften.* Munich: Druckenmüller, 1894–1972.
RDAM   Recherches. Beirut: Dar al-Mashreq.
RlA   E. Ebeling et al., eds. *Reallexikon der Assyriologie und der vorderasiatischen Archäolo-
       gie.* Berlin: De Gruyter, 1928–.

RPOA   *Les Religions du Proche-Orient asiatique: Textes babyloniens, ougaritiques, hittites,* présentés et traduits par R. Labat et al. Paris: Fayard et Denoël, 1970.

SC   Sources chrétiennes. Paris: Cerf, 1941–.

SE   M. Gigante, ed. *La Scuola di Epicuro.* Naples: Bibliopolis, 1976.

SVF   H. von Arnim, ed. *Stoicorum Veterum Fragmenta.* 4 vols. Leipzig: Teubner, 1903–5.

TD   H. Hemmer and P. Lejay, eds. Textes et documents pour l'étude historique du christianisme. Paris: Picard, 1904–.

ThWAT   G. J. Botterweck et al., eds. *Theologisches Wörterbuch zum Alten Testament.* Stuttgart: Kohlhammer, 1973–.

VEP   Vivliothiki Ellinôn Paterôn. Athens: Apostoliki Diakonia tis ekklisias tis Ellados.

YM   Y. Tzvi Langermann, ed. and trans. *Yemenite Midrash: Philosophical Commentaries on the Torah.* San Francisco: Harper, 1996.

Primary Sources

Alain de Lille. *Anticlaudianus,* ed. R. Bossuat. Paris: Vrin, 1955.

Aristotle. *De caelo,* ed. P. Moraux. CUF, 1965.

———. *Nicomachaean Ethics,* ed. I. Bywater. OCT, 1894.

———. *Metaphysica,* ed. W. Jaeger. OCT, 1957. Eng. ed.: *The Works of Aristotle,* vol. 8, *Metaphysica,* 2d ed. Trans. by W. D. Ross. Oxford: Clarendon, 1928.

———. *Parts of Animals,* trans. by A. L. Peck. LCL, 1955.

Augustine. Bibliothèque augustinienne, *Oeuvres de saint Augustin.* Paris: Desclée De Brouwer, 1947–.

———. *Confessiones,* ed. E. Tréhorel and G. Bouissou. 2 vols. BA 14, 1962.

———. *Enarrationes in Psalmos,* ed. E. Dekkers and J. Fraipont. CCSL 38–40, 1956.

———. *De civitate Dei, post recensionem monachorum ordinis sancti Benedicti.* Paris: Gaume, 1838.

———. *De genesi contra Manichaeos.* Eng. trans.: *Saint Augustine* On Genesis: *Two Books on Genesis against the Manichees and on the Literal Interpretation of Genesis: An Unfinished Book,* trans. by Roland J. Teske. Washington, D.C.: Catholic University of America Press, 1991.

Averroës. *Tafsīr mā ba'd al-Ṭabī'a, Grand commentaire de la Métaphysique d'Aristote,* ed. M. Bouyges. 4 vols. [1938–52]. Beirut: Dar al-Machreq, 1967–73.

———. *Tahāfut al-Tahāfut, L'incohérence de l'incohérence,* ed. M. Bouyges [1930]. Beirut, 1987; Eng. trans. by S. Van den Bergh. London: Luzac, 1954.

Avicenna. *al-Šifā', al-Ilāhiyyāt* [*Metaphysics*], ed. G. C. Anawati and S. Za'îd. Cairo, 1960; Fr. trans. By G. C. Anawati. 2 vols. Paris: Vrin, 1978–85.

———. *Kitāb al-Najāt,* ed. M. Fakhry. Beirut: Dār al-Afāq al-jadīda, 1985.

Bahya ben Joseph ibn Paquda. *Al-Hidāja 'ilā Farā'iḍ al-Qulūb.* Ar. text ed. by A. S. Yahuda. Leiden: Brill, 1912; Eng. trans.: *The Book of Direction to the Duties of the Heart,* introduction, trans., and notes by Menahem Mansoor with Sara Arenson and Shoshana Dannhauser (London: Routledge and Kegan Paul, 1973).

Bernard of Clairvaux. *Opera,* ed. J. Leclercq et al. 8 vols. Rome: Editiones Cistercienses, 1957–77.

Bernard of Tours, or Bernardus Silvestris. *Cosmographia,* ed. P. Dronke. Leiden: Brill, 1978; *The Cosmographia,* ed. and trans. by W. Weatherbee. New York, Columbia University Press, 1973.

Bible. *Revised Standard Version of The Holy Bible.* Cleveland: World, 1962.

al-Biruni. *In den Gärten der Wissenschaft: Ausgewählte Texte,* trans. and with commentary by Gotthard Strohmaier, 2d ed. Leipzig: Reclam, 1991.

Boëthius. *De consolatione philosophiae,* ed. and Eng. trans. By S. J. Tester. LCL, 1973.

Bonaventure. *Opera Omnia.* Quaracchi: College of St. Bonaventure, 1882–.

Brethren of Purity. *Rasā'il Iẖwān al-Ṣafā',* ed. Bustani. 4 vols. Beirut: Dar Beyrouth, n.d.

"Hermes Trismegistus." *Corpus Hermeticum,* text prepared by A. D. Nock and trans. by A.-J. Festugière. 4 vols. CUF, 1946–54.

Cicero. *De natura deorum,* ed. and Eng. trans. By H. Rackham. LCL, 1933.

———. *De finibus bonorum et malorum,* ed. T. Schiche [1915]. BT, 1961. Eng. trans. By H. Rackham. LCL, 1914.

Clement of Alexandria. *Extraits de Théodote,* ed. and trans. by F. Sagnard. SC 23, 1970.

Crescas, Hasday. *Light of the Lord* [Hebr.], ed. S. Pisar. Jerusalem: Sifrey Ramot, 1990.

Dante. *La Divina Commedia,* ed. and with commentary by G. A. Scartazzini, editio minor. Milan: Hoepli, 1893.

———. *Monarchy,* ed. and trans. by Prue Shaw. New York: Cambridge University Press, 1996.

Descartes. *Oeuvres,* ed. C. Adam and P. Tannery. 12 vols. Paris: Cerf, 1897–1913.

Diogenes of Oenoanda. *The Fragments,* trans. and commentary by C. W. Chilton. London: Oxford University Press, 1971.

———. *The Epicurean Inscription: Diogenes of Oinoanda,* ed. with introduction and notes by Martin F. Smith. Naples: Bibliopolis, 1993.

Meister Eckhart. *Die deutschen Werke,* ed. and trans. by Josef Quint. Stuttgart: Kohlhammer, 1963–; Fr. trans.: *Traités et sermons,* ed. and trans. by A. de Libera. Paris: Garnier-Flammarion, 1993.

al-Farabi. *On the Perfect State: Abū Naṣr al-Fārābī's Mabādi' Arā' Ahl al-Madīna al-Fāḍila,* ed. and trans. by R. Walzer. Oxford: Clarendon, 1985; *Idées des habitants de la cité vertueuse,* ed. and trans. by Y. Karam et al. Beirut: Commission libanaise pour la traduction des chefs-d'oeuvre; Cairo: IFAO, 1980.

Fontenelle. *Entretiens sur la pluralité des mondes habités* [1687], in *Oeuvres complètes, II (1686–1688).* Paris: Fayard, 1991.

Galileo. *Dialogo sui due massimi sistemi del mondo* [1632], in Edizione nazionale, vol. 7 (1897), 27–489; Fr. trans. By R. Fréreux and F. De Gandt. Paris: Seuil, 1992 [pages from the original included].

Genesis Rabbah. Midrash Bereshit Rabba. Critical edition with notes and commentary by J. Theodor and Ch. Albeck [Hebr.], 2d ed. Jerusalem: Wahrmann, 1965.

Gersonides. *The Wars of the Lord* [Hebr.] Riva di Trento, 1560; Leipzig, 1866. Eng. trans. by S. Feldman. 2 vols. Philadelphia: Jewish Publication Society, 1984–87.

al-Ghazâlî. *Iḥyā' 'ulūm id-Dīn.* 5 vols. Beirut: Dar al-kotob al-Ilmiyah, 1996.

Grosseteste, Robert. *Hexaëmeron,* ed. R. C. Dales and S. Gieben. Oxford: Oxford University Press for the British Academy, 1982.

Halevi, Judah. *The Book of Refutation and Proof of the Despised Faith: The Book of the Khazars-Kuzari,* ed. D. H. Baneth and H. Ben Shanimai. Jerusalem: Magnes, 1977; Fr. trans.: *Le Kuzari: Apologie de la religion méprisée,* ed. and trans. by C. Touati. Louvain: Peeters, 1994.

Heidegger, Martin. *Gesamtausgabe, II. Abteilung: Vorlesungen 1919–1944.* Frankfurt-am-Main: Klostermann, 1975–.

———. *Sein und Zeit;* Eng. trans.: *Being and Time,* trans. by John Macquarrie and Edward Robinson. New York: Harper and Row, 1962.

Hippolytus. *Refutationis Omnium Haeresium librorum decem quae supersunt,* ed. L. Duncker and F. G. Schneidewin. Göttingen: Dieterich, 1859.

Homer. *The Iliad,* trans. by Richmond Lattimore. Chicago: University of Chicago Press, 1951.

Humboldt, Alexander von. *Kosmos: Entwurf einer physischen Weltbeschreibung* [1845], ed. and commentary by H. Beck. 2 vols. Darmstadt: Wissenschaftliche Buchgesellschaft, 1993.

Hume, David. *Dialogues concerning Natural Religion,* in *Principal Writings on Religion,* ed. J. C. A. Gaskin. Oxford: Oxford University Press, 1993.

Ibn Bājja. *Opera Metaphysica,* ed. Majid Fakhry, 2d ed. Beirut: Dar an-Nahar, 1991.

Ibn Ezra, Abraham. *Reader: Annotated Texts with Introductions and Commentaries,* ed. by

Israel Levin [Hebr.]. New York and Tel Aviv: I. Matz Hebrew Classics—I. E. Kiev Library Foundation, 1985.

Ibn Ṭufayl. *Ḥayy ben Yaqdhân: Roman philosophique.* Ar. text with Fr. trans. by Leon Gauthier, 2d ed. Beirut: Imprimerie catholique, 1936.

Johannes Scotus Eriugena. *De divisione naturae. PL* 122: 441a–1022c.

Kant, Immanuel. *Werke in sechs Bänden,* ed. W. Weischedel. Darmstadt: Wissenschaftliche Buchgesellschaft, 1983.

———. *Kritik der praktischen Vernunft,* ed. K. Vorlander. Hamburg: Meiner, 1929; Eng. trans.: *Critique of Practical Reason, and Other Ethical Treatises,* trans. by Thomas Kingsmill Abbott. London: Longmans, 1909.

al-Kindi. *Rasā'il . . . falsafiyya,* ed. M. A. Abū Rida. 2 vols. Cairo: Dār al-Fikr al-ʿArabī, 1950–53.

Koran, ed. and trans. by Danielle Masson. Beirut: Dar al-Kitab al-Lubnāni. Fr. trans. by R. Blachère, *Le Coran.* 3 vols. Paris: Maisonneuve, 1949–50. Eng. trans. by N. J. Dawood. New York: Penguin, 1999.

Leopardi, G. *Operette Morali,* ed. by Paolo Ruffilli. Milan: Garzanti, 1984.

Maimonides. *The Guide of the Perplexed* [Ar.], ed. Y. Joel. Jerusalem: Junovitch, 1929; Eng. trans. with introduction and notes by Shlomo Pines, with an introductory essay by Leo Strauss. Chicago: University of Chicago Press, 1963; Fr. trans.: *Guide des égarés,* trans. by S. Munk. 3 vols. [1856–66]. Paris: Maisonneuve, 1970.

Marcus Aurelius. *The Meditations,* ed. and trans. by A. S. L. Farquharson. 2 vols. [1944]. Oxford: Clarendon, 1968.

Mill, John Stuart. "On Nature," in *The Collected Works,* vol. 10: *Essays on Ethics, Religion and Society,* ed. J. M. Robson. Toronto: University of Toronto Press; London: Routledge & Kegan Paul, 1969.

Montaigne. *Les Essais,* ed. by P. Villey. 3 vols. Paris: Alcan, 1930.

Musset, Alfred de. *La Confession d'un enfant du siècle* [1836], ed. D. Leuwers. Paris, Garnier-Flammarion, 1993.

Nietzsche, Friedrich. *Sämtliche Werke, Kritische Studien-ausgabe,* ed. G. Colli and M. Montinari. 15 vols. Munich: DTV; Berlin, De Gruyter, 1980.

Origen. *Vier Bücher von den Prinzipien,* ed. and trans. by H. Görgemanns and H. Karpp, 3d ed. Darmstadt: Wissenschaftliche Buchgesellschaft, 1992.

Pascal, Blaise. *Pensées,* in *Oeuvres . . . publiées . . .* by L. Brunschvicg, vols. 12–14. Paris: Hachette, 1921.

Plato. *Gorgias.* Eng. trans. by W. R. M. Lamb. LCL, 1925.

———. *The Republic.* Eng. trans. by Allan Bloom. New York: Basic Books, 1968.

———. *Timaeus,* ed. A. Rivaud. CUF, 1925; trans. by L. Brisson, *Timée-Critias.* Paris: Garnier-Flammarion, 1992.Eng. trans. by Francis M. Cornford, *Plato's Cosmology: The "Timaeus" of Plato.* Indianapolis: Hackett, 1997.

Plotinus. *Opera,* ed. P. Henry and H.-R. Schwyzer. 3 vols. Paris: Desclée De Brouwer; Brussels: L'Édition universelle, 1951–73.

Proclus. *In Platonis Timaeum Commentaria,* ed. E. Diehl. 3 vols. BT, 1903–6; Fr. trans. by A.-J. Festugière. 4 vols. Paris: Vrin, 1966.

Razi. *Opera Philosophica fragmentaque quae supersunt,* ed. P. Kraus. Cairo, 1939.

Saadia Gaon. *The Book of Beliefs and Opinions,* original Arabic and Hebrew trans. by Joseph Qāfiḥ. Jerusalem: Sura, 1970; Eng. trans. from the Arabic and from the Hebrew by Samuel Rosenblatt. New Haven: Yale University Press, 1948.

Sade, Marquis de. *Oeuvres complètes,* ed. A. Le Brun and J.-J. Pauvert. Paris: Pauvert, 1986–91.

Schopenhauer, Arthur. *Sämtliche Werke,* ed. W. Fr. von Löhneysen. 5 vols. Darmstadt: Wissenschaftliche Buchgesellschaft, 1982.

Seneca. *Ad Lucilium Epistulae morales,* ed. L. D. Reynolds. 2 vols. OCT, 1965.

———. *Questions naturelles,* ed. and trans. by P. Oltramare. 2 vols. CUF, 1929.

Spinoza, Baruch. *Opera quotquot reperta sunt,* ed. J. Van Vloten and J. P. N. Land, 3d ed. 4 vols. The Hague: Nijhoff, 1914.

Themistius. *Discorsi,* ed. R. Maisano. Turin: UTET, 1995.

Thomas Aquinas. *Summa contra gentiles.* Rome: Editio Leonina Manualis, 1934.

———. *Summa theologica.* 5 vols. Paris: Lethielleux, 1939.

Secondary Sources

Abrams, M. H. *The Mirror and the Lamp: Romantic Theory and the Critical Tradition.* Oxford: Oxford University Press, 1953.

Allen, James P. *Genesis in Egypt: The Philosophy of Ancient Egyptian Creation Accounts.* New Haven: Yale University Press, 1988.

Allers, Rudolf. "Microcosmus from Anaximander to Paracelsus." *Traditio* 2 (1944): 319–407.

Al-Qāḍi, Wadād. "The term 'Khalīfa' in early exegetical literature." *Welt des Islams* 28 (1988): 392–411.

Alt, Karin. *Philosophie gegen Gnosis: Plotins Polemik in seiner Schrift II 9.* Stuttgart: Steiner, 1990.

———. *Weltflucht und Weltbejahung: Zur Frage des Dualismus bei Plutarch, Numenios, Plotin.* Stuttgart: Steiner, 1993.

Altmann, Alexander. "The Delphic Maxim in Medieval Islam and Judaism." *Studies in Religious Philosophy and Mysticism,* 1–40. London: Routledge and Kegan Paul, 1969.

D'Alverny, Marie-Thérèse. "Le cosmos symbolique du xiiᵉ siècle." *Archives d'histoire doctrinale et littéraire du Moyen Âge* 20 (1953): 31–81.

D'Alverny, Marie-Thérèse, and Françoise Hudry. "Al-Kindi: De radiis." *Archives d'histoire doctrinale et littéraire du Moyen Âge* 41 (1974): 139–260.

Andrae, Tor. *Les Origines de l'islam et le christianisme,* trans. J. Roche. Paris: Maisonneuve, 1955.

André, Jean-Marie. *La Philosophie à Rome.* Paris: PUF, 1977.

Aptowitzer, V. "Die Anteilnahme der physischen Welt an den Schicksalen des Menschen." *Monatsschrift für Geschichte und Wissenschaft des Judentums* 28 (1920): 227–31, 305–13; 29 (1921):71–87, 164–87.

Arendt, Hannah. *Condition de l'homme moderne,* trans. G. Fradier. Paris: Calmann-Levy, 1961; Eng. ed. *The Human Condition.* Chicago: University of Chicago Press, 1998.

Arkoun, Mohammed. *Essais sur la pensée islamique.* Paris: Maisonneuve et Larose, 1973.

Assmann, Aleida. *Die Legitimität der Fiktion: Ein Beitrag zur Geschichte der literarischen Kommunikation.* Munich: Fink, 1980.

Assmann, Jan. *Maât: L'Égypte pharaonique et l'idée de justice sociale.* Conférences, essais et leçons du Collège de France. Paris: Julliard, 1989.

———. *Ma'at: Gerechtigkeit und Unsterblichkeit im Alten Ägypten.* Munich: Beck, 1990.

———. "Magische Weisheit: Wissensformen im ägyptischen Kosmotheismus." *Stein und Zeit: Mensch und Gesellschaft im alten Ägypten,* 59–75. Munich: Fink, 1991.

Aubenque, Pierre. *La Prudence chez Aristote,* 2d ed. Paris: PUF, 1976.

Bādāwī, 'Abdurrahmān. *Aristoteles apud Arabes* [Ar. 1947]. Kuwait, 1980.

———. *Les Néo-platoniciens chez les Arabes* [Ar. 1954]. Kuwait, 1977.

———. *Plotinus apud Arabes* [Ar. 1955]. Kuwait, 1977.

———. *Traités philosophiques par al-Kindī—al-Fārābī—Ibn Bajjah-Ibn 'Adyy* [Ar. 1968]. Beirut: Dar al-Andaloss, 1983.

———. *Platon en terre d'islam.* [Ar. 1973]. Beirut: Al-Andaloss, 1980.

Baer, Yitzhaq. *Untersuchungen über Quellen und Komposition des Schebet Jehuda.* Berlin: Schwetschke, 1923.

——— [Fritz I.]. "New Notes on Shebet-Jehuda" [Hebr.]. *Tarbiẓ* 6 (1934): 152–79.

Ballabriga, Alain. *Le Soleil et le Tartare: L'image mythique du monde en Grèce archaïque.* Paris: EHESS, 1986.

Baltes, Matthias. *Die Weltentstehung des platonischen Timaios nach den antiken Interpreten.* Leiden: Brill, 1976–78.

Balthasar, Hans Urs von. *Kosmische Liturgie: Das Weltbild Maximus' des Bekenners*, 2d ed. Einsiedeln: Johannes, 1961.

Barr, James. *Biblical Words for Time*, 2d ed. London: SCM Press, 1969.

Bausani, Alessandro. "Niẓāmī di Gangia e la 'pluralità dei mondi.'" *Rivista degli studi orientali* 46 (1971): 197–215.

Beauchamp, Paul. *Création et séparation: Etude exégétique du chapitre premier de la Genèse.* Paris: Desclée De Brouwer, 1969.

Beierwaltes, Werner. *Denken des Einen: Studien zur neuplatonischen Philosophie und ihrer Wirkungs-geschichte.* Frankfurt: Klostermann, 1985 [reviewed in *Philosophische Rundschau* (1988): 329–34].

Berman, Lawrence. "The Political Interpretation of the Maxim: 'The Purpose of Philosophy is the Imitation of God.'" *Studia Islamica* 15 (1961): 53–61.

Benardete, Seth. "On Plato's *Timaeus* and Timaeus' Science-Fiction." *Interpretation* 2 (1971): 21–63.

Bernath, Klaus. "Thomas von Aquin und die Erde." In A. Zimmermann, ed., *Miscellanea Mediaevalia*, vol. 19: *Thomas van Aquin, Werke und Wirkung im Licht neuerer Forschung*, 175–91. Berlin: De Gruyter, 1988.

Besançon, Alain. *L'Image interdite: Une histoire intellectuelle de l'iconoclasme.* Paris: Fayard, 1994.

Bettetini, Maria. *La misura delle case: Struttura e modelli dell' universo secondo Agostino d'Ippona.* Milan: Rusconi, 1994.

Betz, Hans Dieter. "Kosmogonie und Ethik in der Bergpredigt." *Zeitschrift für Theologie und Kirche* 81 (1984): 139–71.

Bianchi, Luca. "Onnipotenza divina e ordine del mondo fra XIII e XIV secolo." *Medioevo* 10 (1984): 105–53.

Biard, Joël. "L'unité du monde selon Guillaume d'Ockham (ou la logique de la cosmologie ockhamiste)." *Vivarium* 22 (1984): 63–83.

Bickel, Susanne. *La Cosmogonie égyptienne avant le Nouvel Empire.* Fribourg: Éditions universitaires; Göttingen: Vandenhoeck & Ruprecht, 1994.

Biemel, Walter. *Le Concept de monde chez Heidegger* [1950]. Paris: Vrin, 1981.

Biese, Alfred. *Die Entwicklung des Naturgefühls bei den Griechen.* Kiel: Lipsius & Teicher, 1882.

———. *Die Entwicklung des Naturgefühls bei den Römern.* Kiel: Lipsius & Teicher, 1884.

———. *Die Entwicklung des Naturgefühls im Mittelalter und in der Neuzeit.* Leipzig: Veit, 1888.

Bietenhard, Hans. *Die himmlische Welt im Urchristentum und Spätjudentum.* Tübingen: Mohr, 1951.

Blumenberg, Hans. "'Nachahmung der Natur': Zur Vorgeschichte der Idee des schöpferischen Menschen" [1957]. *Wirklichkeiten in denen wir leben*, 55–103. Stuttgart: Reclam, 1981.

———. *Paradigmen zu einer Metaphorologie* [1960]. Frankfurt: Suhrkamp, 1998.

———. "Contemplator coeli." In D. Gerhardt, ed. , *Orbis scriptus, D. Tschizewskij zum 70. Geburtstag*, 113–24. Munich: Fink, 1966.

———. *Schiffbruch mit Zuschauer, Paradigma einer Daseinsmetapher.* Frankfurt: Suhrkamp, 1979.

———. *Die Genesis der kopernikanischen Welt* [1975]. 3 vols. Frankfurt: Suhrkamp, 1981.

———. *Die Lesbarkeit der Welt* [1983]. Frankfurt: Suhrkamp, 1986.

———. *Das Lachen der Thrakerin: Eine Urgeschichte der Theorie.* Frankfurt: Suhrkamp, 1987.

———. *Die Legitimität der Neuzeit: Erneuerte Ausgabe.* Frankfurt: Suhrkamp, 1988. [See also Brague 1995.]

———. *Die Vollzähligkeit der Sterne.* Frankfurt: Suhrkamp, 1997.

Böhm, Walter. *Johannes Philoponos: Grammatikos von Alexandrien (6. Jh. n. Chr.): Ausgewählte Schriften übersetzt, eingeleitet und kommentiert von W. B.* Munich: Schöningh, 1967.

Boll, Franz. *Kleine Schriften zur Sternkunde des Altertums.* Leipzig: Koehler & Amelang, 1950.

Borst, Arno. *Die Katharer.* Stuttgart: Anton Hiersemann, 1953.

Bosch i Veciana, Antoni. "Aproximació al concepte de kosmos en el quart evangeli." *Revista catalana de teologia* 4 (1979): 259–84.

Bottéro, Jean. *Mésopotamie: L'écriture, la raison et les dieux.* Paris: Gallimard, 1987. Eng. trans.: *Mesopotamia: Writing, Reasoning, and the Gods,* trans. by Zainab Bahrani and Marc Van De Mieroop. Chicago: University of Chicago Press, 1992.

Bottéro, Jean, and Samuel N. Kramer. *Lorsque les dieux faisaient l'homme: Mythologie méso-potamienne.* Paris: Gallimard, 1989.

Boulnois, Olivier, ed. *La Puissance et son ombre: De Pierre Lombard à Luther.* Paris: Aubier, 1994.

Boyde, Patrick. *Dante, Philomythes and Philosopher: Man in the Cosmos.* Cambridge: Cambridge University Press, 1981.

Brague, Rémi. "La phénoménologie comme voie d'accès au monde grec: Note sur la critique de la *Vorhandenheit* comme modèle ontologique dans la lecture heideggérienne d'Aristote." In J.-L. Marion, ed., *Phénoménologie et métaphysique,* 247–73. Paris: PUF, 1984.

———. "The Body of the Speech: A New Hypothesis on the Compositional Structure of Timaeus' Monologue." In D. O'Meara, ed., *Platonic Investigations,* 53–83. Washington, D.C.: Catholic University of America Press, 1985.

———. *Aristote et la question du monde: Essai sur le contexte cosmologique et anthropologique de l'ontologie.* Paris: PUF, 1988.

———. "L'expérience biblique du monde et l'idée de création." *Création et salut.* Brussels: Publications des facultés universitaires Saint-Louis , no. 47 (1989), 105–20.

———. "Le déni d'humanité: Sur le jugement: 'ces gens ne sont pas des hommes' dans quelques textes antiques et médiévaux." *Lignes 12, Penser le racisme* (1990a): 217–32.

———. "Joseph Conrad et la dialectique des Lumières: Le mal dans 'Coeur des tenebres.'" *Les Études philosophiques* (1990b): 21–36.

———. "Le récit du commencement: Une aporie de la raison grecque." In J.-F. Mattei, ed., *La Naissance de la raison en Grèce: Actes du congrès de Nice, mai 1987,* 23–31. Paris: PUF, 1990c.

———. "La cosmologie finale du *Sophiste* (265b4–e6)." In P. Aubenque, ed., *Études sur le "Sophiste" de Platon,* 269–88. Naples: Bibliopolis, 1991.

———. "Verité: Problematique moderne et spiritualité." *DS,* vol. 16 (1992), cols. 444–53.

———. "L'anthropologie de l'humilité." in R. Brague, ed., *Saint Bernard et la Philosophie,* 129–52. Paris: PUF, 1993a.

———. *Europe, la voie romaine.* Paris: Critérion, 1993b.

———. "Geozentrismus als Demütigung des Menschen." *Internationale Zeitschrift für Philosophie* 1 (1994a): 2–25.

———. "Cosmos et éthique: La fin d'un paradigme." *Acta Institutionis Philosophiae et Estheticae (Tokyo), Eco-ethica et civilisatio moderna,* 12 (1994b): 53–64.

———. "La Galaxie Blumenberg." *Le Débat* 83 (1995): 173–86.

———. "Are We at Home in the World?" In L. Rouner, ed., *The Longing for Home,* 95–111. Notre-Dame: University of Notre-Dame Press, 1996.

———. "Cosmological Mysticism: The Imitation of the Heavenly Bodies in Ibn Tufayl's *Hayy ibn Yaqzan." Graduate Faculty Philosophy Journal* (New School for Social Research, New York), no. 19–20 (1997a): 91–102.

———. "Deux versions du microcosme: Être le monde en petit ou devenir le monde en grand." In A. Hasnawi, ed., *Perspectives arabes et médiévales sur la tradition scientifique et philosophique grecque,* 523–34. Paris: Institut du monde arabe; Louvain: Peeters, 1997b.

———. "Geocentrism as a Humiliation for Man." *Medieval Encounters* 3 (1997c): 187–210.

———. "Le problème de l'homme moderne." In G. Laforest and P. de Lara, eds., *Charles Taylor et l'interprétation de l'identité moderne.* Entretiens de Cerisy, June 1995, 217–29. Paris: Cerf, 1998.

———. "Le Monde moral." In N.-L. Cordero, ed., *Ontologie et dialogue: Hommage à Pierre Aubenque,* 189–96. Paris: Vrin, 2000.

———. "L'Idée de curiosité dans le judaïsme et l'islam pré-modernes: Pour ouvrir un dossier." In G. Freudenthal et al., eds., *Torah et science: Perspectives historiques et théoriques: Etudes offertes à Charles Touati,* 131–46. Paris: Peeters, 2001.

———. "L'homme du monde." In P. Kemp, ed., *Monde et mondanéité* (forthcoming).

Brinkmann, Hennig. *Mittelalterliche Hermeneutik.* Tübingen: Niemeyer, 1980.

Broadie, Alexander, and John MacDonald. "The Ancient Near Eastern and Greek Concepts of Universal Order." *Prudentia* 9 (1977a): 1–14.

———. "The Concept of Cosmic Order in Egypt in Dynastic and Roman Times." *L'Antiquité classique* 47 (1977b): 106–28.

Brunner-Traut, Emma. *Frühformen des Erkennens: Aspektive im alten Ägypten,* 2d ed. Darmstadt: Wissenschaftliche Buchgesellschaft, 1992 [reviewed in *Le Temps des savoirs: La Dénomination* 1 (2000), 251–54].

Buchner, Hartmut. *Eros und Sein: Erörterungen zu Platons Symposion.* Bonn: Bouvier, 1965 [reviewed in *RPhLouvain* (1973), 151–59].

Bultmann, Rudolf. *Theologie des Neuen Testaments.* Tübingen: Mohr, 1954.

Bultot, Robert. *Christianisme et valeurs humaines.* A: *La doctrine du mépris du monde en Occident, de S. Ambroise à Innocent III,* vol. 4: *Le XIe siècle, part 1. Pierre Damien; part 2. Jean de Fécamp, Hennann Contract, Roger de Caen, Anselme de Canterbury.* Louvain: Nauwelaerts, 1963–64.

Casevitz, Michel. "À la recherche du Kosmos." *Le Temps de la réflexion,* no. 10, *Le Monde* (1989): 97–119.

Cassin, Barbara. *L'Effet sophistique.* Paris: Gallimard, 1995.

Champeaux, Gérard de, and Dom Sebastien Sterckx. *Introduction au monde des symboles.* Saint-Léger-Vauban, Yonne: Zodiaque, 1966.

Charles, R. H. *The Apocrypha and Pseudepigrapha of the Old Testament.* Oxford: Clarendon, 1913.

Chenu, Marie-Dominique. *La Théologie au douzième siècle,* 2d ed. Paris: Vrin, 1966.

Chiesa, Bruno. *Creazione e caduta dell'uomo nell'esegesi giudeo-araba medievale.* Brescia: Paideia, 1989.

Clavier, Paul. *Kant, les idées cosmologiques.* Paris: PUF, 1997.

Collingwood, R. G. *The Idea of Nature.* Oxford: Oxford University Press, 1945.

Colomer, Eugenio. "Individuo y cosmo en Nicolas de Cusa." *Nicolas de Cusa en el V Centenario de su muerte (1464–1964),* 1: 67–88. Madrid: Instituto "Luis Vives" de Filosofia, 1967.

Cormier, Philippe. *Généalogie de personne.* Paris: Critérion, 1994.

Cornford, Francis Macdonald. *Plato's Cosmology: The "Timaeus" of Plato, translated with a running commentary.* London: Routledge & Kegan Paul, 1937.

Costantini, Michel. *La Génération Thalès.* Paris: Critérion, 1992.

Couliano, Ioan Peter. "The Gnostic Revenge: Gnosticism and Romantic Literature." In J. Taubes, ed., *Religionstheorie und Politische Theologie,* vol. 2: *Gnosis und Politik,* 290–306. Munich: Schöningh & Fink, 1984.

———. *Les Gnoses dualistes d'Occident: Histoire et mythes.* Paris: Plon, 1990.

Courcelle, Pierre. *La "Consolation de philosophie" dans la tradition littéraire: Antecedents et postérité de Boèce.* Paris: Études augustiniennes, 1967.

Cropsey, Joseph. "The Whole as Setting for Man: On Plato's *Timaeus.*" *Interpretation* 17 (1989–90): 165–91.

Crowe, Michael J. *The Extraterrestrial Life Debate, 1750–1900: The Idea of a Plurality of Worlds from Kant to Lowell.* Cambridge: Cambridge University Press, 1988.

Curtius, Ernst Robert. *Europäische Literatur und lateinisches Mittelalter* [1953]. Berne: Francke, 1973.

Dales, Richard C. "The De-Animation of the Heavens in the Middle Ages." *Journal of the History of Ideas* 41 (1980): 531–50.

Daniélou, Jean. *Essai sur le mystère de l'histoire.* Paris: Éditions du Seuil, 1953.

Davidson, Herbert Alan. "The Study of Philosophy as a Religious Obligation." In S. D. Goitein, ed., *Religion in a Religious Age,* 53–68. Cambridge, Mass.: Association for Jewish Studies, 1974.

Deichgräber, Karl. *Natura varie ludens, ein Nachtrag zum griechischen Naturbegriff.* Stuttgart: Steiner, 1954.

Depraz, Natalie. "Le statut phénoménologique du monde dans la gnose: du dualisme a la non-dualité." *Laval théologique et philosophique* 52 (1996): 625–47.

Deprun, Jean. "Sade et la philosophie biologique de son temps" [1968]. *De Descartes au romantisme: Études historiques et thématiques,* 133–47. Paris: Vrin, 1987.

DeWitt, Norman Wentworth. *Epicurus and His Philosophy.* Minneapolis: University of Minnesota Press, 1954.

Dewitte, Jacques. "Du refus à la réconciliation: À propos de l'acosmisme gnostique." *Le Temps de la réflexion,* no. 10, *Le Monde* (1989): 151–73.

Dick, Steven J. *Plurality of Worlds: The Origins of the Extraterrestrial Life Debate from Democritus to Kant.* Cambridge: Cambridge University Press, 1982.

Dickerman, Sherwood Owen. *De argumentis quibusdam apud Xenophontem, Platonem et Aristotelem obviis e structura hominis et animalium petitis.* Halle: Wischan & Burkhardt, 1909.

Diels, Hermann. "Himmels- und Höllenfahrten von Homer bis Dante." *Neue Jahrbücher* (1922): 239–53.

Dierauer, Urs. *Tier und Mensch im Denken der Antike: Studien zur Tierpsychologie, Anthropologie und Ethik.* Amsterdam: Gruner, 1977.

Dihle, Albrecht. *The Theory of Will in Classical Antiquity.* Berkeley: University of California Press, 1982.

Dodds, Eric Robertson. *Paiens et chétiens dans un âge d'angoisse.* Translated by Henri-Dominique Saffrey. Claix: La Pensée Sauvage, 1979. (Later ed. of Eng. orig.: *Pagan and Christian in an Age of Anxiety: Some Aspects of Religious Experience from Marcus Aurelius to Constantine.* Cambridge: Cambridge University Press, 1990.)

Drekmeier, Charles. *Kingship and Community in Early India.* Stanford: Stanford University Press, 1962.

Edsman, Carl-Martin. *"Arbor inversa:* Heiland, Welt und Mensch als Himmelspflanzen." In K. Rudolph, ed., *Festschrift Walter Baetke dargebracht zu seinem 80. Geburtstag am 28. März 1964,* 85–109. Weimar: Bohlaus, 1966.

Ego, Beate. *Im Himmel und auf Erden: Studien zum Verhältnis von himmlischer und irdischer Welt im rabbinischen Judentum.* Tübingen: Mohr, 1989.

Ehrard, Jean. *L'Idée de nature en France dans la première moitié du XVIIᵉ siècle* [1963]. Paris: Albin Michel, 1994.

Elsas, Christoph. *Neuplatonische und gnostische Weltablehnung in der Schule Plotins.* Berlin: De Gruyter, 1975.

Erren, Manfred. *Die Phainomena des Aratos von Soloi.* Wiesbaden: Steiner, 1967.

Fascher, Erich, "Abraham, ΦΥΣΙΟΛΟΓΟΣ und ΦΙΛΟΣΘΕΟΥ: Eine Studie zur außerbiblischen Abrahamtradition im Anschluß an Deuteronomium 4, 19." In A. Stuiber, and A. Hermann, eds., *Mullus: Festschrift Theodor Klauser,* 111–24. *Jahrbuch für Antike und Christentum.* Ergänzungsband 1. Münster: Aschendorffsche Verlagsbuchhandlung, 1964.

Fazzo, Silvia, and Hillary Wiesner. "Alexander of Aphrodisias in the Kindi-Circle and in al-Kindi's Cosmology." *Arabic Sciences and Philosophy* 3 (1993): 119–53.

Feldman, Seymour. "The End of the Universe in Medieval Jewish Philosophy." *Association for Jewish Studies Review* 11 (1986): 53–77.

Festugière, André-Jean. *L'Idéal religieux des Grecs et l'Évangile.* Paris: Gabalda, 1932.

———. *La Révélation d'Hermès Trismégiste,* vol. 2: *Le Dieu cosmique.* Paris: Gabalda, 1949.

———. *Les Trois "Protreptiques" de Platon: Euthydème, Phédon, Epinomis.* Paris: Vrin, 1973.

Fontaine, Resianne. "Why is the Sea Salty? The Discussion of Salinity in Hebrew Texts of the Thirteenth Century." *Arabic Sciences and Philosophy* 5 (1995): 195–218.

Fox, Michael V. "Aging and Death in Qohelet 12." *Journal for the Study of the Old Testament* 42 (1988): 55–77.

Freudenthal, Gad. "(Al-)chemical Foundations for Cosmological Ideas: Ibn Sina on the

Geology of an Eternal World." in S. Unguru, ed., *Physics, Cosmology and Astronomy, 1300–1700: Tension and Accommodation*, 47–73. Dordrecht: Kluwer, 1991.

———. "Sauver son âme ou sauver les phénomènes: Sotériologie, épistémologie et astronomie chez Gersonide." In Gad Freudenthal, ed., *Studies on Gersonides: A Fourteenth-Century Jewish Philosopher-Scientist*, 317–52. Leiden: Brill, 1992.

———. "Maimonides' Stance on Astrology in Context: Cosmology, Physics, Medicine and Providence." In F. Rosner, ed., *Moses Maimonides: Physician, Scientist and Philosopher*, 77–90, 244–49. Northvale, N.J.: Jason Aronson, 1993.

Friedrich, Hugo. *Die Struktur der modernen Lyrik: Von Baudelaire bis zur Gegenwart.* Hamburg: Rowohlt, 1956.

Früchtel, Ursula. *Die kosmologischen Vorstellungen bei Philo von Alexandrien: Ein Beitrag zur Geschichte der Genesisexegese.* Leiden: Brill, 1968.

Funkenstein, Amos. *Theology and the Scientific Imagination from the Middle Ages to the Seventeenth Century.* Princeton: Princeton University Press, 1986.

———. *Perceptions of Jewish History.* Berkeley and Los Angeles: University of California Press, 1993.

Furley, David. *Cosmic Problems: Essays on Greek and Roman Philosophy of Nature.* Cambridge: Cambridge University Press, 1989.

Gaiser, Konrad. *Platon und die Geschichte.* Stuttgart: Frommann, 1961.

Galston, Myriam. *Politics and Excellence: The Political Philosophy of Alfarabi.* Princeton: Princeton University Press, 1990.

Gardet, Louis. *Dieu et la destinée de l'homme.* Les Grands Problèmes de la théologie musulmane. Paris: Vrin, 1967.

Ginzburg, Carlo. *Il Formaggio e i vermi: Il cosmo di un mugnaio del' '500.* Turin: Einaudi, 1976. [French trans. by M. Aymard. Paris: Flammarion, 1980.]

Gladigow, Burkhard. *Sophia und Kosmos: Untersuchungen zur Frühgeschichte von sophos und sophia.* Hildesheim: Olms, 1965.

Goldschmidt, Victor. *Le Système stoïcien et l'idée de temps.* Paris: Vrin, 1953.

———. *Platonisme et pensée contemporaine.* Paris: Aubier, 1970.

Goodman, Lenn E. "Râzî's Myth of the Fall of Soul: Its Function in His Philosophy." In G. Hourani, ed., *Essays on Islamic Philosophy and Science*, 25–40. Albany: SUNY Press, 1975.

Granada, Miguel A. *Cosmología, religión y politica en el renacimiento: Ficino, Savonarola, Pomponazzi, Maquiavelo.* Barcelona: Anthropos, 1988.

Granel, Gérard. *Traditionis traditio.* Paris: Gallimard, 1972.

Grant, Edward. "Cosmology." In D.C. Lindberg, ed., *Science in the Middle Ages*, 265–302. Chicago: University of Chicago Press, 1978.

———. "Celestial Matter: A Medieval and Galilean Cosmological Problem." *Journal of Medieval and Renaissance Studies* 13 (1983): 157–86.

———. "Medieval and Renaissance Scholastic Conceptions of the Influence of the Celestial Region on the Terrestrial." *Journal of Medieval and Renaissance Studies* 17 (1987): 1–23.

———. "Celestial Incorruptibility in Medieval Cosmology, 1200–1687." In S. Unguru, ed., *Physics, Cosmology and Astronomy, 1300–1700: Tension and Accommodation*, 101–27. Dordrecht: Kluwer, 1991.

———. *Planets, Stars and Orbs: The Medieval Cosmos, 1200–1687.* Cambridge: Cambridge University Press, 1994.

Gregory, Tullio. *Platonismo medievale: Studi e ricerche.* Rome: Istituto Storico Italiano per il Medio Evo, 1958.

———. *Mundana Sapientia: Forme di conoscenza nella cultura medievale.* Rome, Edizioni di storia e letteratura, 1992.

Groethuysen, Bernard. *Philosophische Anthropologie.* Munich: Oldenburg, 1928. French trans.: Paris: Gallimard, 1953.

Groh, Ruth, and Dieter Groh. "Petrarca und der Mont Ventoux." *Merkur* 46 (1992): 290–307.

Gruber, Joachim. *Kommentar zu Boethius De consolatione philosophiae.* Berlin: De Gruyter, 1978.

Guillaumont, Antoine. "Le dépaysement comme forme d'ascèse dans le monachisme ancien" [1968]. *Aux origines du monachisme chrétien: Pour une phénoménologie du monachisme,* 89–116. Bégrolles-en-Mauge: Abbaye de Bellefontaine, 1979.

Gutas, Dimitri. *Avicenna and the Aristotelian Tradition: Introduction to Reading Avicenna's Philosophical Works.* Leiden: Brill, 1988.

Hadot, Pierre. "Physique et poésie dans le *Timée* de Platon." *Revue de théologie et de philosophie* 115 (1983): 113–33.

———. "Le sage et le monde." *Le Temps de la réflexion,* no. 10, *Le Monde* (1989): 175–88.

———. *Qu'est-ce que la philosophie antique?* Paris: Gallimard, 1995.

Haebler, Claus. "Kosmos: eine etymologischwortgeschichtliche Untersuchung." *Archiv für Begriffsgeschichte* 11 (1967): 101–18.

Hahn, Étienne. "Hadîth cosmogonique et Aggada." *Revue des études juives* 101 (1937): 53–72.

Hallyn, Fernand. *La Structure poétique du monde: Copernic, Kepler.* Paris: Éditions du Seuil, 1987.

Halm, Heinz. *Kosmologie und Heilslehre der frühen Ismāʿīliya: Eine Studie zur islamischen Gnosis.* Wiesbaden: Steiner, 1978.

Happ, Heinz. "Kosmologie und Metaphysik bei Aristoteles: Ein Beitrag zum Transzendenzproblem." In K. Flasch , ed., *Parusia: Studien zur Philosophie Platons und zur Problemgeschichte des Platonismus, Festgabe für J. Hirschberger,* 155–87. Frankfurt: Minerva, 1965.

———. "Weltbild und Seinslehre bei Aristoteles." *Antike und Abendland: Beiträge zum Verständnis der Griechen und Römer und ihres Nachlebens* 14 (1968): 72–91.

Harvey, Steven. "The Hebrew Translation of Averroes' Prooemium to His Long Commentary on Aristotle's Physics." *Proceedings of the American Academy for Jewish Research* 52 (1985): 55–84.

Harvey, Warren Zeev. "Averroès et Maïmonide sur le devoir de considération philosophique (iʿtibār)" [Hebr.]. *Tarbiz* 58 (1988): 75–83.

———. "Sur Averroès, Maïmonide et la cité idéale" [Hebr.]. *Iyyunim be-sugiyyôt pilosofiyyôt,* 19–31. Jerusalem: Académie des Sciences d'Israel, 1992.

Heinemann, Isaac. "Die Lehre von der Zweckbestimmung des Menschen im griechischrömischen Altertum und im jüdischen Mittelalter." *Bericht des jüdisch-theologischen Seminars . . . für das Jahr 1925.* Breslau, 1926.

Heinen, Anton M. *Islamic Cosmology: A Study of As-Suyuti's al-Hay'a as-sanīya fī 'l-hay'a as-sunnīya.* Beirut: Steiner, 1982.

Helm, Rudolf. *Lukian und Menipp.* Leipzig: Teubner, 1906.

Henrich, Dieter. *Ethik zum nuklearen Frieden.* Frankfurt: Suhrkamp, 1990.

Henry, Anne, ed. *Schopenhauer et la création littéraire en Europe.* Paris: Méridiens Klincksieck, 1989.

Hering, C. J. "Gratian on Equity." *Studia Gratiana* 2 (1954): 94–113.

Hommel, H. "Mikrokosmos." *Rheinisches Museum für Philologie,* NF 92 (1943): 56–89.

Hornung, Erik. *Geist der Pharaonenzeit.* Munich: DTV, 1992.

Houtman, Cornelis. *Der Himmel im Alten Testament: Israels Weltbild und Weltanschauung.* Leiden: Brill, 1993.

Idel, Moshe. *Le Golem,* trans. by C. Aslanoff. Paris: Cerf, 1992.

Jachimowicz, Edith. "Islamic Cosmology." In C. Blacker, ed., *Ancient Cosmologies,* 143–71. London: Allen & Unwin, 1975.

Jacob, Christian. "Dédale géographe: Regard et voyage aériens en Grèce." *Lalies: Actes des sessions de linguistique et de littérature.* 147–64. Paris: PENS, 1984.

Jacobsen, Thorkild. "Mesopotamia." In H. Frankfort, et al., *Before Philosophy: The Intellectual Adventure of Ancient Man. An Essay on Speculative Thought in the Ancient Near East,* 137–234. London: Penguin, 1949.

Jenni, Ernst Samuel. *Das Wort 'olam im Alten Testament.* Berlin: Topelmann, 1953.

Jonas, Hans. *Gnosis und spätantiker Geist,* part 1: *Die mythologische Gnosis,* 2d ed. Göttingen: Vandenhoeck & Ruprecht, 1954.

Jones, Howard. *The Epicurean Tradition.* London: Routledge, 1989.

Kalkavage, Peter. "The Song of Timaeus." *The St. John's Review* (1985): 56–67.

Kellner, Menachem. "On the Status of the Astronomy and Physics in Maimonides' Mishneh Torah: A Chapter in the History of Science." *British Journal for the History of Science* 24 (1991): 453–63.

Kerchensteiner, Jula. *Kosmos: Quellenkritische Untersuchungen zu den Vorsokratikern.* Munich: Beck, 1962.

Kirk, Geoffrey Stephen, ed. *Heraclitus: The Cosmic Fragments.* Cambridge: Cambridge University Press, 1962.

Klingner, Fritz. *De Boetii Consolatione Philosophiae.* Berlin, 1921.

Koschorke, Albrecht. *Die Geschichte des Horizonts: Grenze und Grenzüberschreitung in literarischen Landschaftsbildern.* Frankfurt: Suhrkamp, 1990.

Koyré, Alexandre. *From the Closed World to the Infinite Universe.* Baltimore: The Johns Hopkins University Press, 1957. French ed.: *Du monde clos a l'univers infini,* trans. by R. Tarr, Hermann. Paris: PUF, 1962.

———. *La Revolution astronomique: Copernic, Kepler, Borelli.* Paris: Hermann, 1961. English ed.: trans. by R. E. W. Maddison. Ithaca: Cornell University Press, 1973.

Kranz, Walther. *Kosmos.* Archiv für Begriffsgeschichte, vol. 2, part 1. Bonn: H. Bouvier, 1955.

Kraus, Paul. *Jābir ibn Hayyān: Contribution à l'histoire des idées scientifiques dans l'islam,* vol. 2: *Jābir et la science grecque* [1942]. Paris: Belles Lettres, 1986.

Kurdzialek, Marian. "Der Mensch als Abbild des Kosmos." *Miscellanea Mediaevalia* 8 (1971): 35–75.

Lackner, Wolfgang. "Zum Lehrbuch der Physik des Nikephoros Blemmydes." *Byzantinische Forschungen* 4 (1972): 157–69.

Lämmli, Franz. *Vom Chaos zum Kosmos: Zur Geschichte einer Idee.* 2 vols. Basel: F. Reinhardt, 1962.

Lambert, W. G. "The Cosmology of Sumer and Babylon." In C. Blacker, ed., *Ancient Cosmologies,* 42–65. London: Allen & Unwin, 1975.

Landau, Yehuda. *The Desire of Matter towards Form in Aristotle's Philosophy* [Hebr.]. University of Tel Aviv, 1972 [reviewed in *Les Études philosophiques* (1983): 274–78].

Langermann, Yitzhak Tzvi. "Some Astrological Themes in the Thought of Abraham ibn Ezra." In I. Twersky, ed., *Rabbi Abraham Ibn Ezra: Studies in the Writings of a Twelfth-Century Polymath,* 28–85. Cambridge: Harvard University Press, 1993.

Langlois, Charles-Victor. *La Connaissance de la nature et du monde au Moyen Âge d'apres quelques écrits français à l'usage des laïcs.* Paris: Hachette, 1911.

Lazarus-Yafeh, Hava. *Studies in al-Ghazzali.* Jerusalem: Magnes, 1975.

Legrand, Joseph, S.J. *L'Univers et l'homme dans la philosophie de saint Thomas.* 2 vols. Paris: Desclée De Brouwer, 1946.

Lerner, Michel-Pierre. *Le Monde des spheres.* 1. *Genèse et triomphe d'une représentation cosmique;* 2. *La Fin du cosmos classique.* Paris: Belles Lettres, 1996–97.

Leroi-Gorhan, André. *Le Geste et la Parole: Technique et langage.* Paris: Albin Michel, 1964.

Le Roy Ladurie, Emmanuel. *Montaillou, village occitan de 1294 à 1324.* Paris: Gallimard, 1975.

Levine, Hillel. "Paradise Not Surrendered: Jewish Reactions to Copernicus and the Growth of Modern Science." In R. S. Cohen, ed., *Epistemology, Methodology and the Social Sciences,* 203–25. Dordrecht: Reidel, 1983.

Lewis, Bernard. *The Muslim Discovery of Europe.* New York: W. W. Norton, 1982. French ed.: *Comment l'Islam a découvert l'Europe,* trans. A. Pélissier. Paris: La Découverte, 1984.

Lewis, C. S. *The Discarded Image: An introduction to medieval and Renaissance literature.* Cambridge: Cambridge University Press, 1964.

———. *Studies on Words.* 2d ed. Cambridge: Cambridge University Press, 1967.

Lieberman, Saul. *Hellenism in Jewish Palestine: Studies in the Literary Transmission, Beliefs and*

Manners of Palestine in the 1st Century B.C.E–IV Century C.E. New York: Jewish Theological Seminary, 1950.

Liebeschütz, Hans. "Kosmologische Motive in der Bildungswelt der Frühscholastik." *Vorträge der Bibliothek Warburg*, vol. 3: *1923/24*, 83–148. Berlin: Teubner, 1926.

Lingat, Robert. *Les Sources du droit dans le système traditionnel de l'inde.* The Hague: Mouton, 1967.

Litt, Thomas. *Les Corps célestes dans l'univers de s. Thomas d'Aquin.* Louvain: Nauwelaerts, 1963.

Lloyd, Geoffrey E. R. "Greek Cosmologies" and "Science and Morality in Greco-Roman Antiquity." *Methods and Problems in Greek Science: Selected Papers*, 141–63 and 352–71. Cambridge: Cambridge University Press, 1991.

L'Orange, Hans Peter, *Studies on the Iconography of Cosmic Kingship in the Ancient World* [1953]. New Rochelle, N.Y.: Caratzas Bros., 1982.

Lovejoy, Arthur O. *The Great Chain of Being: A Study of the History of an Idea* [1936]. Cambridge: Harvard University Press, 1950.

Löw, Immanuel. *Die Flora der Juden* [1928–34]. 4 vols. Hildesheim: Olms, 1967.

Löwith, Karl. "Mensch und Menschenwelt" [1960a]. *Mensch und Menschenwelt: Beiträge zur Anthropologie (Sämtliche Schriften, I)*, ed. Klaus Stichweh, 295–328. Stuttgart: Metzler, 1981.

———. *Der Weltbegriff der neuzeitlichen Philosophie.* Heidelberg: Winter, 1960b.

Lubac, Henri de. *Surnaturel: Études historiques.* Paris: Aubier, 1946.

———. *Pic de La Mirandole: Études et discussions.* Paris: Aubier, 1974.

Macklem, Michael. *The Anatomy of the World: Relations between Natural and Moral Law from Donne to Pope.* Minneapolis: University of Minnesota Press, 1958.

Mahdi, Muhsin. "Alfarabi against Philoponus." *Journal of Near Eastern Studies* 26 (1967): 233–60.

Malamoud, Charles. "Cosmologie prescriptive: Observations sur le monde et le non-monde dans l'Inde ancienne." *Le Temps de la réflexion*, no. 10, *Le Monde* (1989): 303–25.

Malter, Henry. *Saadia Gaon: His Life and Works.* Philadelphia: Jewish Publication Society, 1921.

Manent, Pierre. *Naissances de la politique moderne: Machiavel, Hobbes, Rousseau.* Paris: Payot, 1977.

Mansfeld, Jaap. "Bad World and Demiurge: A 'Gnostic' Motif from Parmenides and Empedocles to Lucretius and Philo." In R. Van den Broeck, ed., *Studies in Gnosticism and Hellenistic Religions: Festschrift G. Quispel*, 261–314. Leiden: Brill, 1981.

———. "Peri Kosmou: A Note on the History of a Title." *Vigiliae Christianae* 46 (1992): 391–411.

Marcus, W. "Typen altchristlicher Kosmologie in den Genesis-Kommentaren." *Philosophisches Jahrbuch der Görres-Gesellschaft* 65 (1956): 106–19.

Marejko, Jean. *Cosmologie et politique: L'influence de la révolution scientifique sur la formation des régimes politiques modernes.* Lausanne: L'Age d'homme, 1989.

Maróth, Miklos. *Die Araber und die antike Wissenschaftstheorie.* Budapest: Akadémiai Kiadó, 1994.

Marquard, Odo. *Schwierigkeiten mit der Geschichtsphilosophie: Aufsätze* [1973]. Frankfurt: Suhrkamp, 1982.

———. *Apologie des Zufälligen: Philosophische Studien.* Stuttgart: Reclam, 1986.

Martineau, Emmanuel. *Malevitch et la philosophie.* Lausanne: L'Age d'homme, 1977.

Masson, Denise. *Monothéisme coranique et monothéisme biblique: Doctrines comparées.* Paris: Desclée De Brouwer, 1976.

Mattéi, Jean-François. *L'Ordre du monde: Platon—Nietzsche—Heidegger.* Paris: PUF, 1989.

Maurer, Armand. "Ockham on the Possibility of a Better World." *Mediaeval Studies* 38 (1976): 291–312.

McEvoy, James. *The Philosophy of Robert Grosseteste.* Oxford: Clarendon Press, 1982.

McKenzie, John L. "God and Nature in the Old Testament." *Catholic Biblical Quarterly* 14 (1952): 18–39, 124–45.

Meier, Fritz. "Der 'Urknall', eine Idee des Abû Bakr ar-Râzi." *Oriens* 33 (1991): 1–21.

Merleau-Ponty, Jacques, and Bruno Morando. *Les Trois Étapes de la cosmologie.* Paris: Laffont, 1971.

Michot, Jean R. *La Destinée de l'homme selon Avicenne: Le retour à Dieu (ma'ād) et l'imagination.* Louvain: Peeters, 1986.

Miethke, Jürgen. *Ockhams Weg zur Sozialphilosophie.* Berlin: De Gruyter, 1969.

Mittelstrass, Jürgen. *Die Rettung der Phänomene: Ursprung und Geschichte eines antiken Forschungsprinzips.* Berlin: De Gruyter, 1962.

Murray, Gilbert. *Five Stages of Greek Religion.* New York: Columbia University Press, 1925.

Nazzaro, A. "Gnothi seauton nell' epistemologia filoniana." *Annali della facolta di lettere e filosofia* (Naples), 12 (1969–70): 49–86.

———. "Nota a Filone, De Migratione Abrahami, 8." *Rivista di filologia classica* (Turin), 98 (1970): 188–93.

Needham, Joseph. *Science and Civilisation in China,* vol. 3: *Mathematics and the Sciences of the Heaven and the Earth.* Cambridge: Cambridge University Press, 1959.

Nicholson, Reynold Alleyne. *Studies in Islamic Mysticism.* Cambridge: Cambridge University Press, 1921.

Nicolson, Marjorie H. *The Breaking of the Circle: Studies in the Effect of the "New Science" upon Seventeenth-Century Poetry,* rev. ed. New York: Columbia University Press, 1960.

Niditch, Susan. "The Cosmic Man: Man as Mediator in Rabbinic Literature." *Journal of Jewish Studies* 34 (1983): 137–46.

Norden, Eduard. *Agnostos theos: Untersuchungen zur Formengeschichte religioser Rede.* Leipzig:, Teubner, 1913.

North, John David. "Celestial Influence—The major Premise of Astrology." In P. Zambelli, ed., *"Astrologi hallucinati": Stars and the End of the World in Luther's Time,* 45–100. New York: De Gruyter, 1986.

———. "Medieval Concepts of Celestial Influence: A Survey." In P. Curry, ed., *Astrology, Science and Society: Historical Essays,* 5–17. Woodbridge: Boydell Press, 1987.

———. *Chaucer's Universe.* Oxford: Clarendon, 1988.

Nutkiewicz, Michael. "Maimonides on the Ptolemaic System: The Limits of Our Knowledge." *Comitatus* 9 (1978): 63–72.

Obolensky, Dmitri. *The Bogomils: A Study in Balkan Neo-Manichaeism.* Cambridge: Cambridge University Press, 1948.

O'Brien, Denis. *Théodicée plotinienne, théodicée gnostique.* Leiden: Brill, 1993.

Orbán, Arpad Peter. *Les Dénominations du monde chez les premiers auteurs chrétiens.* Nijmegen: Dekker & Van De Vegt, 1970.

Ormsby, Eric Linn. *Theodicy in Islamic Thought: The Dispute over Al-Ghazali's "Best of Possible Worlds."* Princeton: Princeton University Press, 1984.

Ort, Lodewijk Josephus Rudolf. *Mani: A Religio-historical Description of His Personality.* Leiden: Brill, 1967.

Osler, Margaret J., ed. *Atoms, Pneuma and Tranquillity: Epicurean and Stoic Themes in European Thought.* Cambridge: Cambridge University Press, 1991.

Pabst, Bernhard. *Atomtheorien des lateinischen Mittelalters.* Darmstadt: Wissenschaftliche Buchgesellschaft, 1994.

Panofsky, Erwin. *Idea: Ein Beitrag zur Begriflsgeschichte der älteren Kunsttheorie* [1924]. Berlin: Hessling, 1975.

Parel, Anthony. *The Machiavellian Cosmos.* New Haven: Yale University Press, 1992.

Paret, Rudi. *Der Koran: Kommentar und Konkordanz,* 2d ed. Stuttgart: Kohlhammer, 1977.

Parsons, Wilfrid, S.J. "'Lest Men Like Fishes.'" *Traditio* 3 (1945): 380–88.

Pellegrino, Michele. "Il 'topos' dello 'status rectus' nel contesto filosofico e biblico (A proposito di Ad Diognetum 10, 1–2)." In A. Stuiber and A. Hermann, eds., *Mullus: Festschrift Theodor Klauser,* 273–81. *Jahrbuch für Antike und Christentum.* Ergänzungsband 1. Münster: Aschendorffsche Verlagsbuchhandlung, 1964.

Pépin, Jean. *Théologie cosmique et théologie chrétienne (Ambroise, Exam. I I,* 1–4). Paris: PUF, 1964.

Pétrement, Simone. *Le Dieu séparé. Les origines du gnosticisme.* Paris: Cerf, 1984.

Pidoux, G. "Un aspect négligé de la justice dans l'Ancien Testament: Son aspect cosmique." *Revue de théologie et de philosophie* (Lausanne), 4 (1954): 283–88.

Pines, Shlomo, ed. *Beiträge zur islamischen Atomenlehre.* Berlin: Grafenhainichen, 1936.

————. *Studies in the History of Jewish Philosophy: The Transmission of Texts and Ideas* [Hebr.]. Jerusalem: Mosad Bialik, 1977.

————. *Studies in Abu'l Barakât al-Baghdâdî: Physics and Metaphysics* (Collected Works, vol. 1). Jerusalem: Magnes; Leiden: Brill, 1979.

Pines, Shlomo, and Zeev Harvey. "To see the stars and constellations" [Hebr.]. *Mehqarey Yerushalayim be-Makhsheveth Israel* 3, no. 4 (1984): 507–11.

Platti, Emilio. "Une cosmologie chrétienne." *Mideo* 15 (1982): 75–118.

Plumley, J. M. "The Cosmology of Ancient Egypt." In C. Blacker, ed., *Ancient Cosmologies,* 17–41. London: Allen & Unwin, 1975.

Pöhlmann, Egert. "Der Mensch—das Mangelwesen? Zum Nachwirken antiker Anthropologie bei Arnold Gehlen." *Archiv für Kulturgeschichte* 52 (1970): 297–312.

Pomian, Krzysztof. "Astrology as a Naturalistic Theology of History." In P. Zambelli, ed., *"Astrologi hallucinati": Stars and the End of the World in Luther's Time,* 29–43. New York: De Gruyter, 1986.

Preus, Anthony. "Man and Cosmos in Aristotle: Metaphysics A and the Biological Works." In D. Devereux and P. Pellegrin, eds., *Biologie, logique et métaphysique chez Aristote: Actes du Séminaire C.N.R.S.-N.S.F., Oléron, 28 juin–3 juillet 1987,* 471–90. Paris: CNRS, 1990.

Probst, J. H. "Le sentiment de la nature chez Ramon Lulle." *Estudis franciscans* 48 (1936): 234–43.

Proust, Dominique. *L'Harmonie des spheres.* Paris: Dervy-Livres, 1990.

Puech, Henri-Charles. *En quête de la gnose,* 1. *La Gnose et le temps.* Paris: Gallimard, 1978.

————. *Sur le manichéisme et autres essais.* Paris: Flammarion, 1979.

Puhvel, Jaan. "The Origins of Greek Kosmos and Latin Mundus." *American Journal of Philology* 97 (1976): 154–67.

Quispel, Gilles. *Gnostic Studies,* vol. 1. Istanbul: Nederlands Historisch-Archaeologisch Instituut in het Nabie Oosten, 1974.

Randi, Eugenio. "Talpe e extraterrestri: Un inedito di Agostino Triunfo di Ancona sulla pluralita dei mondi." *Rivista di storia della filosofia* 44 (1989): 311–26.

Reitzenstein, Richard, and H. H. Schaeder. *Studien zum antiken Synkretismus aus Iran und Griechenland.* 2 vols. Leipzig: Teubner, 1926.

Richter, Gerhard. *Theodoros Dukas Laskaris, der natürliche Zusammenhang: Ein Zeugnis vom Stand der byzantinischen Philosophie in der Mitte des 13. Jahrhunderts.* Amsterdam: Adolf M. Hakkert, 1989.

Rico, Francisco. *El pequeño mundo del hombre: Varia fortuna de una idea en las letras españolas.* Edición corregida y aumentada. Madrid: Alianza Editorial, 1988.

Ritter, Hellmut. *Das Meer der Seele: Mensch, Welt und Gott in den Geschichten des Fariduddin 'Attar,* Nachdruck mit Zusätzen und Verbesserungen. Leiden: Brill, 1978.

Ritter, Joachim. "Die Lehre vom Ursprung und Sinn der Theorie bei Aristoteles" [1953]. *Metaphysik und Politik: Studien zu Aristoteles und Hegel,* 9–32. Frankfurt: Suhrkamp, 1977.

————. "Landschaft: Zur Funktion des Ästhetischen in der modernen Gesellschaft." *Subjektivität: Sechs Aufsätze,* 141–63, 172–90. Frankfurt: Suhrkamp, 1974.

Robinson, H. Wheeler. *Inspiration and Revelation in the Old Testament.* Oxford: Clarendon, 1946.

Rosenmeyer, Thomas G. *Senecan Drama and Stoic Cosmology.* Berkeley and Los Angeles: University of California Press, 1989.

Ruderman, David B. *Jewish Thought and Scientific Discovery in Early Modern Europe.* New Haven: Yale University Press, 1995.

Rudler, Gustave. *La Jeunesse de Benjamin Constant, 1767–1794: Le disciple du XVIIIᵉ siècle*, Utilitarisme et pessimisme, Mme de Charrière. Paris: A. Colin, 1909.

Rutherford, R. B. *The Meditations of Marcus Aurelius: A Study.* Oxford: Clarendon, 1989.

Saint Girons, Baldine. *Fiat lux: Une philosophie du sublime.* Paris: Quai Voltaire, 1993.

Salem, Jean. *Tel un Dieu parmi les hommes: L'éthique d'Épicure.* Paris: Vrin, 1989.

———. *Démocrite: Grains de poussière dans un rayon de soleil.* Paris: Vrin, 1996.

Sambursky, Shmuel. *The Physical World of Late Antiquity.* London: Routledge & Kegan Paul, 1962.

Sarfatti, Gad Ben-Ami. "Talmudic Cosmography" [Hebr.]. *Tarbiz* 35 (1965–66): 137–48.

Schabert, Tilo. *Die Architektur der Welt: Eine kosmologische Lektüre architektonischer Formen.* Munich: Fink, 1997.

Schaeder, Hans Heinrich. "Die islamische Lehre vom Vollkommenen Menschen, ihre Herkunft und ihre dichterische Gestaltung." *Zeitschrift der Deutschen Morgenländischen Gesellschaft* 79 (1925): 192–268.

Schaefer, Alexander. "The Position and Function of Man in the Created World according to Saint Bonaventure." *Franciscan Studies* 20 (1960): 261–316; 21 (1961): 233–382.

Schimmel, Annemarie. *Mystische Dimensionen des Islam: Die Geschichte des Sufismus.* Cologne: Diederichs, 1985.

———. *Und Muhammad ist sein Prophet: Die Verehrung des Propheten in der islamischen Frömmigkeit,* 2d ed. Munich: Diederichs, 1989.

Schlier, Heinrich. *Religionsgeschichtliche Untersuchungen zu den Ignatius-Briefen.* Giessen: Töpelmann, 1929.

———. *Essais sur le Nouveau Testament,* trans. A. Liefooghe. Paris: Cerf, 1968.

Schmid, Hans Heinrich. *Wesen und Geschichte der Weisheit: Eine Untersuchung zur altorientalischen und israelitischen Weisheitsliteratur.* Berlin: Töpelmann, 1966.

———. *Gerechtigkeit als Weltordnung: Hintergrund und Geschichte des alttestamentlichen Gerechtigkeitsbegriff.* Tübingen: Mohr, 1968.

Schmid, Wolfgang, "Christus als Naturphilosoph bei Arnobius." In J. Derbolav et al., eds., *Erkenntnis und Verantwortung: Festschrift für Theodor Litt,* 264–84. Düsseldorf: Schwann, 1961.

Schmidt, Albert-Marie. *La Poésie scientifique en France au seizième siècle: Ronsard–Maurice Scève–Baïf–Belleau–Du Bartas–Agrippa d'Aubigne.* Paris: Albin Michel, 1938.

Schoedel, William R. *A Commentary on the Letters of Ignatius of Antioch.* Philadelphia: Fortress, 1985.

Scholem, Gershom. "An Inquiry in the Kabbala of R. Isaac ben Jacob Hacohen. II: The Evolution of the Doctrine of the Worlds in the Early Kabbala" [Hebr.]. *Tarbiz* 2 (1931): 415–42; 3 (1931): 33–66.

———. *Kabbalah.* Jerusalem: Keter, 1974.

Schuhl, Pierre-Maxime. "Un cauchemar de Platon" [1953]. In *Études platoniciennes,* 85–89. Paris: PUF, 1960.

Schwabl, Hans. "Zur Mimesis bei Arat: Prooimion und Parthenos." In R. Hanslick et al., eds., *Antidosis: Festschrift für W Kraus,* 336–56. Vienna: Bohlau, 1972.

Schweizer, Hans Rudolf. *Ästhetik als Philosophie der sinnlichen Erkenntnis. Eine Interpretation der "Aesthetica" A. G. Baumgartens mit teilweiser Wiedergabe des lateinischen Textes und deutscher Übersetzung.* Basel: Schwabe, 1973 [reviewed in *Archives de Philosophie* (1977): 657–60].

Sèd, Nicolas, *La Mystique cosmologique juive.* Paris: EHESS and Mouton, 1981.

Shahar, Shulamit. "Catharism and the Beginnings of the Kabbalah in Languedoc: Elements Common to the Catharic Scriptures and the Book Bahir" [Hebr.]. *Tarbiz* 40 (1971): 483–507.

Shattuck, Roger. *Forbidden Knowledge: From Prometheus to Pornography.* New York: St. Martin's, 1996.

Shea, William R. "Galileo, Scheiner, and the Interpretation of Sunspots." *Isis* 61 (1970): 498–519.

Silverstein, Theodore. "The Fabulous Cosmogony of Bernardus Silvestris." *Modern Philology* 46 (1948): 92–116.

Simson, Otto von. *The Gothic Cathedral: Origins of Gothic Architecture and the Medieval Concept of Order,* 3d ed. Princeton: Princeton University Press, 1988.

Sloterdijk, Peter. *Weltfremdheit.* Frankfurt: Suhrkamp, 1993.

Smith, Jonathan Z. *Map Is Not Territory: Studies in the History of Religions.* Leiden: Brill, 1978.

Smith, Martin Ferguson, ed. *The Epicurean Inscription: Diogenes of Oinoanda.* Naples: Bibliopolis, 1993.

Smith, Richard. "The Modern Relevance of Gnosticism." In *NHL,* 532–49.

Sorabji, Richard. *Time, Creation and the Continuum.* London: Duckworth, 1983.

Souiller, Didier. *Calderón et le grand théâtre du monde.* Paris: PUF, 1992.

Speyer, Heinrich. *Die biblischen Erzählungen im Qoran* [1931]. Hildesheim: Olms, 1961.

Spitzer, Leo. *Classical and Christian Ideas of World Harmony: Prolegomena to an Interpretation of the Word "Stimmung."* Baltimore: The Johns Hopkins University Press, 1963.

Stadelmann, Luis I. J., S.J. *The Hebrew Conception of the World: A Philological and Literary Study.* Rome: Pontifical Biblical Institute, 1970.

Staiger, Emil. *Die Zeit als Einbildungskraft des Dichters: Untersuchungen zu Gedichten von Brentano, Goethe und Keller* [1939]. Munich, DTV, 1976.

Steinen, Wolfram von den. *Der Kosmos des Mittelalters: Von Karl dem Großen zu Bernhard von Clairvaux,* 2d ed. Bern: Francke, 1967.

Stern, Samuel Miklos. "The Earliest Cosmological Doctrines of Ismâ'ilism." In *Studies in Early Ismâ'ilism,* 3–29. Jerusalem: Magnes; Leiden: Brill, 1983.

Strack, H. L., and P. Billerbeck. *Kommentar zum Neuen Testament aus Talmud und Midrash,* t. 1. Munich: Beck, 1922.

Strauss, Leo. *Natural Right and History.* Chicago: University of Chicago Press, 1953.

———. *Socrates and Aristophanes.* London: Basic Books, 1966.

———. *Liberalism Ancient and Modern.* London: Basic Books, 1968.

———. *Xenophon's Socrates.* Ithaca: Cornell University Press, 1972.

———. "On the Interpretation of Genesis." *L'Homme: Revue française d'anthropologie* 21 (1981): 536.

———. *The Rebirth of Classical Political Rationalism: An Introduction to the Thought of Leo Strauss: Essays and Lectures by Leo Strauss,* ed. T. L. Pangle. Chicago: University of Chicago Press, 1989.

Striker, Gisela. "Following Nature: A Study in Stoic Ethics." *Oxford Studies in Ancient Philosophy* 9 (1991): 1–73.

Stroumsa, Gedalyahu Guy. "Aher: A Gnostic." In B. Layton, ed., *The Rediscovery of Gnosticism,* 2: 808–18. Leiden: Brill, 1980–81.

———. *Another Seed: Studies in Gnostic Mythology.* Leiden: Brill, 1984.

———. *Savoir et salut.* Paris: Cerf, 1992.

Szlezák, Thomas. "Psyche–Polis–Kosmos: Bemerkungen zur Einheit des platonischen Denkens." in E. Rudolph, ed., *Polis und Kosmos: Naturphilosophie und politische Philosophie bei Platon,* 26–42. Darmstadt: Wissenschaftliche Buchgesellschaft, 1996.

Tarán, Leonardo. "The Creation Myth in Plato's *Timaeus,*" in J.-P. Anton et al., eds., *Essays in Ancient Greek Philosophy,* 372–407. Albany: SUNY Press, 1971.

Tardieu, Michel. *Codex de Berlin.* Paris: Cerf, 1984.

———. "Sābiens coraniques et 'Sābiens' de Harrān." *Journal asiatique* 274 (1986): 1–44.

Taub, Liba Chaia. *Ptolemy's Universe: The Natural Philosophical and Ethical Foundations of Ptolemy's Astronomy.* La Salle, Ill.: Open Court, 1993.

Taubes, Jacob. *Vom Kult zur Kultur: Bausteine zu einer Kritik der historischen Vernunft: Gesammelte Aufsätze zur Religions- und Geistesgeschichte,* ed. A. and J. Assmann et al. Munich, Fink, 1996.

Taylor, Alfred Edward. *A Commentary on Plato's "Timaeus."* Oxford: publisher, 1928.

Taylor, Charles. *Sources of the Self: The Making of the Modern Identity.* Cambridge: Harvard University Press, 1989 [cf. Brague 1998].

Touati, Charles. *La Pensée philosophique et théologique de Gersonide.* Paris: Minuit, 1973.

Tov, Emanuel. "The Rabbinic Tradition Concerning the "Alterations" Inserted into the Greek Pentateuch and Their Relation to the Original Text of the LXX." *Journal for the Study of Judaism in the Persian, Hellenistic and Roman Period* 15 (1984): 65–89.

Tuzet, Hélène. *Le Cosmos et l'imagination.* Paris: Corti, 1965.

Unger, Rudolf. "'Der bestimte Himmel über mir . . .': Zur geschichtlichen Deutung eines Kant-Wortes." In *Immanuel Kant: Festschrift zur zweiten Jahrhundertfeier seines Geburtstages,* ed. by the Albertus-Universität in Königsberg i. Pr., 241–70. Leipzig: Dieterich, 1924

Urbach, Ephraim E. *The Sages: Their Concepts and Beliefs,* trans. by I. Abrahams. 2 vols. Jerusalem: Magnes, 1979.

Vajda, Georges. "La philosophie et la théologie de Joseph Ibn Caddiq." *Archives d'histoire doctrinale et littéraire du Moyen Âge* 17 (1949): 93–181.

———. *Juda ben Nissim Ibn Maïka, philosophe juif marocain.* Institut des hautes études marocaines, collection Hespéris, 15. Paris: Larose, 1954.

———. *Isaac Albalag, averroiste juif, traducteur et annotateur d'Al-Ghâzâli.* Paris: Vrin, 1960.

———. *Recherches sur la philosophie et la kabbale dans la pensée juive du Moyen Âge.* Paris: Mouton, 1962.

Verhaeghe, J. *Het mensbeeld in de Aristotelische Ethiek.* Verhandelingen van de Koninklijke Academie voor Wetenschappen, Letteren en Schone Kunsten van België, Klasse der Letteren, vol. 42, no. 94. Brussels, 1980 [reviewed in *Les Études philosophiques* (1985): 440–44].

Vlastos, Gregory. *Studies in Greek Philosophy,* vol. 1: *The Presocratics,* ed. Daniel W. Graham. Princeton: Princeton University Press, 1995.

Voegelin, Eric. *Order and History,* vol. 1: *Israel and Revelation.* Baton Rouge: Louisiana State University Press, 1956.

Volz, Paul. *Die Eschatologie der jüdischen Gemeinde im neutestamentlichen Zeitalter.* Tübingen: Mohr, 1934.

Walker, Paul E. *Early Philosophical Shiism: The Ismaili Neoplatonism of Abū Ya'qūb al-Sijistānī.* Cambridge: Cambridge University Press, 1993.

Wallace-Hadrill, David Sutherland. *The Greek Patristic View of Nature.* Manchester: Manchester University Press; New York: Barnes & Noble, 1968.

Weiss, Hans-Friedrich. *Untersuchungen zur Kosmologie des hellenistischen und palestinischen Judentums.* Berlin: Akademie Verlag, 1966.

Weisser, Ursula. *Das "Buch über das Geheimnis der Schöpfung" von Pseudo-Apollonios von Tyana.* Berlin: De Gruyter, 1980.

Wensinck, Arent Jan. "On the Relation between Ghazali's Cosmology and His Mysticism." *Mededeelingen der koninklijke akademie van wetenschappen te Amsterdam, Afdeeling Letterkunde, Rubriek A* 75 (1933): 183–209.

Werner, Karl. "Die Kosmologie und Naturlehre des scholastischen Mittelalters mit spezieller Beziehung auf Wilhelm von Conches." *Sitzungsberichte der kaiserlichen Akademie der Wissenschaften, Philosophisch-historische Klasse* 75 (1873): 309–403.

———. "Kosmologie und allgemeine Naturlehre des Roger Bacon." *Sitzungsberichte der kaiserlichen Akademie der Wissenschaften, Philosophisch-historische Klasse* 94 (1879): 489–612.

Wewers, Gerd A. "Die Wissenschaft von der Natur im rabbinischen Judentum: Ein Beitrag zur Hermeneutik theologischen Denkens und zum Wirklichkeitsbegriff in diesem Denken." *Kairos: Zeitschrift für Religionswissenschaft und Theologie* 14 (1972): 1–21.

Widengren, Geo. "Macrocosmos–Microcosmos speculation in the Rasa'il Ikhwan al-Safa and some Hurufi texts." *Archivio di filosofia* (1980): 297–312.

Wilson, Catherine. *The Invisible World: Early Modern Philosophy and the Invention of the Microscope.* Princeton: Princeton University Press, 1995.

Wilson, John. "Egypt." In H. Frankfort et al., *Before Philosophy: The Intellectual Adventure of Ancient Man: An Essay on Speculative Thought in the Ancient Near East* [1946], 39–133. London: Penguin, 1949.

Wlosok, Antonie. *Laktanz und die philosophische Gnosis: Untersuchungen zu Geschichte und Terminologie der gnostischen Erlösungsvorstellung.* Abhandlungen der Heidelberger Akademie der Wissenschaften, Philosophisch-historische Klasse. 1960–62.

Zahlten, J. *Creatio Mundi: Darstellungen der sechs Schöpfungstage und naturwissenschaftliches Weltbild im Mittelalter.* Stuttgart: Klett-Cotta, 1979.

Zambelli, Paola. "Le stelle 'sorde e mute' ed i loro 'motori' alle origini della scienza moderna? Un case-study storiografico." In B. Mojsisch et al., eds., *Historia Philosophiae Medii Aevi: Studien zur Geschichte der Philosophie des Mittelalters (Festschrift für Kurt Flasch zu seinem 60. Geburtstag),* 1099–1117. Amsterdam: Gruner, 1991.

Zonta, Mauro. *La filosofia antica nel medioevo ebraico: Le traduzioni ebraiche medievali dei testi filosofici antichi.* Brescia, Paideia, 1996 [reviewed in *Bulletin de philosophie médiévale, II, Archives de philosophie* 61 (1998): 25–27].

Index

Abrahamic model, 51, 60, 70, 154; divine proximity and, 155–60; end of world and, 168–70; equality of providence and, 161–63; fall of man and, 167–68; Gnosticism and, 83–84, 155; God's position to world, 157–60; man's dignity and, 163–65; reversed microcosm and, 165–66; Socratism and, 78–82

Abû Hatim, 83

Abuya, Elisha ben, 69

Achamoth, 65

Adam, 95–96, 159–60, 170

Adam qadmon, 63

Aetius, 37

affliction *(penthos)*, 163

Aher, 69

aiōn, 11–12, 55

Akkadian, 12, 17

Alfred (king), 138

Alain of Lille, 139–42, 178

Albalag, Isaac, 89

alchemy, 127

Alexander of Aphrodisias, 76, 109, 116, 118, 123–24, 127

Alexander of Lycopolis, 108

alienation *(xeniteia)*, 84

All, the, 17–18, 66

Allah, 56–61, 83, 181

Almagest (Ptolemy), 127–28

Ambrose of Milan, 168

al-'Āmirī, Abū'l-Hasan, 76

Anaxagoras, 19, 31–32

anthropology, 2, 10; cosmology and, 5–6; erect posture and, 99–101; influences, 96–99; and *kosmos*, 18–25; microcosms, 93–96; physical prefiguration of, 93–101; rejection of, 75–76

Anticlaudianus (Alain of Lille), 139–40

Antiochus of Ascalon, 123

Anytos, 132

apocalyptic literature, 51–52, 168–80

Apocrypha, 56

Archimedes, 14

Arendt, Hannah, 227

Aristotle, 86, 98, 126–27, 142, 152, 179, 213, 217; celestial is divine, 122; and comets, 186–87;

and contemplation objects, 121–22; and divine omnipotence, 180–82; and equality of providence, 161; ethics, 109, 125; and incompleteness, 171; and man's posture, 99–100; and new astronomy, 188–90; and Socrates, 22–23, 30; and spheres, 41; and technology, 210; two types of matter, 89

Arnold, Matthew, 195–96, 203

Assmann, Jan, 15–16, 230n.39

astrology, 164

astronomy, 24, 33, 39, 51; Abraham and, 80; Brethren of Purity and, 128; celestial observations and, 134–51; effects of new, 186–200; God and, 189, 191–93, 197–98; Kepler and, 97; Nietzsche and, 189–90; primacy of sky and, 126–30; religion and, 186–89; star of Magi, 156

ataraxia (disturbances), 38–40

Athenagoras, 157

Athens, 44, 111–12

Atomists: Democritus and, 36–37; Epicureanism and, 38–41; Lucretius and, 42–43; physics and, 36–39

Atum, 13

Augustine, 91; and celestial bodies, 139–40; contemplation of nature, 174–75; and end of world, 168; ethics, 107, 110; and idolatry, 158; man's posture and, 101

Aurelius, Marcus, 76–78, 151–52, 170, 218

Averroes, 89–90, 103, 118, 172

Avicebron, 89

Avicenna, 1, 76, 179, 239n.7; and celestial bodies, 143–44, 150; ethics, 110–11, 251nn. 103–4; metaphysics, 251n.104

awareness, 69

Axial Age *(Achsenzeit)*, 11–12

Baal, 50

Babylon, 18, 46

Bacon, Francis, 127, 164, 175

Bacon, Roger, 187

Baghdadi, Abd al-Latif, al-, 106

Bāquillānī, Kalâm, al-, 160

Bar Qappara, 150